Chapter 20

In the morning : The Butler, Cogitating

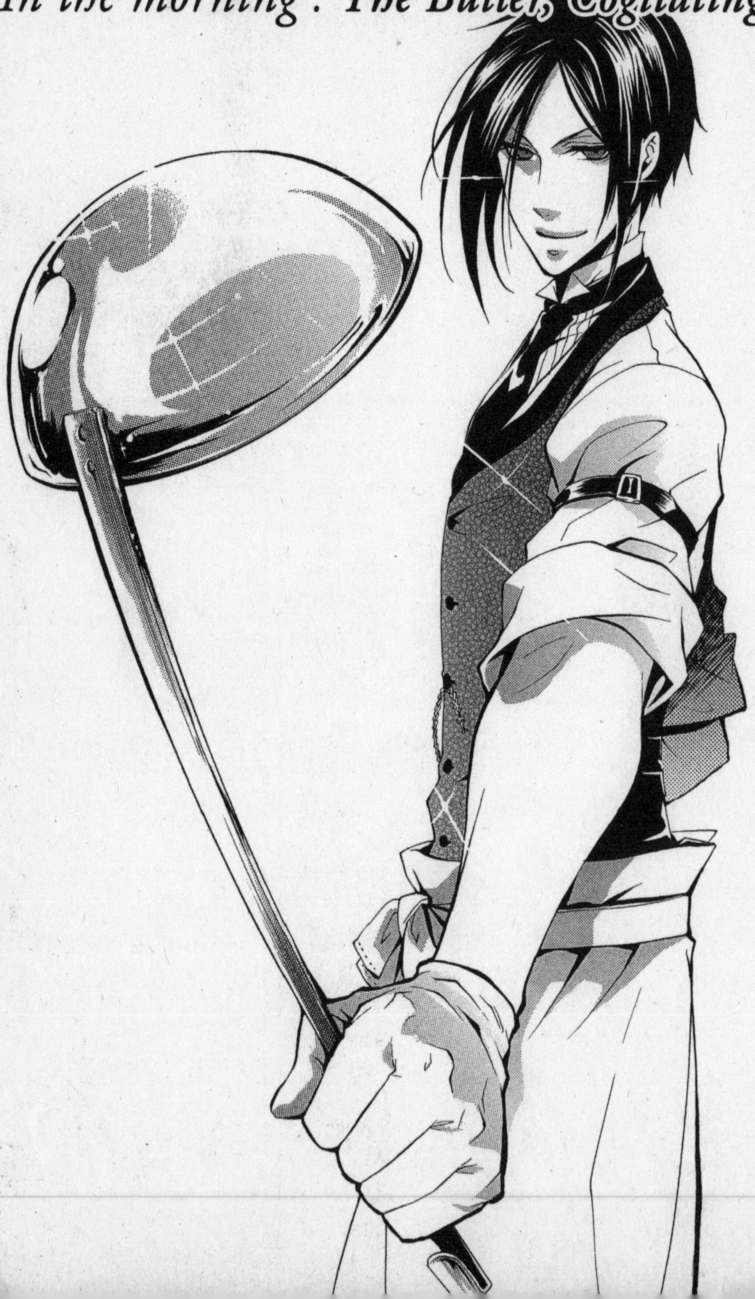

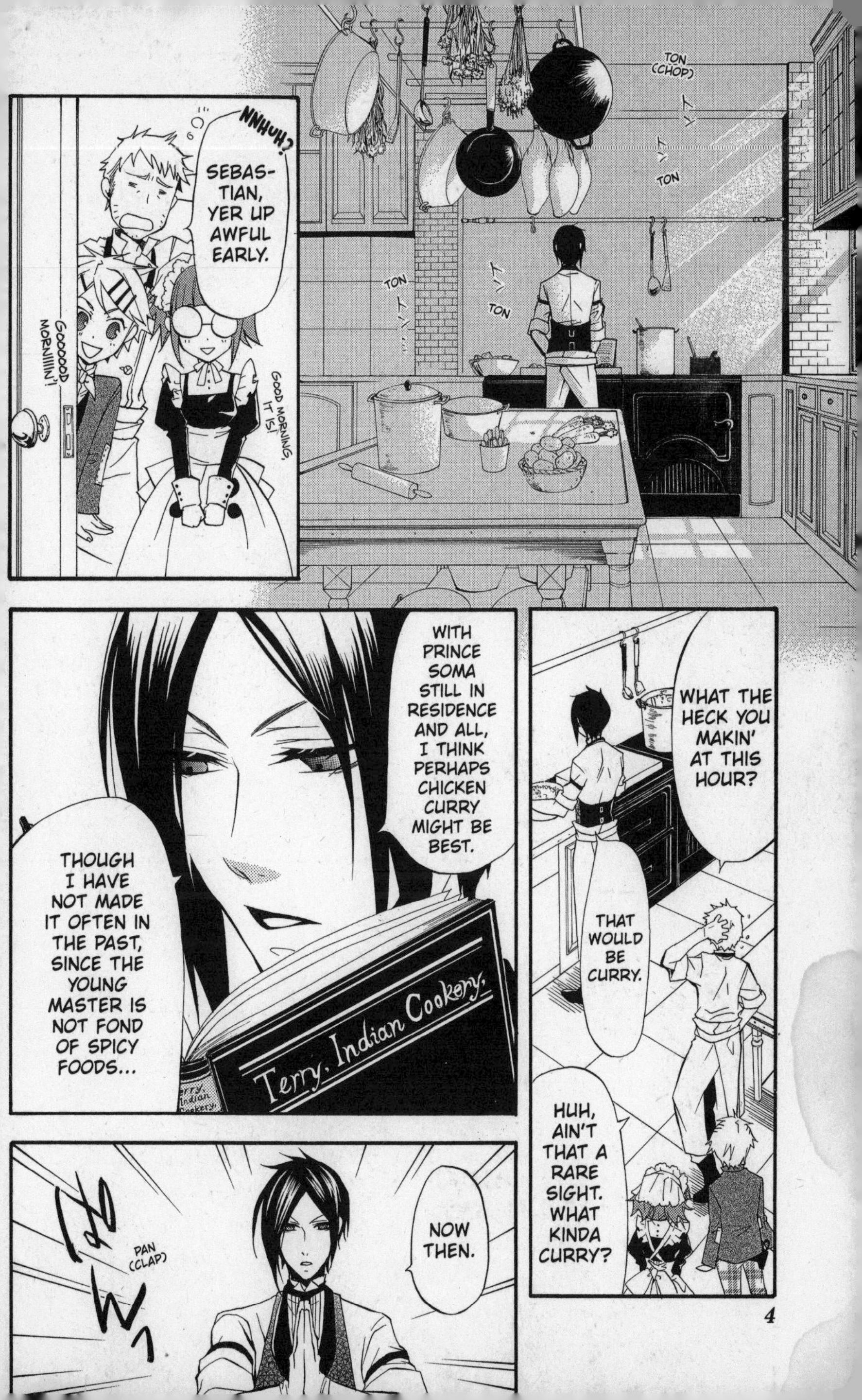
TON (CHOP)
TON
TON
TON
NNHUH?
SEBAS-TIAN, YER UP AWFUL EARLY.
GOOD MORNING, IT IS!
GOOOOOD MORNIIIIN'!
WHAT THE HECK YOU MAKIN' AT THIS HOUR?
THAT WOULD BE CURRY.
HUH, AIN'T THAT A RARE SIGHT. WHAT KINDA CURRY?
WITH PRINCE SOMA STILL IN RESIDENCE AND ALL, I THINK PERHAPS CHICKEN CURRY MIGHT BE BEST.
THOUGH I HAVE NOT MADE IT OFTEN IN THE PAST, SINCE THE YOUNG MASTER IS NOT FOND OF SPICY FOODS...
Terry. Indian Cookery.
NOW THEN.
PAN (CLAP)

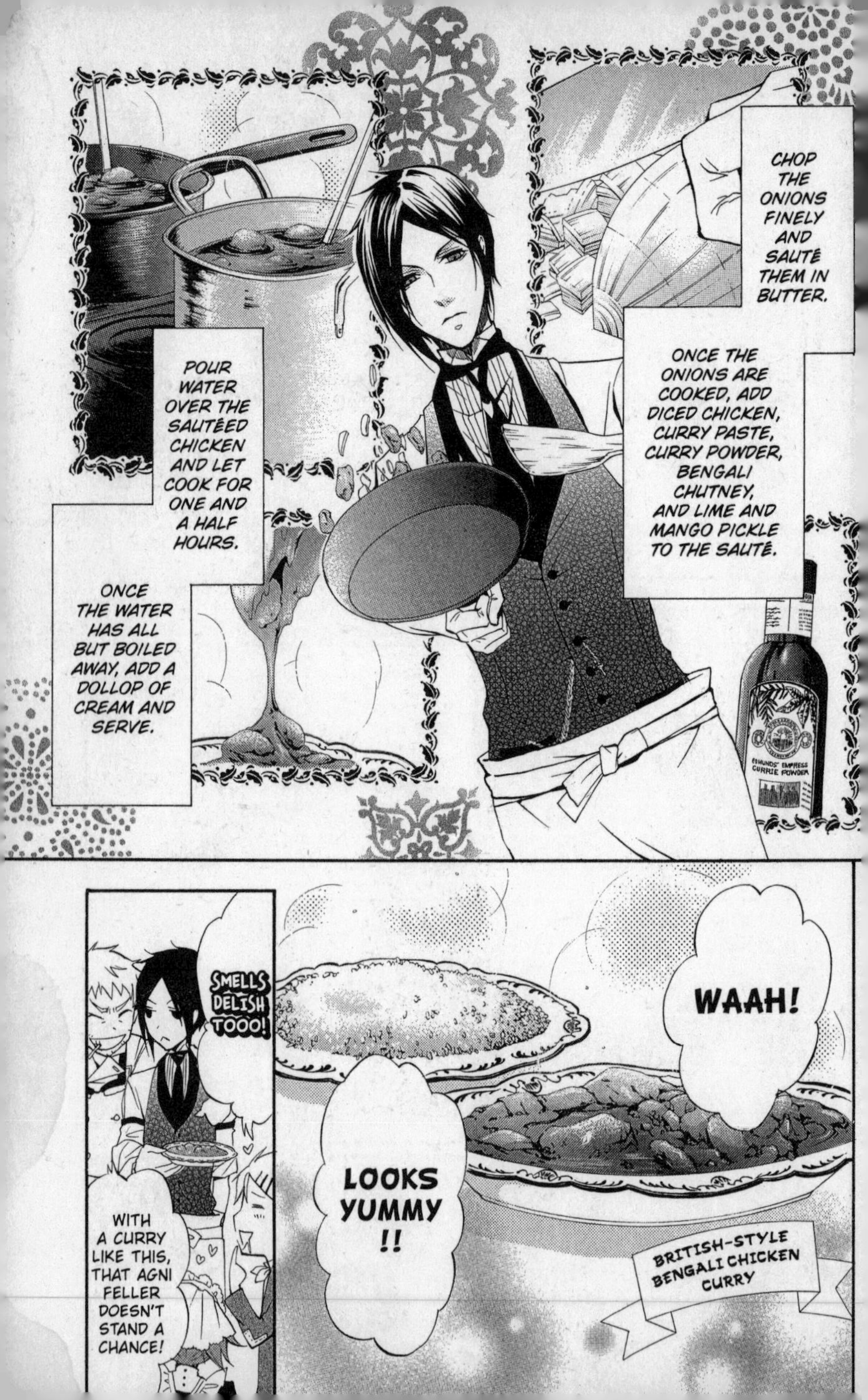
CHOP THE ONIONS FINELY AND SAUTÉ THEM IN BUTTER.
ONCE THE ONIONS ARE COOKED, ADD DICED CHICKEN, CURRY PASTE, CURRY POWDER, BENGALI CHUTNEY, AND LIME AND MANGO PICKLE TO THE SAUTÉ.
EDMUNDS' EMPRESS CURRIE POWDER
POUR WATER OVER THE SAUTÉED CHICKEN AND LET COOK FOR ONE AND A HALF HOURS.
ONCE THE WATER HAS ALL BUT BOILED AWAY, ADD A DOLLOP OF CREAM AND SERVE.
WAAH!
LOOKS YUMMY !!
BRITISH-STYLE BENGALI CHICKEN CURRY
SMELLS DELISH TOOO!
WITH A CURRY LIKE THIS, THAT AGNI FELLER DOESN'T STAND A CHANCE!

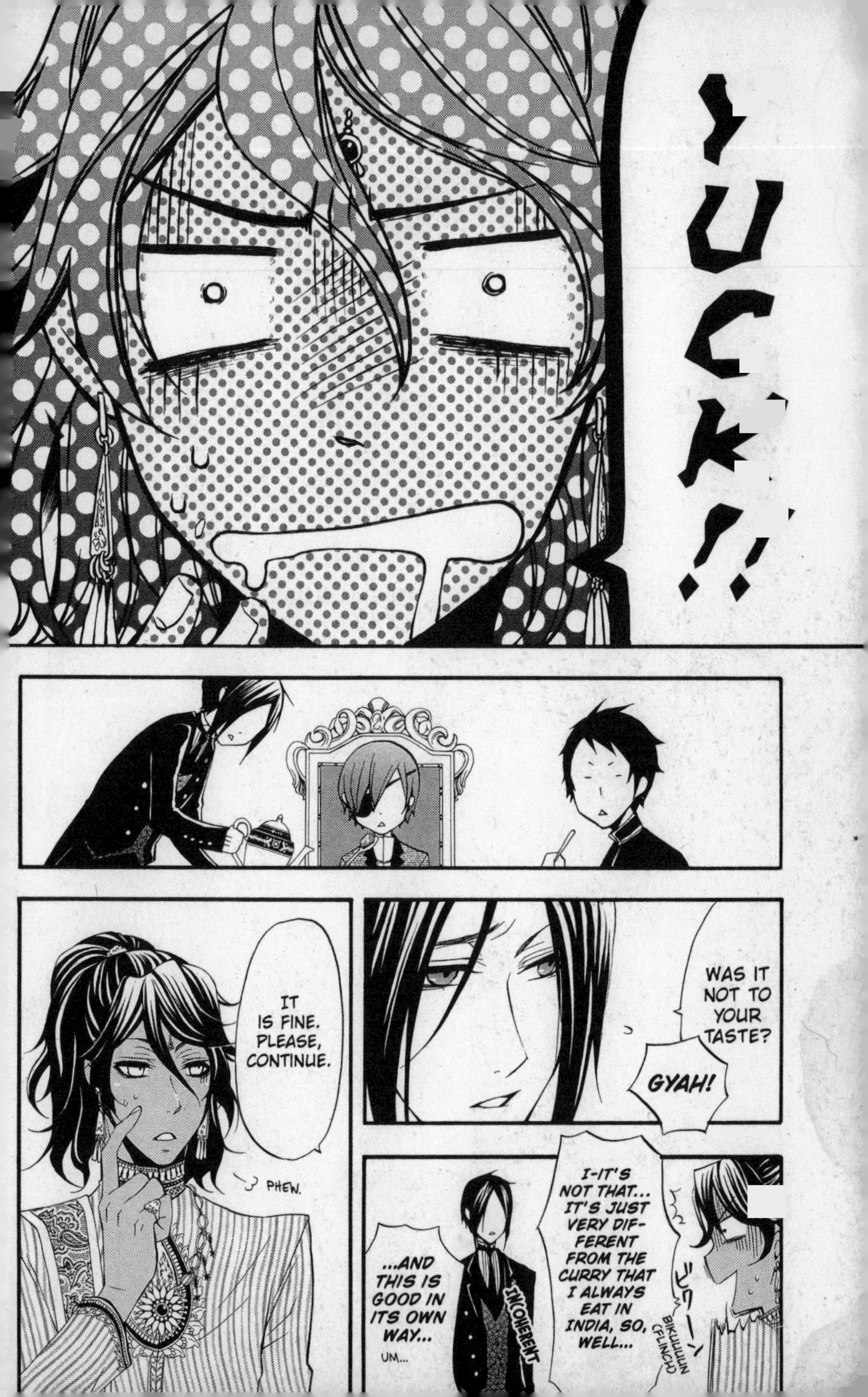
YUCK!!
WAS IT NOT TO YOUR TASTE?
GYAH!
BIKUUUUN (FLINCH)
I-IT'S NOT THAT... IT'S JUST VERY DIF-FERENT FROM THE CURRY THAT I ALWAYS EAT IN INDIA, SO, WELL...
INCOHERENT
...AND THIS IS GOOD IN ITS OWN WAY...
UM...
IT IS FINE. PLEASE, CONTINUE.
PHEW.

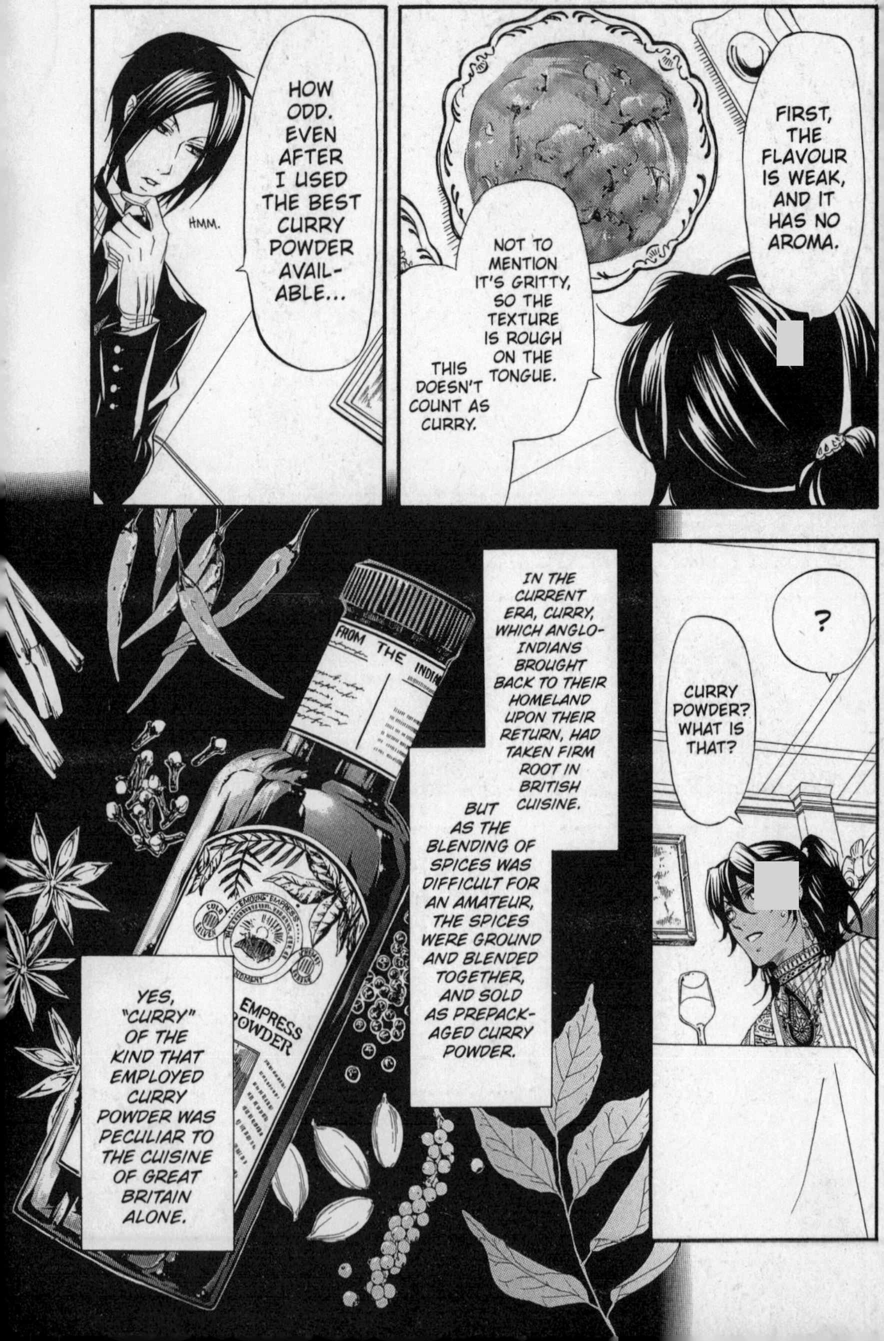
FIRST, THE FLAVOUR IS WEAK, AND IT HAS NO AROMA.
NOT TO MENTION IT'S GRITTY, SO THE TEXTURE IS ROUGH ON THE TONGUE.
THIS DOESN'T COUNT AS CURRY.
HOW ODD. EVEN AFTER I USED THE BEST CURRY POWDER AVAIL-ABLE...
HMM.
?
CURRY POWDER? WHAT IS THAT?
IN THE CURRENT ERA, CURRY, WHICH ANGLO-INDIANS BROUGHT BACK TO THEIR HOMELAND UPON THEIR RETURN, HAD TAKEN FIRM ROOT IN BRITISH CUISINE.
BUT AS THE BLENDING OF SPICES WAS DIFFICULT FOR AN AMATEUR, THE SPICES WERE GROUND AND BLENDED TOGETHER, AND SOLD AS PREPACK-AGED CURRY POWDER.
YES, "CURRY" OF THE KIND THAT EMPLOYED CURRY POWDER WAS PECULIAR TO THE CUISINE OF GREAT BRITAIN ALONE.

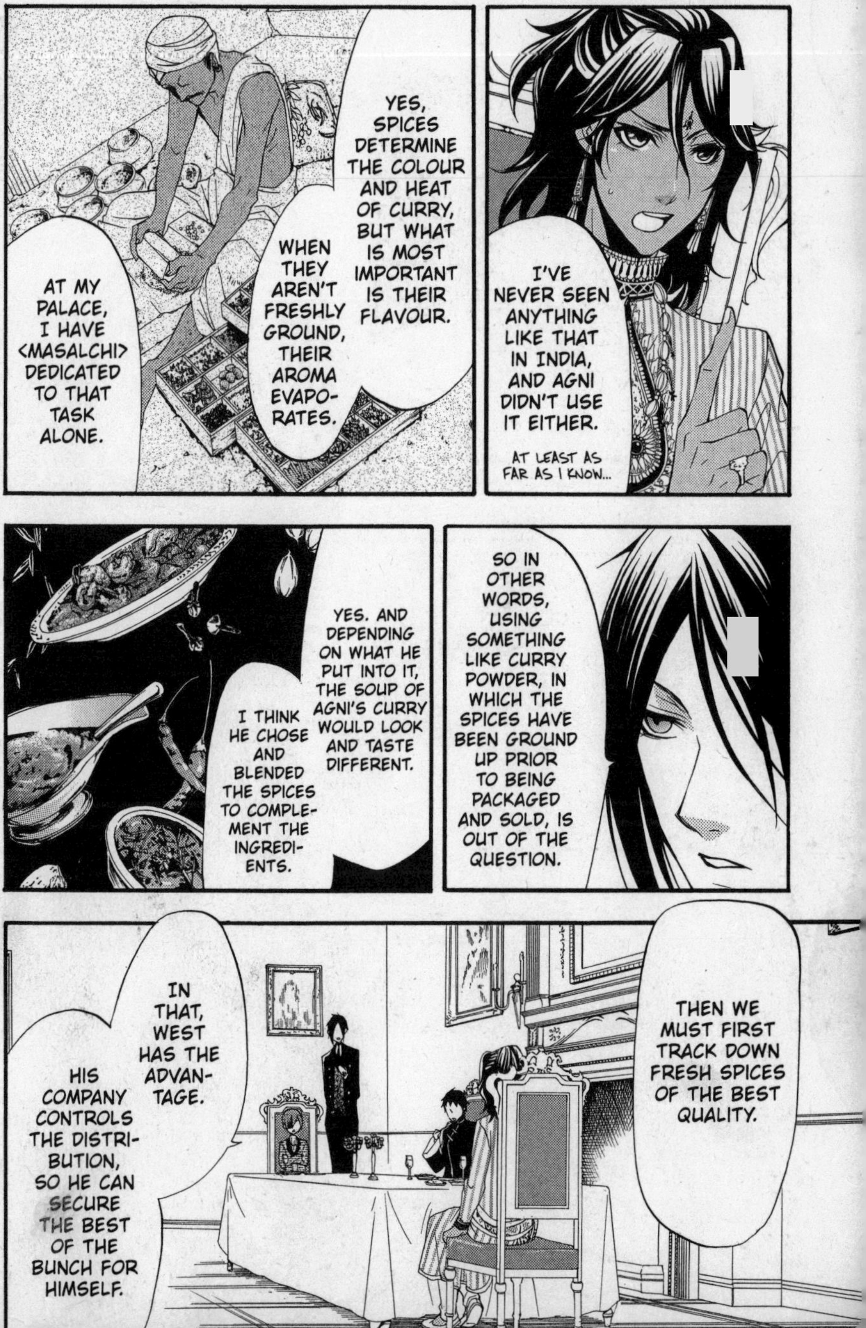
I'VE NEVER SEEN ANYTHING LIKE THAT IN INDIA, AND AGNI DIDN'T USE IT EITHER.
AT LEAST AS FAR AS I KNOW...
YES, SPICES DETERMINE THE COLOUR AND HEAT OF CURRY, BUT WHAT IS MOST IMPORTANT IS THEIR FLAVOUR.
WHEN THEY AREN'T FRESHLY GROUND, THEIR AROMA EVAPO-RATES.
AT MY PALACE, I HAVE <MASALCHI> DEDICATED TO THAT TASK ALONE.
SO IN OTHER WORDS, USING SOMETHING LIKE CURRY POWDER, IN WHICH THE SPICES HAVE BEEN GROUND UP PRIOR TO BEING PACKAGED AND SOLD, IS OUT OF THE QUESTION.
YES. AND DEPENDING ON WHAT HE PUT INTO IT, THE SOUP OF AGNI'S CURRY WOULD LOOK AND TASTE DIFFERENT.
I THINK HE CHOSE AND BLENDED THE SPICES TO COMPLE-MENT THE INGREDI-ENTS.
THEN WE MUST FIRST TRACK DOWN FRESH SPICES OF THE BEST QUALITY.
IN THAT, WEST HAS THE ADVAN-TAGE.
HIS COMPANY CONTROLS THE DISTRI-BUTION, SO HE CAN SECURE THE BEST OF THE BUNCH FOR HIMSELF.

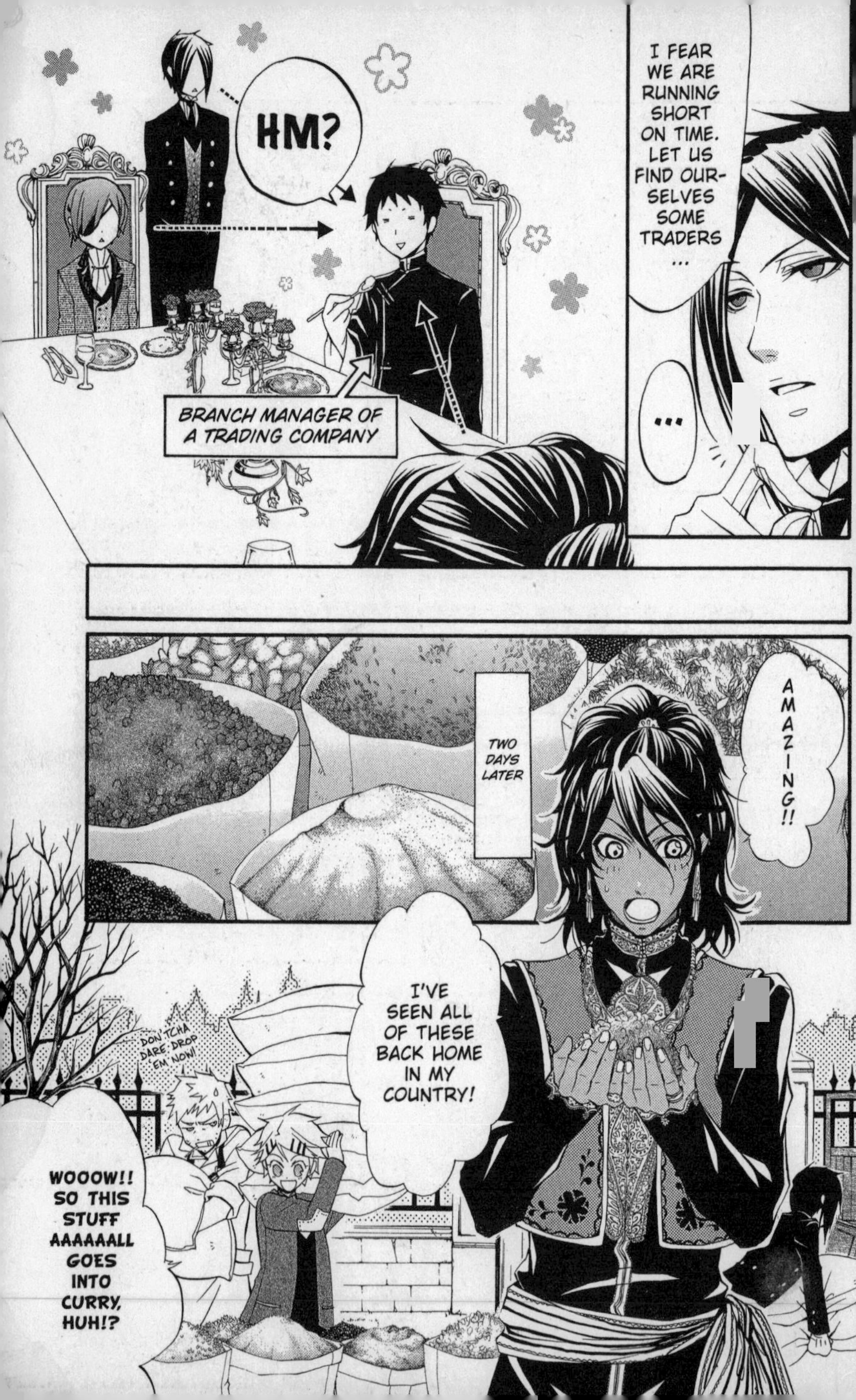

I FEAR WE ARE RUNNING SHORT ON TIME. LET US FIND OURSELVES SOME TRADERS ...
...
HM?
BRANCH MANAGER OF A TRADING COMPANY
AMAZING!!
TWO DAYS LATER
I'VE SEEN ALL OF THESE BACK HOME IN MY COUNTRY!
DON'TCHA DARE DROP 'EM NOW!
WOOOW!! SO THIS STUFF AAAAAALL GOES INTO CURRY, HUH!?

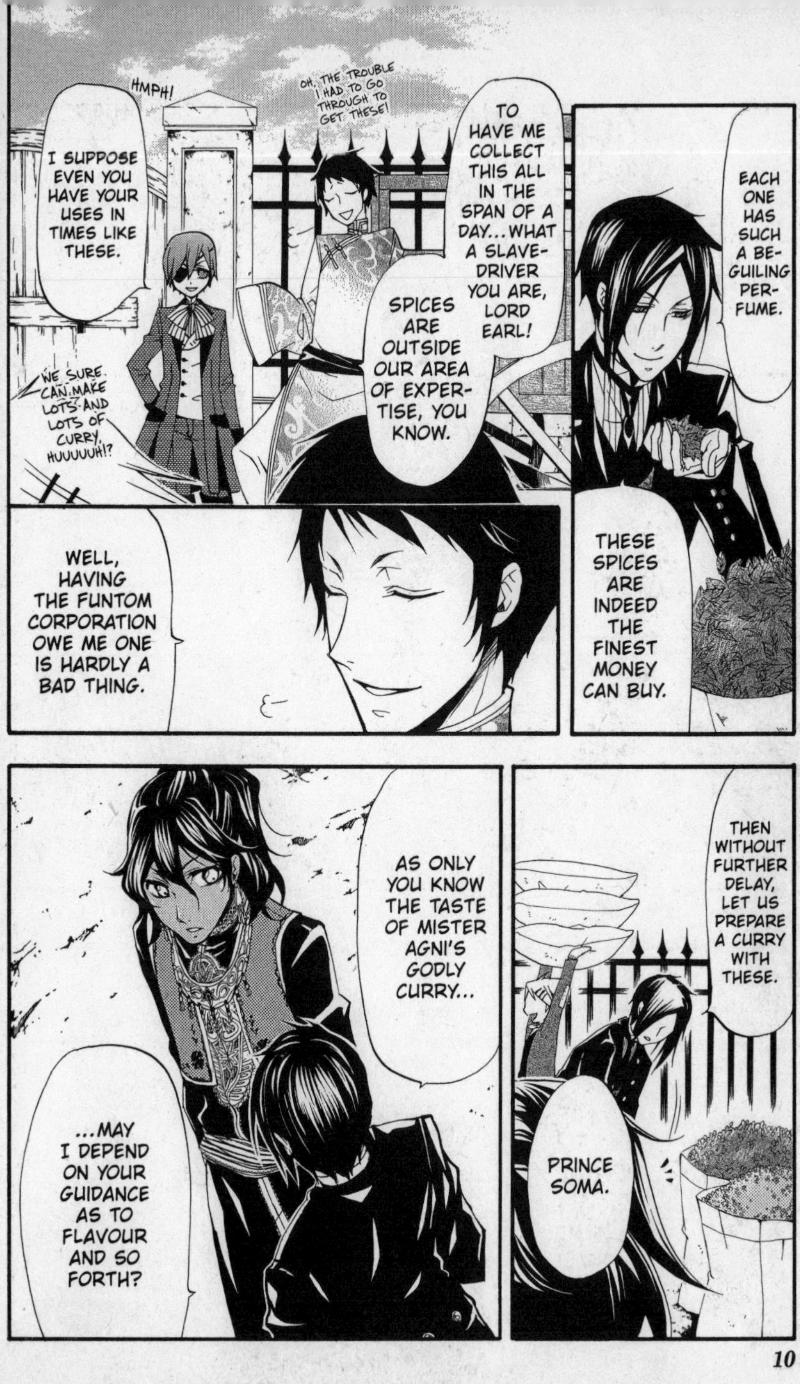
EACH ONE HAS SUCH A BE-GUILING PER-FUME.
THESE SPICES ARE INDEED THE FINEST MONEY CAN BUY.
TO HAVE ME COLLECT THIS ALL IN THE SPAN OF A DAY... WHAT A SLAVE-DRIVER YOU ARE, LORD EARL!
OH, THE TROUBLE I HAD TO GO THROUGH TO GET THESE!
SPICES ARE OUTSIDE OUR AREA OF EXPER-TISE, YOU KNOW.
HMPH!
I SUPPOSE EVEN YOU HAVE YOUR USES IN TIMES LIKE THESE.
WE SURE CAN MAKE LOTS AND LOTS OF CURRY, HUUUUUH!?
WELL, HAVING THE FUNTOM CORPORATION OWE ME ONE IS HARDLY A BAD THING.
THEN WITHOUT FURTHER DELAY, LET US PREPARE A CURRY WITH THESE.
PRINCE SOMA.
AS ONLY YOU KNOW THE TASTE OF MISTER AGNI'S GODLY CURRY...
...MAY I DEPEND ON YOUR GUIDANCE AS TO FLAVOUR AND SO FORTH?

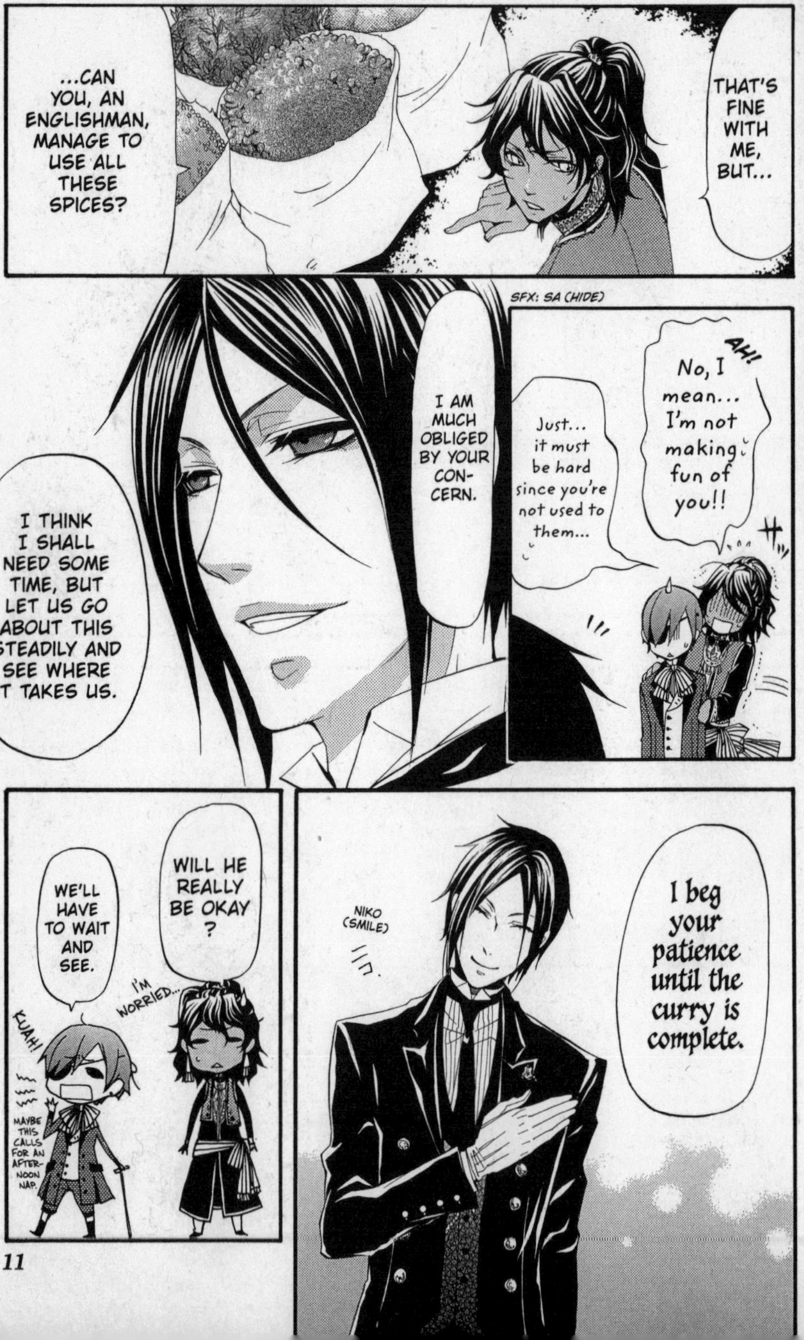
THAT'S FINE WITH ME, BUT...
...CAN YOU, AN ENGLISHMAN, MANAGE TO USE ALL THESE SPICES?
SFX: SA (HIDE)
AH!
No, I mean... I'm not making fun of you!!
Just... it must be hard since you're not used to them...
I AM MUCH OBLIGED BY YOUR CON-CERN.
I THINK I SHALL NEED SOME TIME, BUT LET US GO ABOUT THIS STEADILY AND SEE WHERE IT TAKES US.
NIKO (SMILE)
I beg your patience until the curry is complete.
WILL HE REALLY BE OKAY?
I'M WORRIED...
WE'LL HAVE TO WAIT AND SEE.
KUAH!
MAYBE THIS CALLS FOR AN AFTER-NOON NAP.

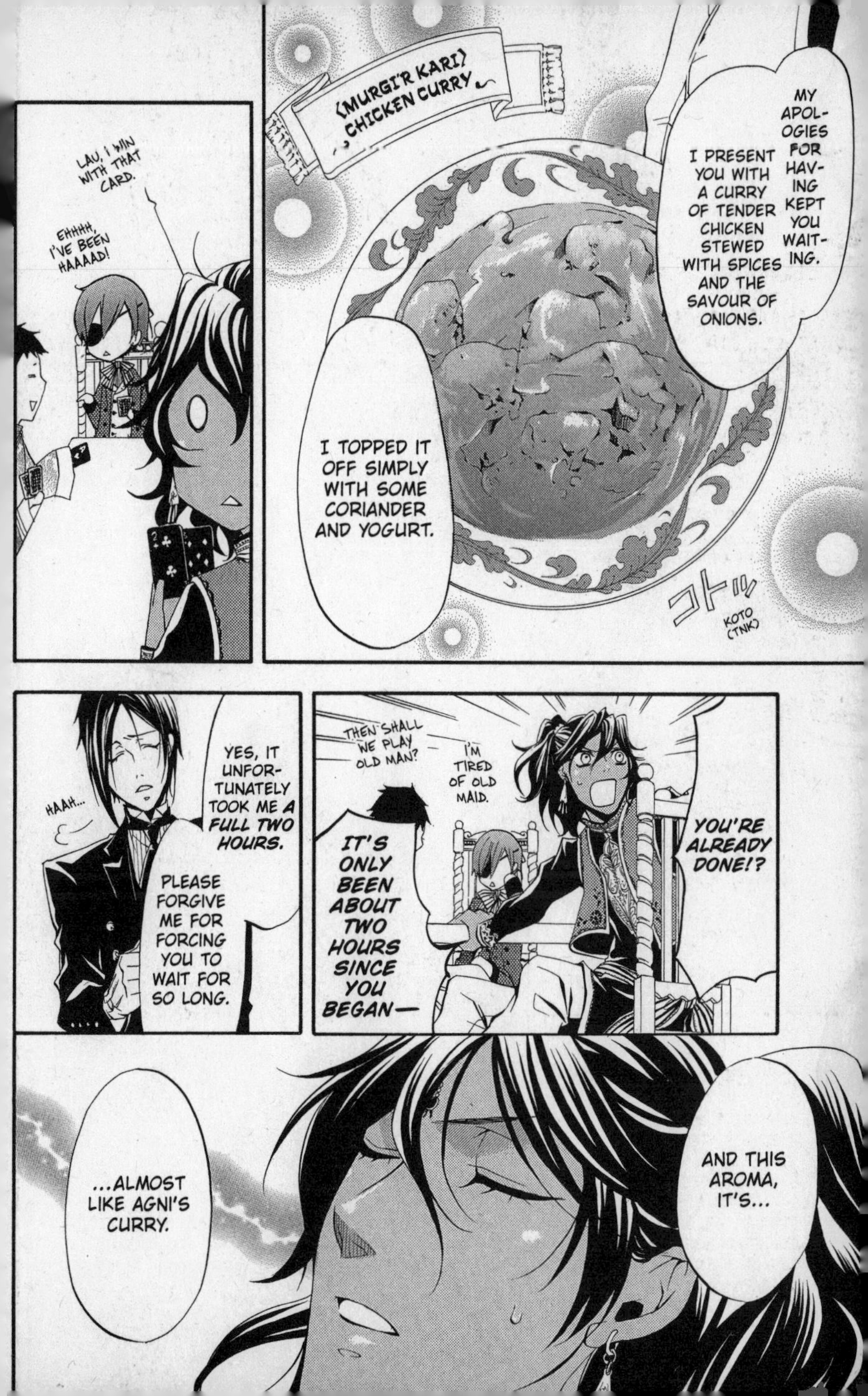

{MURGI'R KARI} CHICKEN CURRY
MY APOLOGIES FOR HAVING KEPT YOU WAITING.
I PRESENT YOU WITH A CURRY OF TENDER CHICKEN STEWED WITH SPICES AND THE SAVOUR OF ONIONS.
I TOPPED IT OFF SIMPLY WITH SOME CORIANDER AND YOGURT.
コトッ
KOTO (TNK)
LAU, I WIN WITH THAT CARD.
EHHHH, I'VE BEEN HAAAAD!
YOU'RE ALREADY DONE!?
I'M TIRED OF OLD MAID.
THEN SHALL WE PLAY OLD MAN?
IT'S ONLY BEEN ABOUT TWO HOURS SINCE YOU BEGAN—
YES, IT UNFORTUNATELY TOOK ME A FULL TWO HOURS.
HAAH...
PLEASE FORGIVE ME FOR FORCING YOU TO WAIT FOR SO LONG.
AND THIS AROMA, IT'S...
...ALMOST LIKE AGNI'S CURRY.

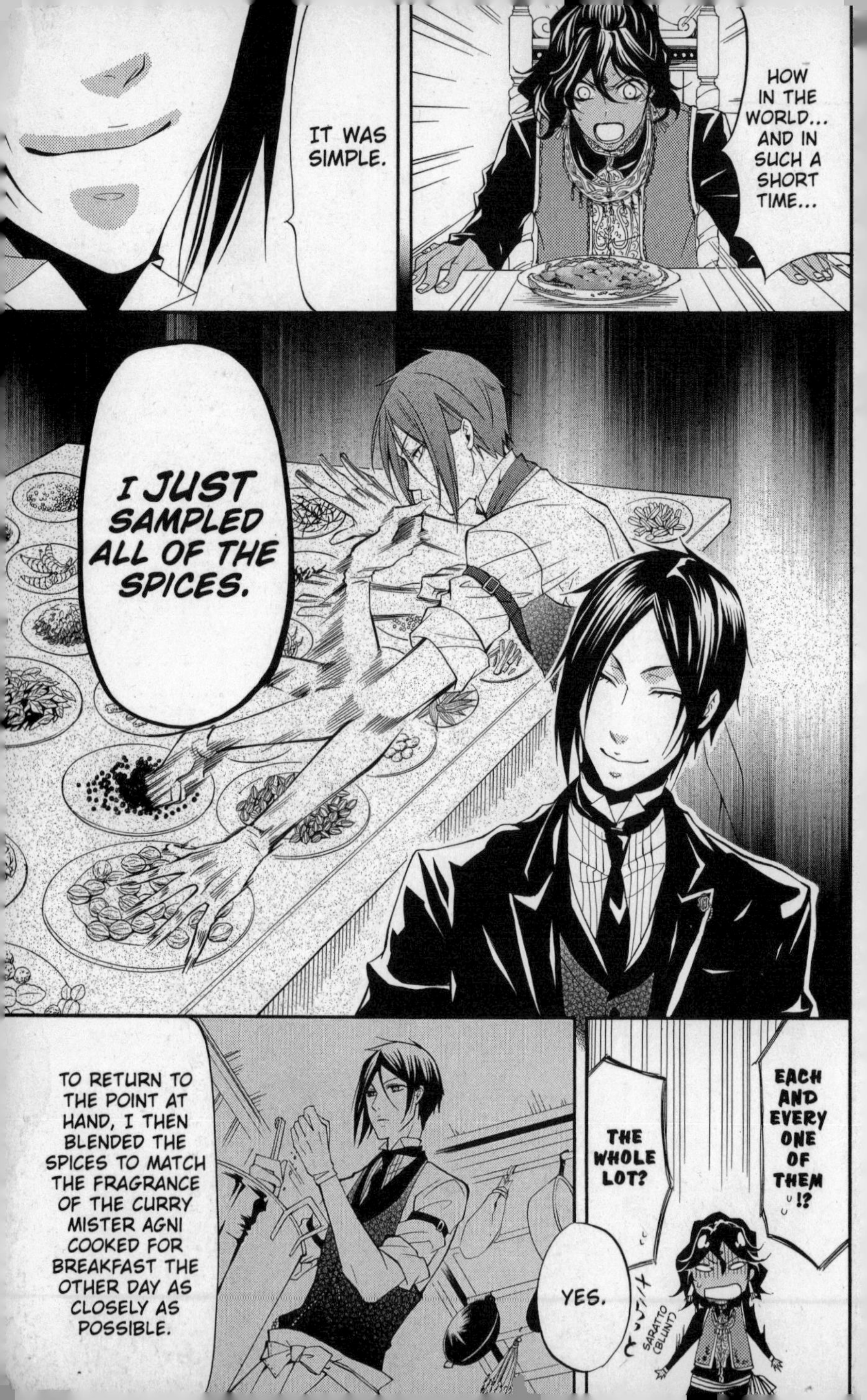
HOW IN THE WORLD... AND IN SUCH A SHORT TIME...
IT WAS SIMPLE.
I JUST SAMPLED ALL OF THE SPICES.
EACH AND EVERY ONE OF THEM!?
THE WHOLE LOT?
YES.
SARATTO (BLLINT)
TO RETURN TO THE POINT AT HAND, I THEN BLENDED THE SPICES TO MATCH THE FRAGRANCE OF THE CURRY MISTER AGNI COOKED FOR BREAKFAST THE OTHER DAY AS CLOSELY AS POSSIBLE.

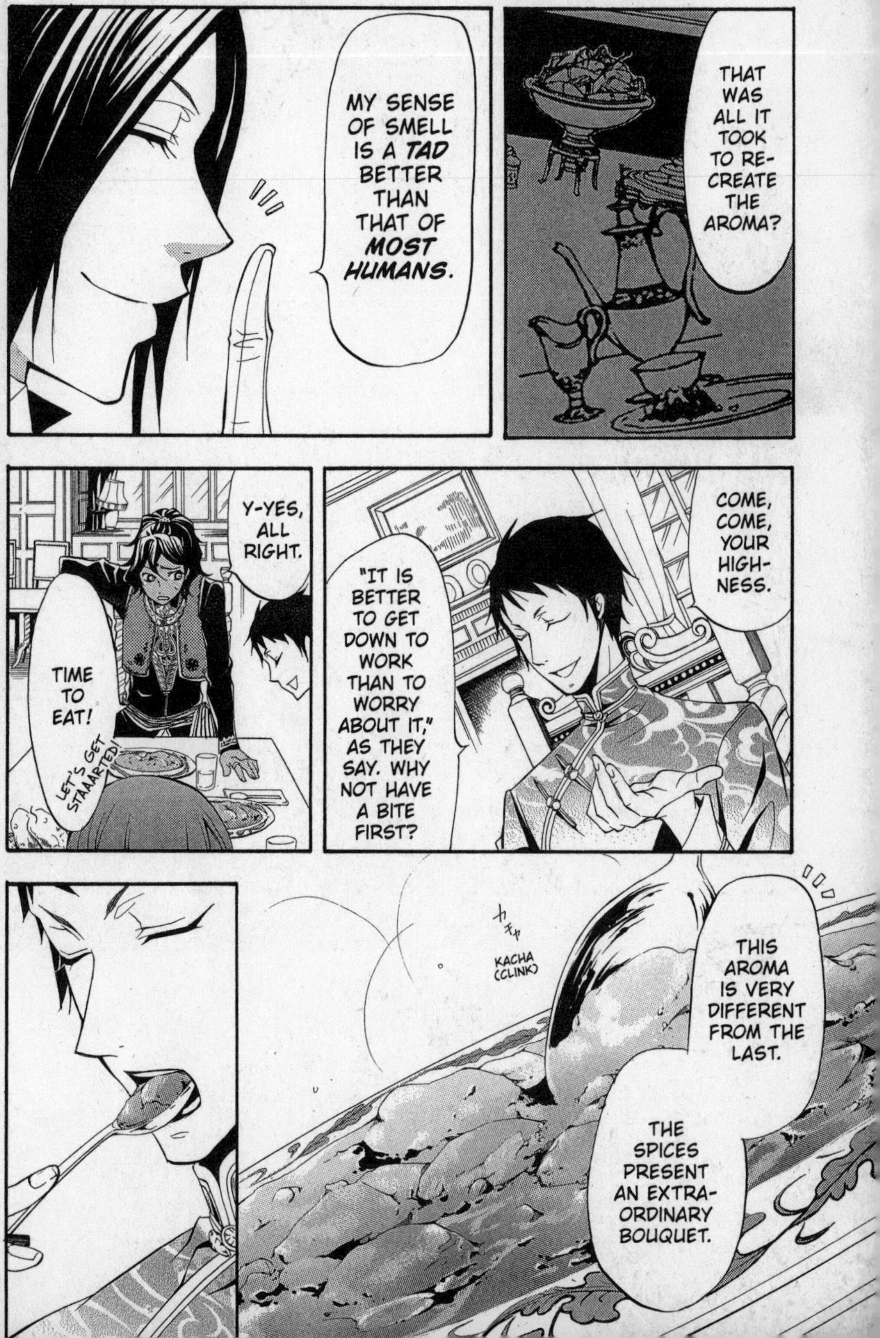
THAT WAS ALL IT TOOK TO RE-CREATE THE AROMA?
MY SENSE OF SMELL IS A *TAD* BETTER THAN THAT OF ***MOST HUMANS***.
COME, COME, YOUR HIGHNESS.
"IT IS BETTER TO GET DOWN TO WORK THAN TO WORRY ABOUT IT," AS THEY SAY. WHY NOT HAVE A BITE FIRST?
Y-YES, ALL RIGHT.
TIME TO EAT!
LET'S GET STAAARTED!
KACHA (CLINK)
THIS AROMA IS VERY DIFFERENT FROM THE LAST.
THE SPICES PRESENT AN EXTRA-ORDINARY BOUQUET.

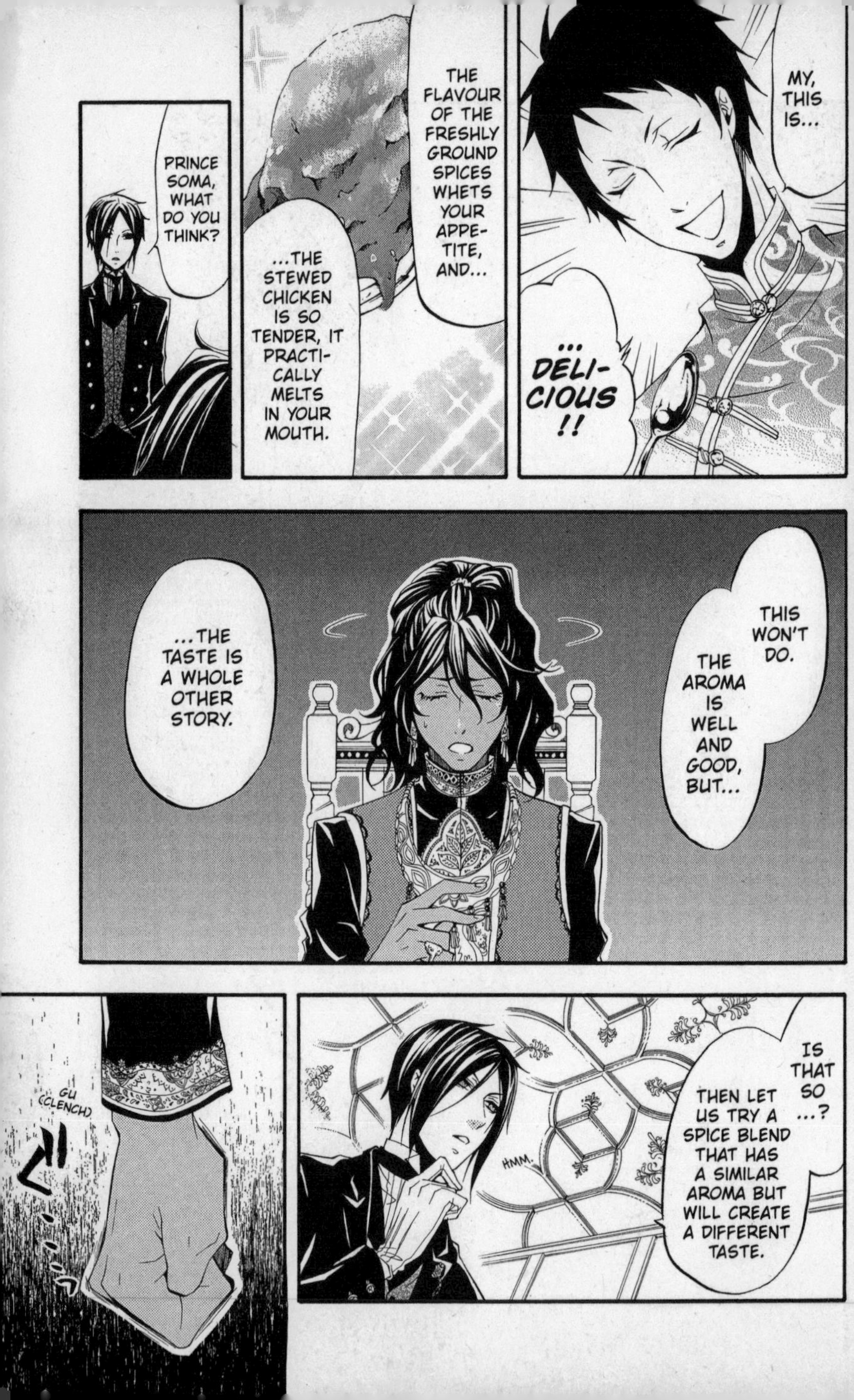
MY, THIS IS...
...DELICIOUS!!
THE FLAVOUR OF THE FRESHLY GROUND SPICES WHETS YOUR APPETITE, AND...
...THE STEWED CHICKEN IS SO TENDER, IT PRACTICALLY MELTS IN YOUR MOUTH.
PRINCE SOMA, WHAT DO YOU THINK?
THIS WON'T DO.
THE AROMA IS WELL AND GOOD, BUT...
...THE TASTE IS A WHOLE OTHER STORY.
IS THAT SO ...?
THEN LET US TRY A SPICE BLEND THAT HAS A SIMILAR AROMA BUT WILL CREATE A DIFFERENT TASTE.
HMM.
GU (CLENCH)

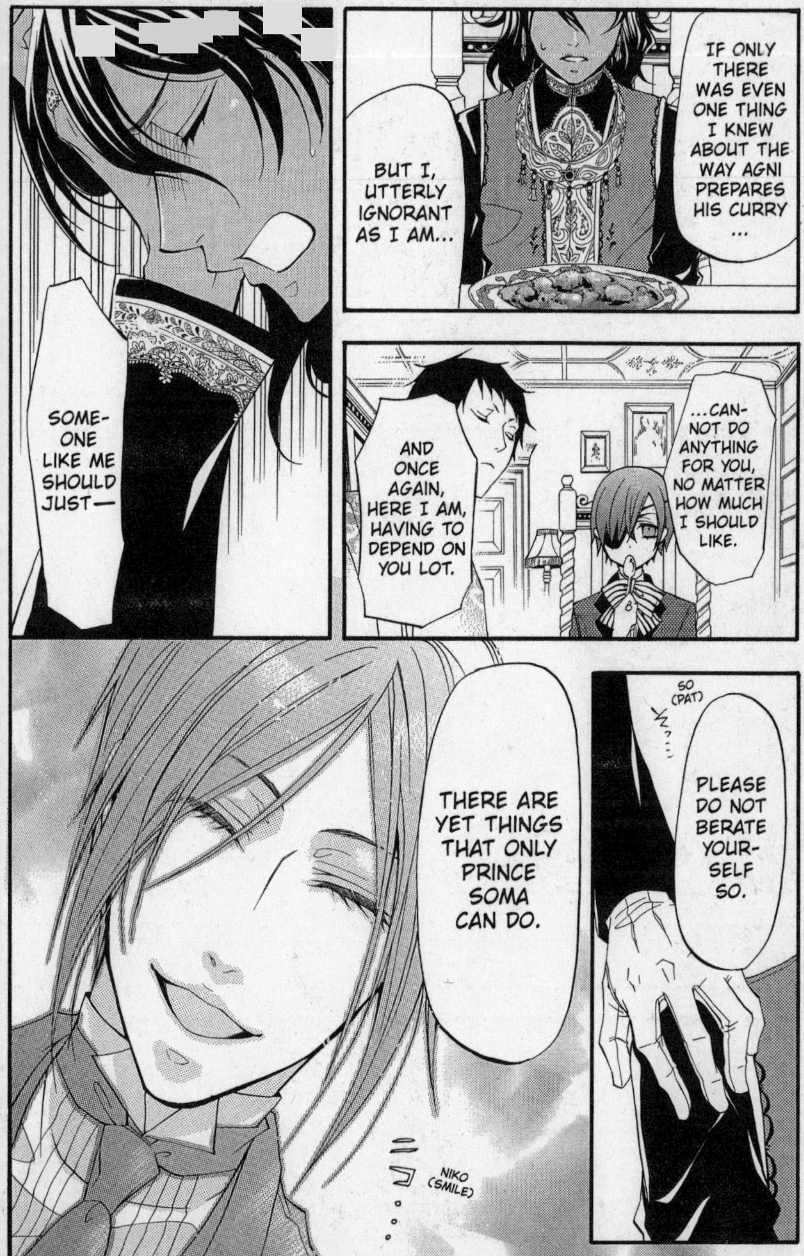
IF ONLY THERE WAS EVEN ONE THING I KNEW ABOUT THE WAY AGNI PREPARES HIS CURRY ...
BUT I, UTTERLY IGNORANT AS I AM...
...CAN-NOT DO ANYTHING FOR YOU, NO MATTER HOW MUCH I SHOULD LIKE.
AND ONCE AGAIN, HERE I AM, HAVING TO DEPEND ON YOU LOT.
SOME-ONE LIKE ME SHOULD JUST—
SO (PAT)
PLEASE DO NOT BERATE YOUR-SELF SO.
THERE ARE YET THINGS THAT ONLY PRINCE SOMA CAN DO.
NIKO (SMILE)

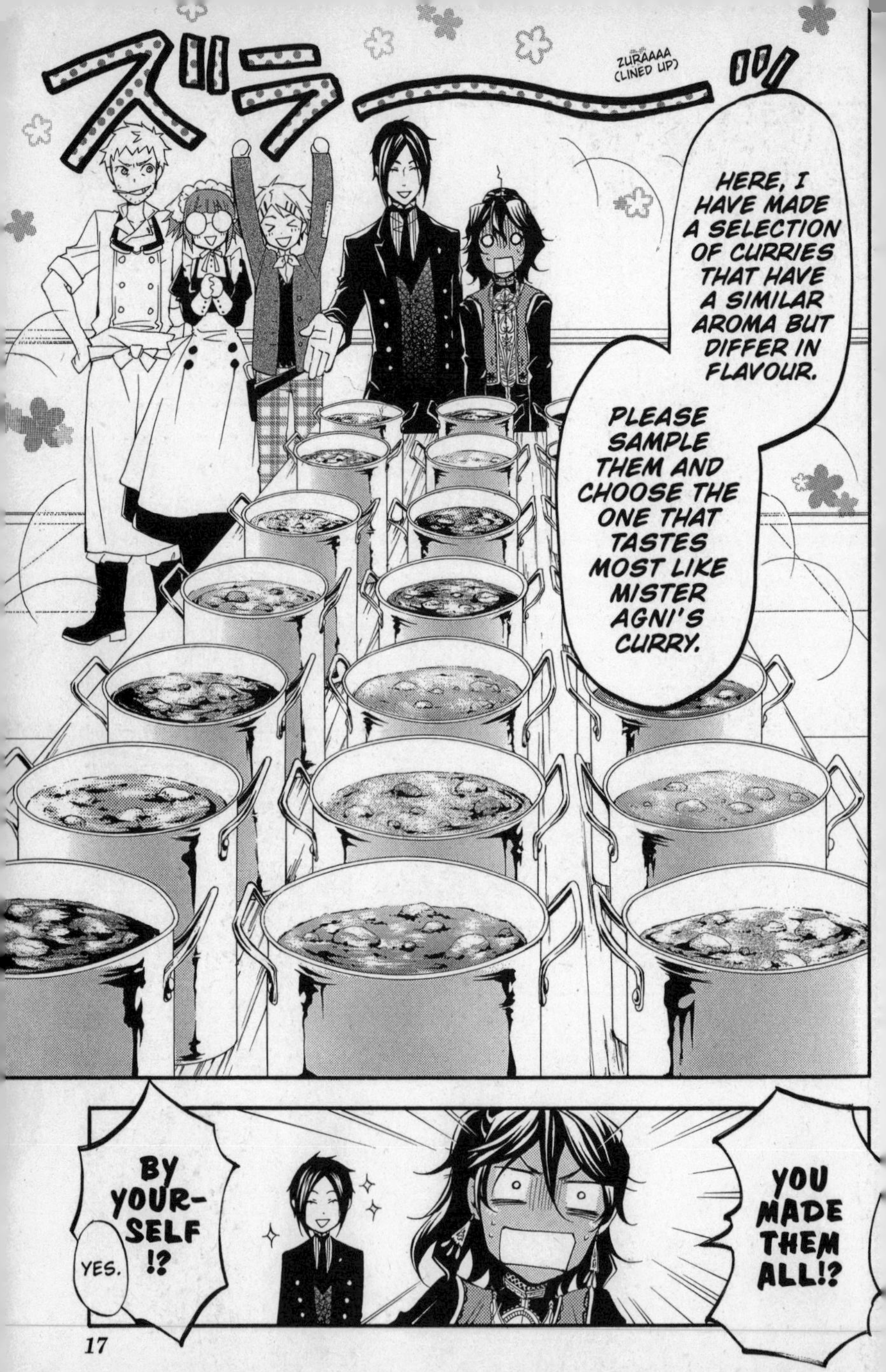
ズラーーッ!
ZURAAAA (LINED UP)
HERE, I HAVE MADE A SELECTION OF CURRIES THAT HAVE A SIMILAR AROMA BUT DIFFER IN FLAVOUR.
PLEASE SAMPLE THEM AND CHOOSE THE ONE THAT TASTES MOST LIKE MISTER AGNI'S CURRY.
YOU MADE THEM ALL!?
BY YOUR-SELF!?
YES.

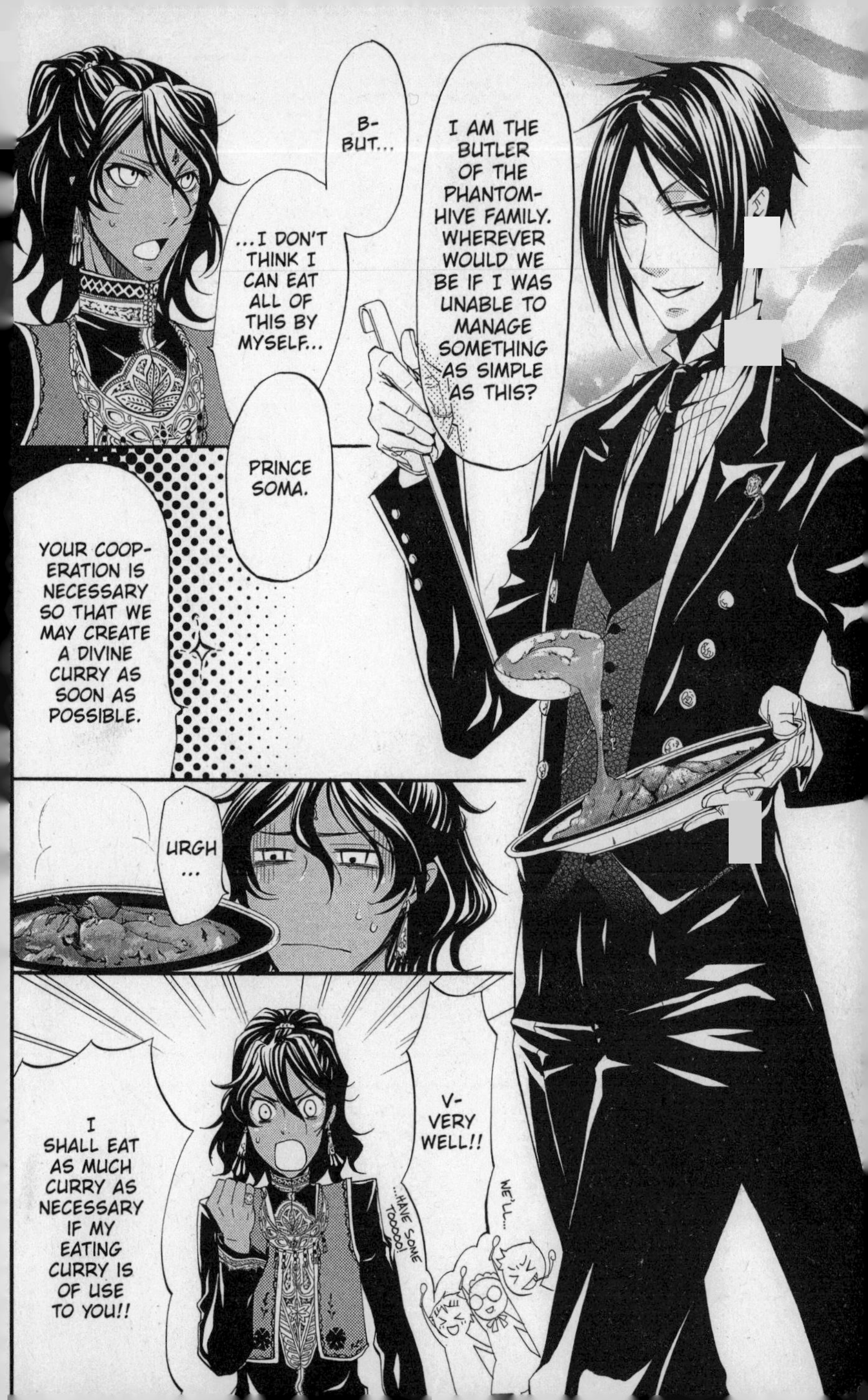
I AM THE BUTLER OF THE PHANTOM-HIVE FAMILY. WHEREVER WOULD WE BE IF I WAS UNABLE TO MANAGE SOMETHING AS SIMPLE AS THIS?
B-BUT...
...I DON'T THINK I CAN EAT ALL OF THIS BY MYSELF...
PRINCE SOMA.
YOUR COOP-ERATION IS NECESSARY SO THAT WE MAY CREATE A DIVINE CURRY AS SOON AS POSSIBLE.
URGH...
V-VERY WELL!!
I SHALL EAT AS MUCH CURRY AS NECESSARY IF MY EATING CURRY IS OF USE TO YOU!!
WE'LL...
...HAVE SOME TOOOOO!

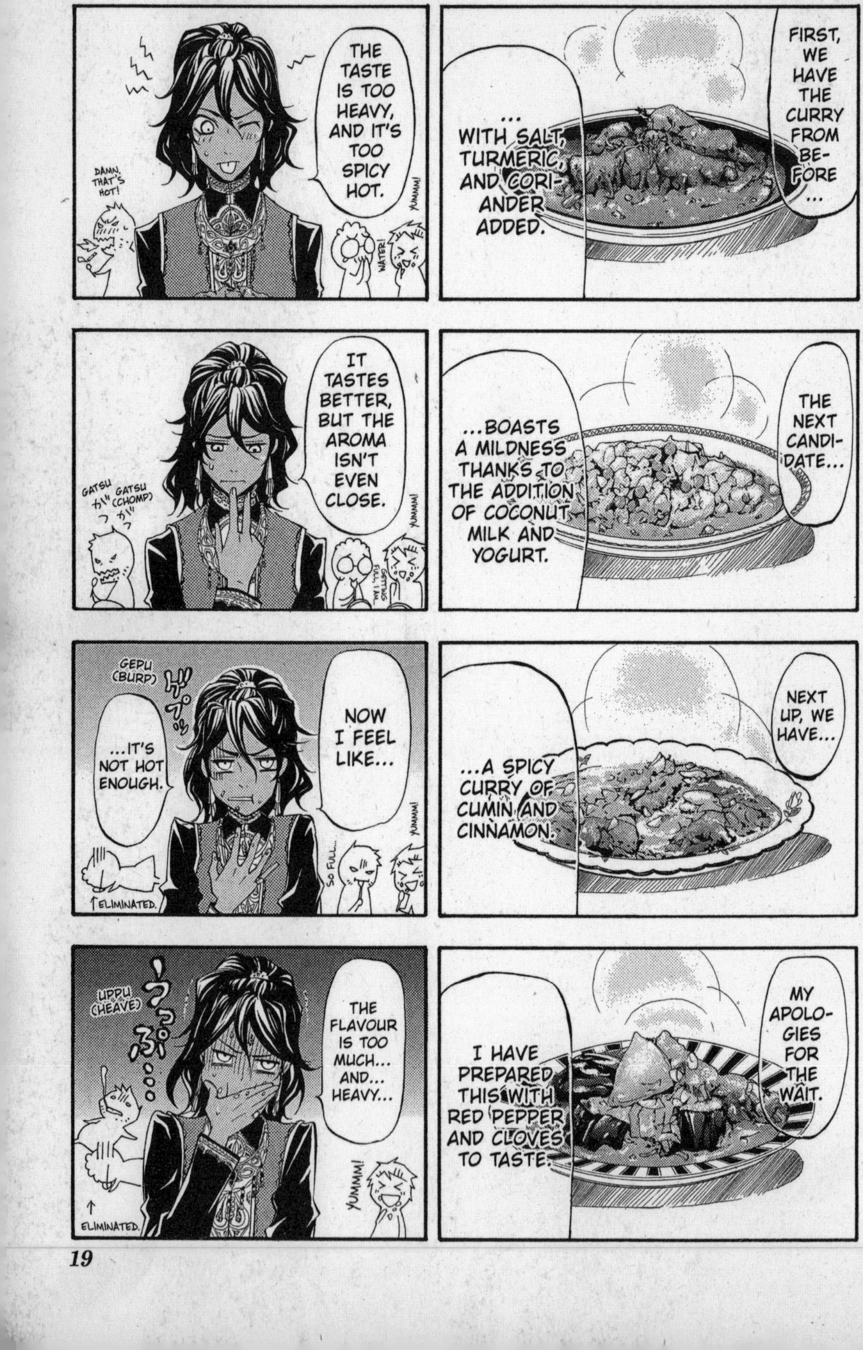
FIRST, WE HAVE THE CURRY FROM BE-FORE...
...WITH SALT, TURMERIC, AND CORI-ANDER ADDED.
THE TASTE IS TOO HEAVY, AND IT'S TOO SPICY HOT.
YUMMM!
WATER!
DAMN, THAT'S HOT!
THE NEXT CANDI-DATE...
...BOASTS A MILDNESS THANKS TO THE ADDITION OF COCONUT MILK AND YOGURT.
IT TASTES BETTER, BUT THE AROMA ISN'T EVEN CLOSE.
YUMMM!
GETTING FULL, I AM.
GATSU GATSU (CHOMP)
NEXT UP, WE HAVE...
...A SPICY CURRY OF CUMIN AND CINNAMON.
NOW I FEEL LIKE...
GEPU (BURP)
...IT'S NOT HOT ENOUGH.
YUMMM!
SO FULL...
ELIMINATED.
MY APOLOGIES FOR THE WAIT.
I HAVE PREPARED THIS WITH RED PEPPER AND CLOVES TO TASTE.
THE FLAVOUR IS TOO MUCH... AND... HEAVY...
UPPU (HEAVE)
YUMMM!
ELIMINATED.

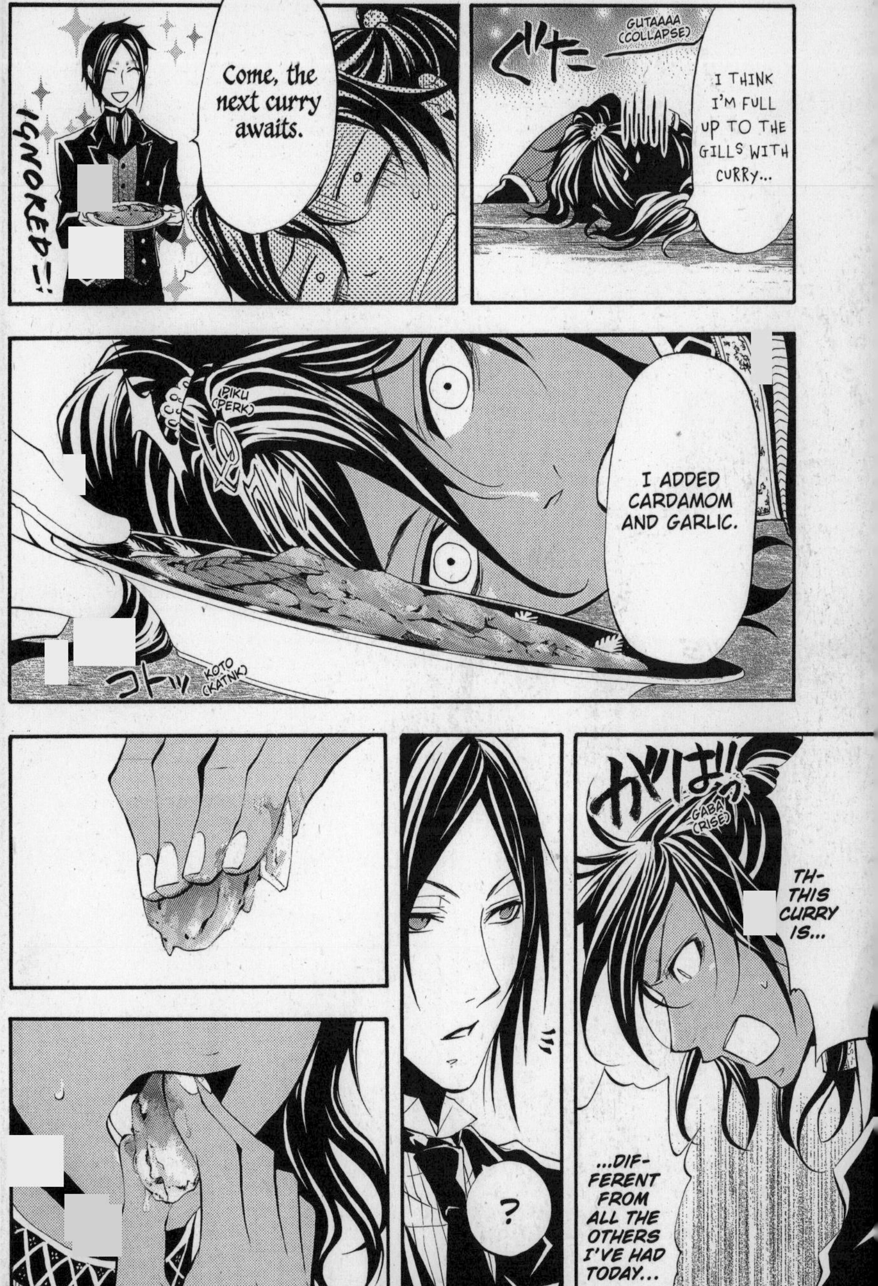
GUTAAAA (COLLAPSE)
I THINK I'M FULL UP TO THE GILLS WITH CURRY...
Come, the next curry awaits.
IGNORED!!
I ADDED CARDAMOM AND GARLIC.
PIKU (PERK)
KOTO (KATNK)
GABA (RISE)
TH-THIS CURRY IS...
...DIF-FERENT FROM ALL THE OTHERS I'VE HAD TODAY...
?

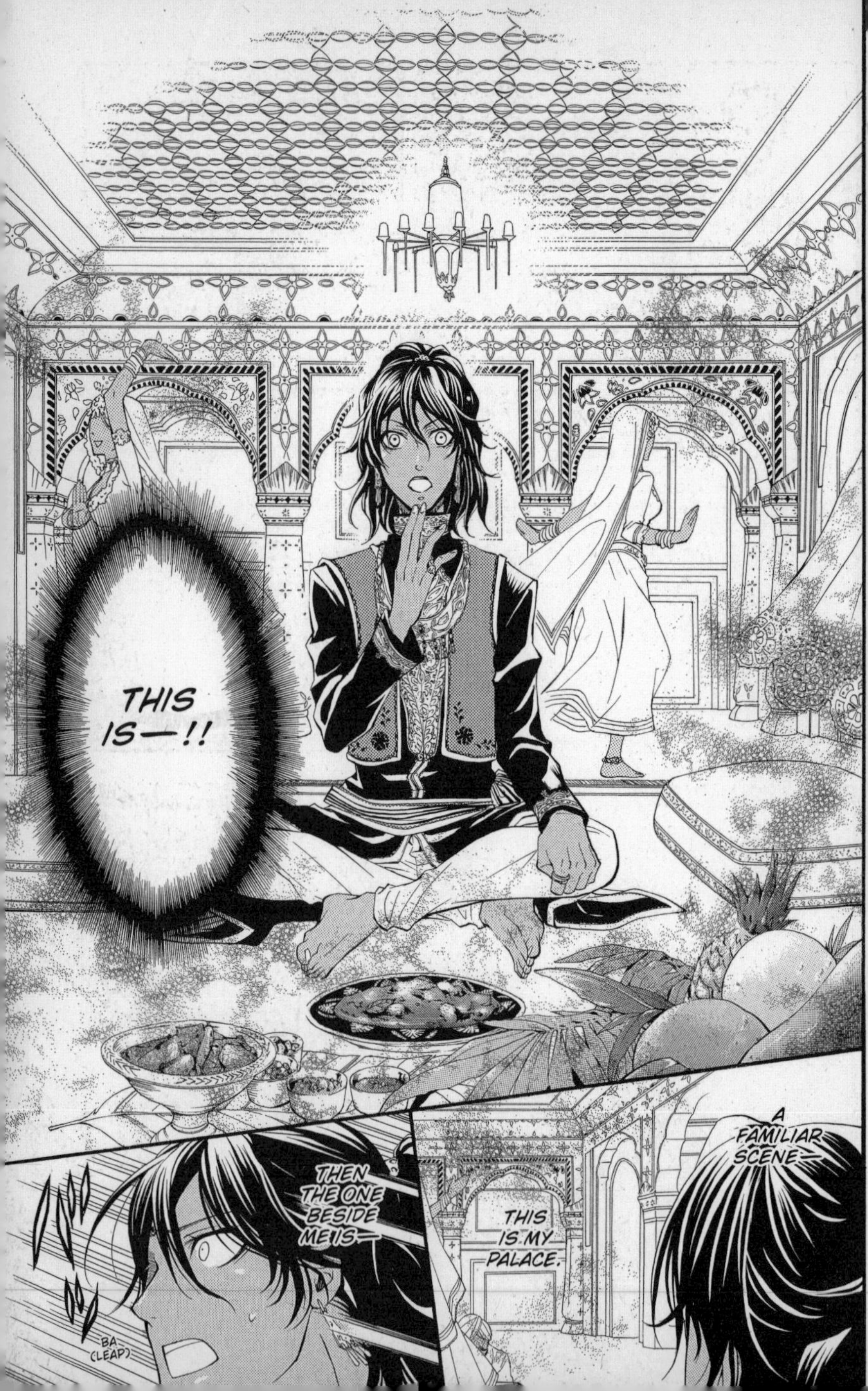
THIS IS—!!
A FAMILIAR SCENE
THIS IS MY PALACE.
THEN THE ONE BESIDE ME IS—
BA (LEAP)

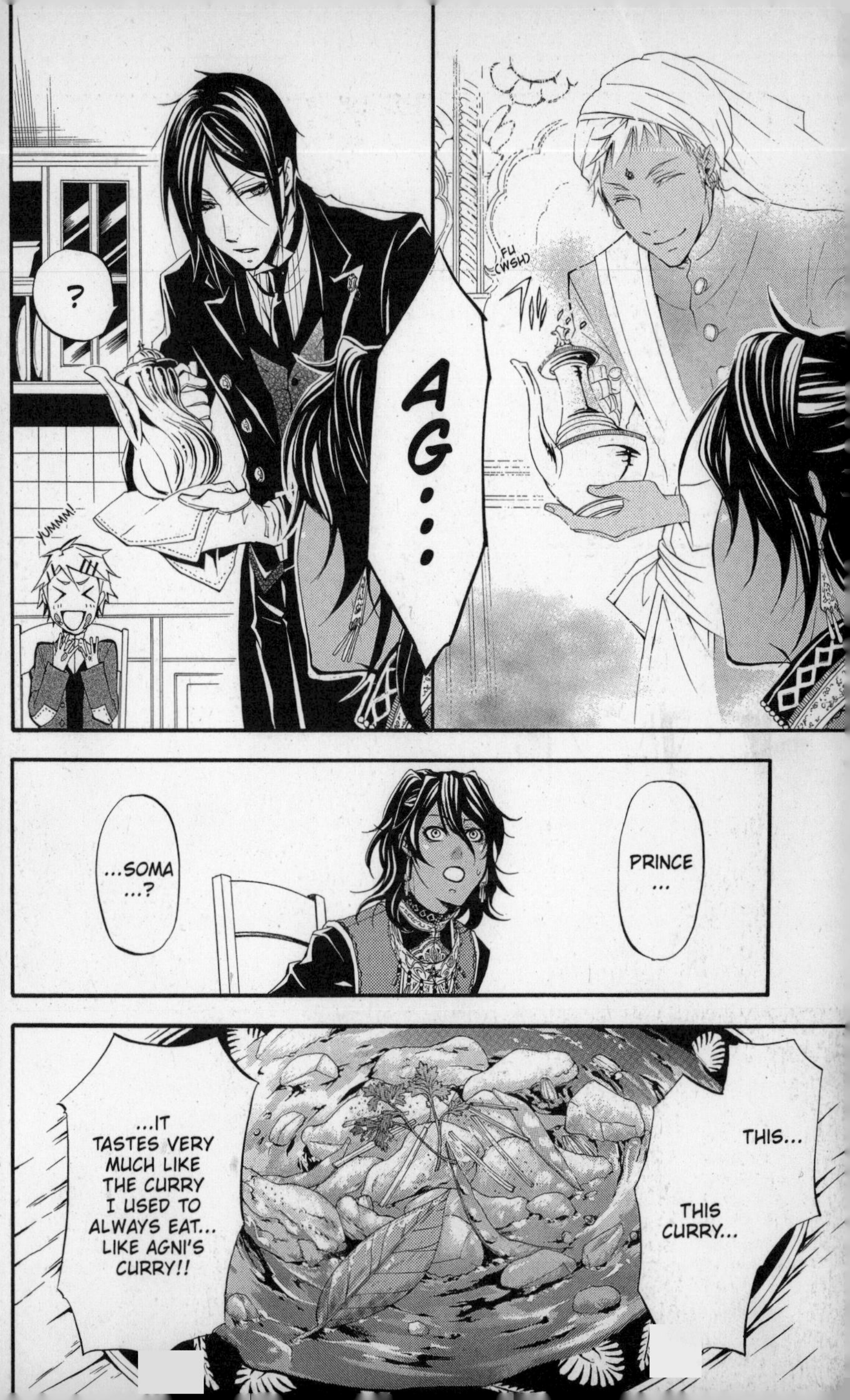
FU (WSH)
AG...
?
YUMMM!
PRINCE ...
...SOMA ...?
THIS...
THIS CURRY...
...IT TASTES VERY MUCH LIKE THE CURRY I USED TO ALWAYS EAT... LIKE AGNI'S CURRY!!

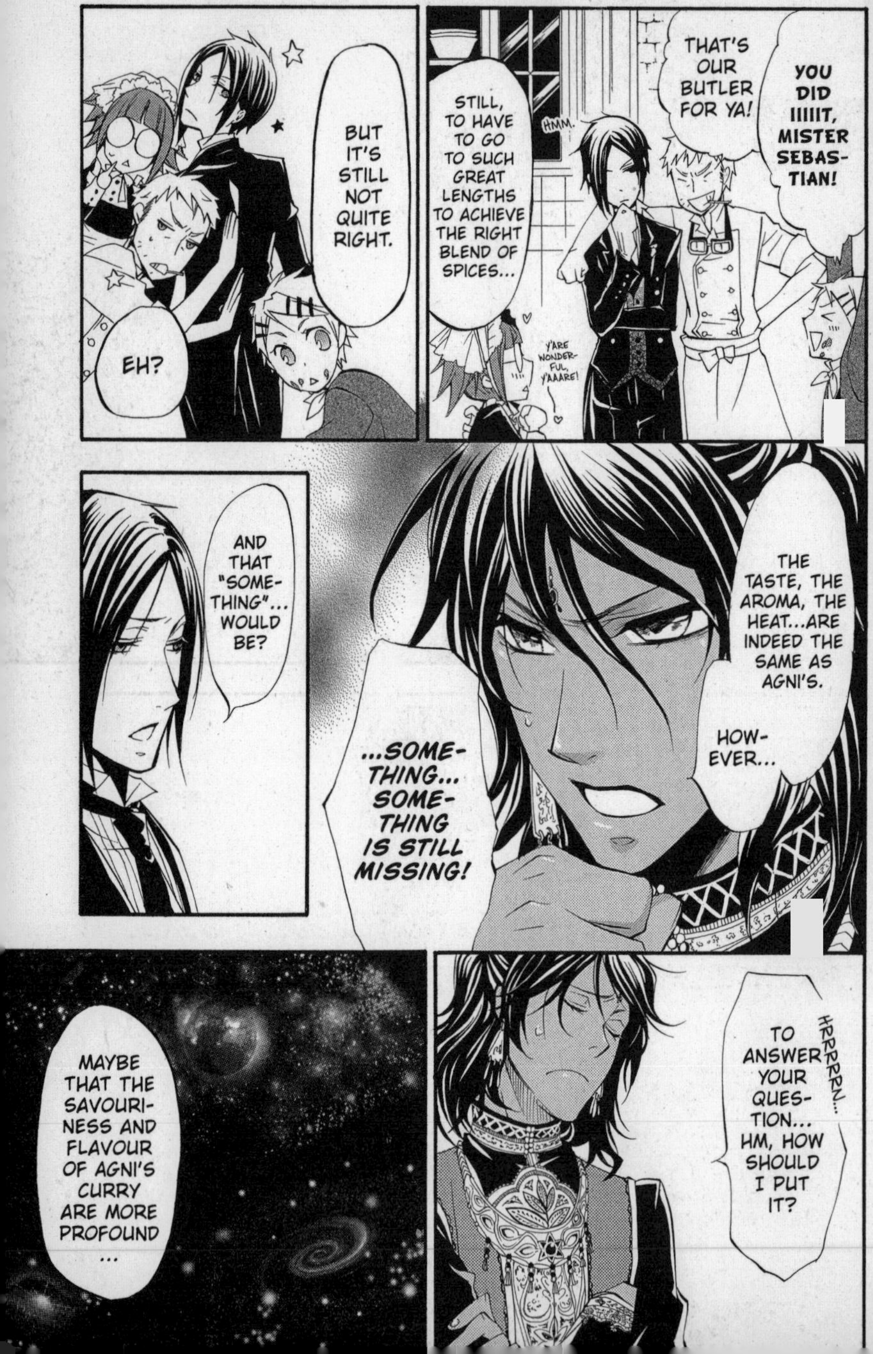
YOU DID IIIIIT, MISTER SEBASTIAN!
THAT'S OUR BUTLER FOR YA!
HMM.
STILL, TO HAVE TO GO TO SUCH GREAT LENGTHS TO ACHIEVE THE RIGHT BLEND OF SPICES...
Y'ARE WONDERFUL, Y'AAARE!
BUT IT'S STILL NOT QUITE RIGHT.
EH?
THE TASTE, THE AROMA, THE HEAT...ARE INDEED THE SAME AS AGNI'S.
HOWEVER...
...SOMETHING... SOMETHING IS STILL MISSING!
AND THAT "SOMETHING"... WOULD BE?
HRRRRRN...
TO ANSWER YOUR QUESTION... HM, HOW SHOULD I PUT IT?
MAYBE THAT THE SAVOURINESS AND FLAVOUR OF AGNI'S CURRY ARE MORE PROFOUND ...

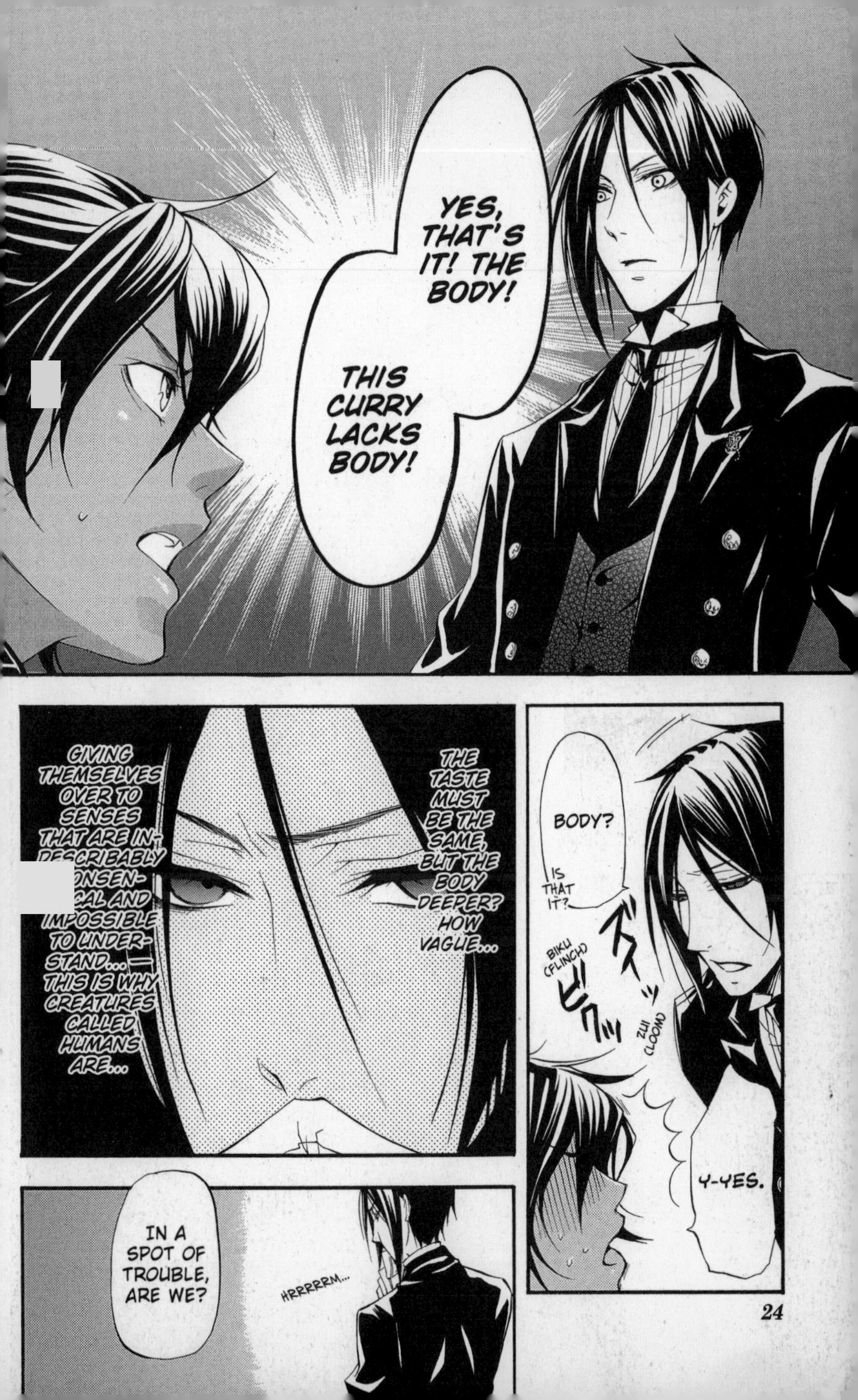
YES, THAT'S IT! THE BODY!
THIS CURRY LACKS BODY!
BODY?
IS THAT IT?
ZUI (LOOM)
BIKU (FLINCH)
Y-YES.
THE TASTE MUST BE THE SAME, BUT THE BODY DEEPER? HOW VAGUE...
GIVING THEMSELVES OVER TO SENSES THAT ARE IN-DESCRIBABLY ONSEN-CAL AND IMPOSSIBLE TO UNDER-STAND... THIS IS WHY CREATURES CALLED HUMANS ARE...
HRRRRRM...
IN A SPOT OF TROUBLE, ARE WE?

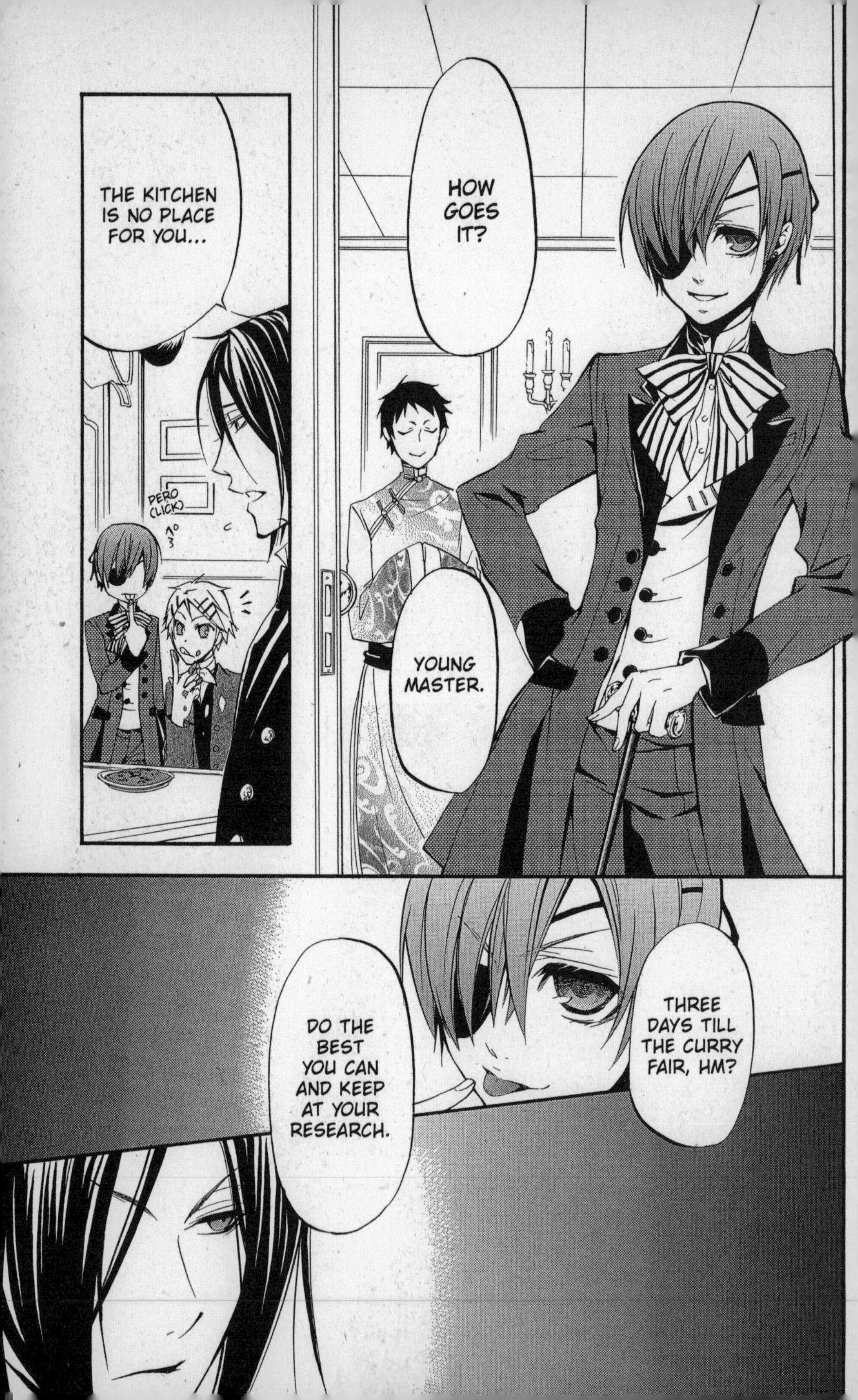
HOW GOES IT?
YOUNG MASTER.
THE KITCHEN IS NO PLACE FOR YOU...
PERO (LICK)
THREE DAYS TILL THE CURRY FAIR, HM?
DO THE BEST YOU CAN AND KEEP AT YOUR RESEARCH.

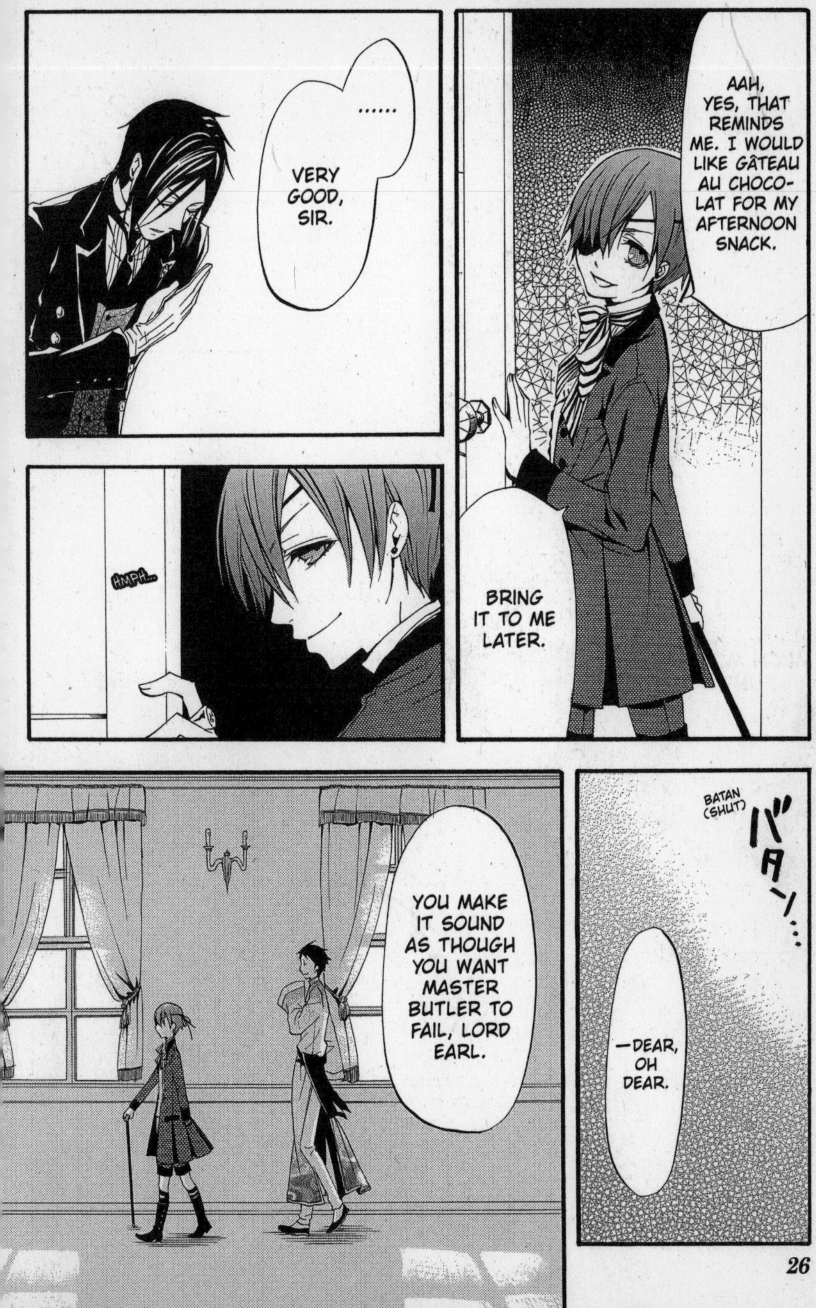
AAH, YES, THAT REMINDS ME. I WOULD LIKE GÂTEAU AU CHOCOLAT FOR MY AFTERNOON SNACK.
BRING IT TO ME LATER.
......
VERY GOOD, SIR.
HMPH...
BATAN (SHUT)
バタン…
—DEAR, OH DEAR.
YOU MAKE IT SOUND AS THOUGH YOU WANT MASTER BUTLER TO FAIL, LORD EARL.

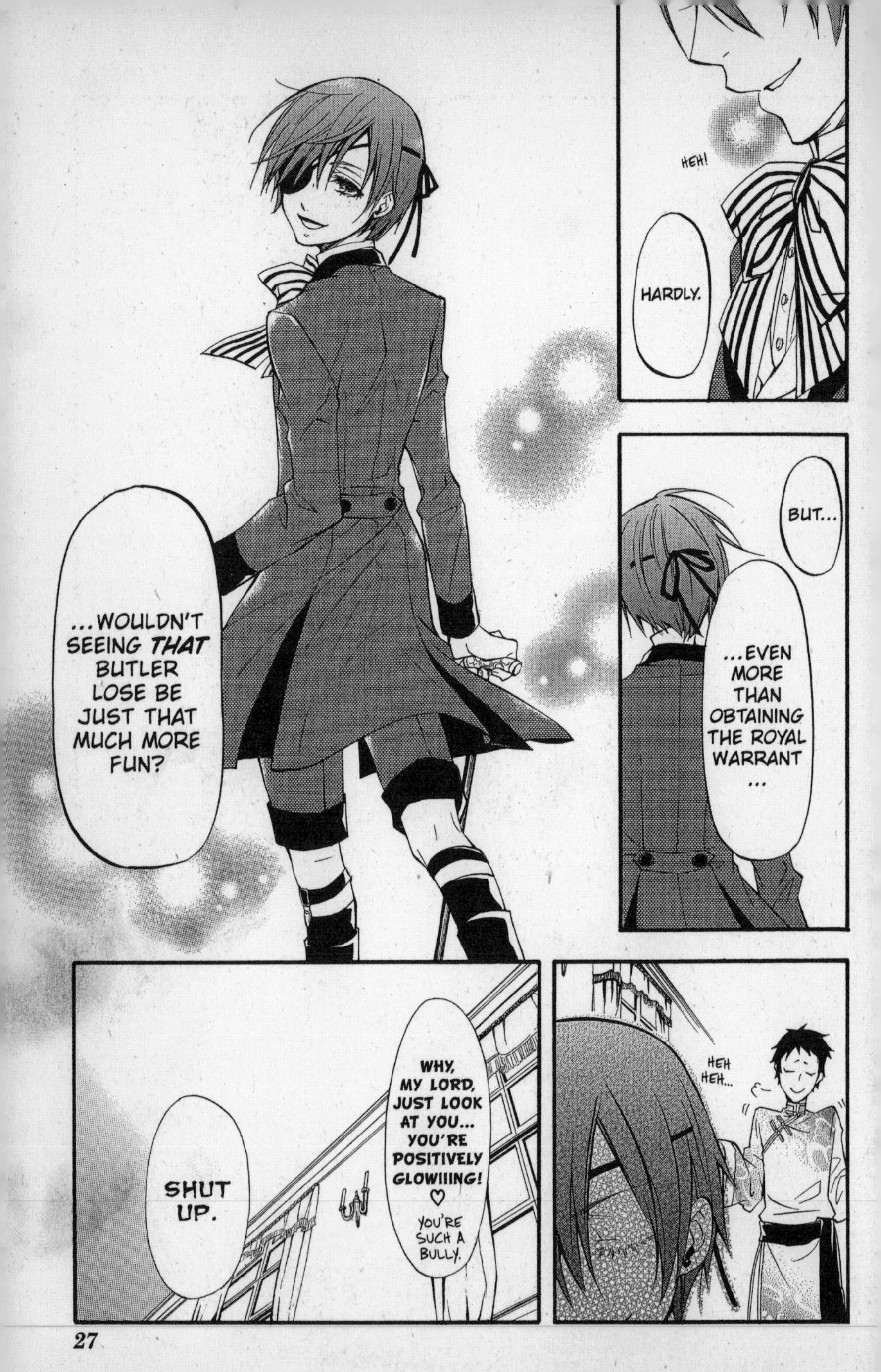
HEH!
HARDLY.
BUT...
...EVEN MORE THAN OBTAINING THE ROYAL WARRANT...
...WOULDN'T SEEING *THAT* BUTLER LOSE BE JUST THAT MUCH MORE FUN?
HEH HEH...
WHY, MY LORD, JUST LOOK AT YOU... YOU'RE POSITIVELY GLOWIIING! ♡
YOU'RE SUCH A BULLY.
SHUT UP.

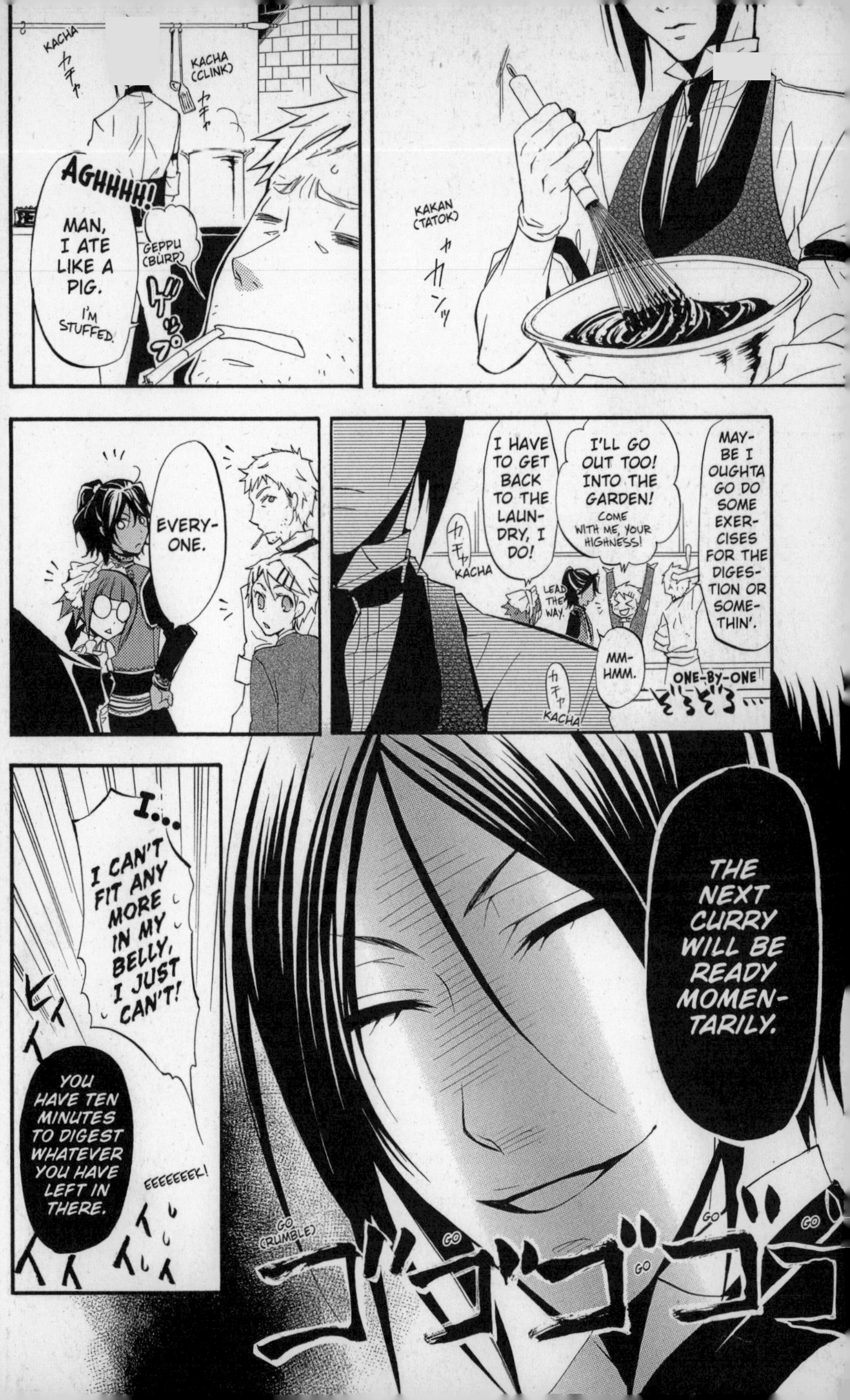
KAKAN (TATOK)
KACHA
KACHA (CLINK)
AGHHHH!
MAN, I ATE LIKE A PIG.
I'M STUFFED.
GEPPU (BURP)
MAY-BE I OUGHTA GO DO SOME EXER-CISES FOR THE DIGES-TION OR SOME-THIN'.
I'LL GO OUT TOO! INTO THE GARDEN!
COME WITH ME, YOUR HIGHNESS!
I HAVE TO GET BACK TO THE LAUN-DRY, I DO!
KACHA
LEAD THE WAY.
MM-HMM.
ONE-BY-ONE
KACHA
EVERY-ONE.
THE NEXT CURRY WILL BE READY MOMEN-TARILY.
GO (RUMBLE)
GO
GO
GO
I...
I CAN'T FIT ANY MORE IN MY BELLY, I JUST CAN'T!
YOU HAVE TEN MINUTES TO DIGEST WHATEVER YOU HAVE LEFT IN THERE.
EEEEEEEK!

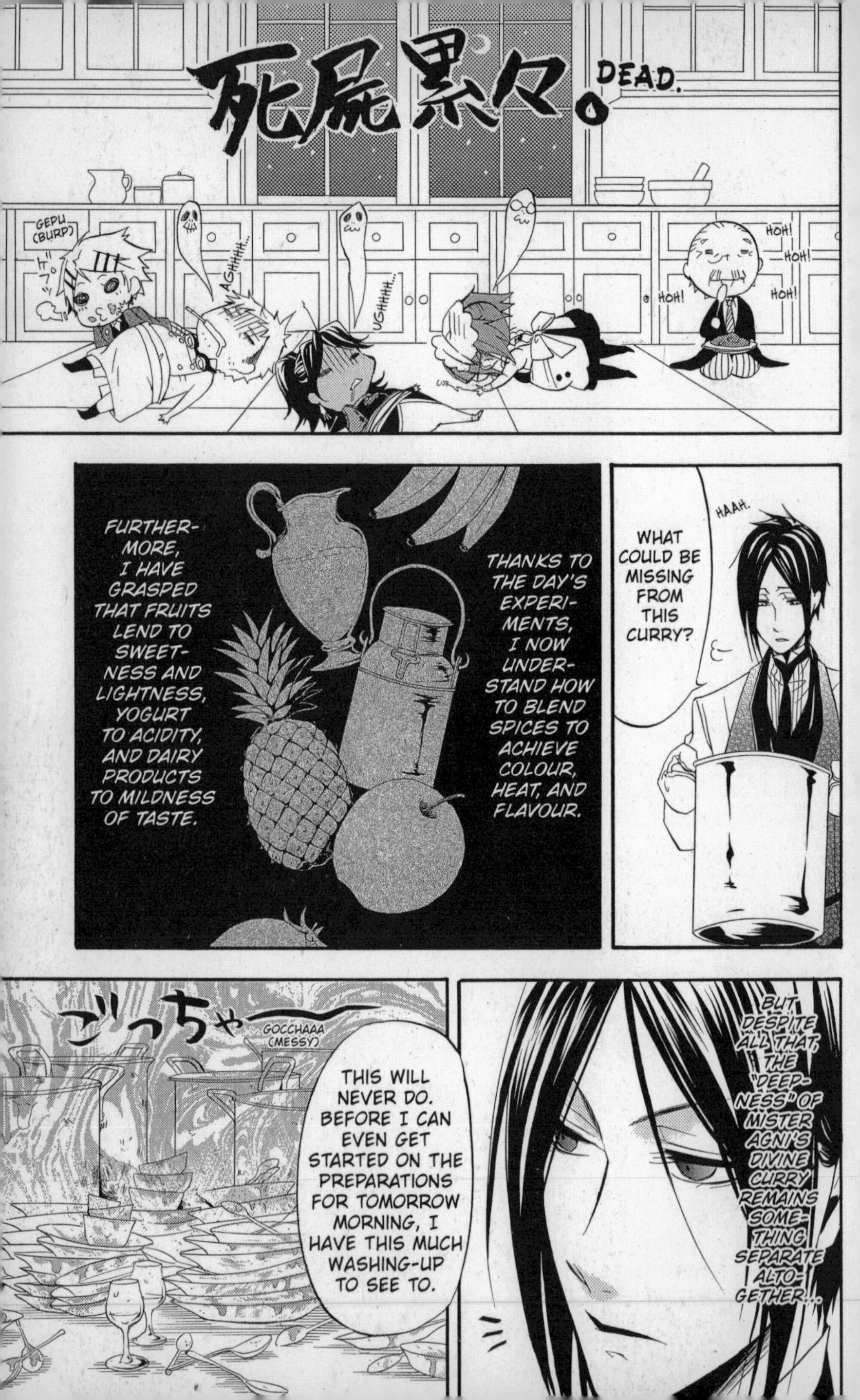

死屍累々。
DEAD.
HOH!
HOH!
HOH!
HOH!
UGHHHH...
AGHHHH...
GEPU (BURP)
HAAH.
WHAT COULD BE MISSING FROM THIS CURRY?
THANKS TO THE DAY'S EXPERIMENTS, I NOW UNDERSTAND HOW TO BLEND SPICES TO ACHIEVE COLOUR, HEAT, AND FLAVOUR.
FURTHERMORE, I HAVE GRASPED THAT FRUITS LEND TO SWEETNESS AND LIGHTNESS, YOGURT TO ACIDITY, AND DAIRY PRODUCTS TO MILDNESS OF TASTE.
BUT DESPITE ALL THAT, THE "DEEPNESS" OF MISTER AGNI'S DIVINE CURRY REMAINS SOMETHING SEPARATE ALTOGETHER...
ごっちゃー
GOCCHAAA (MESSY)
THIS WILL NEVER DO. BEFORE I CAN EVEN GET STARTED ON THE PREPARATIONS FOR TOMORROW MORNING, I HAVE THIS MUCH WASHING-UP TO SEE TO.

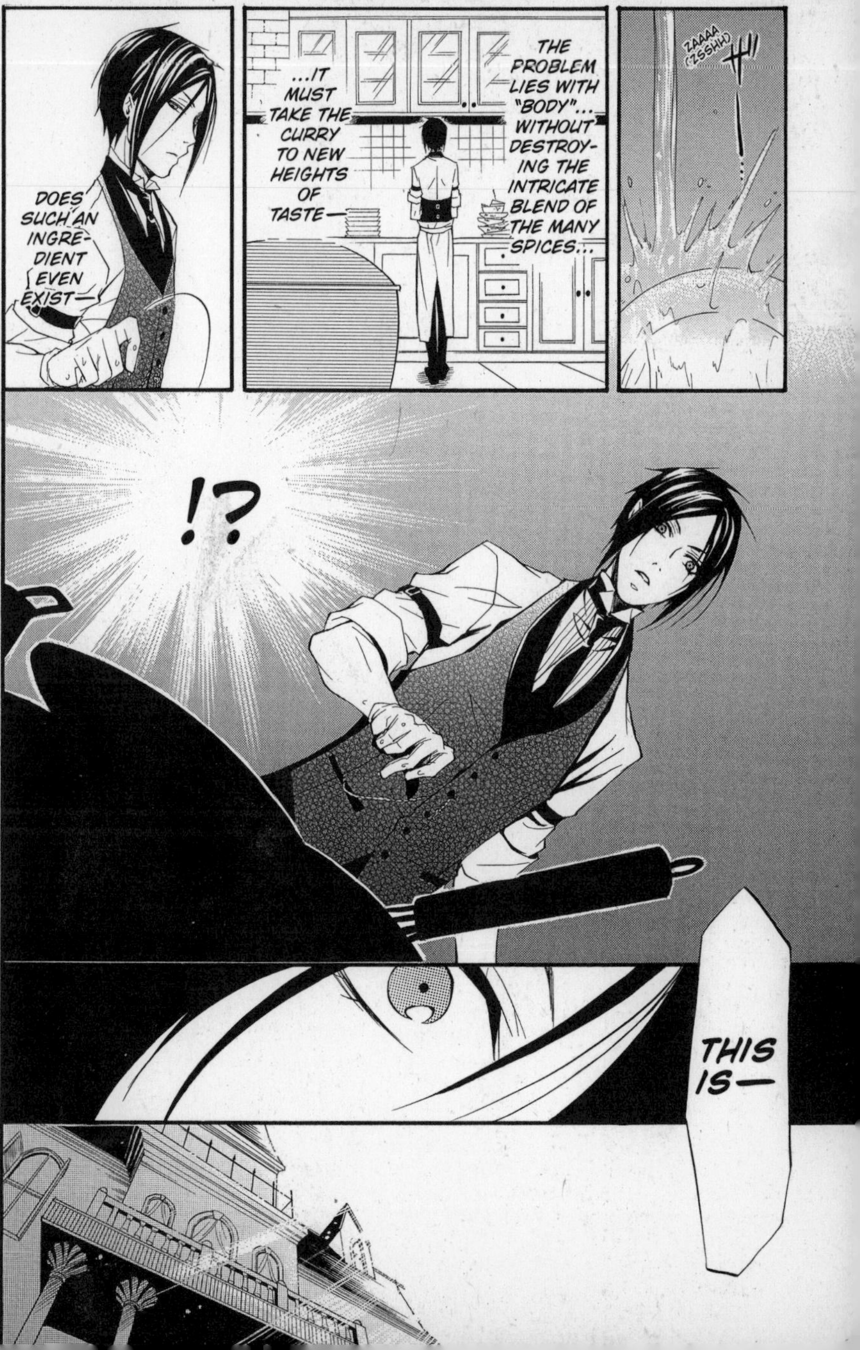
ZAAAA (ZSSHH)
THE PROBLEM LIES WITH "BODY"... WITHOUT DESTROYING THE INTRICATE BLEND OF THE MANY SPICES...
...IT MUST TAKE THE CURRY TO NEW HEIGHTS OF TASTE—
DOES SUCH AN INGREDIENT EVEN EXIST—
!?
THIS IS—

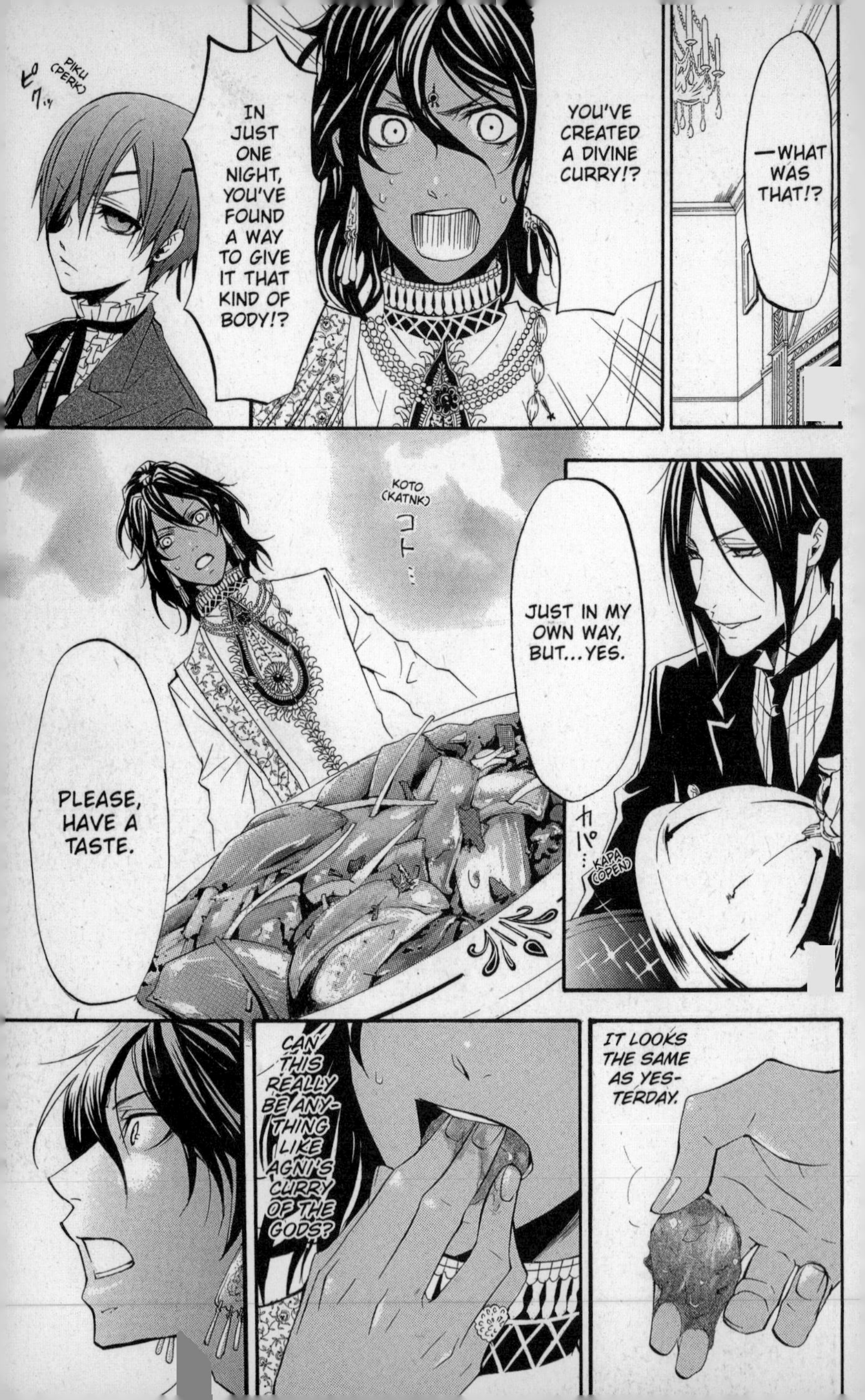
—WHAT WAS THAT!?
YOU'VE CREATED A DIVINE CURRY!?
IN JUST ONE NIGHT, YOU'VE FOUND A WAY TO GIVE IT THAT KIND OF BODY!?
PIKU (PERK)
ピク
KAPA (OPEN)
カパ
JUST IN MY OWN WAY, BUT...YES.
KOTO (KATNK)
コト
PLEASE, HAVE A TASTE.
IT LOOKS THE SAME AS YESTERDAY.
CAN THIS REALLY BE ANYTHING LIKE AGNI'S CURRY OF THE GODS?

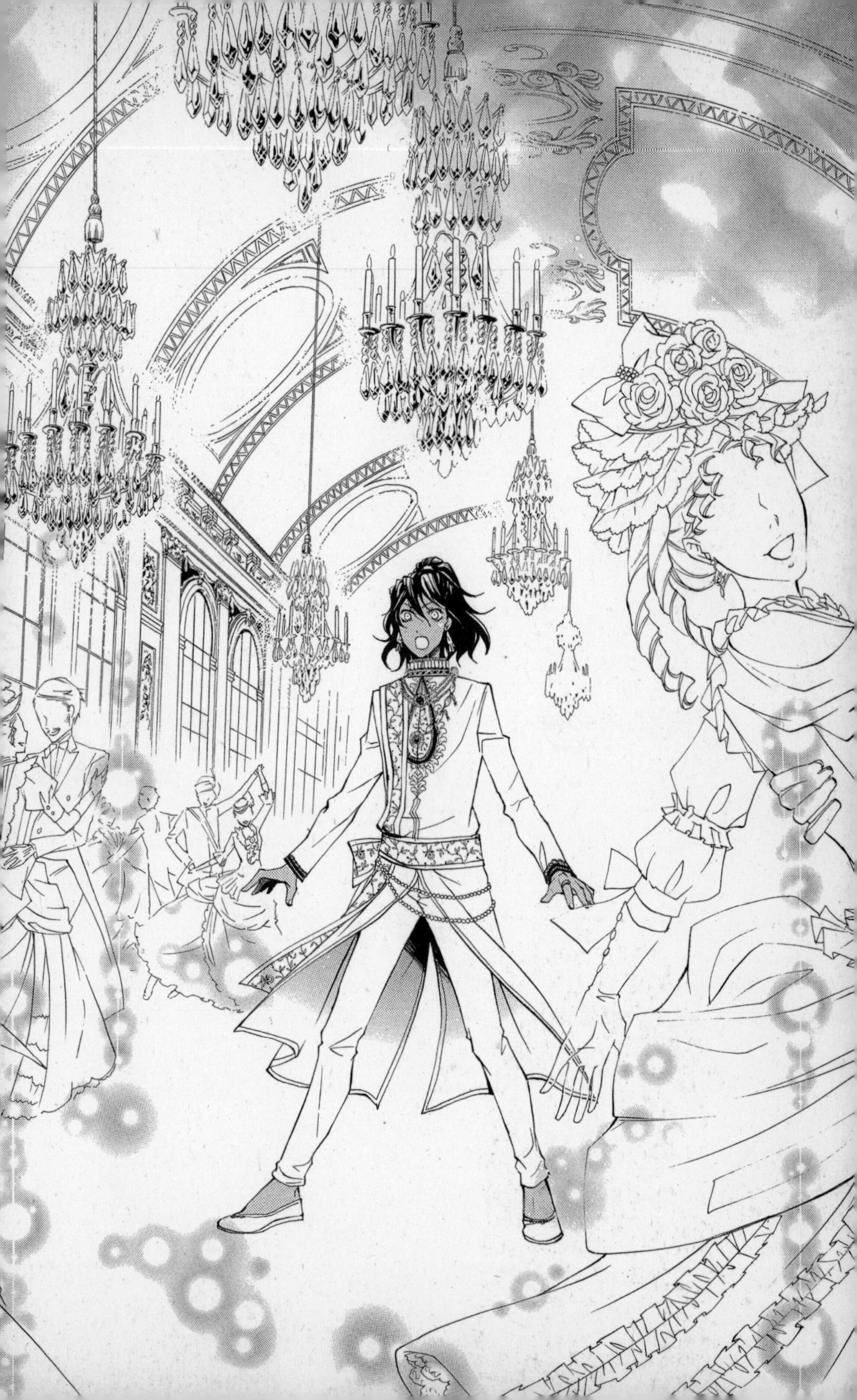

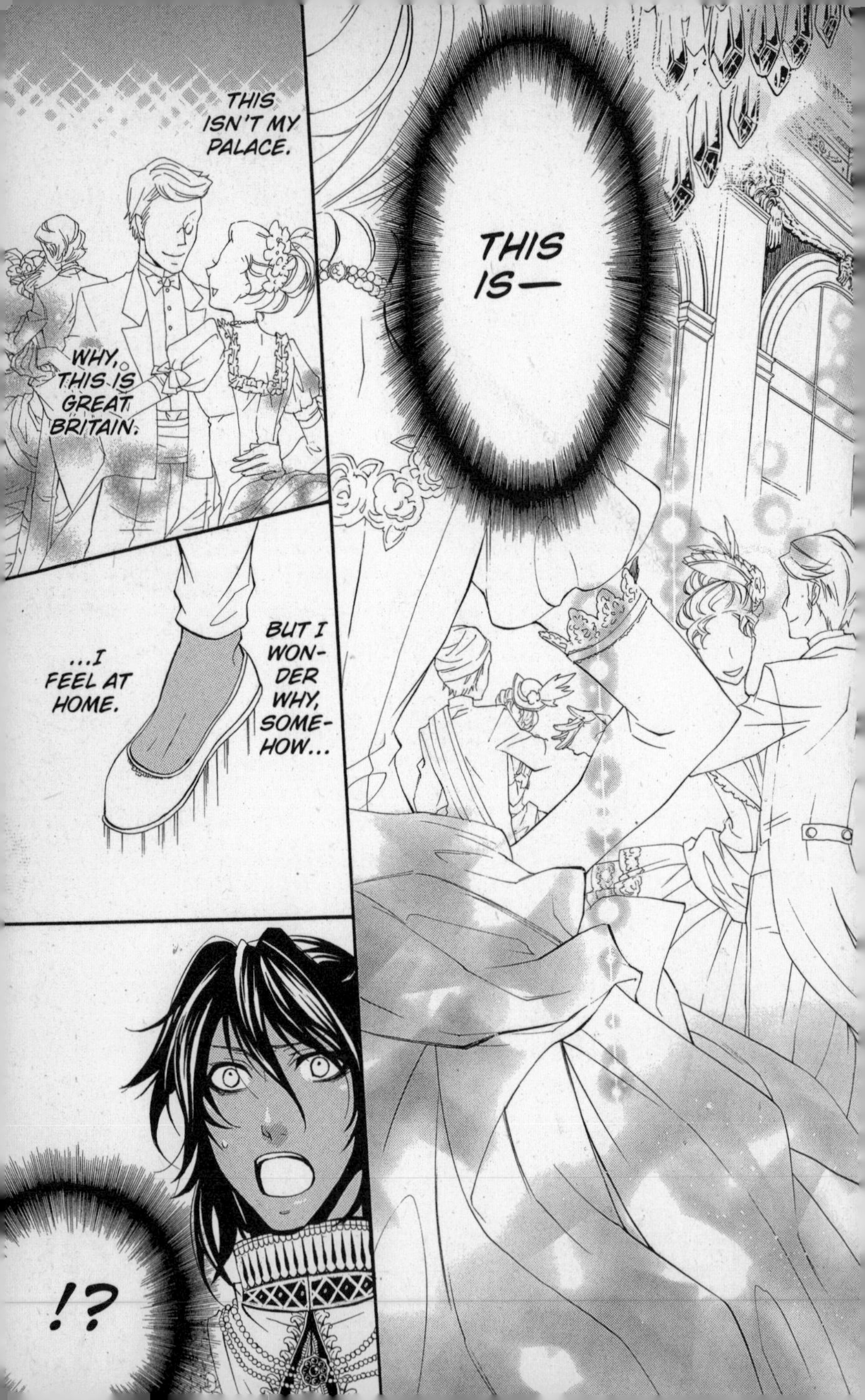
THIS IS—
THIS ISN'T MY PALACE.
WHY, THIS IS GREAT BRITAIN.
BUT I WONDER WHY, SOMEHOW...
...I FEEL AT HOME.
!?

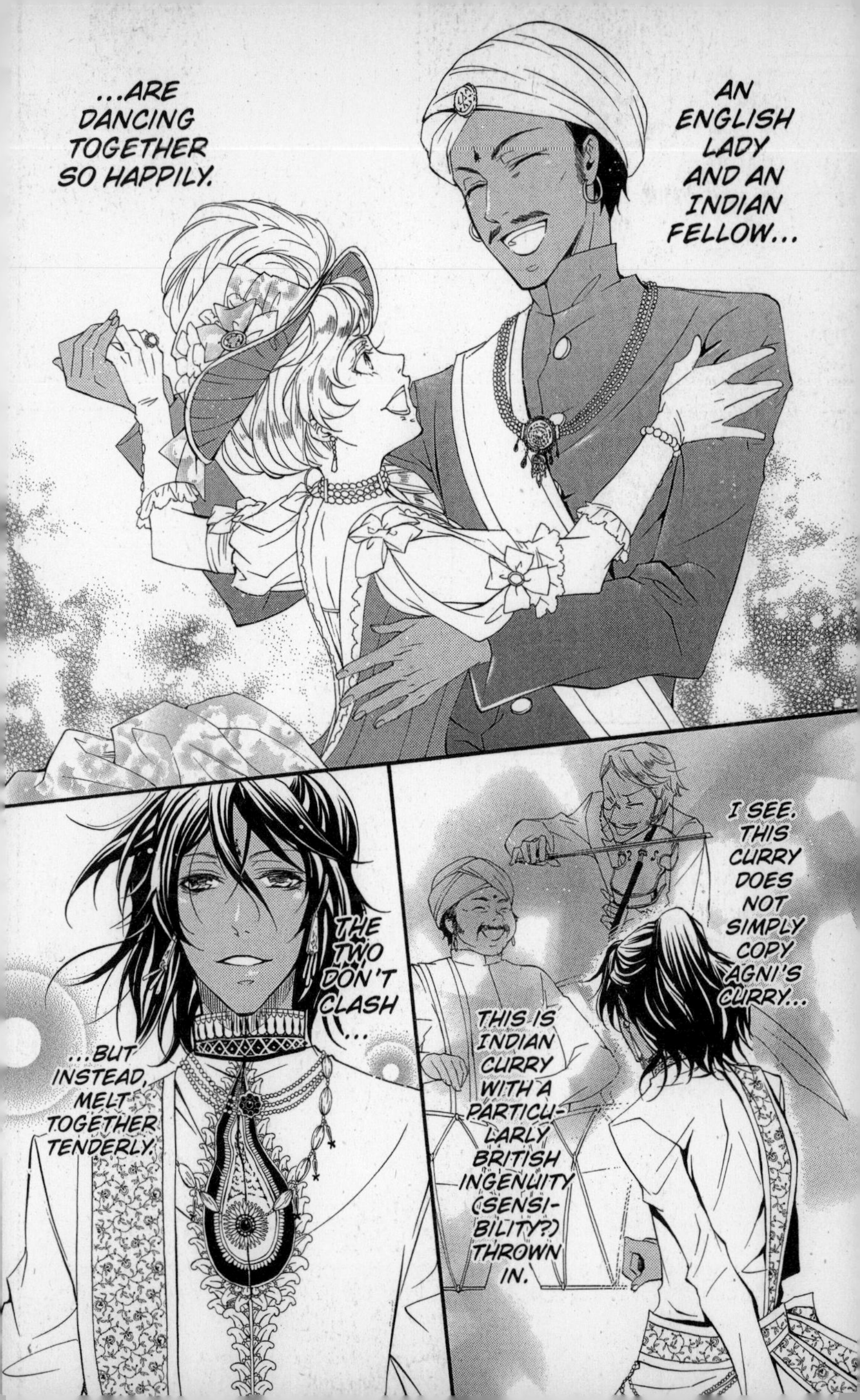
AN ENGLISH LADY AND AN INDIAN FELLOW...
...ARE DANCING TOGETHER SO HAPPILY.
I SEE. THIS CURRY DOES NOT SIMPLY COPY AGNI'S CURRY...
THIS IS INDIAN CURRY WITH A PARTICU-LARLY BRITISH INGENUITY (SENSI-BILITY?) THROWN IN.
THE TWO DON'T CLASH...
...BUT INSTEAD, MELT TOGETHER TENDERLY.

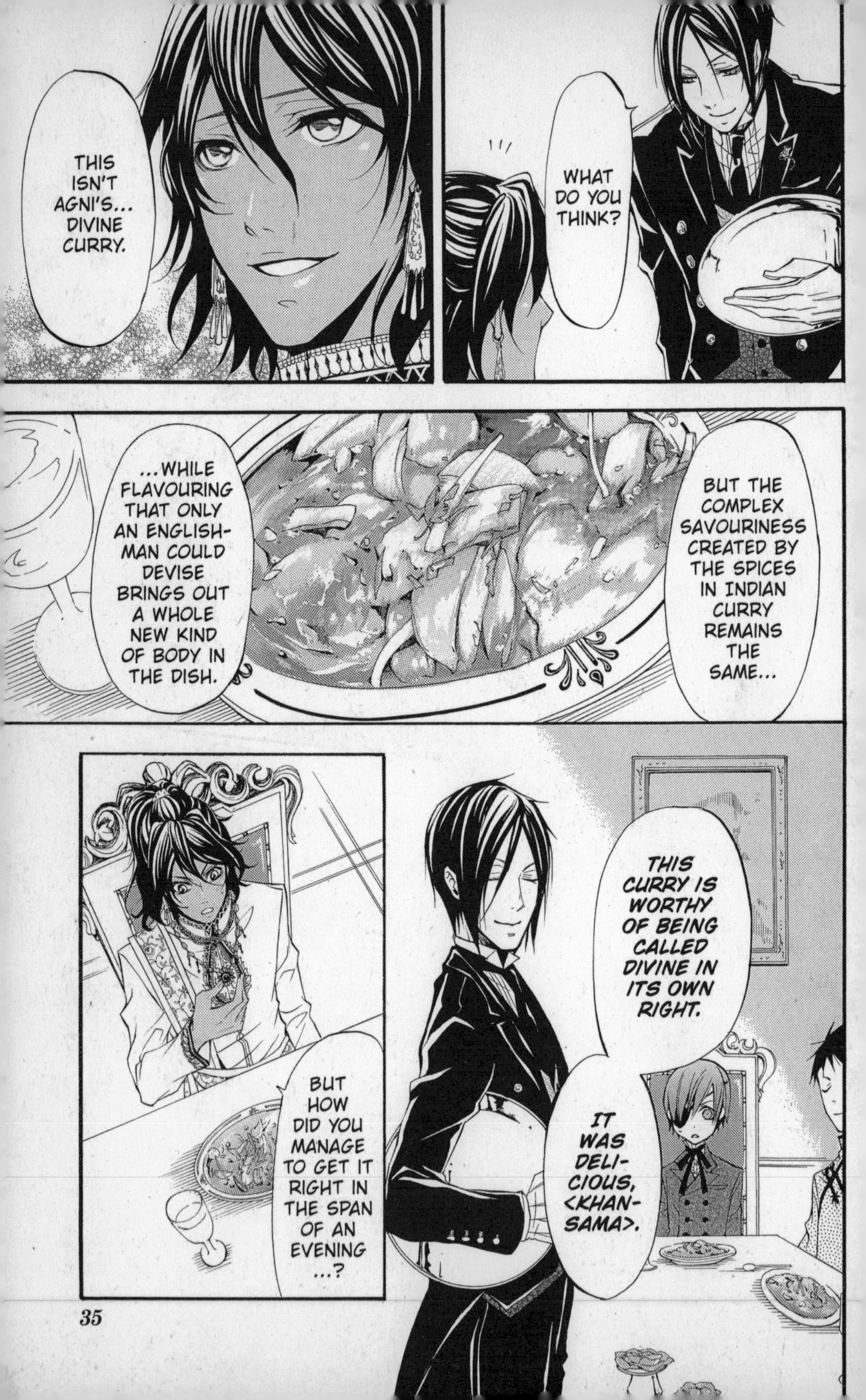
WHAT DO YOU THINK?
THIS ISN'T AGNI'S... DIVINE CURRY.
BUT THE COMPLEX SAVOURINESS CREATED BY THE SPICES IN INDIAN CURRY REMAINS THE SAME...
...WHILE FLAVOURING THAT ONLY AN ENGLISH-MAN COULD DEVISE BRINGS OUT A WHOLE NEW KIND OF BODY IN THE DISH.
THIS CURRY IS WORTHY OF BEING CALLED DIVINE IN ITS OWN RIGHT.
IT WAS DELI-CIOUS, <KHAN-SAMA>.
BUT HOW DID YOU MANAGE TO GET IT RIGHT IN THE SPAN OF AN EVENING ...?

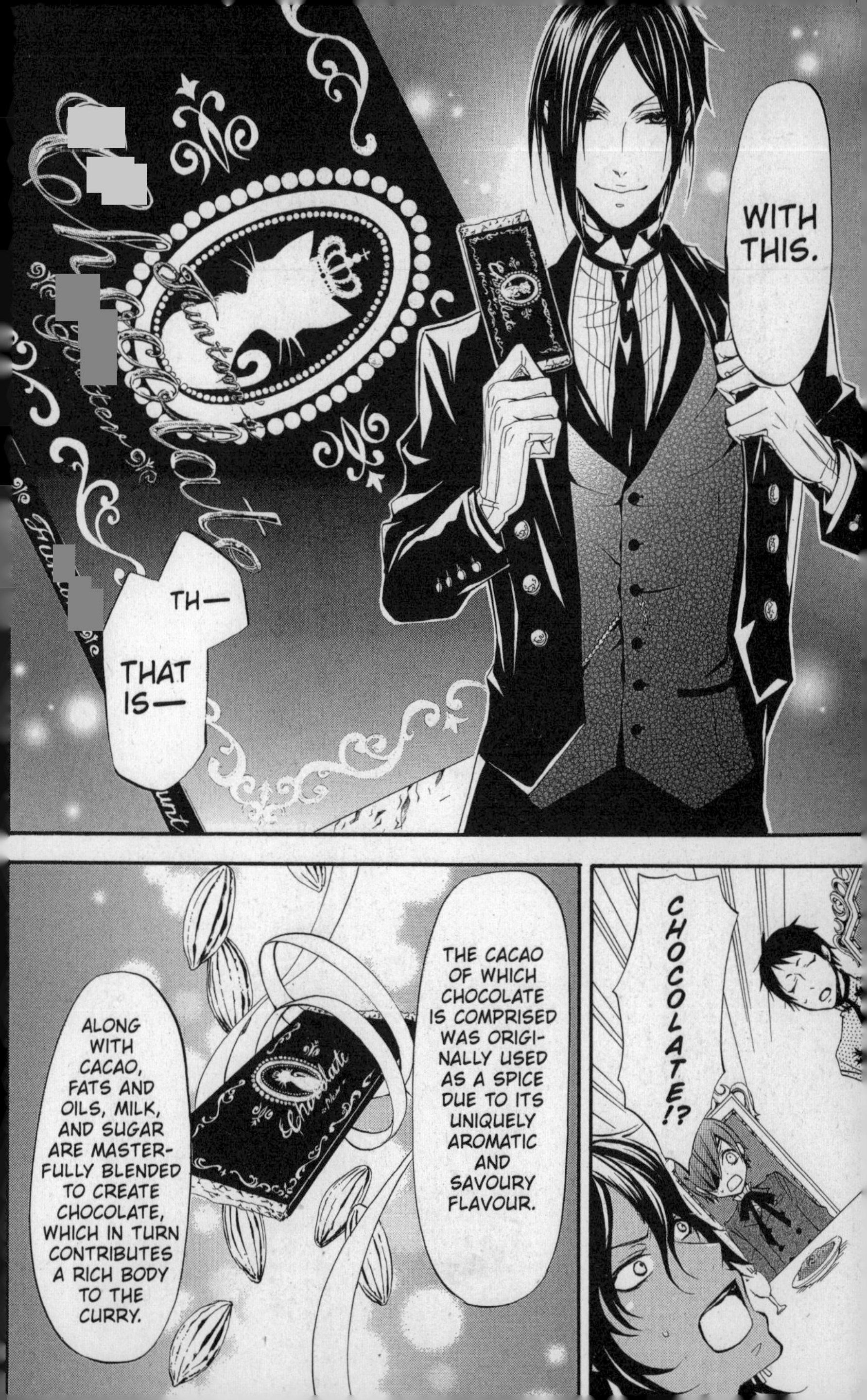
WITH THIS.
TH—
THAT IS—
CHOCOLATE!?
THE CACAO OF WHICH CHOCOLATE IS COMPRISED WAS ORIGI-NALLY USED AS A SPICE DUE TO ITS UNIQUELY AROMATIC AND SAVOURY FLAVOUR.
ALONG WITH CACAO, FATS AND OILS, MILK, AND SUGAR ARE MASTER-FULLY BLENDED TO CREATE CHOCOLATE, WHICH IN TURN CONTRIBUTES A RICH BODY TO THE CURRY.

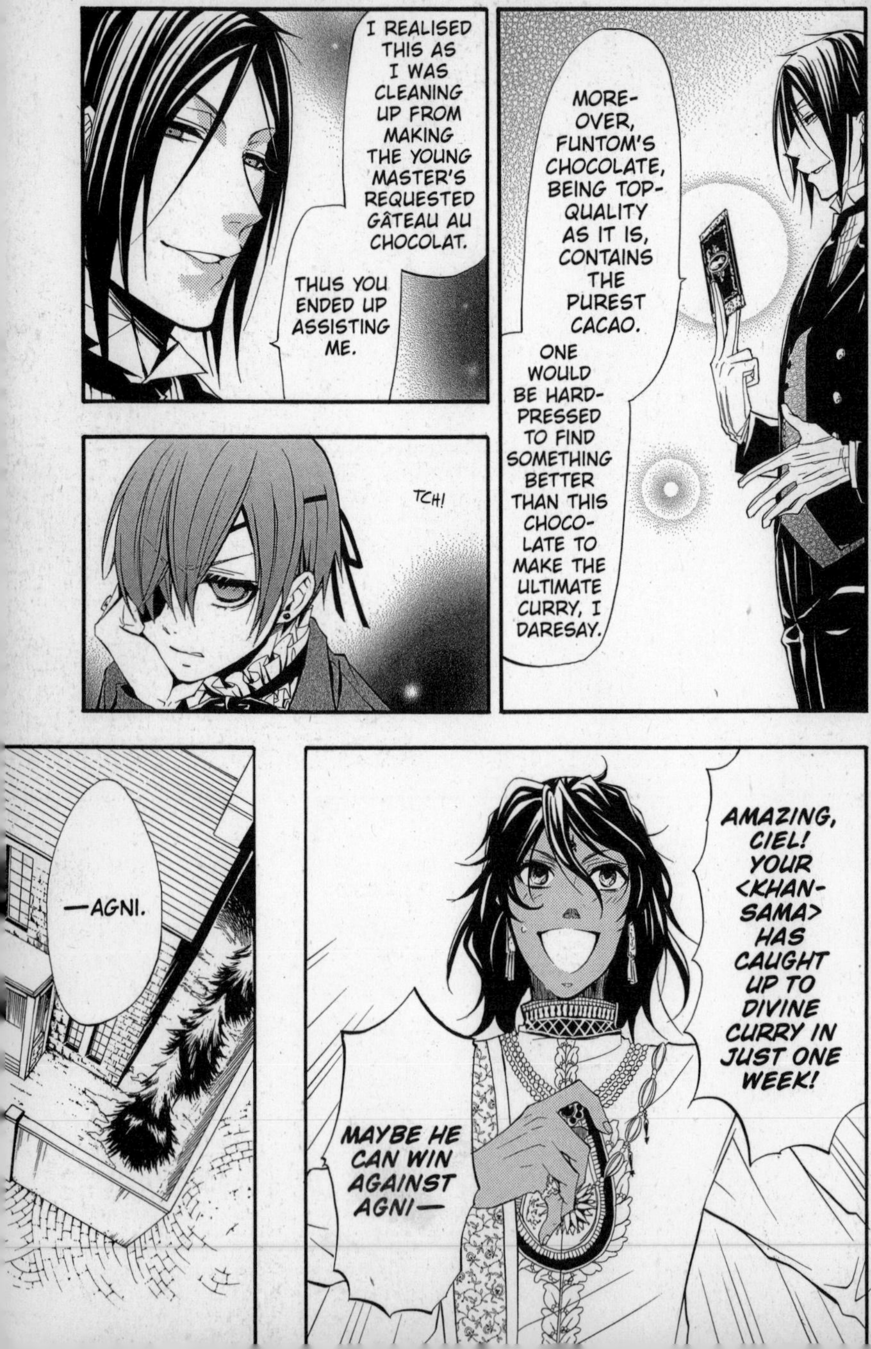
MORE-OVER, FUNTOM'S CHOCOLATE, BEING TOP-QUALITY AS IT IS, CONTAINS THE PUREST CACAO.
ONE WOULD BE HARD-PRESSED TO FIND SOMETHING BETTER THAN THIS CHOCO-LATE TO MAKE THE ULTIMATE CURRY, I DARESAY.
I REALISED THIS AS I WAS CLEANING UP FROM MAKING THE YOUNG MASTER'S REQUESTED GÂTEAU AU CHOCOLAT.
THUS YOU ENDED UP ASSISTING ME.
TCH!
AMAZING, CIEL! YOUR <KHAN-SAMA> HAS CAUGHT UP TO DIVINE CURRY IN JUST ONE WEEK!
MAYBE HE CAN WIN AGAINST AGNI—
—AGNI.

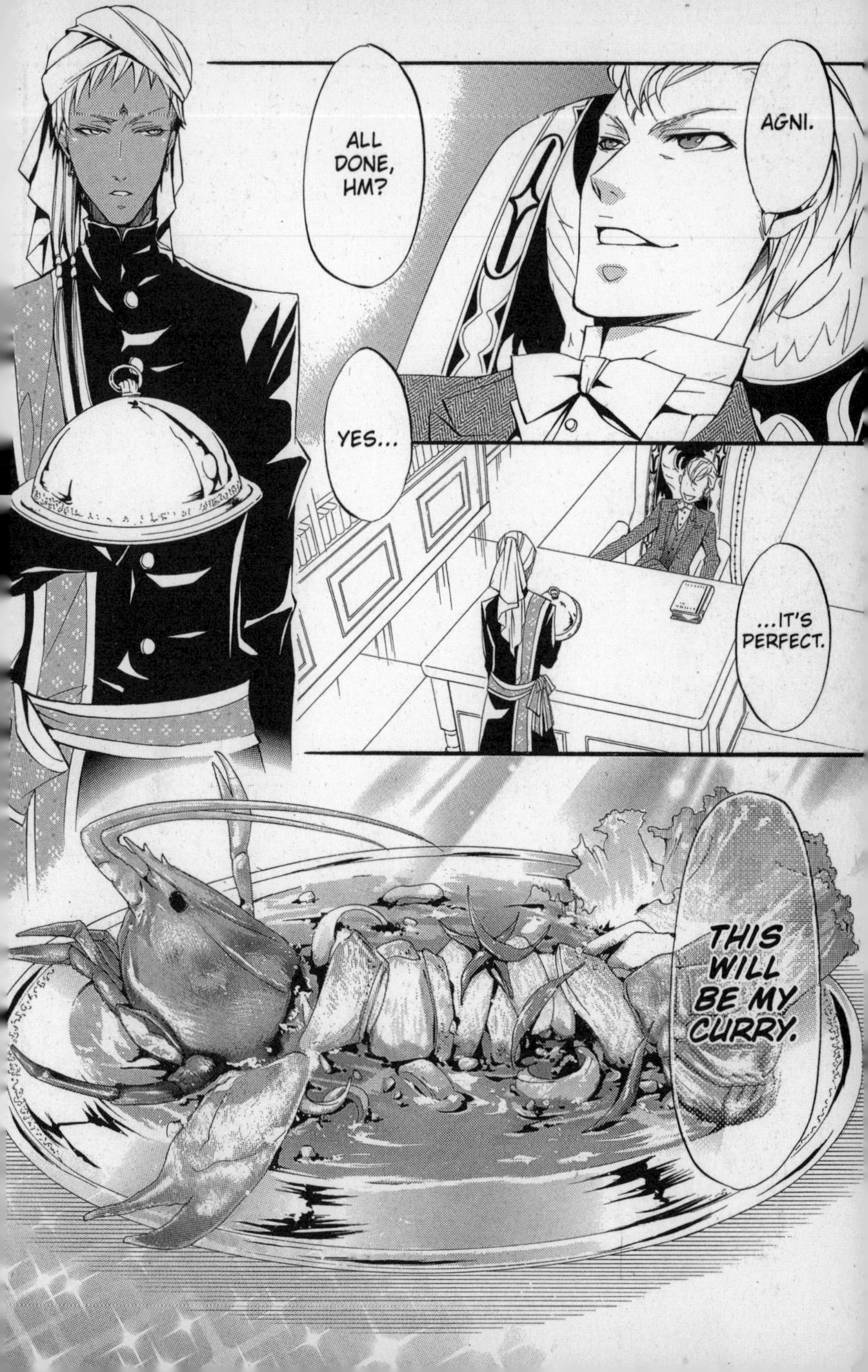
AGNI.
ALL DONE, HM?
YES...
...IT'S PERFECT.
THIS WILL BE MY CURRY.

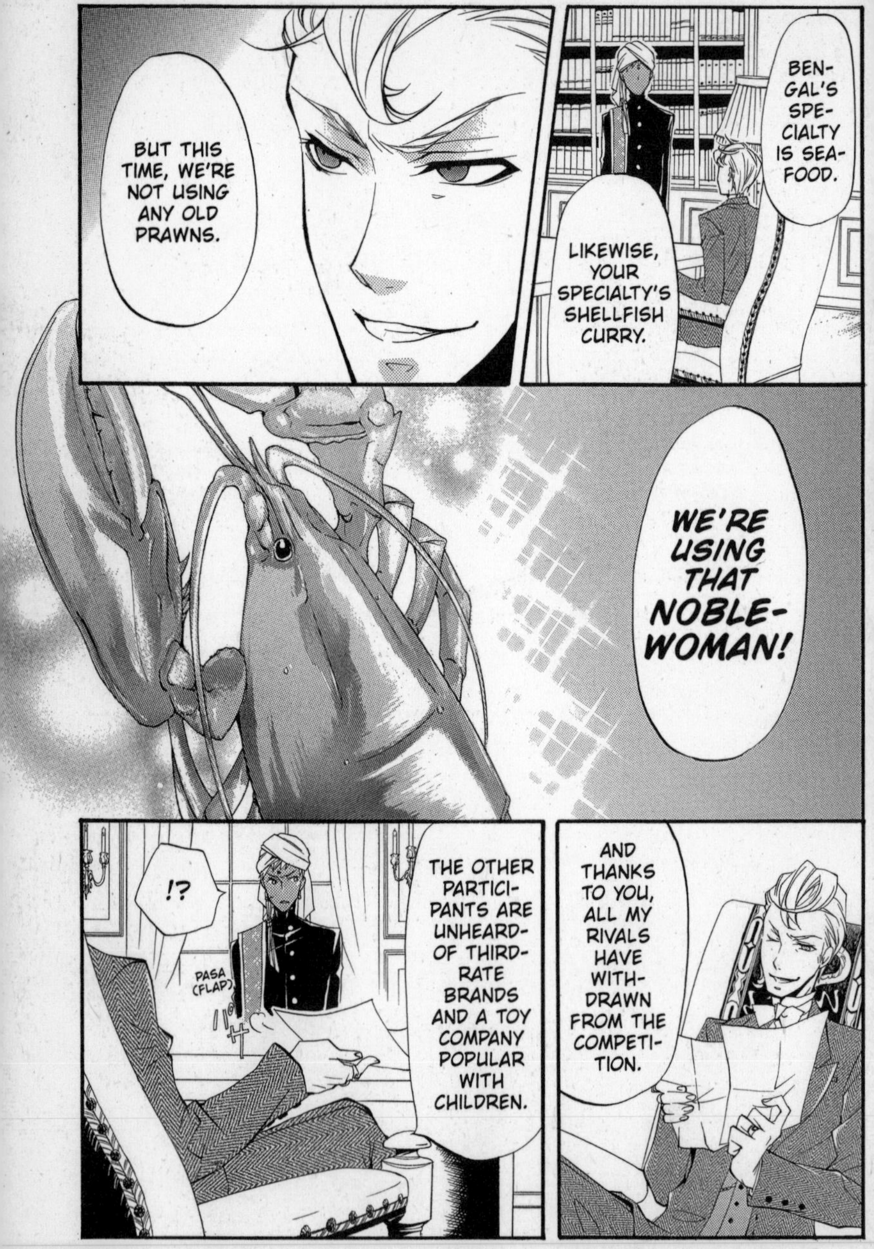
BENGAL'S SPECIALTY IS SEAFOOD.
LIKEWISE, YOUR SPECIALTY'S SHELLFISH CURRY.
BUT THIS TIME, WE'RE NOT USING ANY OLD PRAWNS.
WE'RE USING THAT NOBLEWOMAN!
AND THANKS TO YOU, ALL MY RIVALS HAVE WITHDRAWN FROM THE COMPETITION.
THE OTHER PARTICIPANTS ARE UNHEARD-OF THIRD-RATE BRANDS AND A TOY COMPANY POPULAR WITH CHILDREN.
!?
PASA (FLAP)

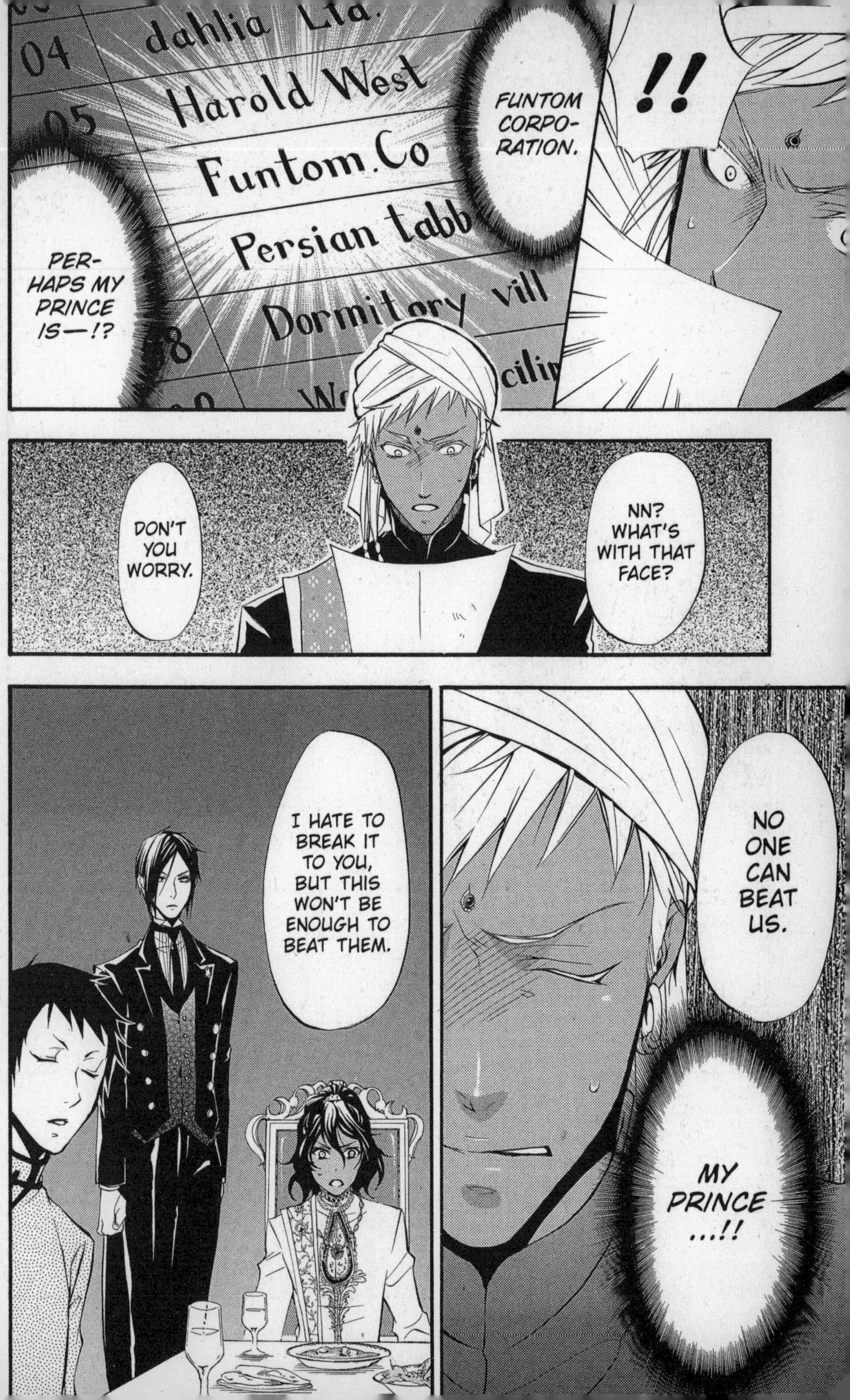

!!
FUNTOM CORPORATION.
04 dahlia
05 Harold West
Funtom.Co
Persian tabb
Dormitory vill
PERHAPS MY PRINCE IS—!?
NN? WHAT'S WITH THAT FACE?
DON'T YOU WORRY.
NO ONE CAN BEAT US.
MY PRINCE ...!!
I HATE TO BREAK IT TO YOU, BUT THIS WON'T BE ENOUGH TO BEAT THEM.

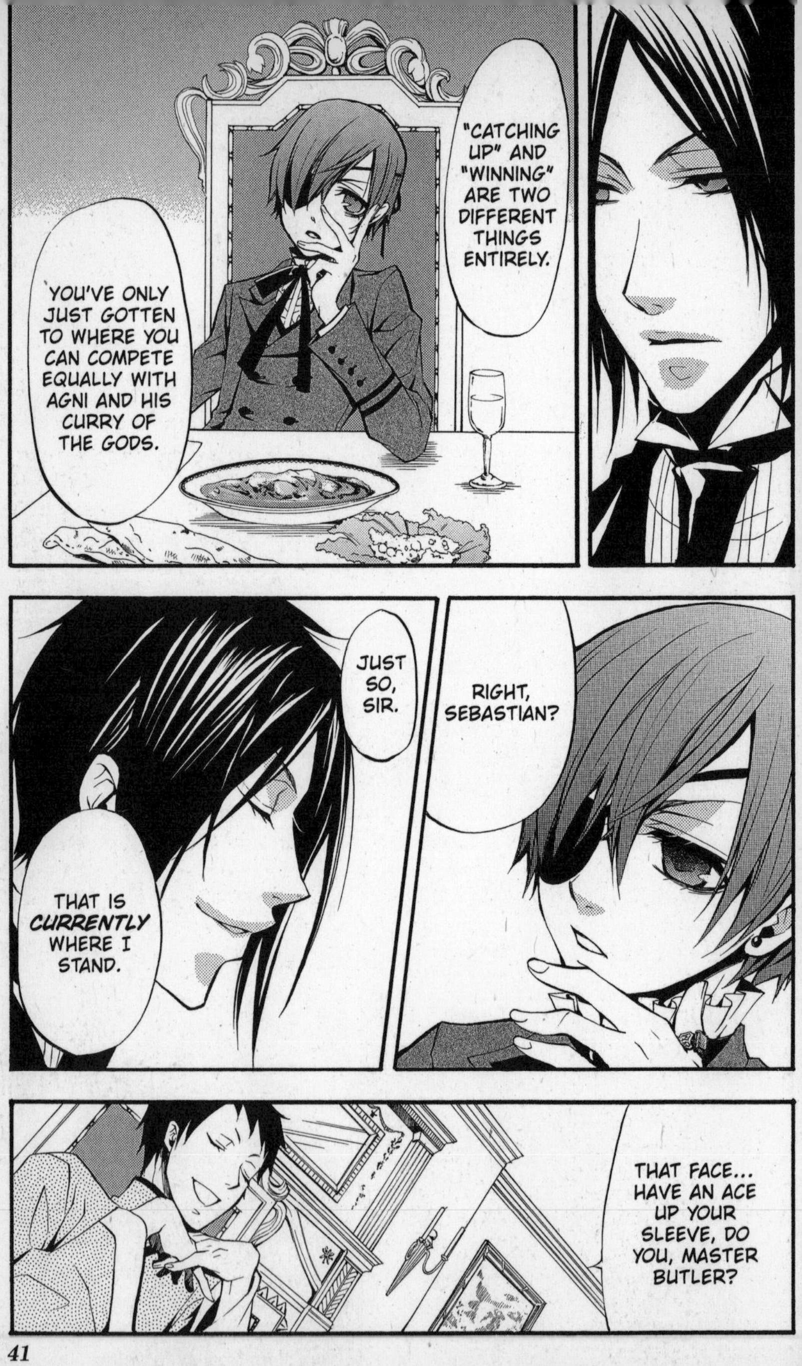
"CATCHING UP" AND "WINNING" ARE TWO DIFFERENT THINGS ENTIRELY.
YOU'VE ONLY JUST GOTTEN TO WHERE YOU CAN COMPETE EQUALLY WITH AGNI AND HIS CURRY OF THE GODS.
RIGHT, SEBASTIAN?
JUST SO, SIR.
THAT IS *CURRENTLY* WHERE I STAND.
THAT FACE... HAVE AN ACE UP YOUR SLEEVE, DO YOU, MASTER BUTLER?

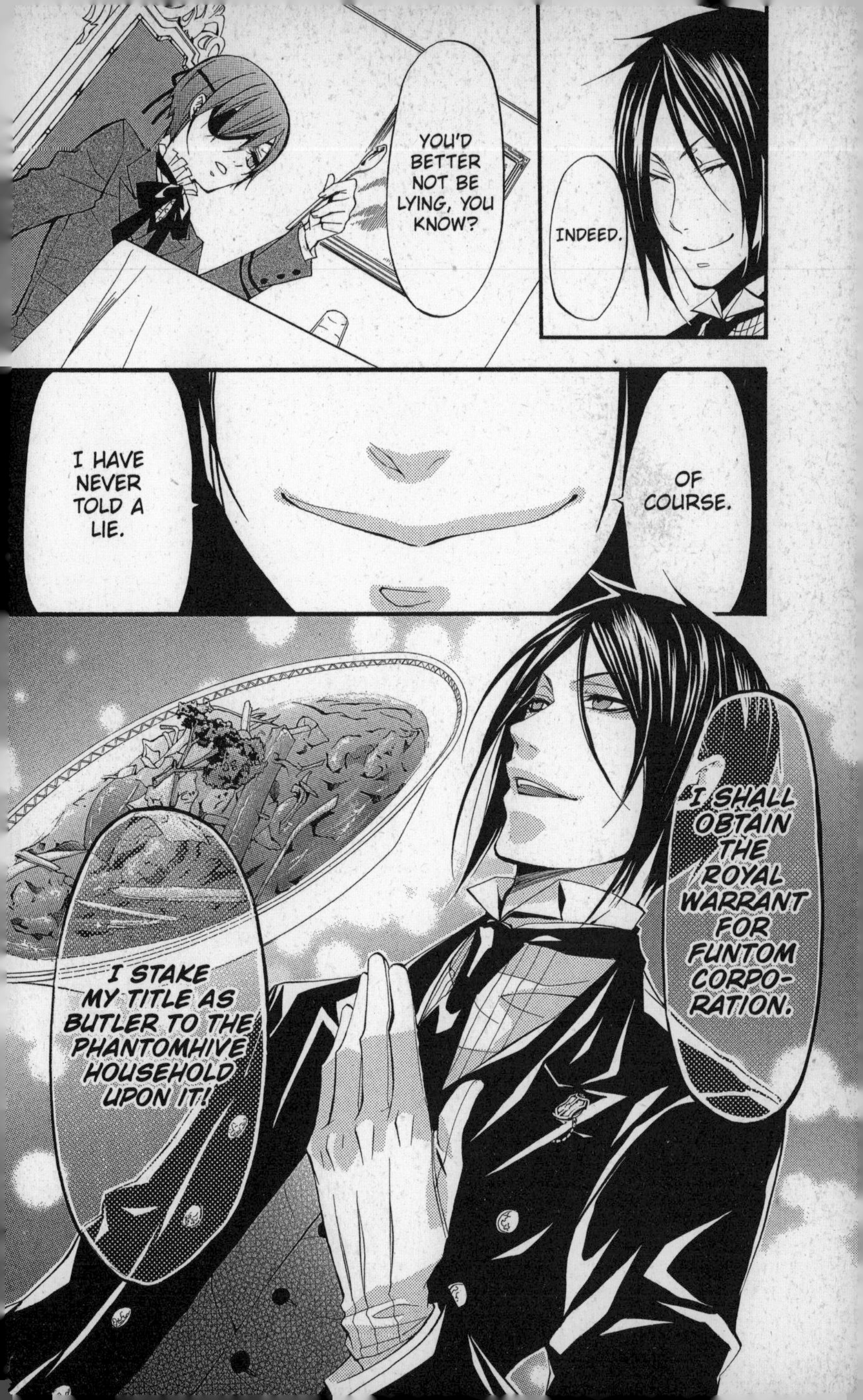
INDEED.
YOU'D BETTER NOT BE LYING, YOU KNOW?
OF COURSE.
I HAVE NEVER TOLD A LIE.
I SHALL OBTAIN THE ROYAL WARRANT FOR FUNTOM CORPO-RATION.
I STAKE MY TITLE AS BUTLER TO THE PHANTOMHIVE HOUSEHOLD UPON IT!

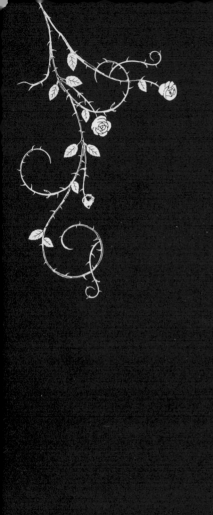

Black Butler

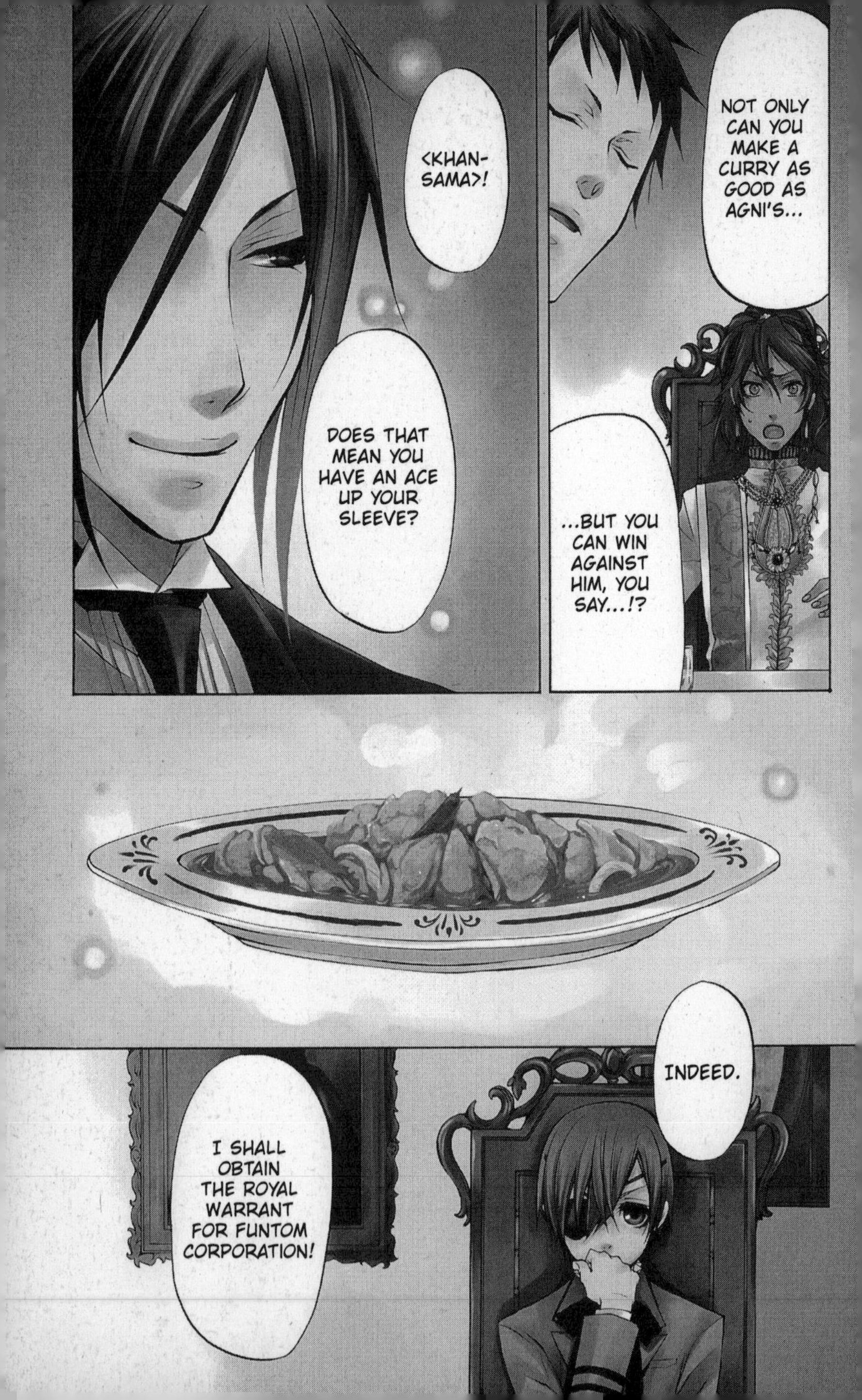
NOT ONLY CAN YOU MAKE A CURRY AS GOOD AS AGNI'S...
...BUT YOU CAN WIN AGAINST HIM, YOU SAY...!?
<KHAN-SAMA>!
DOES THAT MEAN YOU HAVE AN ACE UP YOUR SLEEVE?
INDEED.
I SHALL OBTAIN THE ROYAL WARRANT FOR FUNTOM CORPORATION!

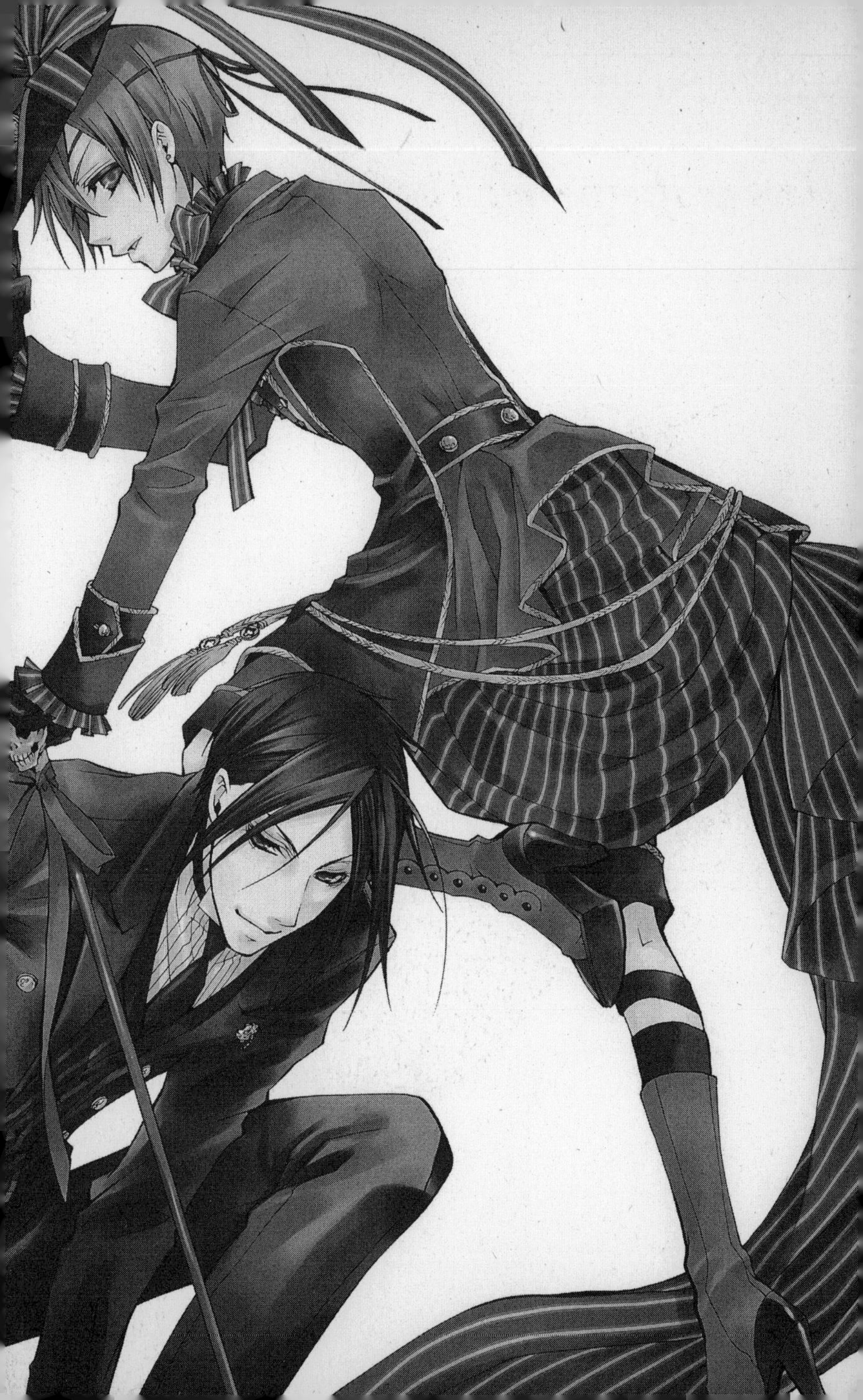

Chapter 21

In the afternoon : The Butler, Competitive

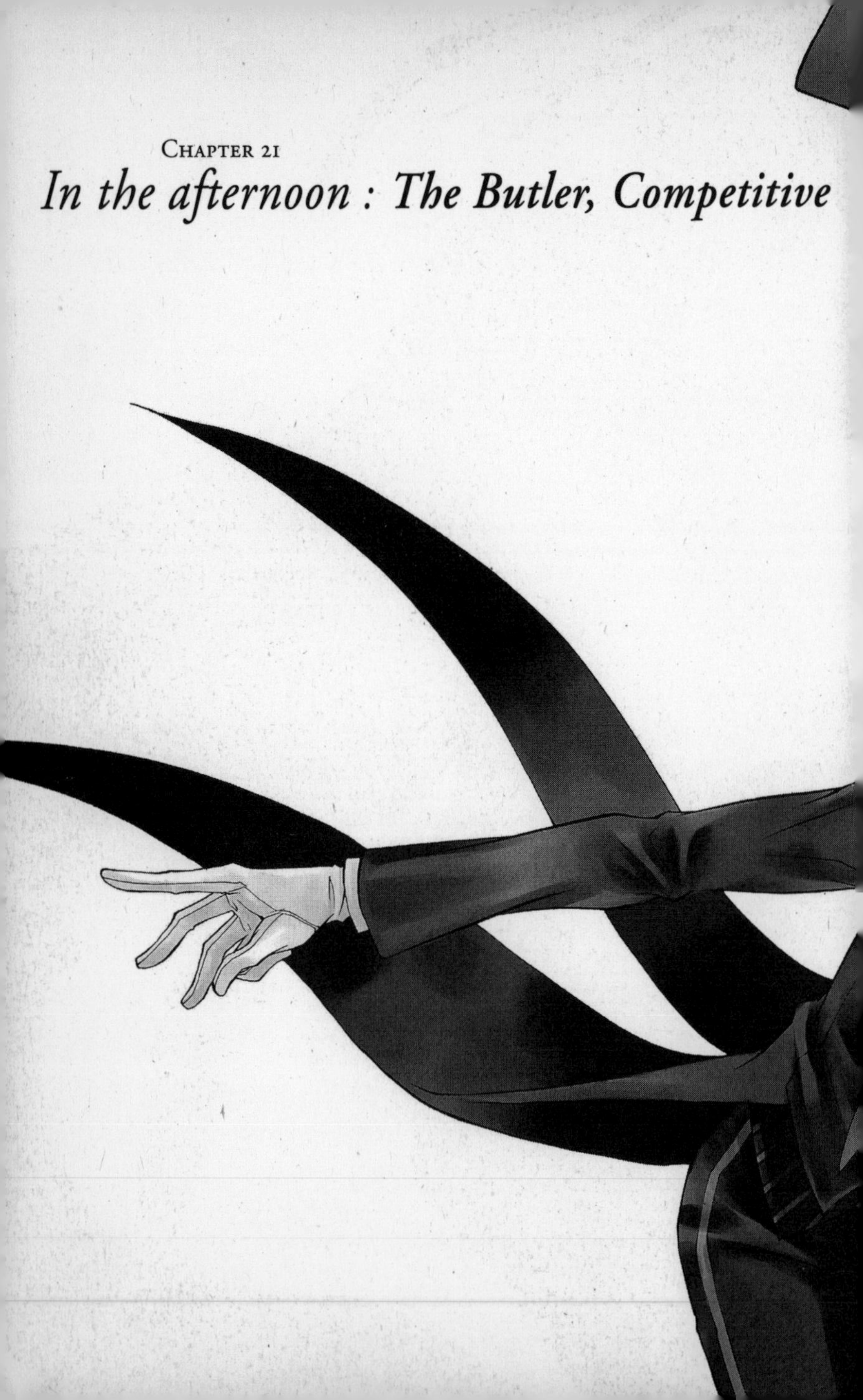

Black Butler

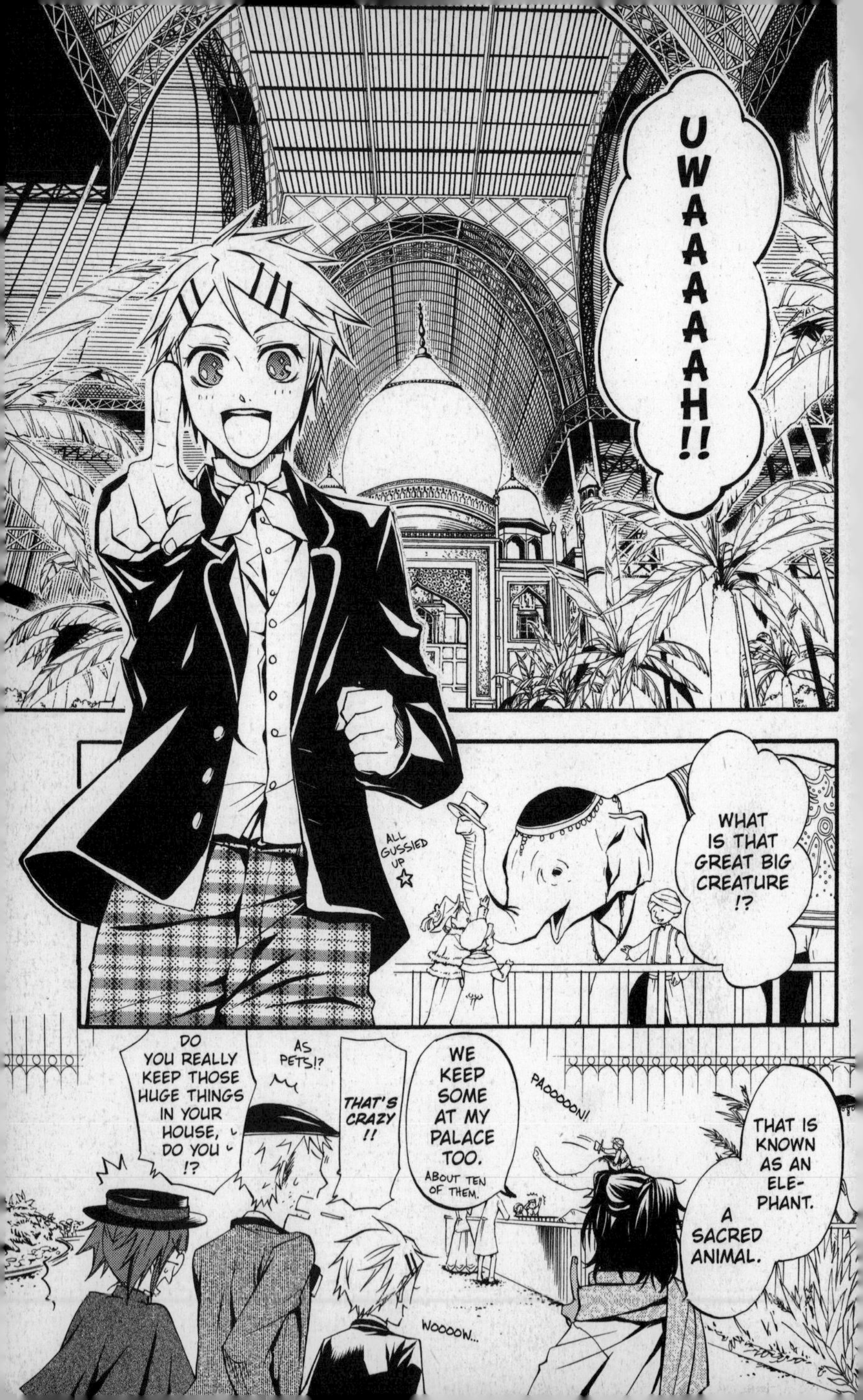
UWAAAAAAH!!
WHAT IS THAT GREAT BIG CREATURE!?
ALL GUSSIED UP ☆
THAT IS KNOWN AS AN ELE-PHANT.
A SACRED ANIMAL.
PAOOOOON!
WE KEEP SOME AT MY PALACE TOO.
ABOUT TEN OF THEM.
THAT'S CRAZY!!
AS PETS!?
DO YOU REALLY KEEP THOSE HUGE THINGS IN YOUR HOUSE, DO YOU!?
WOOOOW...

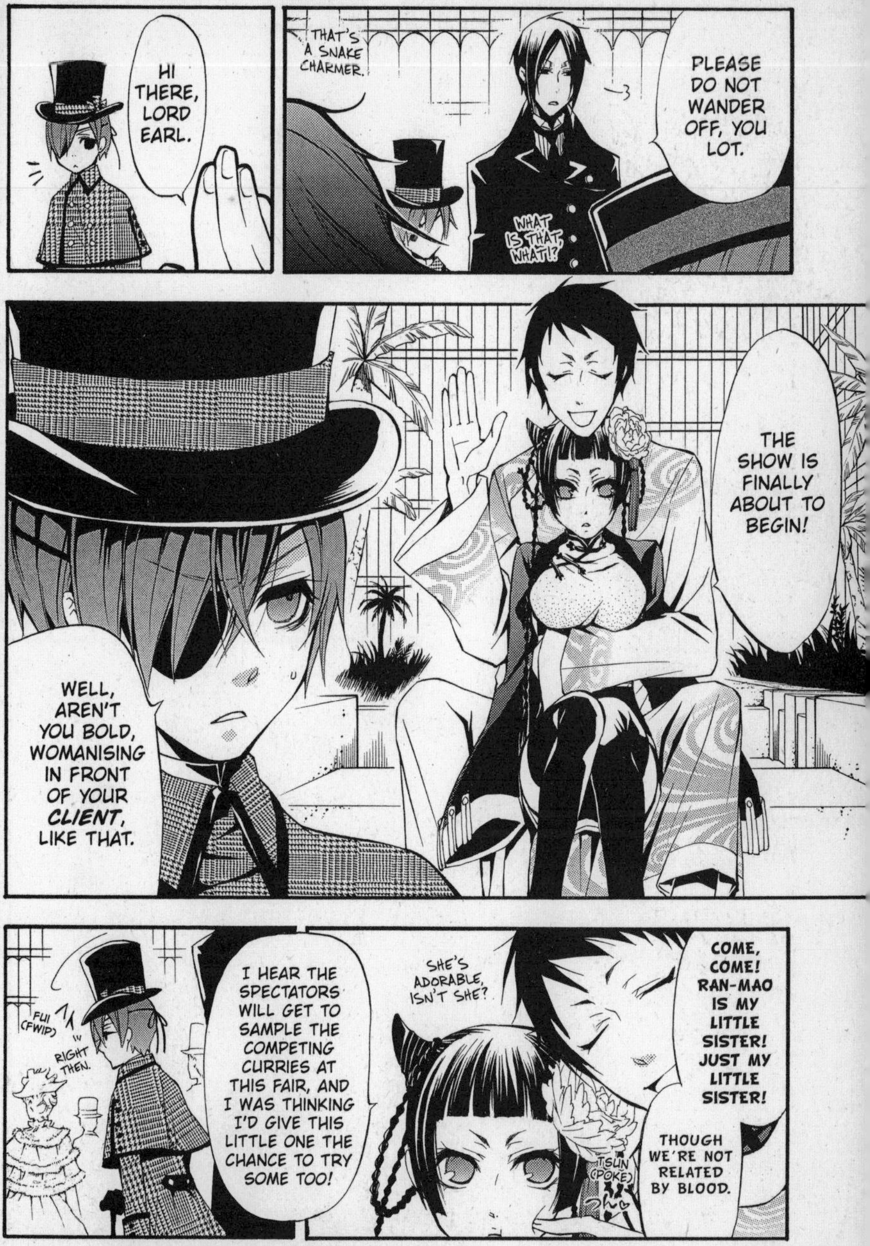
PLEASE DO NOT WANDER OFF, YOU LOT.
WHAT IS THAT, WHAT!?
THAT'S A SNAKE CHARMER.
HI THERE, LORD EARL.
THE SHOW IS FINALLY ABOUT TO BEGIN!
WELL, AREN'T YOU BOLD, WOMANISING IN FRONT OF YOUR *CLIENT*, LIKE THAT.
COME, COME! RAN-MAO IS MY LITTLE SISTER! JUST MY LITTLE SISTER!
SHE'S ADORABLE, ISN'T SHE?
THOUGH WE'RE NOT RELATED BY BLOOD.
TSUN (POKE)
I HEAR THE SPECTATORS WILL GET TO SAMPLE THE COMPETING CURRIES AT THIS FAIR, AND I WAS THINKING I'D GIVE THIS LITTLE ONE THE CHANCE TO TRY SOME TOO!
FUI (FWIP)
RIGHT THEN.

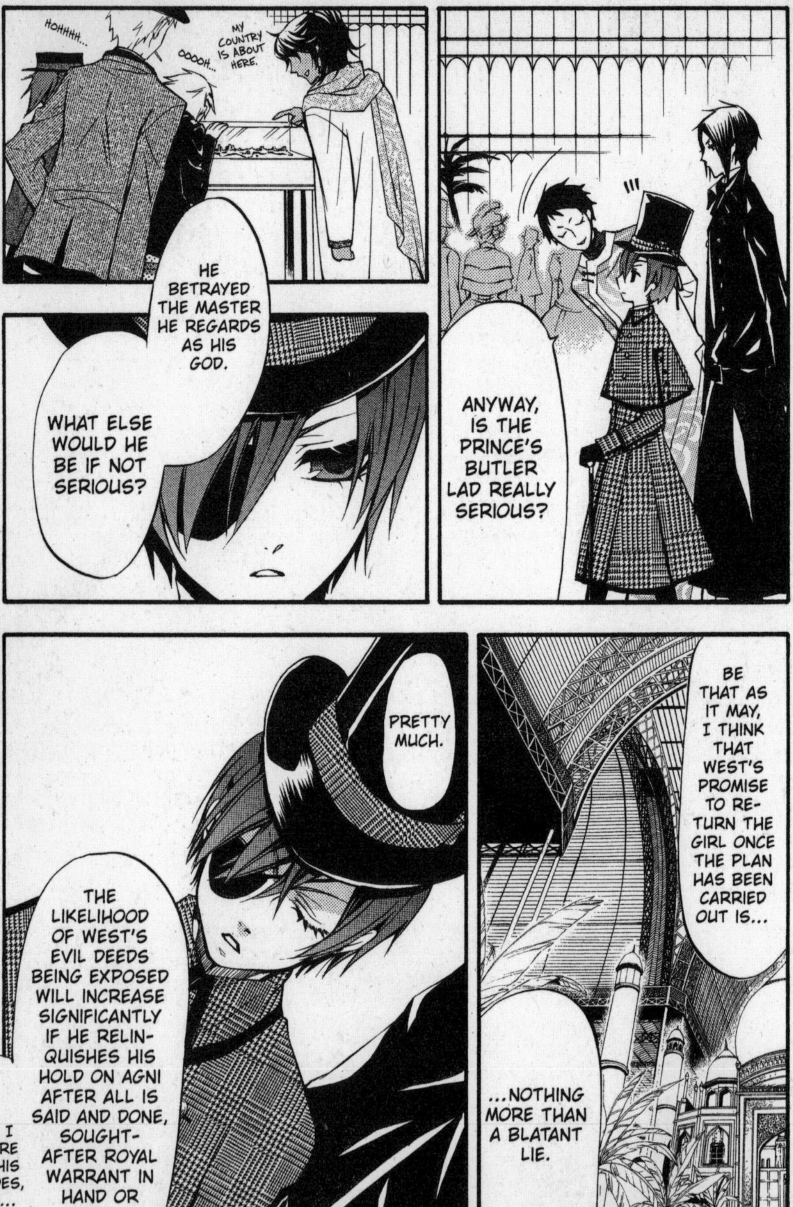

ANYWAY, IS THE PRINCE'S BUTLER LAD REALLY SERIOUS?
MY COUNTRY IS ABOUT HERE.
OOOOH...
HOHHHH...
WHAT ELSE WOULD HE BE IF NOT SERIOUS?
HE BETRAYED THE MASTER HE REGARDS AS HIS GOD.
BE THAT AS IT MAY, I THINK THAT WEST'S PROMISE TO RE-TURN THE GIRL ONCE THE PLAN HAS BEEN CARRIED OUT IS...
...NOTHING MORE THAN A BLATANT LIE.
PRETTY MUCH.
THE LIKELIHOOD OF WEST'S EVIL DEEDS BEING EXPOSED WILL INCREASE SIGNIFICANTLY IF HE RELIN-QUISHES HIS HOLD ON AGNI AFTER ALL IS SAID AND DONE, SOUGHT-AFTER ROYAL WARRANT IN HAND OR NOT.
IF I WERE IN HIS SHOES, I'D...

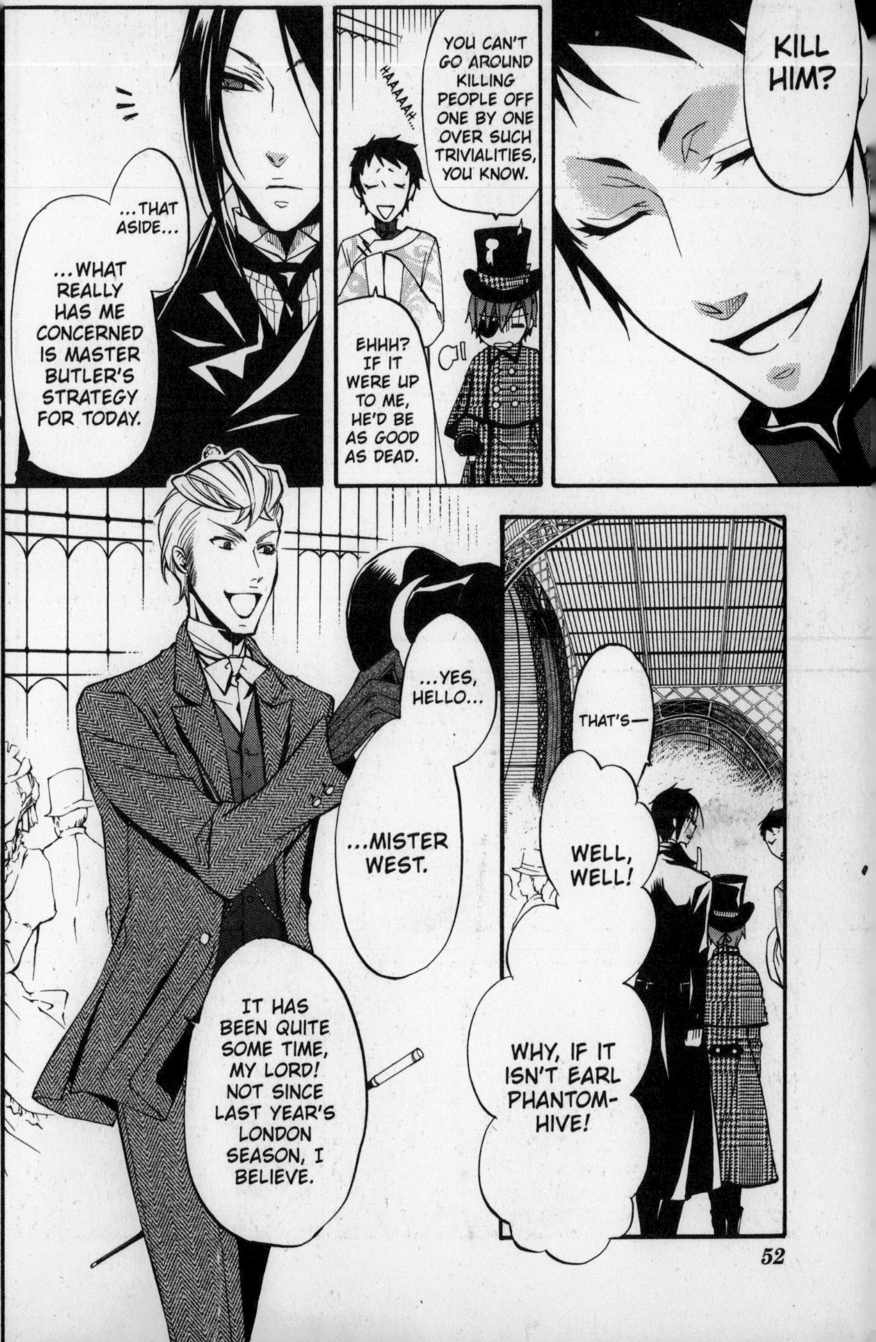
KILL HIM?
YOU CAN'T GO AROUND KILLING PEOPLE OFF ONE BY ONE OVER SUCH TRIVIALITIES, YOU KNOW.
HAAAAAH...
EHHH? IF IT WERE UP TO ME, HE'D BE AS GOOD AS DEAD.
...THAT ASIDE...
...WHAT REALLY HAS ME CONCERNED IS MASTER BUTLER'S STRATEGY FOR TODAY.
THAT'S—
WELL, WELL!
WHY, IF IT ISN'T EARL PHANTOM-HIVE!
...YES, HELLO...
...MISTER WEST.
IT HAS BEEN QUITE SOME TIME, MY LORD! NOT SINCE LAST YEAR'S LONDON SEASON, I BELIEVE.

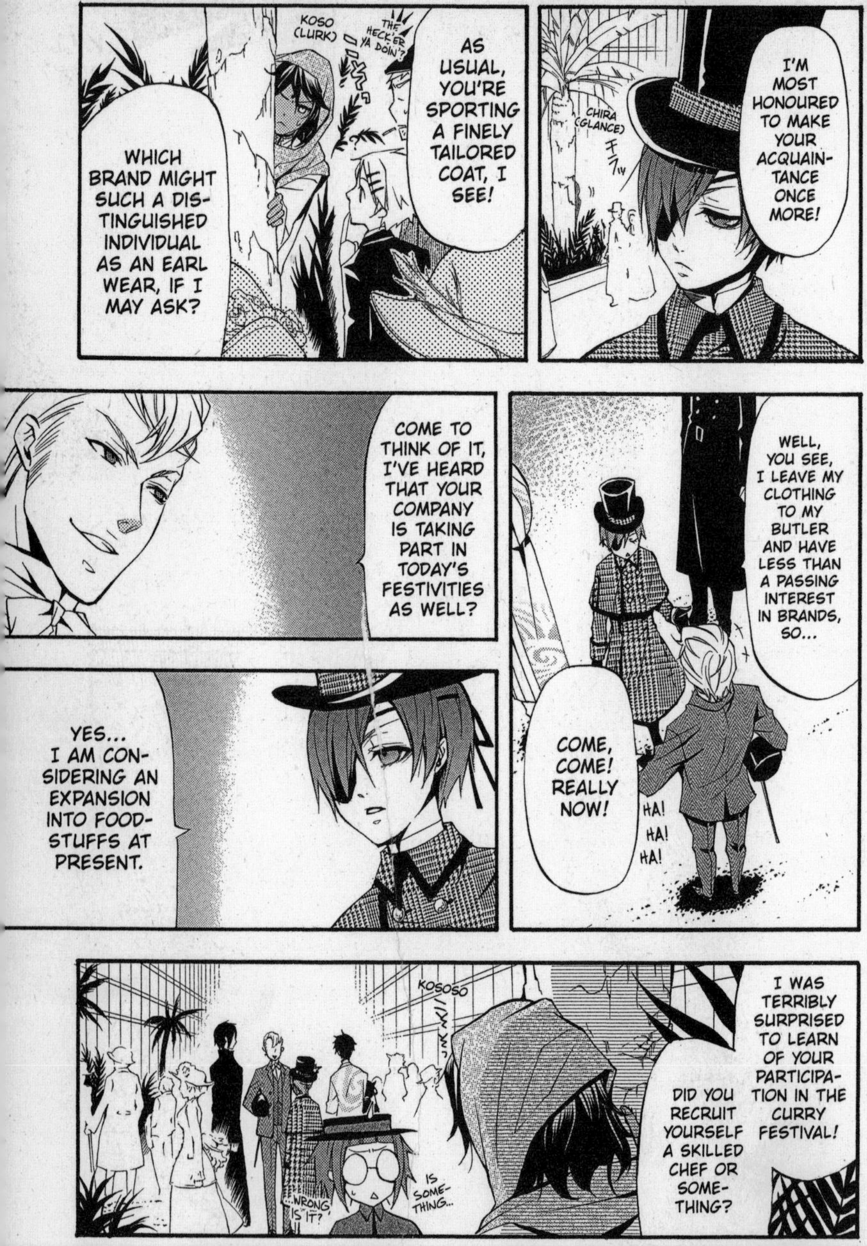
I'M MOST HONOURED TO MAKE YOUR ACQUAINTANCE ONCE MORE!
CHIRA (GLANCE)
AS USUAL, YOU'RE SPORTING A FINELY TAILORED COAT, I SEE!
THE HECK'ER YA DOIN'?
KOSO (LURK)
WHICH BRAND MIGHT SUCH A DISTINGUISHED INDIVIDUAL AS AN EARL WEAR, IF I MAY ASK?
WELL, YOU SEE, I LEAVE MY CLOTHING TO MY BUTLER AND HAVE LESS THAN A PASSING INTEREST IN BRANDS, SO...
COME, COME! REALLY NOW!
HA! HA! HA!
COME TO THINK OF IT, I'VE HEARD THAT YOUR COMPANY IS TAKING PART IN TODAY'S FESTIVITIES AS WELL?
YES... I AM CONSIDERING AN EXPANSION INTO FOODSTUFFS AT PRESENT.
I WAS TERRIBLY SURPRISED TO LEARN OF YOUR PARTICIPATION IN THE CURRY FESTIVAL!
DID YOU RECRUIT YOURSELF A SKILLED CHEF OR SOMETHING?
KOSOSO
IS SOMETHING...
WRONG IS IT?

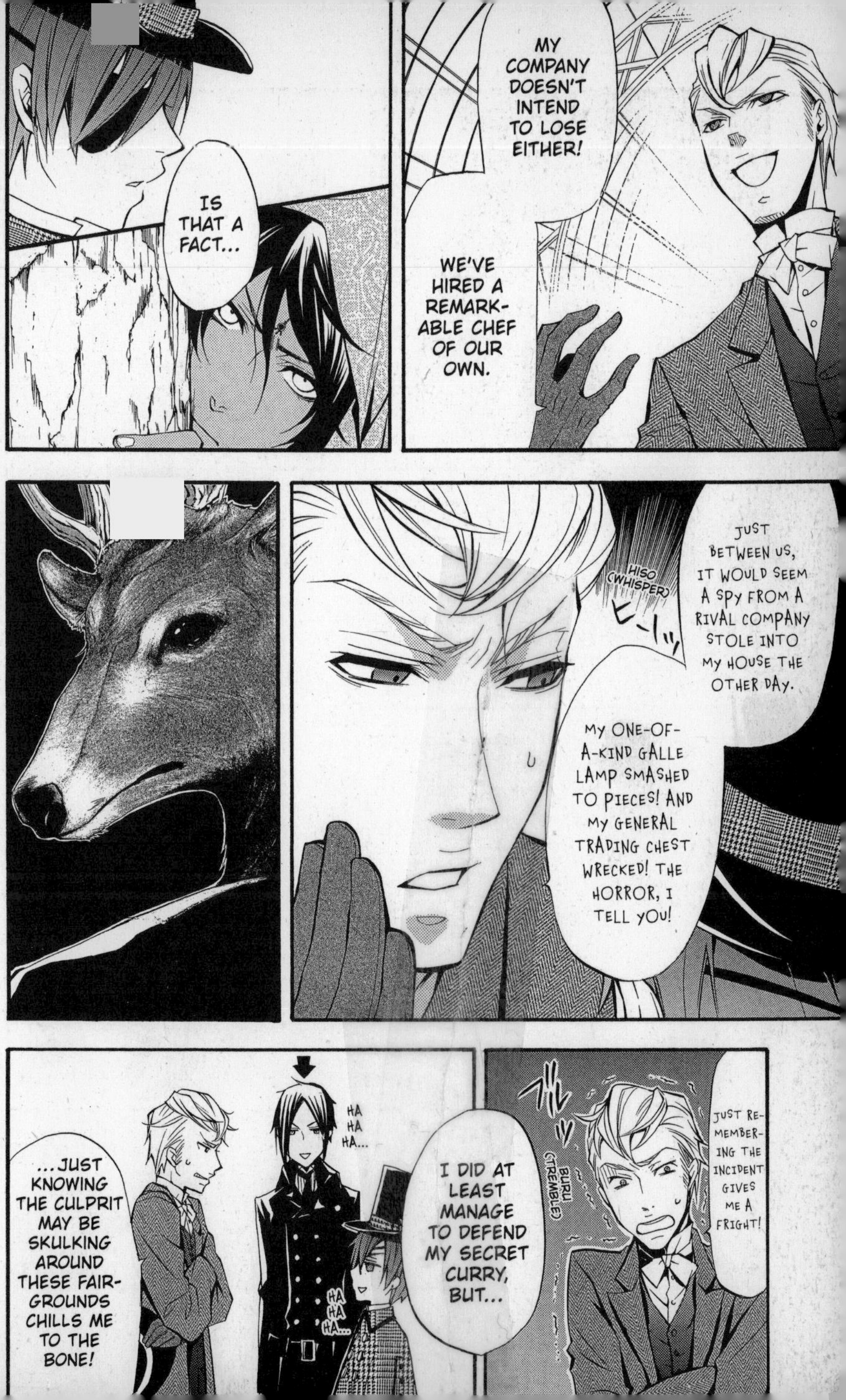
MY COMPANY DOESN'T INTEND TO LOSE EITHER!
WE'VE HIRED A REMARKABLE CHEF OF OUR OWN.
IS THAT A FACT...
HISO (WHISPER)
JUST BETWEEN US, IT WOULD SEEM A SPY FROM A RIVAL COMPANY STOLE INTO MY HOUSE THE OTHER DAY.
MY ONE-OF-A-KIND GALLE LAMP SMASHED TO PIECES! AND MY GENERAL TRADING CHEST WRECKED! THE HORROR, I TELL YOU!
BURU (TREMBLE)
JUST REMEMBERING THE INCIDENT GIVES ME A FRIGHT!
HA HA HA...
I DID AT LEAST MANAGE TO DEFEND MY SECRET CURRY, BUT...
HA HA HA...
...JUST KNOWING THE CULPRIT MAY BE SKULKING AROUND THESE FAIRGROUNDS CHILLS ME TO THE BONE!

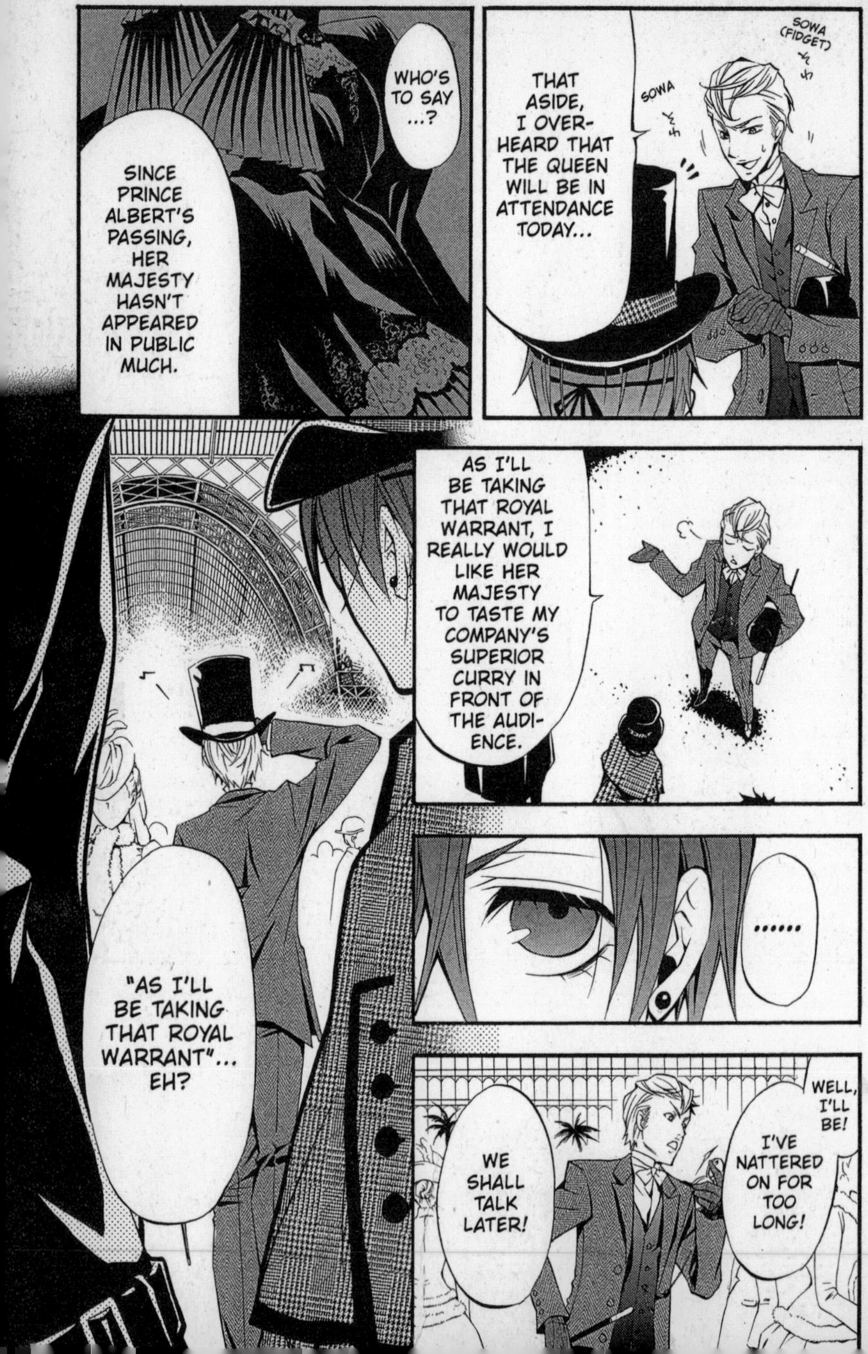
SOWA (FIDGET)
SOWA
THAT ASIDE, I OVER-HEARD THAT THE QUEEN WILL BE IN ATTENDANCE TODAY...
WHO'S TO SAY ...?
SINCE PRINCE ALBERT'S PASSING, HER MAJESTY HASN'T APPEARED IN PUBLIC MUCH.
AS I'LL BE TAKING THAT ROYAL WARRANT, I REALLY WOULD LIKE HER MAJESTY TO TASTE MY COMPANY'S SUPERIOR CURRY IN FRONT OF THE AUDI-ENCE.
......
WELL, I'LL BE!
I'VE NATTERED ON FOR TOO LONG!
WE SHALL TALK LATER!
"AS I'LL BE TAKING THAT ROYAL WARRANT"... EH?

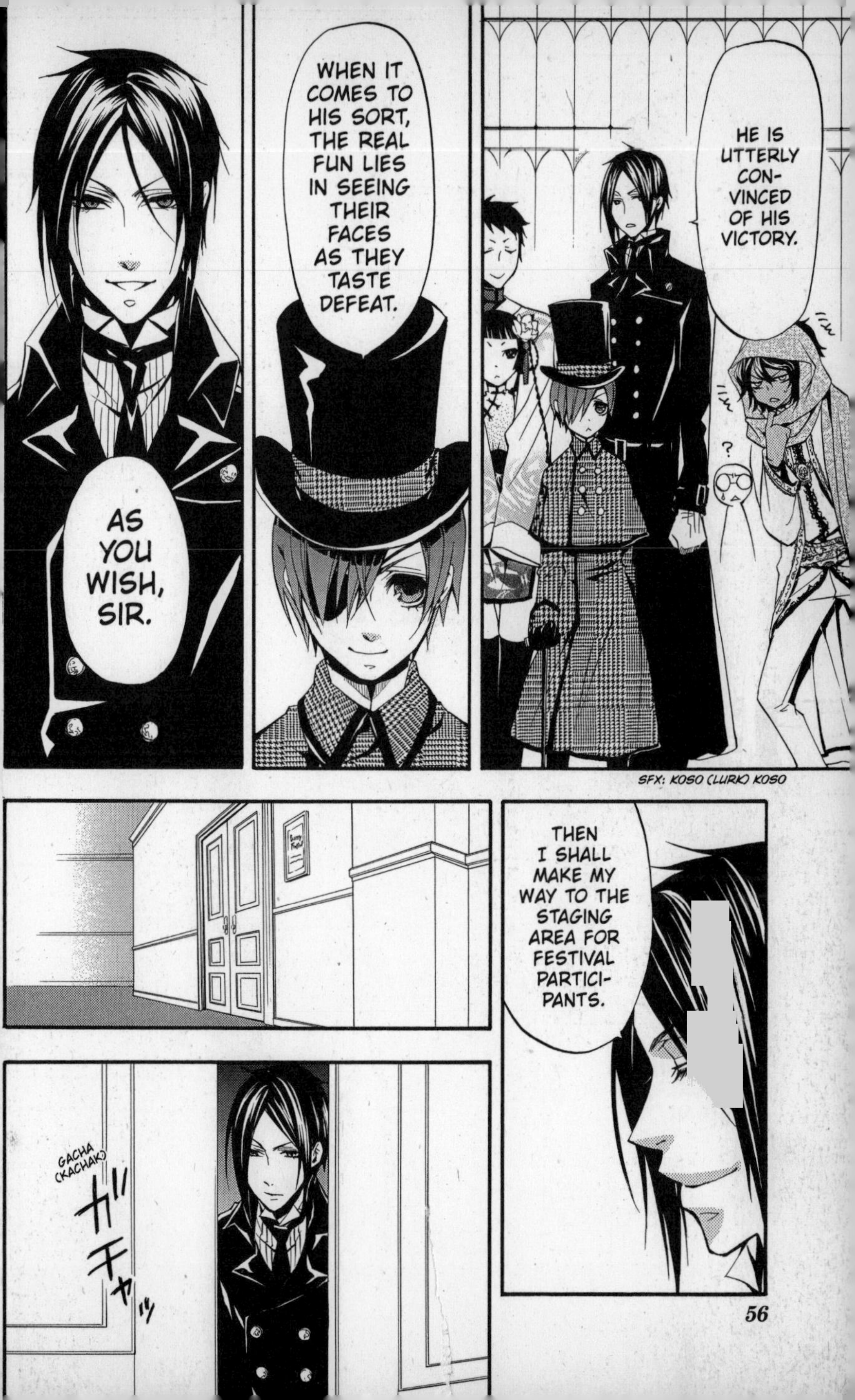
HE IS UTTERLY CON-VINCED OF HIS VICTORY.
WHEN IT COMES TO HIS SORT, THE REAL FUN LIES IN SEEING THEIR FACES AS THEY TASTE DEFEAT.
AS YOU WISH, SIR.
SFX: KOSO (LURK) KOSO
THEN I SHALL MAKE MY WAY TO THE STAGING AREA FOR FESTIVAL PARTICI-PANTS.
GACHA (KACHAK)
ガチャッ

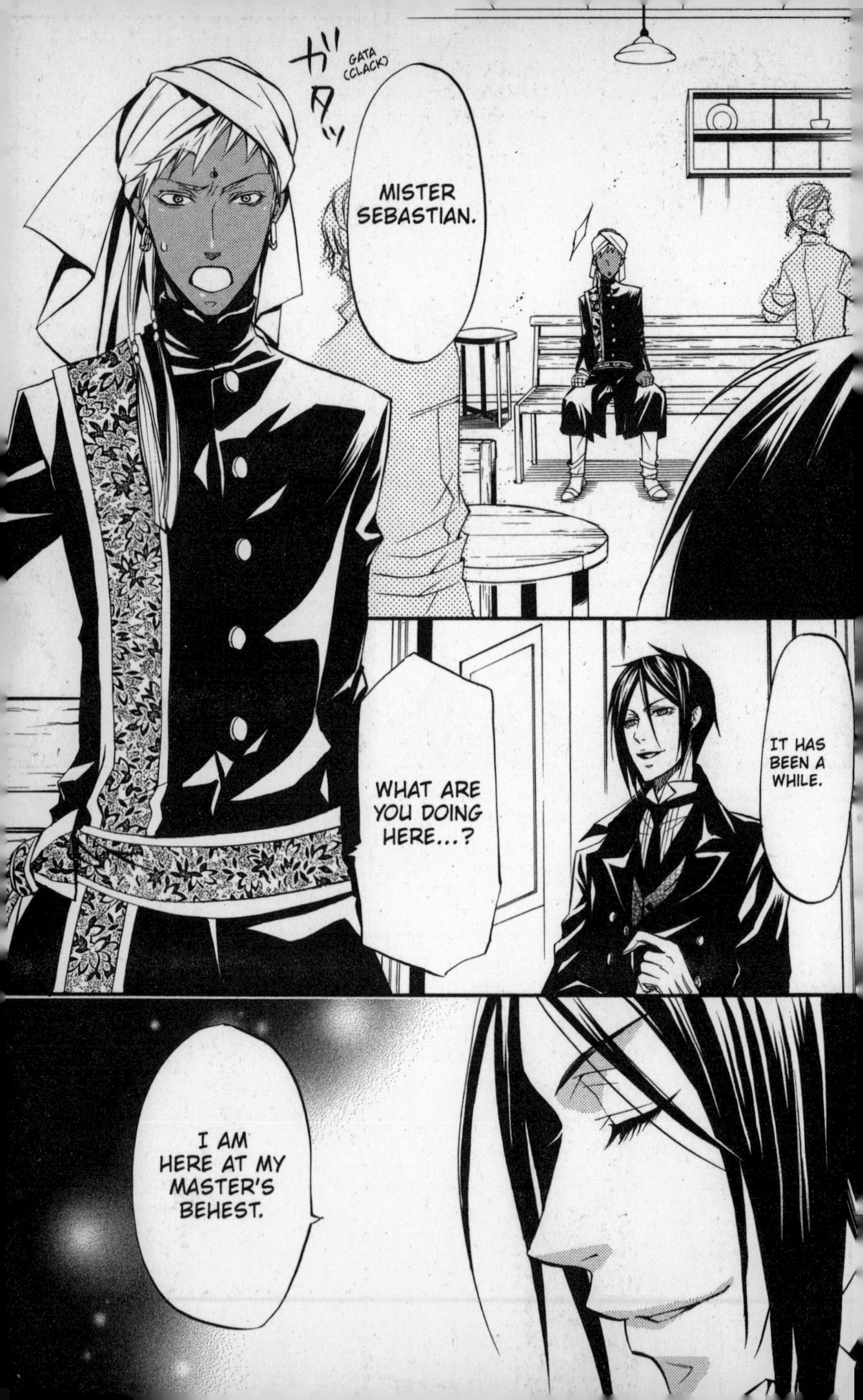
ガタッ
GATA (CLACK)
MISTER SEBASTIAN.
IT HAS BEEN A WHILE.
WHAT ARE YOU DOING HERE...?
I AM HERE AT MY MASTER'S BEHEST.

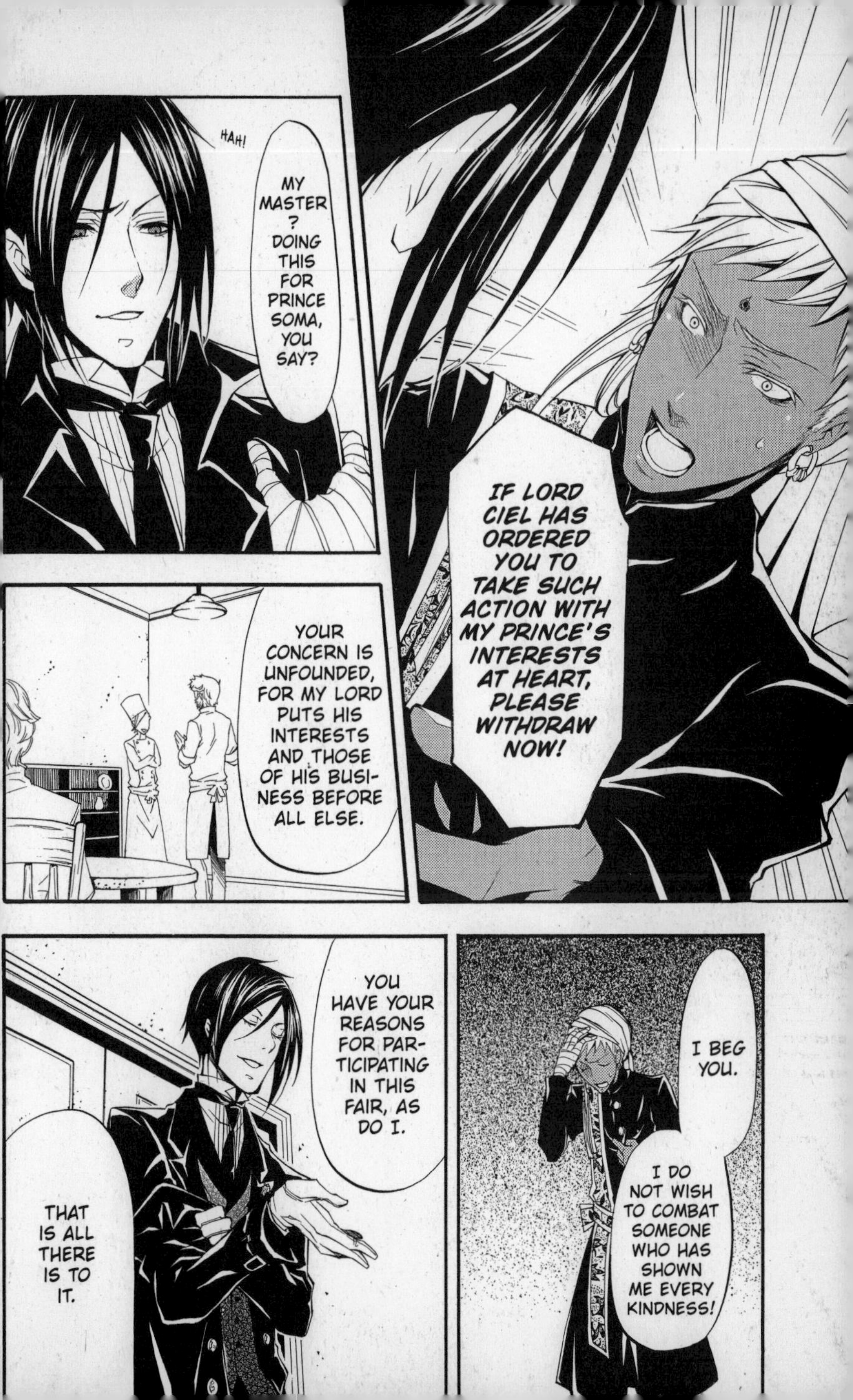
IF LORD CIEL HAS ORDERED YOU TO TAKE SUCH ACTION WITH MY PRINCE'S INTERESTS AT HEART, PLEASE WITHDRAW NOW!
HAH!
MY MASTER? DOING THIS FOR PRINCE SOMA, YOU SAY?
YOUR CONCERN IS UNFOUNDED, FOR MY LORD PUTS HIS INTERESTS AND THOSE OF HIS BUSINESS BEFORE ALL ELSE.
I BEG YOU.
I DO NOT WISH TO COMBAT SOMEONE WHO HAS SHOWN ME EVERY KINDNESS!
YOU HAVE YOUR REASONS FOR PARTICIPATING IN THIS FAIR, AS DO I.
THAT IS ALL THERE IS TO IT.

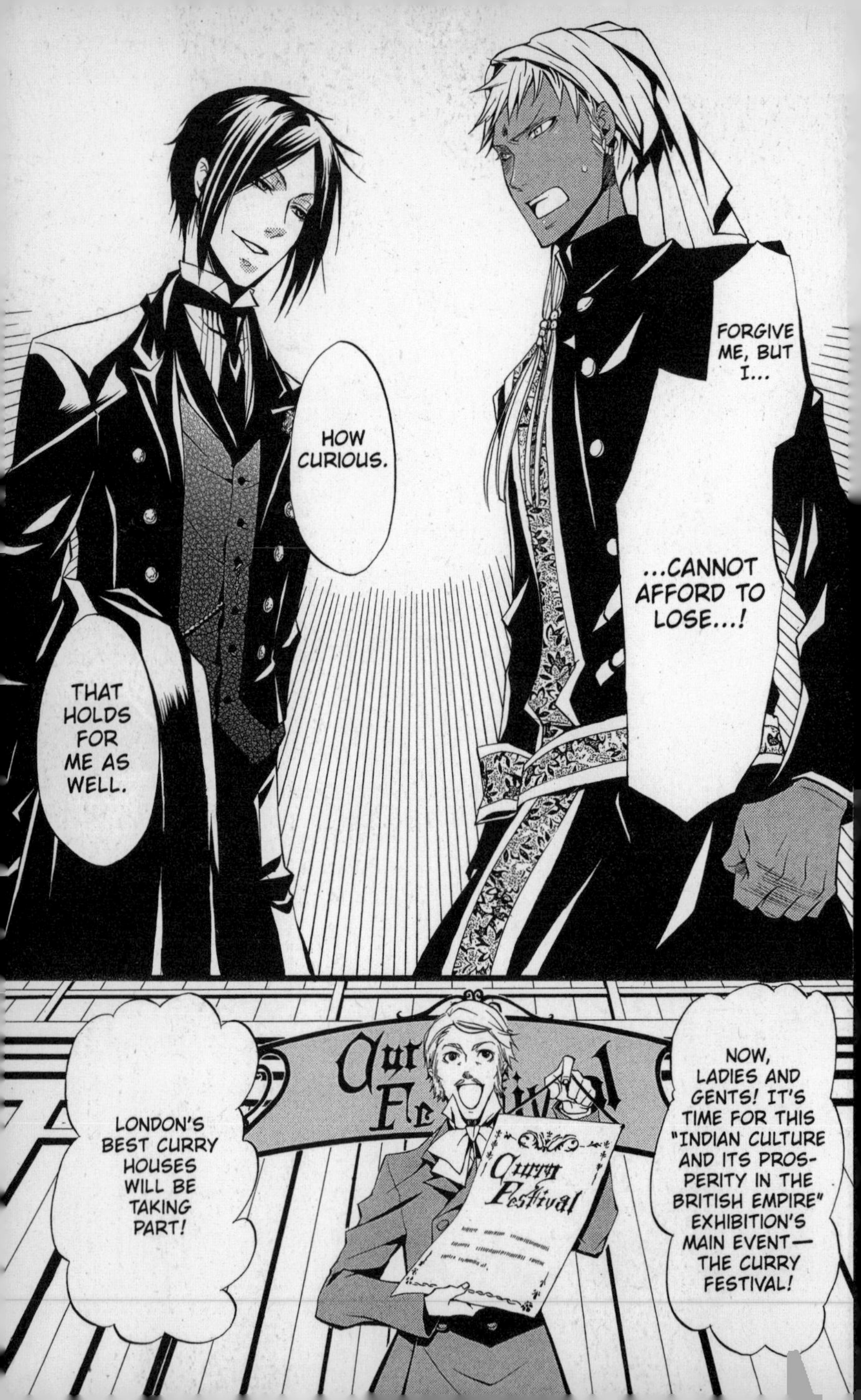
FORGIVE ME, BUT I...
...CANNOT AFFORD TO LOSE...!
HOW CURIOUS.
THAT HOLDS FOR ME AS WELL.
NOW, LADIES AND GENTS! IT'S TIME FOR THIS "INDIAN CULTURE AND ITS PROSPERITY IN THE BRITISH EMPIRE" EXHIBITION'S MAIN EVENT—THE CURRY FESTIVAL!
Curry Festival
LONDON'S BEST CURRY HOUSES WILL BE TAKING PART!

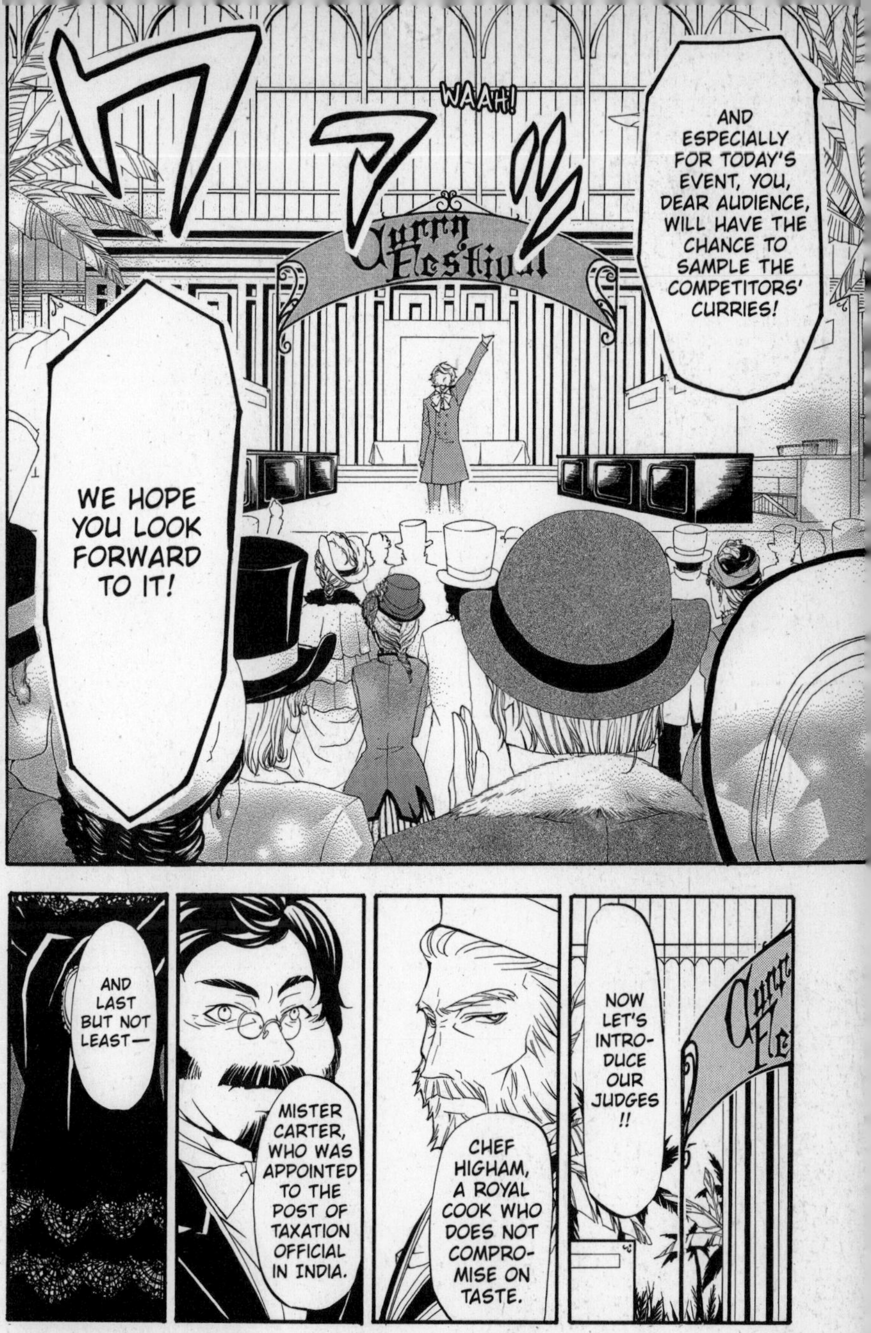
AND ESPECIALLY FOR TODAY'S EVENT, YOU, DEAR AUDIENCE, WILL HAVE THE CHANCE TO SAMPLE THE COMPETITORS' CURRIES!
WAAH!
WE HOPE YOU LOOK FORWARD TO IT!
NOW LET'S INTRO-DUCE OUR JUDGES !!
CHEF HIGHAM, A ROYAL COOK WHO DOES NOT COMPRO-MISE ON TASTE.
MISTER CARTER, WHO WAS APPOINTED TO THE POST OF TAXATION OFFICIAL IN INDIA.
AND LAST BUT NOT LEAST—

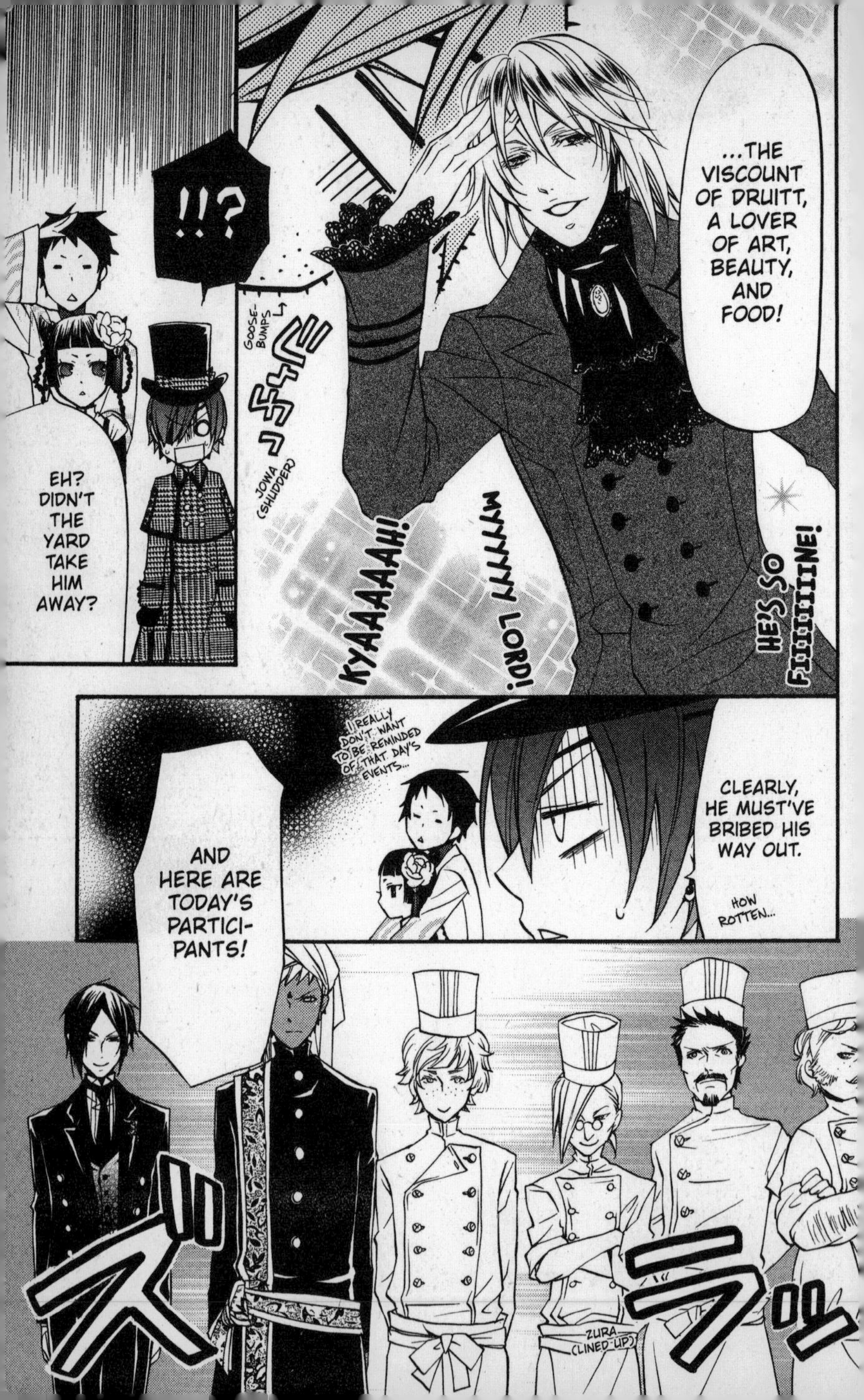
...THE VISCOUNT OF DRUITT, A LOVER OF ART, BEAUTY, AND FOOD!
HE'S SO FIIIIIIIINE!
MYYYYYY LORD!
KYAAAAAAH!
JOWA (SHUDDER)
GOOSE-BUMPS
!!?
EH? DIDN'T THE YARD TAKE HIM AWAY?
CLEARLY, HE MUST'VE BRIBED HIS WAY OUT.
HOW ROTTEN...
I REALLY DON'T WANT TO BE REMINDED OF THAT DAY'S EVENTS...
AND HERE ARE TODAY'S PARTICI-PANTS!
ZURA (LINED UP)

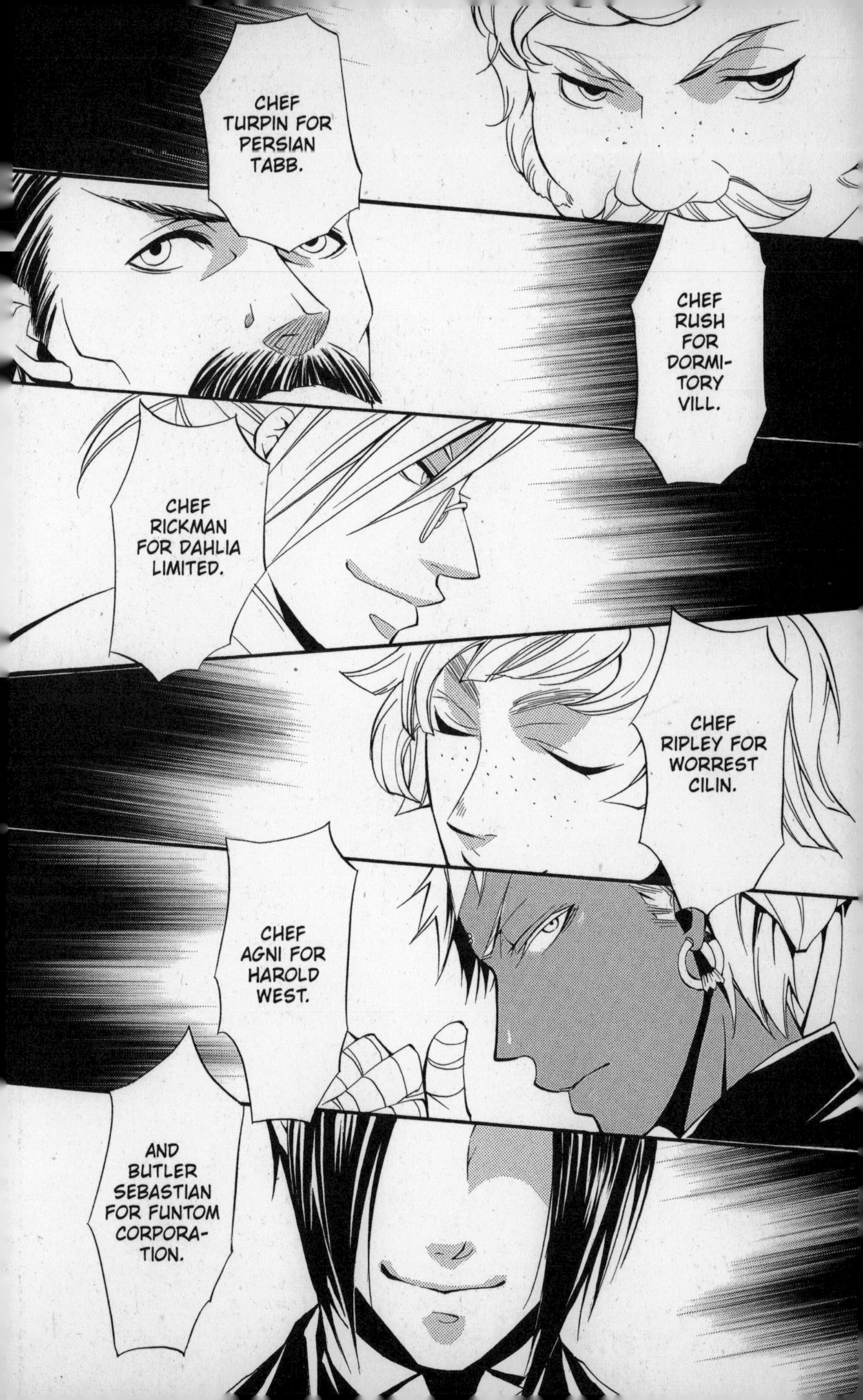
CHEF TURPIN FOR PERSIAN TABB.
CHEF RUSH FOR DORMITORY VILL.
CHEF RICKMAN FOR DAHLIA LIMITED.
CHEF RIPLEY FOR WORREST CILIN.
CHEF AGNI FOR HAROLD WEST.
AND BUTLER SEBASTIAN FOR FUNTOM CORPORATION.

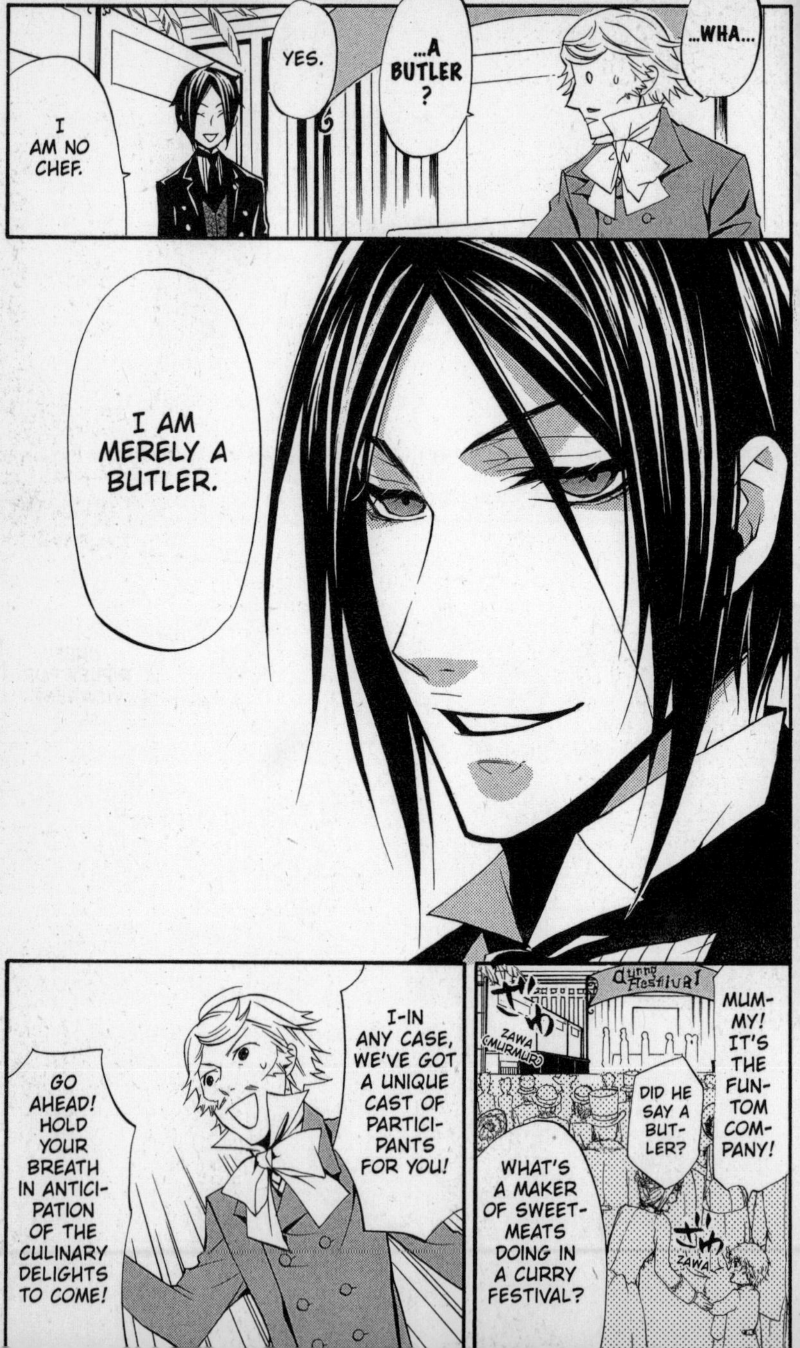
...WHA...
...A BUTLER?
YES.
I AM NO CHEF.
I AM MERELY A BUTLER.
Curry Festival!
MUMMY! IT'S THE FUNTOM COMPANY!
DID HE SAY A BUTLER?
ZAWA (MURMUR)
WHAT'S A MAKER OF SWEETMEATS DOING IN A CURRY FESTIVAL?
ZAWA
I-IN ANY CASE, WE'VE GOT A UNIQUE CAST OF PARTICIPANTS FOR YOU!
GO AHEAD! HOLD YOUR BREATH IN ANTICIPATION OF THE CULINARY DELIGHTS TO COME!

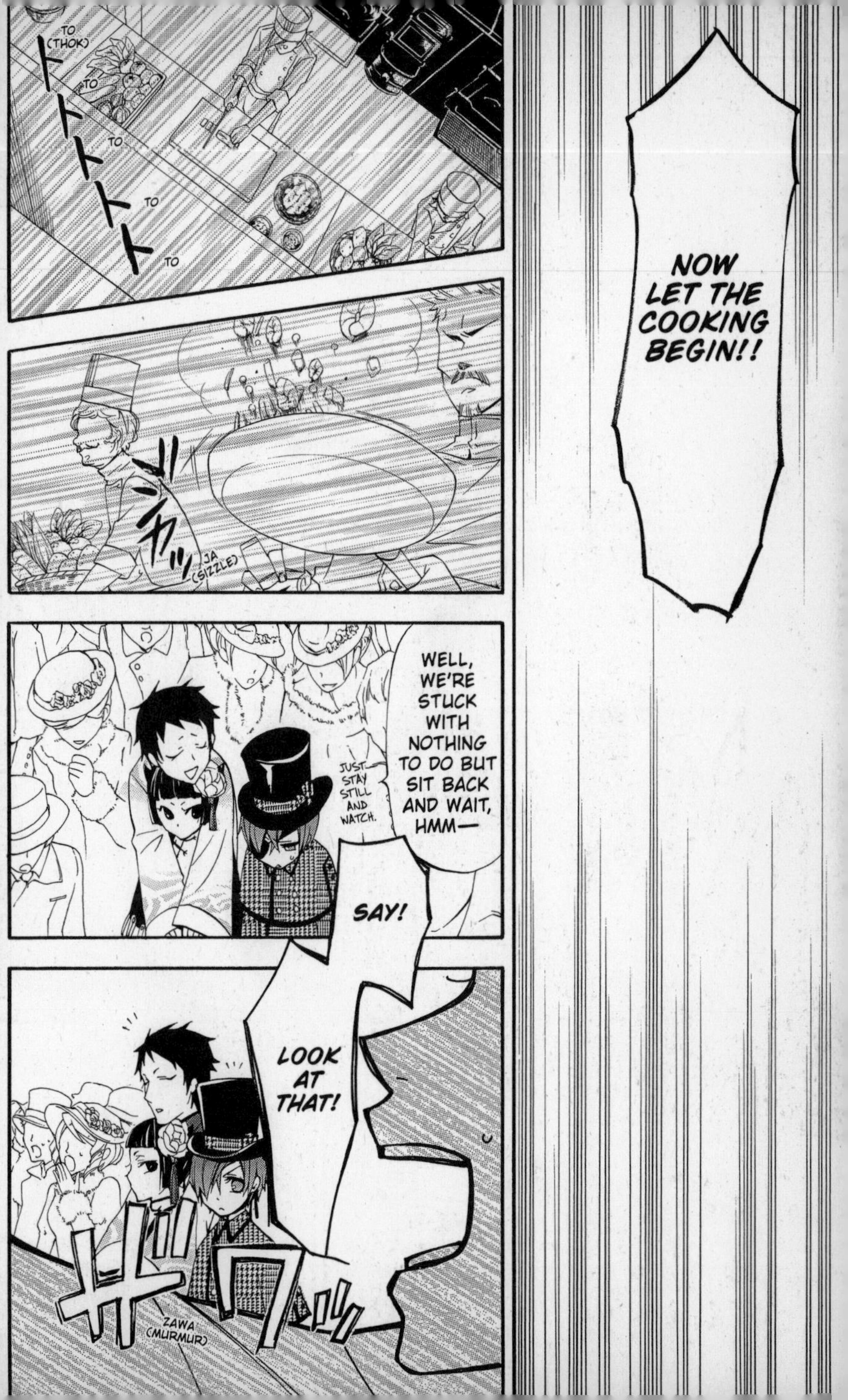
NOW LET THE COOKING BEGIN!!
TO (THOK)
TO
TO
TO
TO
JA (SIZZLE)
WELL, WE'RE STUCK WITH NOTHING TO DO BUT SIT BACK AND WAIT, HMM—
JUST STAY STILL AND WATCH.
SAY!
LOOK AT THAT!
ZAWA (MURMUR)

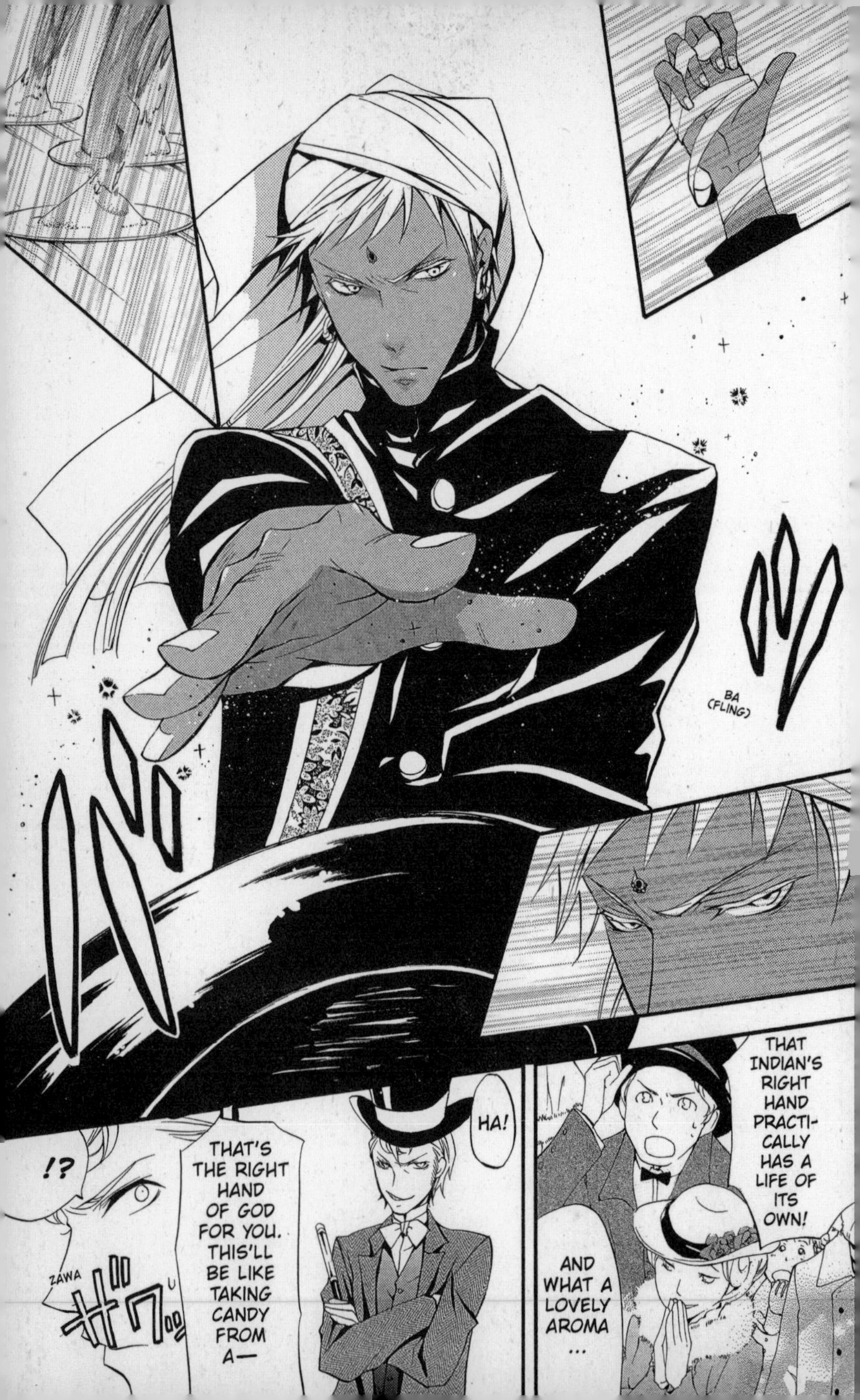
BA (FLING)
THAT INDIAN'S RIGHT HAND PRACTI-CALLY HAS A LIFE OF ITS OWN!
AND WHAT A LOVELY AROMA ...
HA!
THAT'S THE RIGHT HAND OF GOD FOR YOU. THIS'LL BE LIKE TAKING CANDY FROM A—
!?
ZAWA

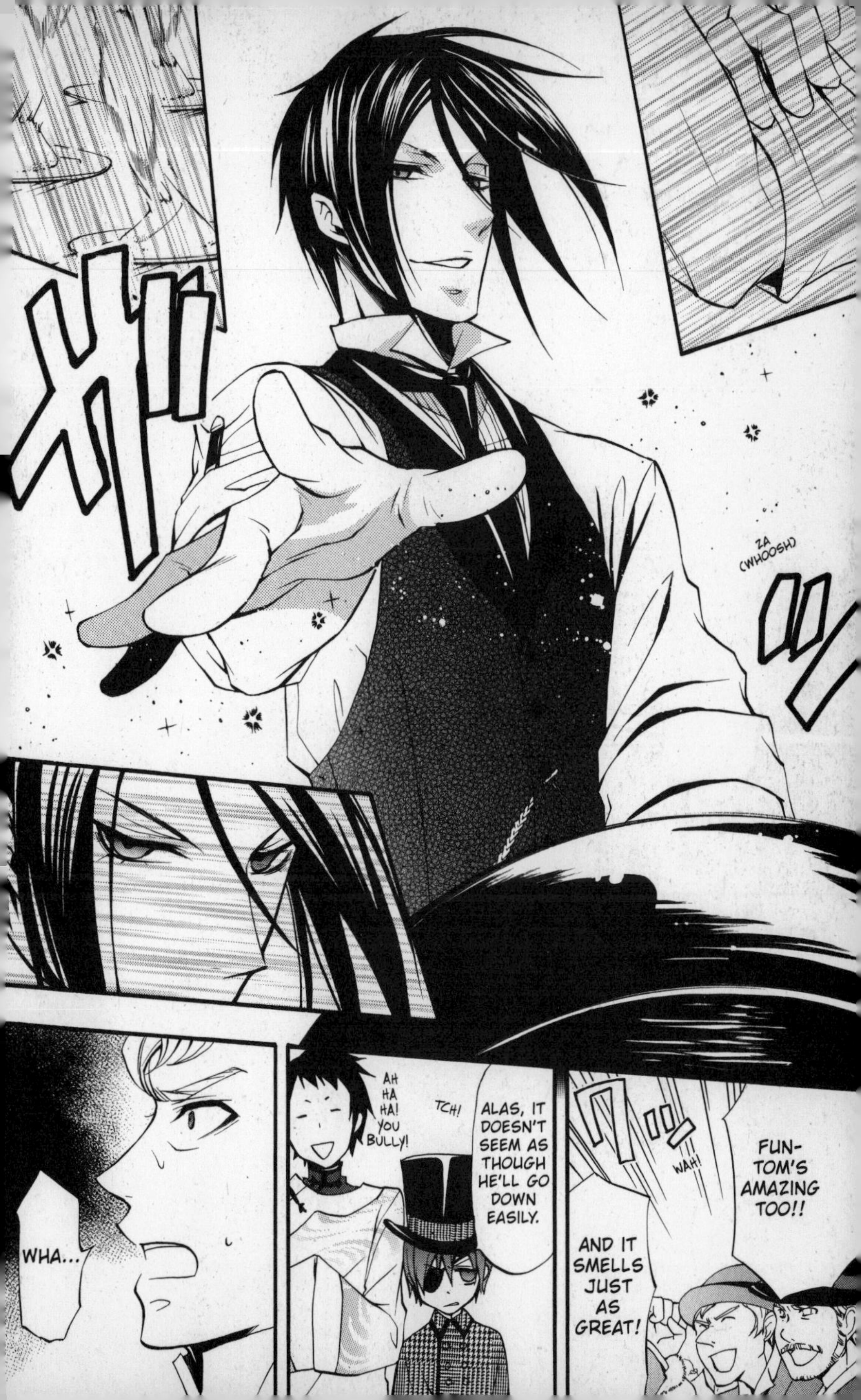
ZA (WHOOSH)
FUN-TOM'S AMAZING TOO!!
WAH!
AND IT SMELLS JUST AS GREAT!
ALAS, IT DOESN'T SEEM AS THOUGH HE'LL GO DOWN EASILY.
TCH!
AH HA HA! YOU BULLY!
WHA...

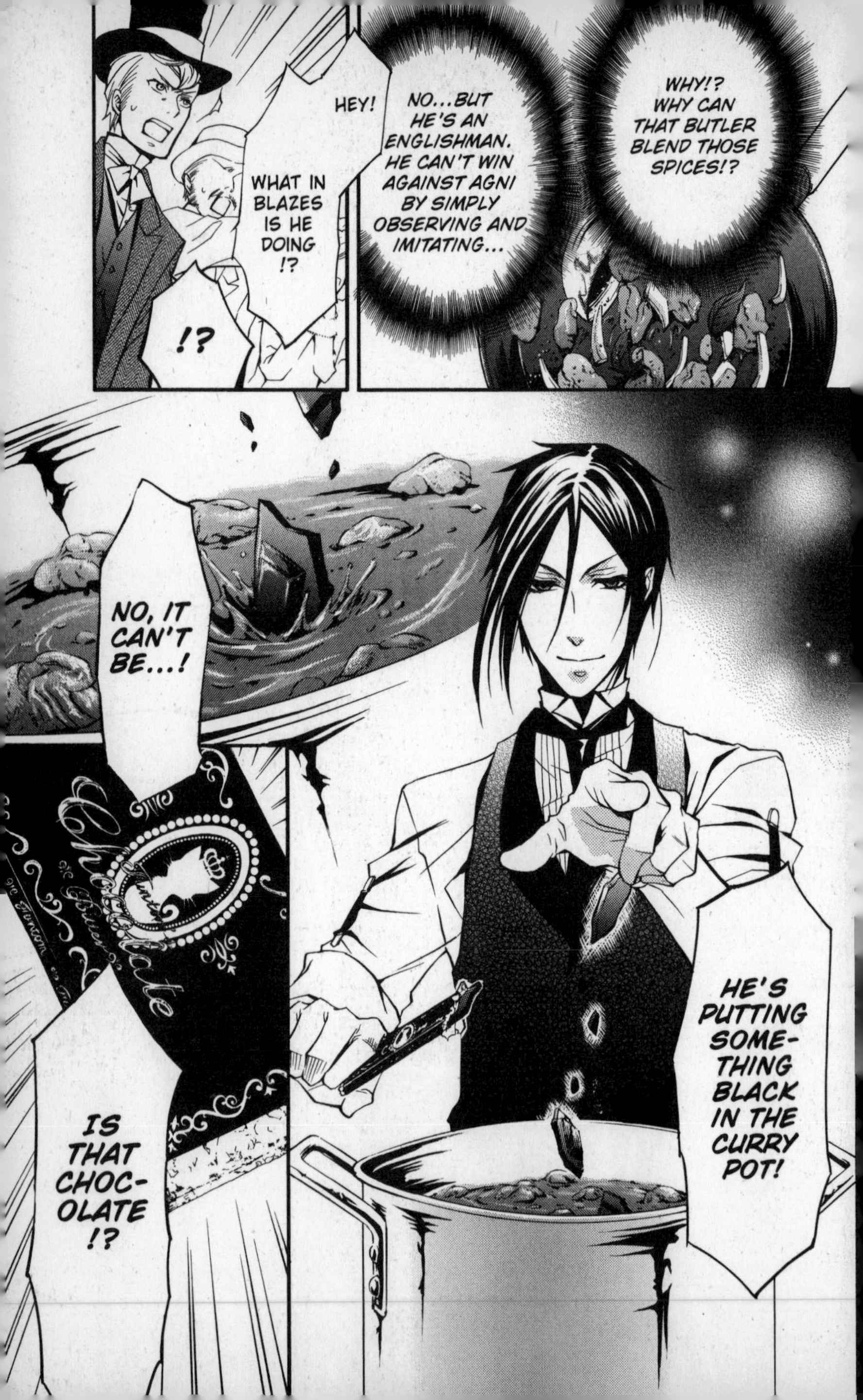
WHY!? WHY CAN THAT BUTLER BLEND THOSE SPICES!?
NO...BUT HE'S AN ENGLISHMAN. HE CAN'T WIN AGAINST AGNI BY SIMPLY OBSERVING AND IMITATING...
HEY!
WHAT IN BLAZES IS HE DOING !?
!?
HE'S PUTTING SOME-THING BLACK IN THE CURRY POT!
NO, IT CAN'T BE...!
IS THAT CHOC-OLATE !?

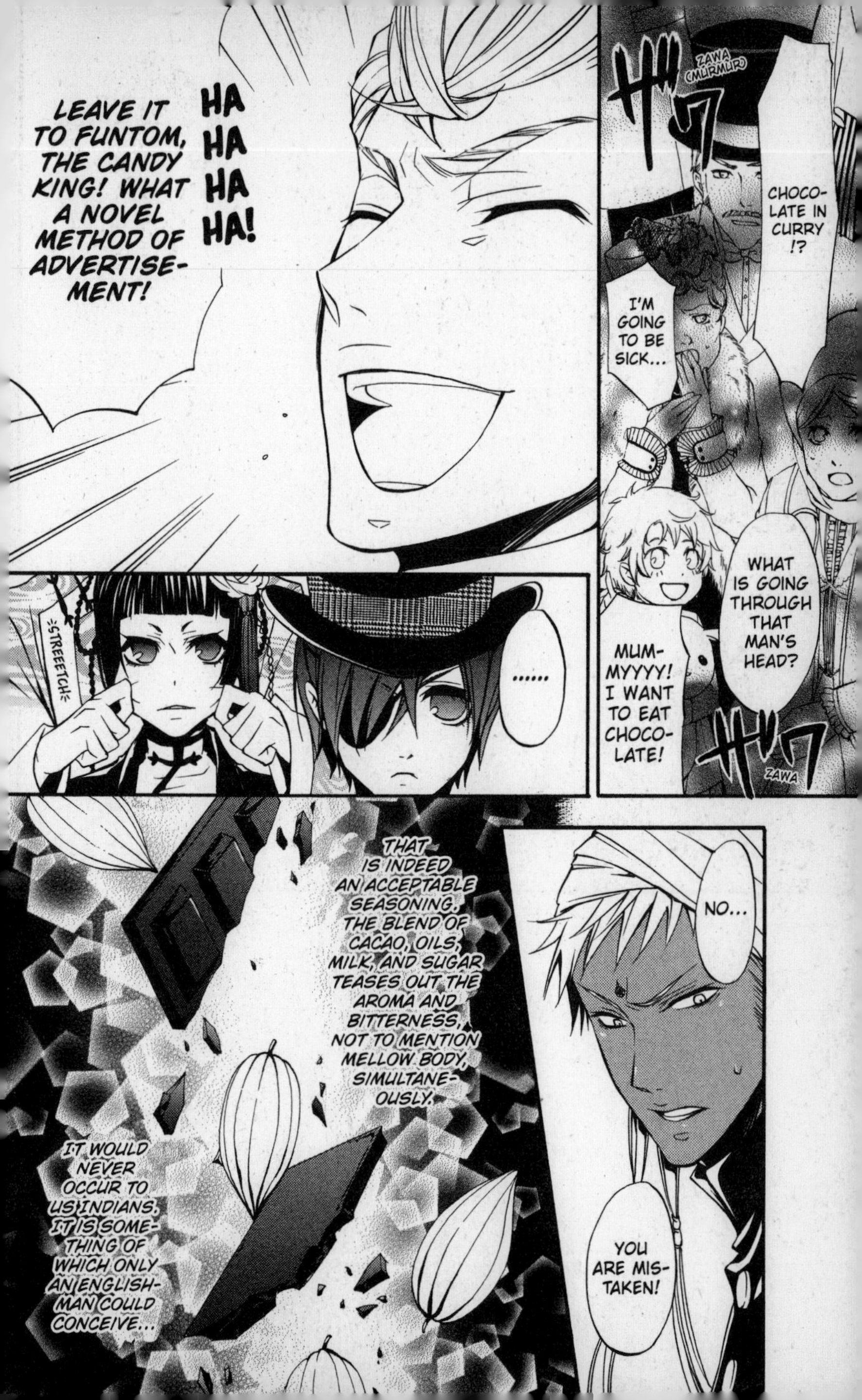
ZAWA (MURMUR)
CHOCOLATE IN CURRY!?
I'M GOING TO BE SICK...
WHAT IS GOING THROUGH THAT MAN'S HEAD?
MUMMYYYY! I WANT TO EAT CHOCOLATE!
ZAWA
HA HA HA HA!
LEAVE IT TO FUNTOM, THE CANDY KING! WHAT A NOVEL METHOD OF ADVERTISEMENT!
......
STREEETCH
NO...
YOU ARE MISTAKEN!
THAT IS INDEED AN ACCEPTABLE SEASONING. THE BLEND OF CACAO, OILS, MILK, AND SUGAR TEASES OUT THE AROMA AND BITTERNESS, NOT TO MENTION MELLOW BODY, SIMULTANEOUSLY.
IT WOULD NEVER OCCUR TO US INDIANS. IT IS SOMETHING OF WHICH ONLY AN ENGLISHMAN COULD CONCEIVE...

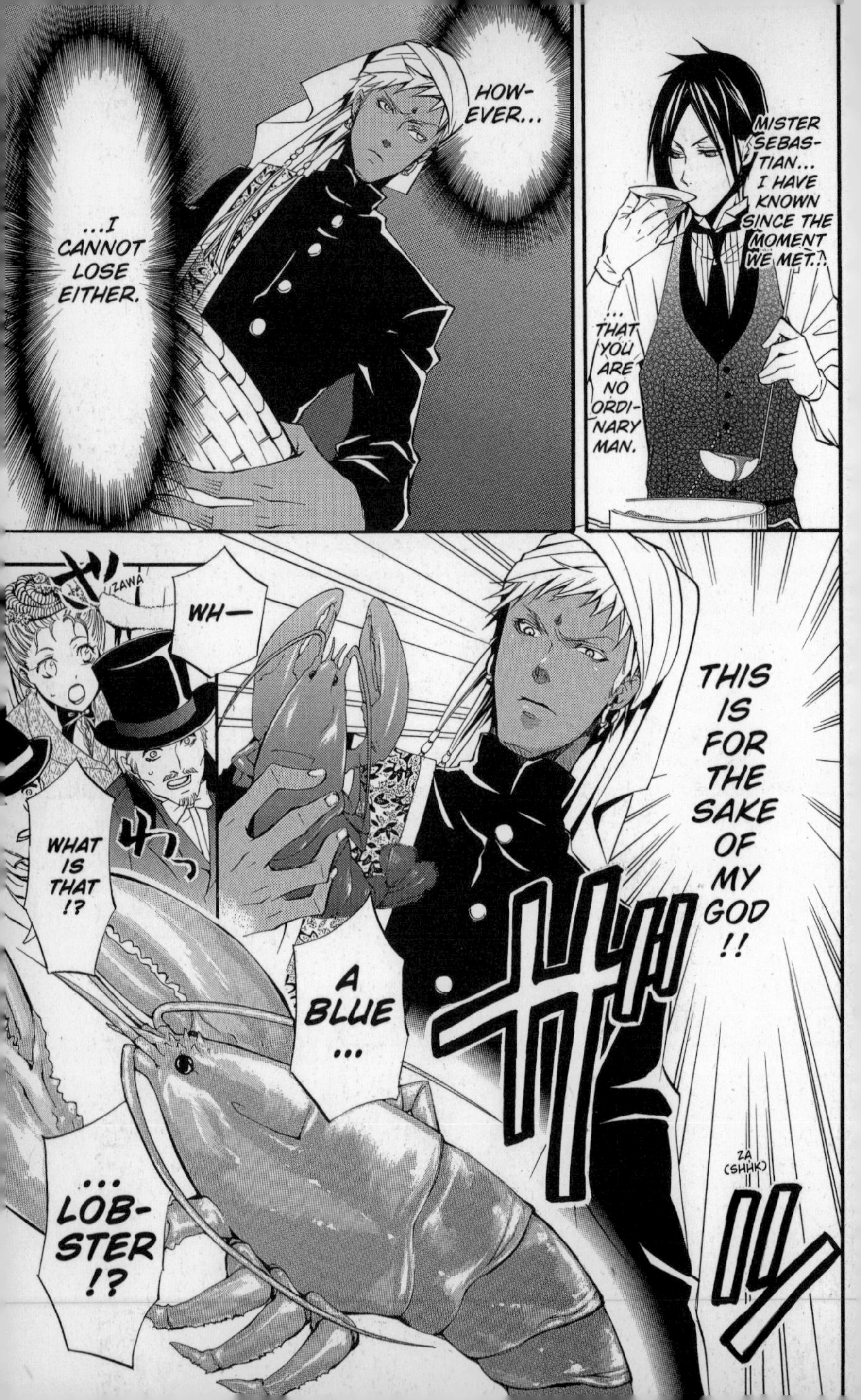
MISTER SEBAS-TIAN... I HAVE KNOWN SINCE THE MOMENT WE MET...
...THAT YOU ARE NO ORDI-NARY MAN.
HOW-EVER...
...I CANNOT LOSE EITHER.
THIS IS FOR THE SAKE OF MY GOD!!
ZA (SHHK)
ZAWA
WH—
WHAT IS THAT!?
A BLUE...
...LÖB-STER!?

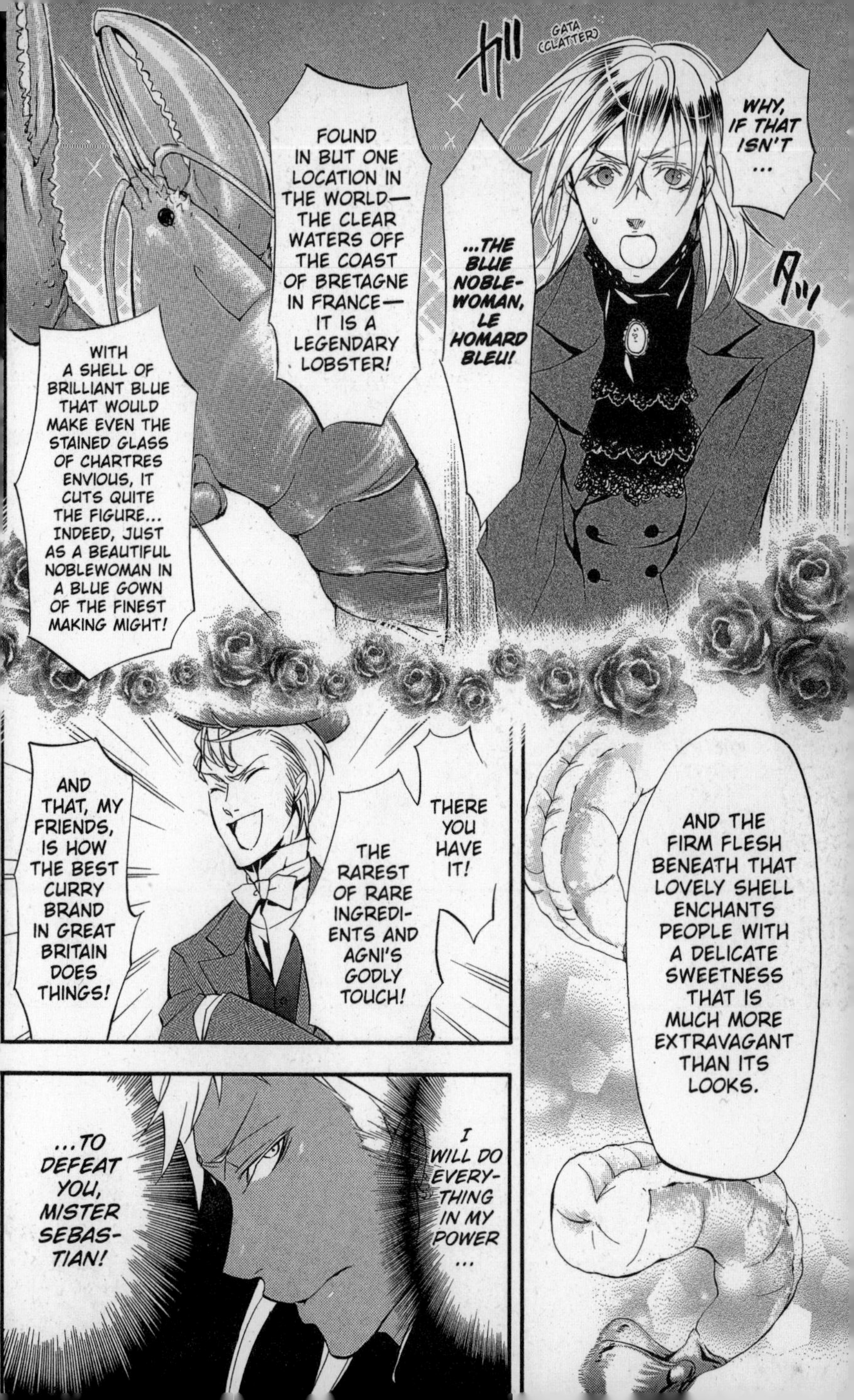

WHY, IF THAT ISN'T ...
GATA (CLATTER)
...THE BLUE NOBLE-WOMAN, LE HOMARD BLEU!
FOUND IN BUT ONE LOCATION IN THE WORLD—THE CLEAR WATERS OFF THE COAST OF BRETAGNE IN FRANCE—IT IS A LEGENDARY LOBSTER!
WITH A SHELL OF BRILLIANT BLUE THAT WOULD MAKE EVEN THE STAINED GLASS OF CHARTRES ENVIOUS, IT CUTS QUITE THE FIGURE... INDEED, JUST AS A BEAUTIFUL NOBLEWOMAN IN A BLUE GOWN OF THE FINEST MAKING MIGHT!
AND THE FIRM FLESH BENEATH THAT LOVELY SHELL ENCHANTS PEOPLE WITH A DELICATE SWEETNESS THAT IS MUCH MORE EXTRAVAGANT THAN ITS LOOKS.
THERE YOU HAVE IT!
THE RAREST OF RARE INGREDI-ENTS AND AGNI'S GODLY TOUCH!
AND THAT, MY FRIENDS, IS HOW THE BEST CURRY BRAND IN GREAT BRITAIN DOES THINGS!
I WILL DO EVERY-THING IN MY POWER ...
...TO DEFEAT YOU, MISTER SEBAS-TIAN!

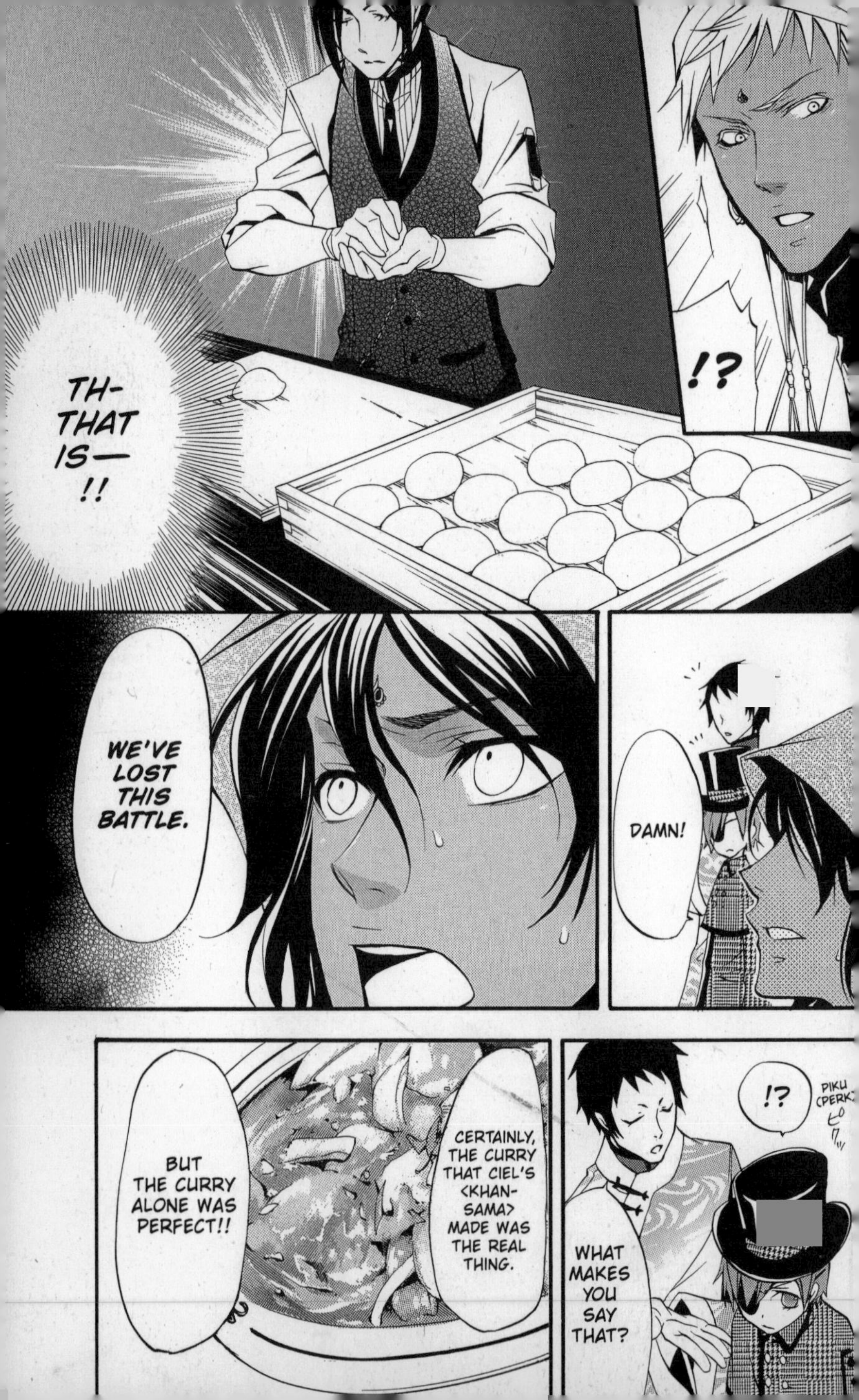
!?
TH-THAT IS—!!
DAMN!
WE'VE LOST THIS BATTLE.
!?
PIKU (PERK)
WHAT MAKES YOU SAY THAT?
CERTAINLY, THE CURRY THAT CIEL'S <KHAN-SAMA> MADE WAS THE REAL THING.
BUT THE CURRY ALONE WAS PERFECT!!

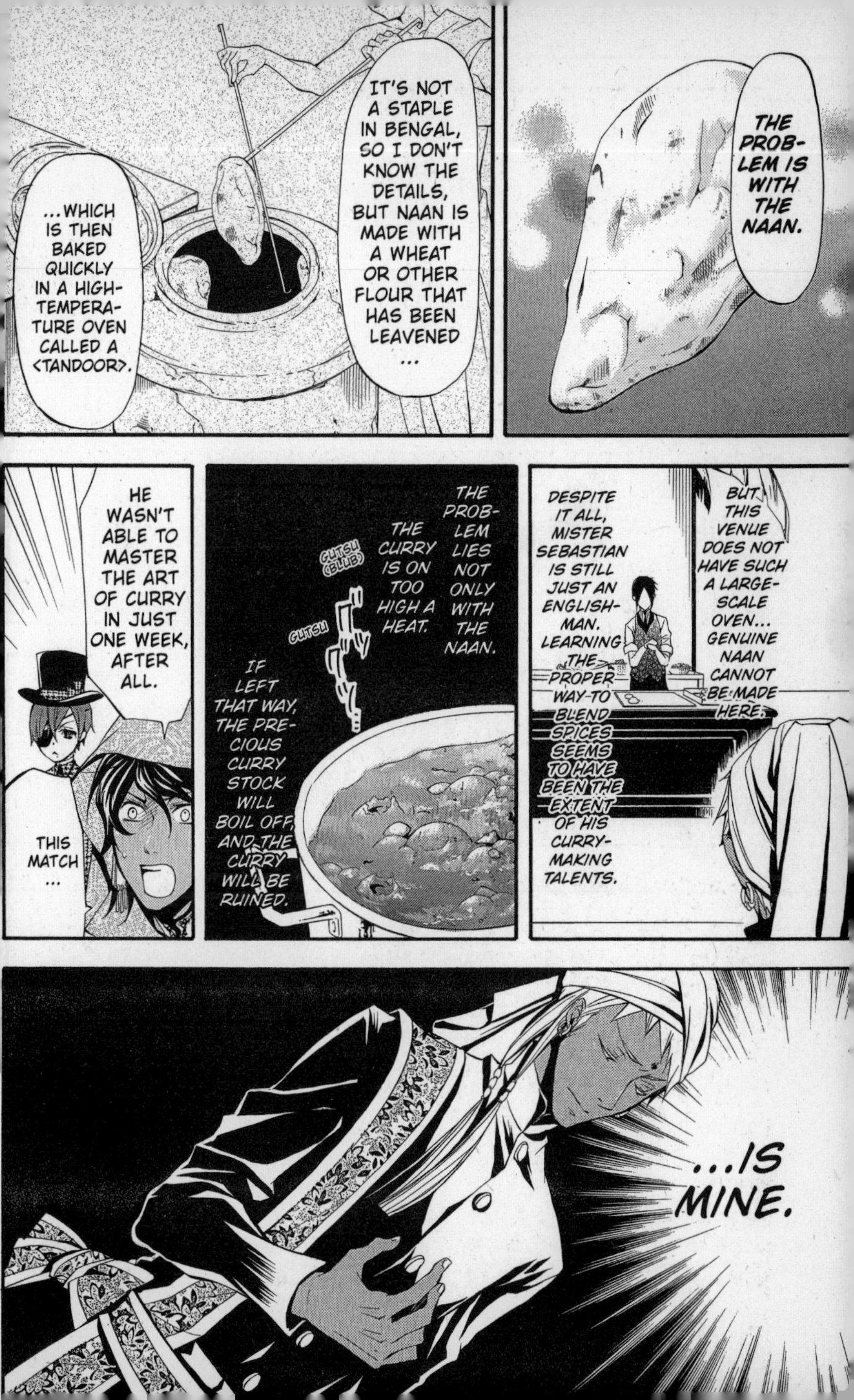
THE PROBLEM IS WITH THE NAAN.
IT'S NOT A STAPLE IN BENGAL, SO I DON'T KNOW THE DETAILS, BUT NAAN IS MADE WITH A WHEAT OR OTHER FLOUR THAT HAS BEEN LEAVENED ...
...WHICH IS THEN BAKED QUICKLY IN A HIGH-TEMPERATURE OVEN CALLED A <TANDOOR>.
BUT THIS VENUE DOES NOT HAVE SUCH A LARGE-SCALE OVEN... GENUINE NAAN CANNOT BE MADE HERE.
DESPITE IT ALL, MISTER SEBASTIAN IS STILL JUST AN ENGLISHMAN. LEARNING THE PROPER WAY TO BLEND SPICES SEEMS TO HAVE BEEN THE EXTENT OF HIS CURRY-MAKING TALENTS.
THE PROBLEM LIES NOT ONLY WITH THE NAAN.
THE CURRY IS ON TOO HIGH A HEAT.
GUTSU (BLUB)
GUTSU
IF LEFT THAT WAY, THE PRECIOUS CURRY STOCK WILL BOIL OFF, AND THE CURRY WILL BE RUINED.
HE WASN'T ABLE TO MASTER THE ART OF CURRY IN JUST ONE WEEK, AFTER ALL.
THIS MATCH ...
...IS MINE.

TIME IS UP!

WE WILL NOW BEGIN THE JUDGING!

Curry Feast

FIRST UP IS PERSIAN TABB'S BEEF CURRY.

コトッ
KOTO (CLINK)

PLEASE ENJOY.

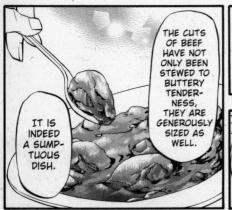

THE CUTS OF BEEF HAVE NOT ONLY BEEN STEWED TO BUTTERY TENDER-NESS, THEY ARE GENEROUSLY SIZED AS WELL.

IT IS INDEED A SUMP-TUOUS DISH.

ぱく
PAKU (CHOMP)

HOWEVER, THE STOCK TASTES FLAT AND HAS NO AROMA, WHICH TELLS ME...

...YOU HAVE USED CURRY POWDER.

THAT A CULINARY PROFESSIONAL WOULD EVEN CONSIDER USING SUCH A THING IS REPREHEN-SIBLE!

EH!? UH-OH...

HE USED IT TOO...

ガーン
GAAAN (SHOCK)

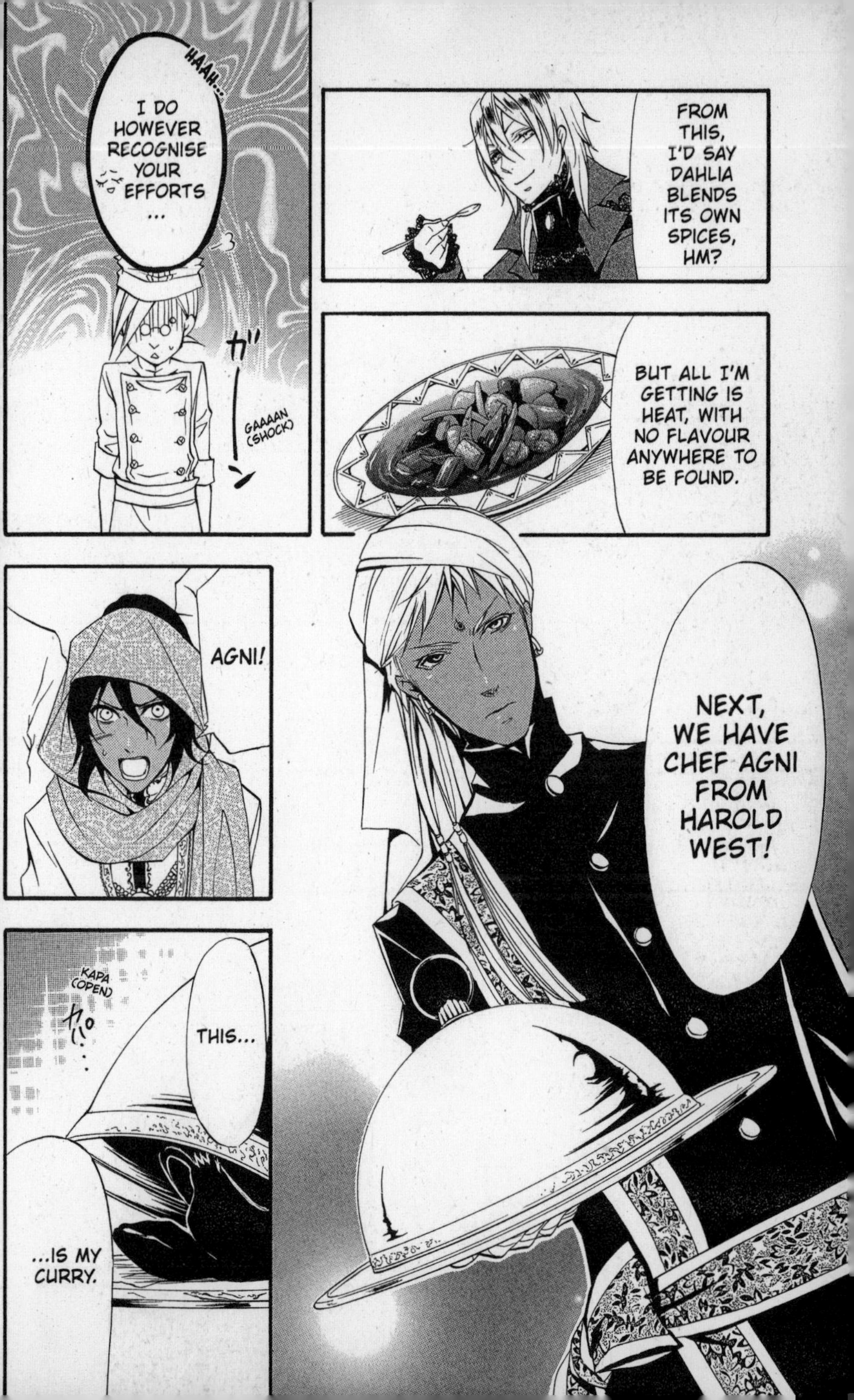
FROM THIS, I'D SAY DAHLIA BLENDS ITS OWN SPICES, HM?
BUT ALL I'M GETTING IS HEAT, WITH NO FLAVOUR ANYWHERE TO BE FOUND.
HAAAH...
I DO HOWEVER RECOGNISE YOUR EFFORTS ...
GAAAAN (SHOCK)
NEXT, WE HAVE CHEF AGNI FROM HAROLD WEST!
AGNI!
KAPA (OPEN)
THIS...
...IS MY CURRY.

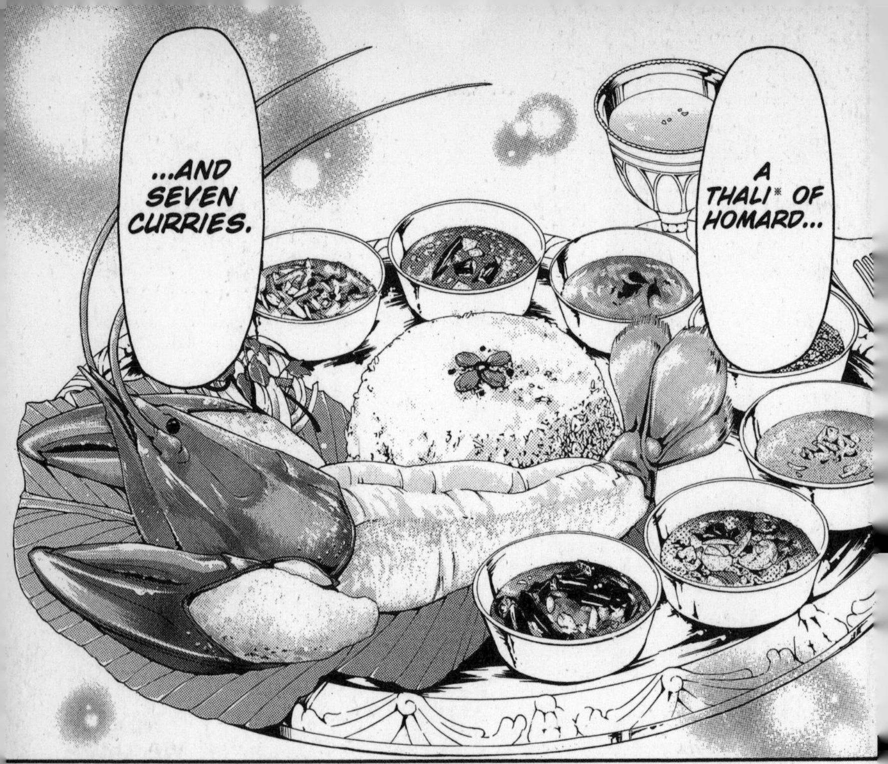
A THALI※ OF HOMARD...
...AND SEVEN CURRIES.

※AN EXTRAVAGANT FOOD PLATTER THAT HAS A VARIETY OF DISHES IN SMALLER BOWLS ARRANGED ON A LARGE PLATE.

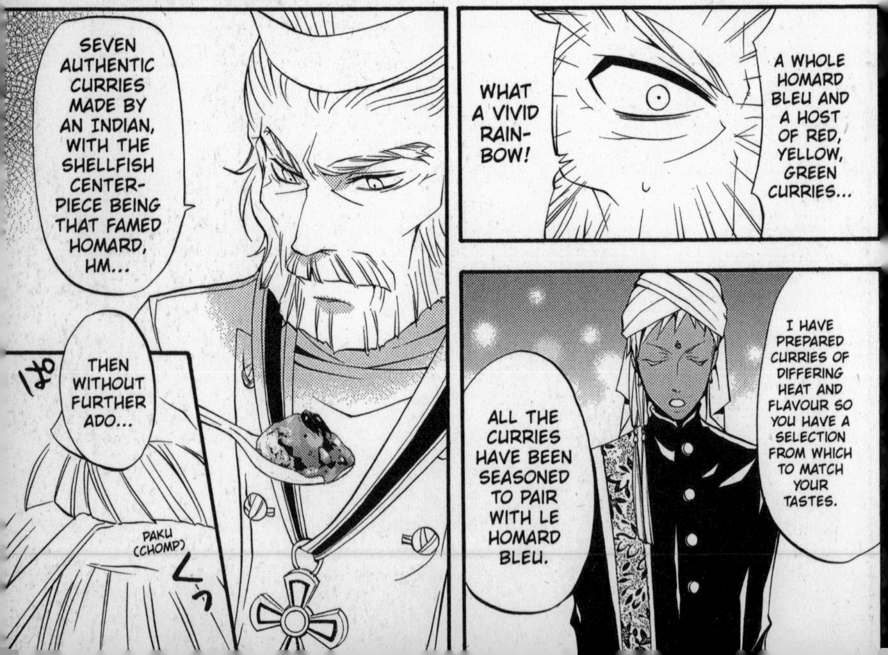
A WHOLE HOMARD BLEU AND A HOST OF RED, YELLOW, GREEN CURRIES...
WHAT A VIVID RAIN-BOW!
I HAVE PREPARED CURRIES OF DIFFERING HEAT AND FLAVOUR SO YOU HAVE A SELECTION FROM WHICH TO MATCH YOUR TASTES.
ALL THE CURRIES HAVE BEEN SEASONED TO PAIR WITH LE HOMARD BLEU.
SEVEN AUTHENTIC CURRIES MADE BY AN INDIAN, WITH THE SHELLFISH CENTER-PIECE BEING THAT FAMED HOMARD, HM...
THEN WITHOUT FURTHER ADO...
PAKU (CHOMP)

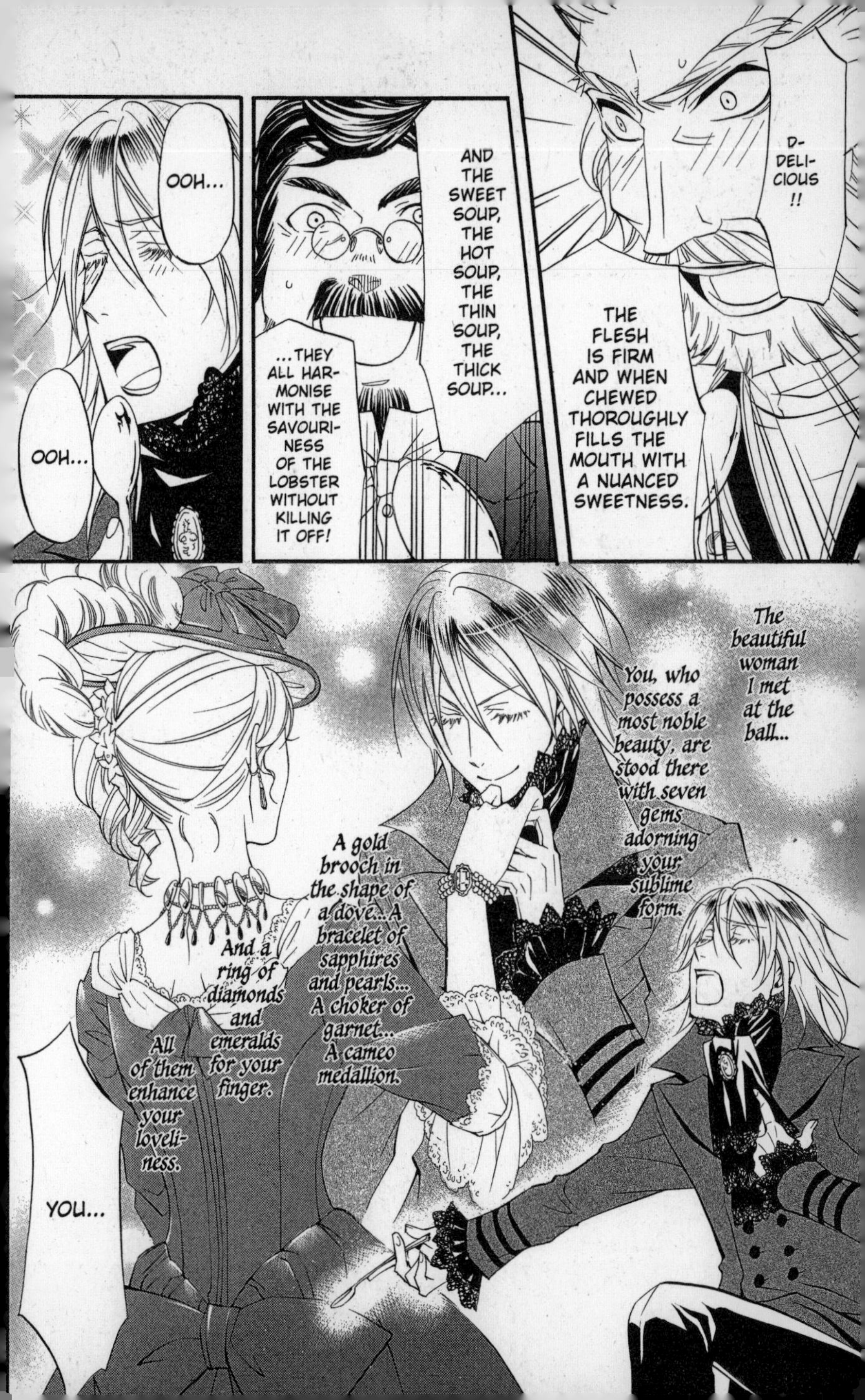
D-DELICIOUS!!
THE FLESH IS FIRM AND WHEN CHEWED THOROUGHLY FILLS THE MOUTH WITH A NUANCED SWEETNESS.
AND THE SWEET SOUP, THE HOT SOUP, THE THIN SOUP, THE THICK SOUP...
...THEY ALL HARMONISE WITH THE SAVOURINESS OF THE LOBSTER WITHOUT KILLING IT OFF!
OOH...
OOH...
The beautiful woman I met at the ball...
You, who possess a most noble beauty, are stood there with seven gems adorning your sublime form.
A gold brooch in the shape of a dove... A bracelet of sapphires and pearls... A choker of garnet... A cameo medallion.
And a ring of diamonds and emeralds for your finger.
All of them enhance your loveliness.
YOU...

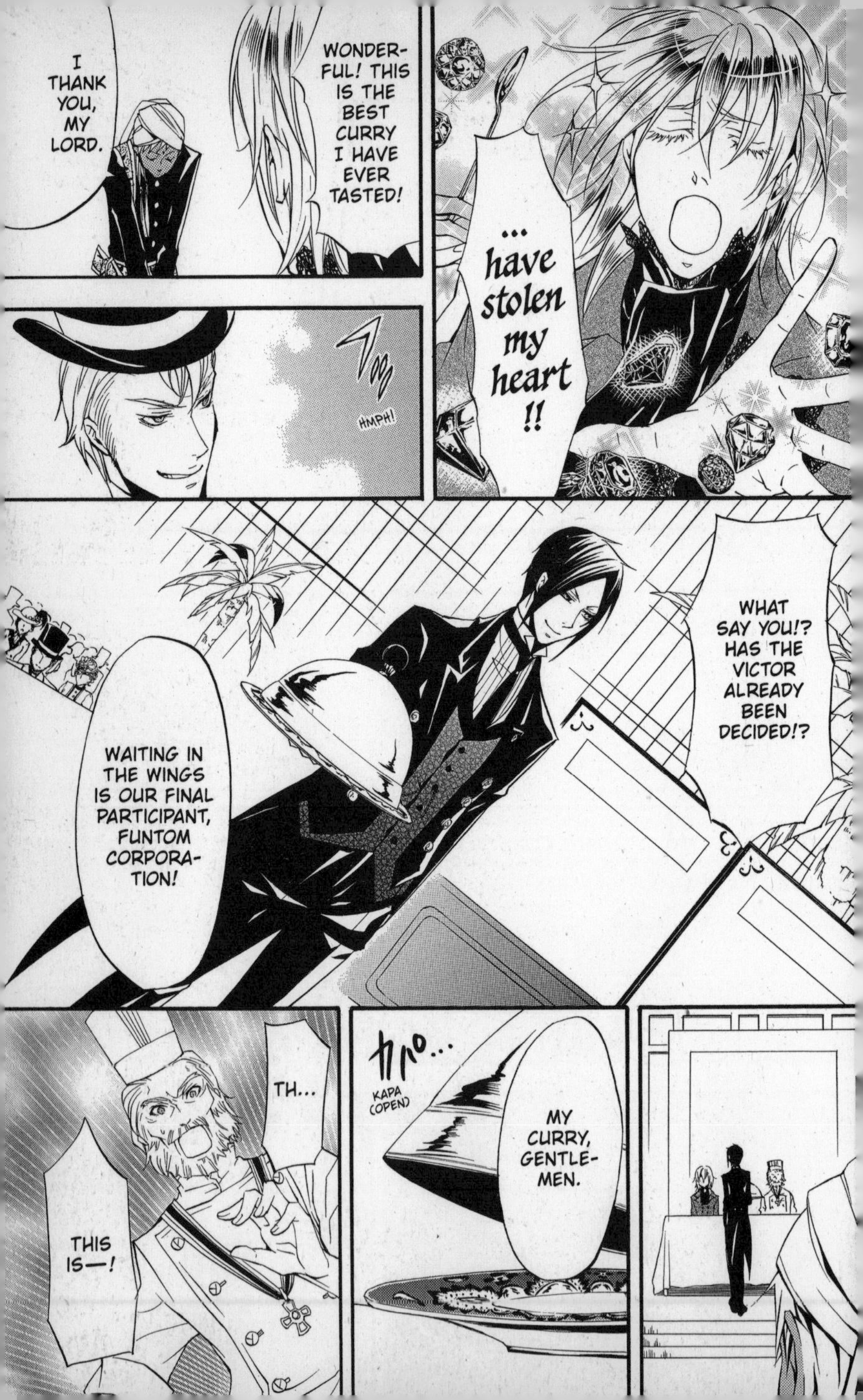
... have stolen my heart!!
WONDERFUL! THIS IS THE BEST CURRY I HAVE EVER TASTED!
I THANK YOU, MY LORD.
HMPH!
WHAT SAY YOU!? HAS THE VICTOR ALREADY BEEN DECIDED!?
WAITING IN THE WINGS IS OUR FINAL PARTICIPANT, FUNTOM CORPORATION!
KAPA (OPEN)
MY CURRY, GENTLEMEN.
TH...
THIS IS—!

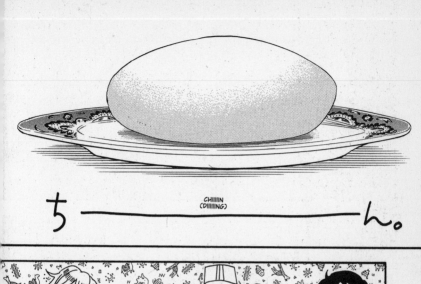

CHIIIIIN
(DIIIIING)

ち ——————————— ん。

POKAAAAN
(STUNNED)

ヒョイ つ
HYOI
(PLUCK)

AH!

YOU
THERE!
WHAT
IS THIS
WHITE
THING
!?

カッ
KA
(FLING)

ARE YOU
TRYING TO
MAKE A
MOCKERY
OF US!?

DOSU
(WHAP)

どすっ

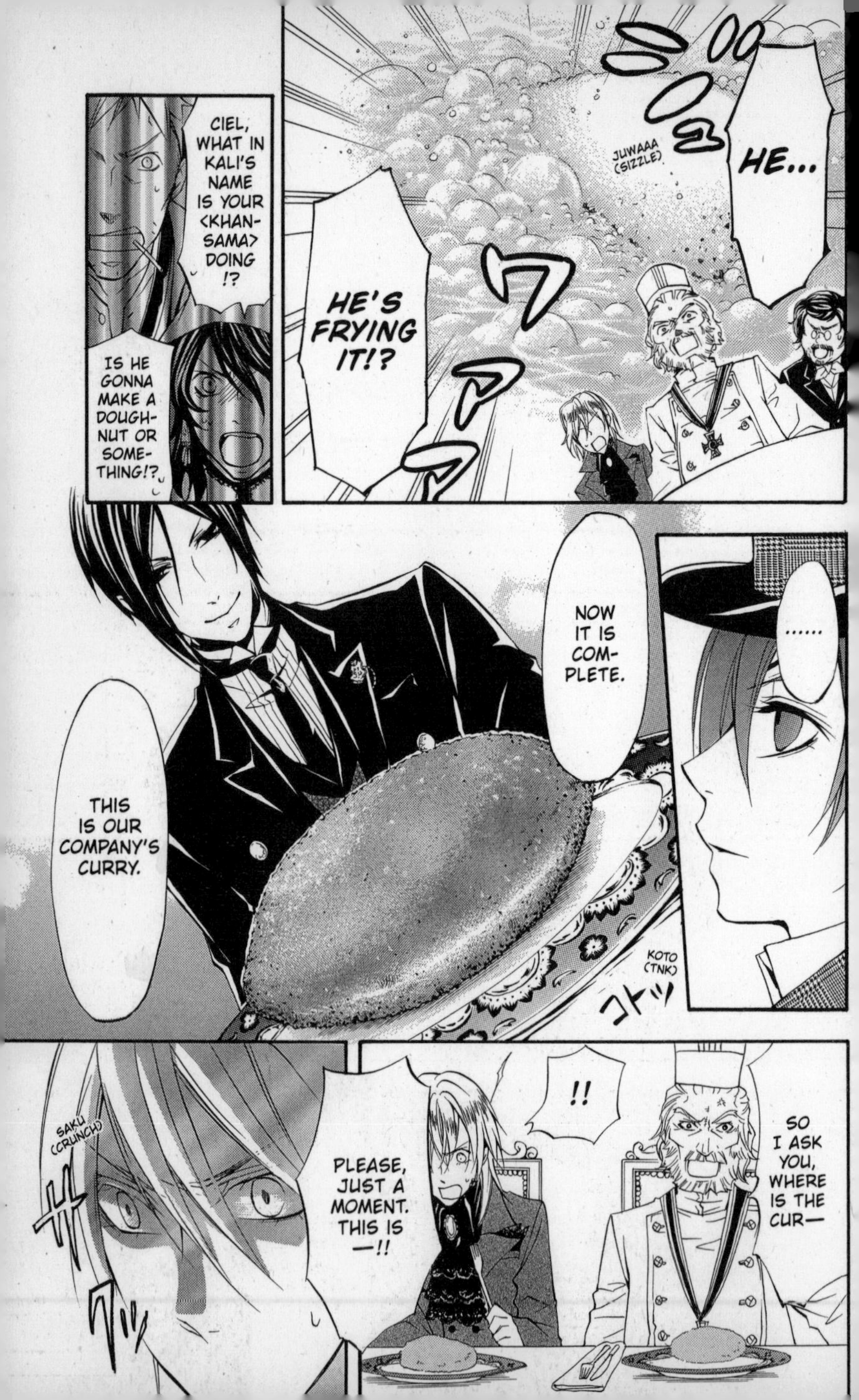
HE...
JUWAAA (SIZZLE)
HE'S FRYING IT!?
CIEL, WHAT IN KALI'S NAME IS YOUR <KHAN-SAMA> DOING !?
IS HE GONNA MAKE A DOUGHNUT OR SOMETHING!?
......
KOTO (TNK)
NOW IT IS COMPLETE.
THIS IS OUR COMPANY'S CURRY.
SO I ASK YOU, WHERE IS THE CUR—
!!
PLEASE, JUST A MOMENT. THIS IS —!!
SAKU (CRUNCH)

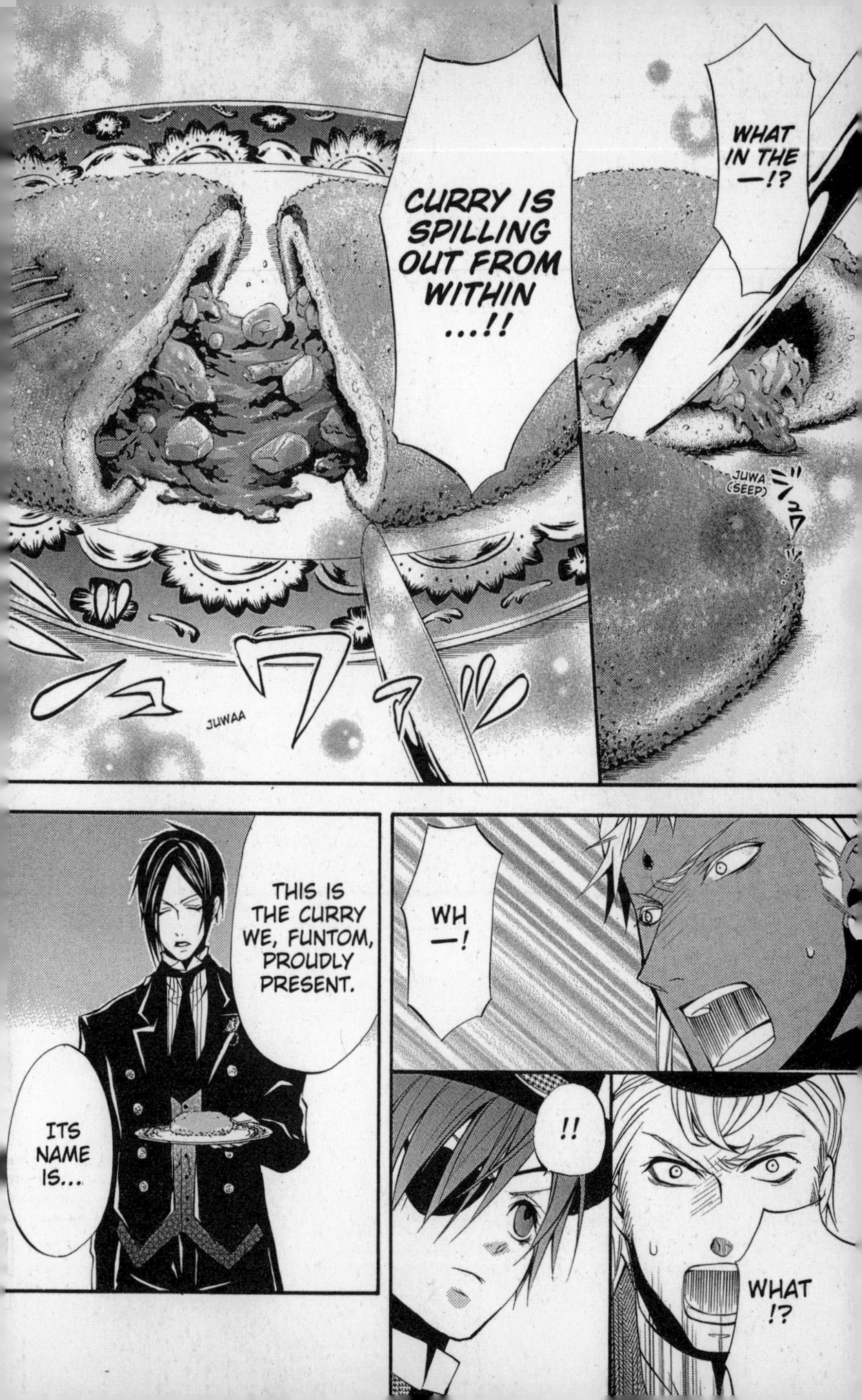
WHAT IN THE —!?
JUWA (SEEP)
CURRY IS SPILLING OUT FROM WITHIN ...!!
JUWAA
WH —!
WHAT !?
!!
THIS IS THE CURRY WE, FUNTOM, PROUDLY PRESENT.
ITS NAME IS...

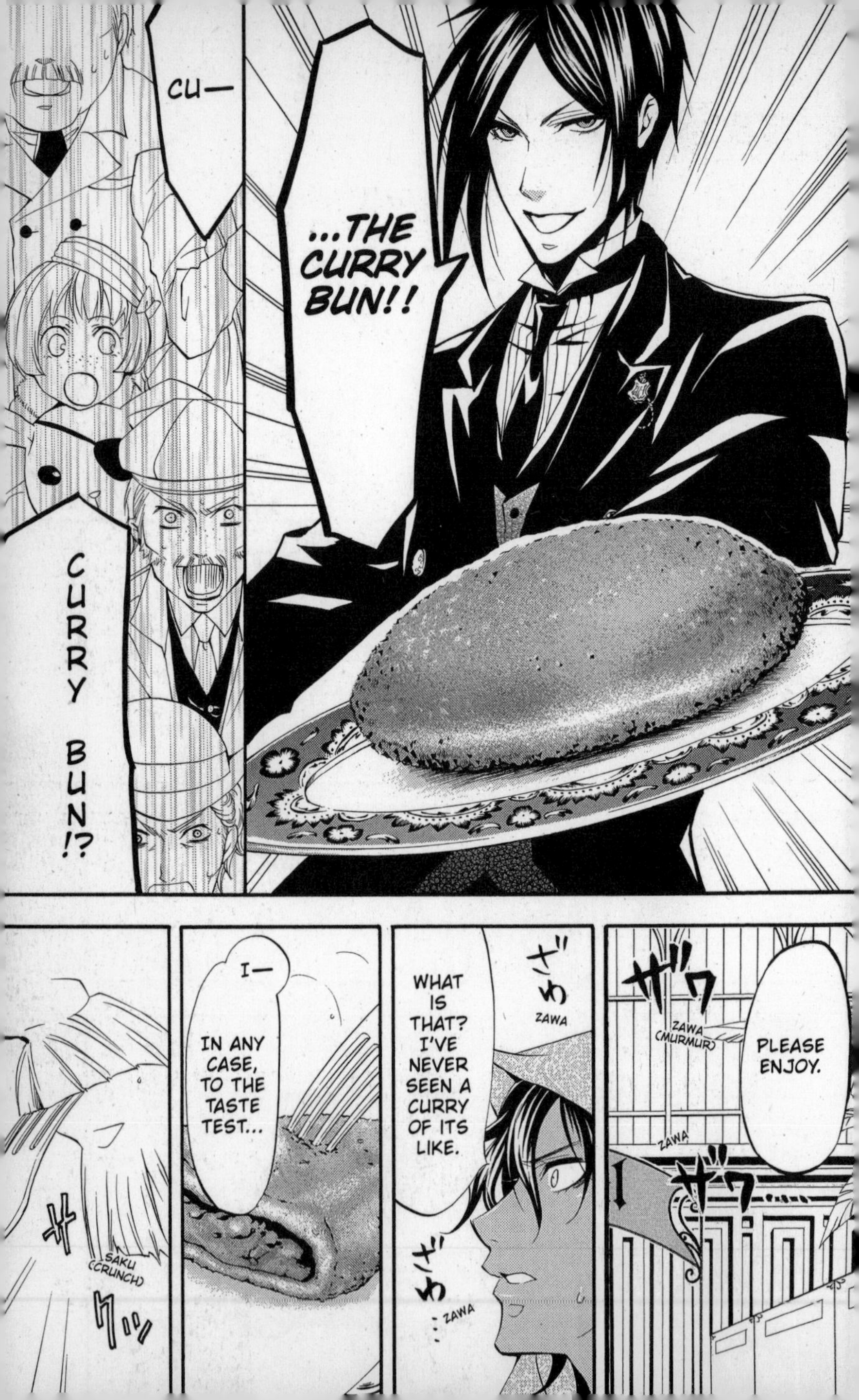
...THE CURRY BUN!!
CU—
CURRY BUN!?
PLEASE ENJOY.
ZAWA (MURMUR)
ZAWA
WHAT IS THAT? I'VE NEVER SEEN A CURRY OF ITS LIKE.
ZAWA
ZAWA
I—
IN ANY CASE, TO THE TASTE TEST...
SAKU (CRUNCH)

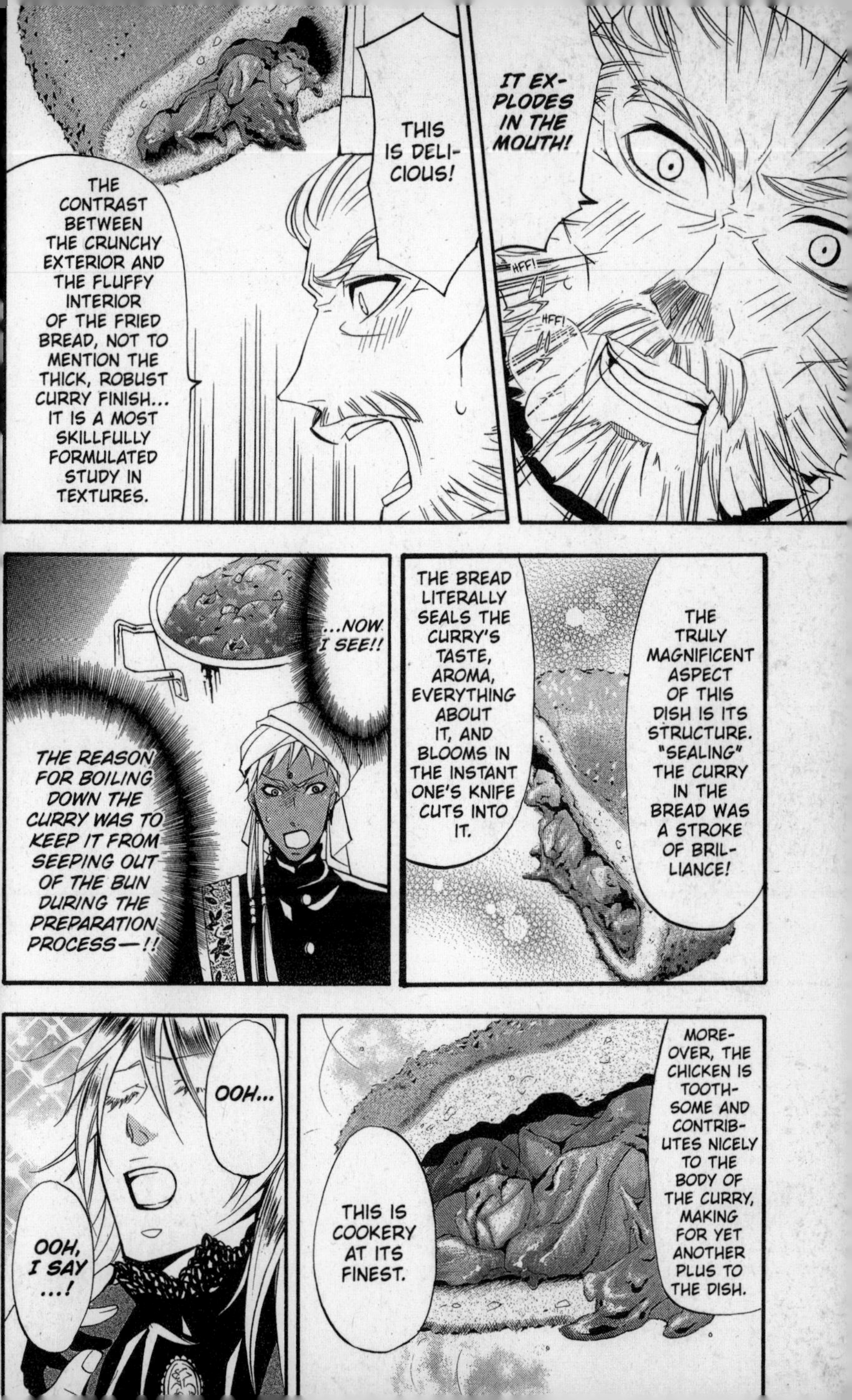
IT EXPLODES IN THE MOUTH!
HFF!
HFF!
THIS IS DELICIOUS!
THE CONTRAST BETWEEN THE CRUNCHY EXTERIOR AND THE FLUFFY INTERIOR OF THE FRIED BREAD, NOT TO MENTION THE THICK, ROBUST CURRY FINISH... IT IS A MOST SKILLFULLY FORMULATED STUDY IN TEXTURES.
THE TRULY MAGNIFICENT ASPECT OF THIS DISH IS ITS STRUCTURE. "SEALING" THE CURRY IN THE BREAD WAS A STROKE OF BRILLIANCE!
THE BREAD LITERALLY SEALS THE CURRY'S TASTE, AROMA, EVERYTHING ABOUT IT, AND BLOOMS IN THE INSTANT ONE'S KNIFE CUTS INTO IT.
...NOW I SEE!!
THE REASON FOR BOILING DOWN THE CURRY WAS TO KEEP IT FROM SEEPING OUT OF THE BUN DURING THE PREPARATION PROCESS—!!
MOREOVER, THE CHICKEN IS TOOTHSOME AND CONTRIBUTES NICELY TO THE BODY OF THE CURRY, MAKING FOR YET ANOTHER PLUS TO THE DISH.
THIS IS COOKERY AT ITS FINEST.
OOH...
OOH, I SAY ...!

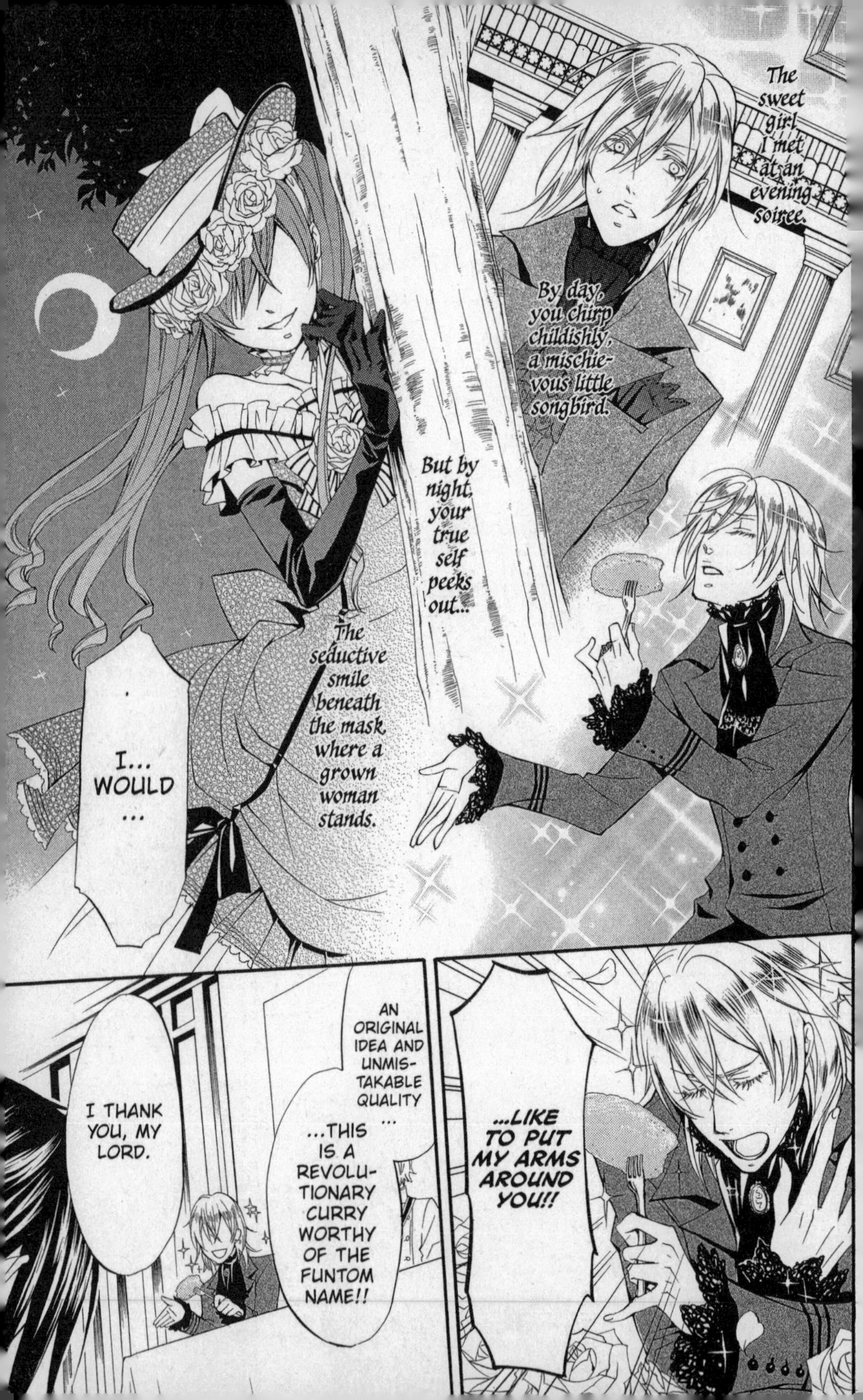
The sweet girl I met at an evening soiree.
By day, you chirp childishly, a mischievous little songbird.
But by night, your true self peeks out...
The seductive smile beneath the mask where a grown woman stands.
I... WOULD ...
...LIKE TO PUT MY ARMS AROUND YOU!!
AN ORIGINAL IDEA AND UNMISTAKABLE QUALITY ...
...THIS IS A REVOLUTIONARY CURRY WORTHY OF THE FUNTOM NAME!!
I THANK YOU, MY LORD.

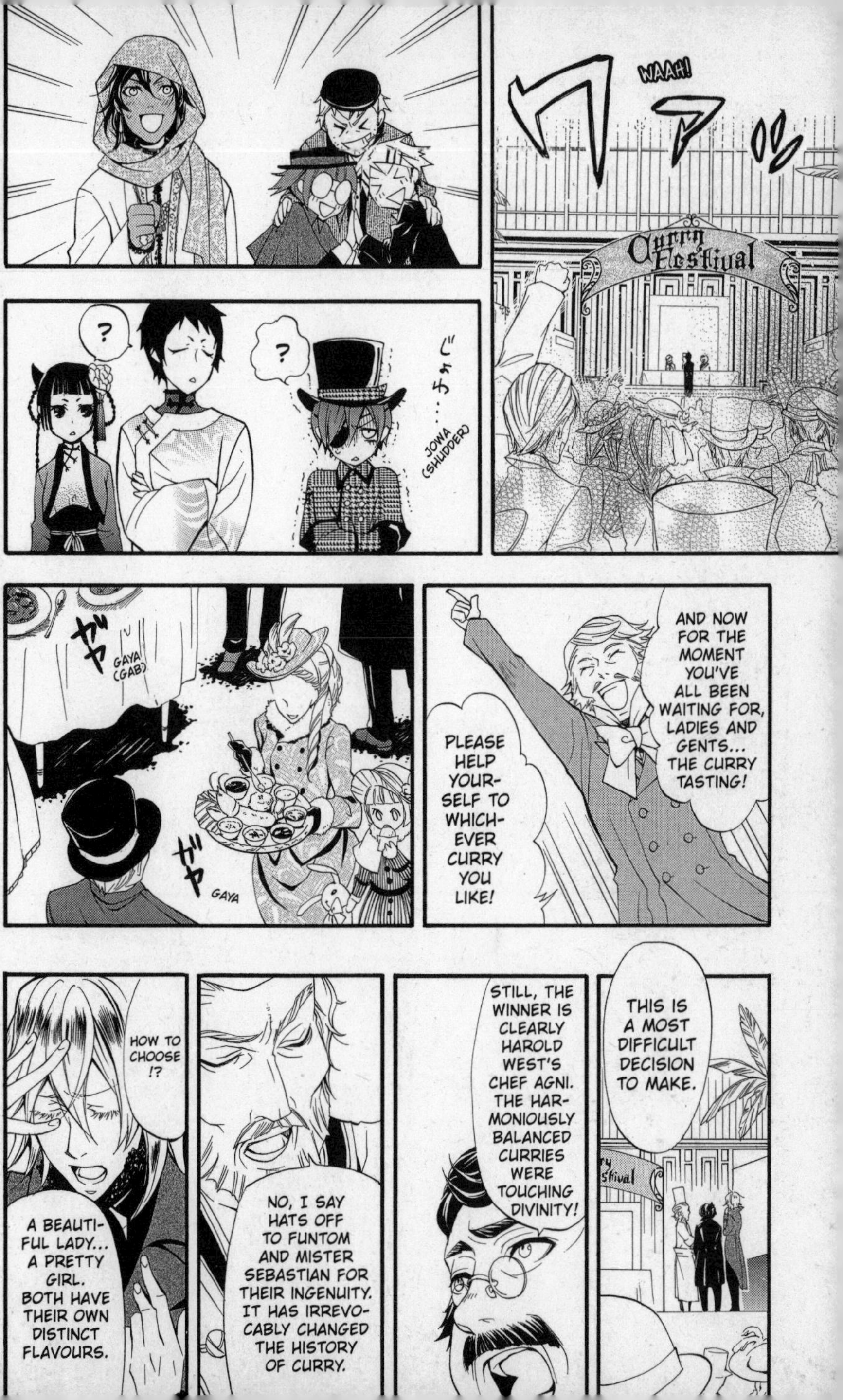
WAAH!
Curry Festival
?
?
JOWA (SHUDDER)
AND NOW FOR THE MOMENT YOU'VE ALL BEEN WAITING FOR, LADIES AND GENTS... THE CURRY TASTING!
PLEASE HELP YOURSELF TO WHICHEVER CURRY YOU LIKE!
ガヤ
GAYA (GAB)
ガヤ
GAYA
THIS IS A MOST DIFFICULT DECISION TO MAKE.
STILL, THE WINNER IS CLEARLY HAROLD WEST'S CHEF AGNI. THE HARMONIOUSLY BALANCED CURRIES WERE TOUCHING DIVINITY!
NO, I SAY HATS OFF TO FUNTOM AND MISTER SEBASTIAN FOR THEIR INGENUITY. IT HAS IRREVOCABLY CHANGED THE HISTORY OF CURRY.
HOW TO CHOOSE!?
A BEAUTIFUL LADY... A PRETTY GIRL. BOTH HAVE THEIR OWN DISTINCT FLAVOURS.

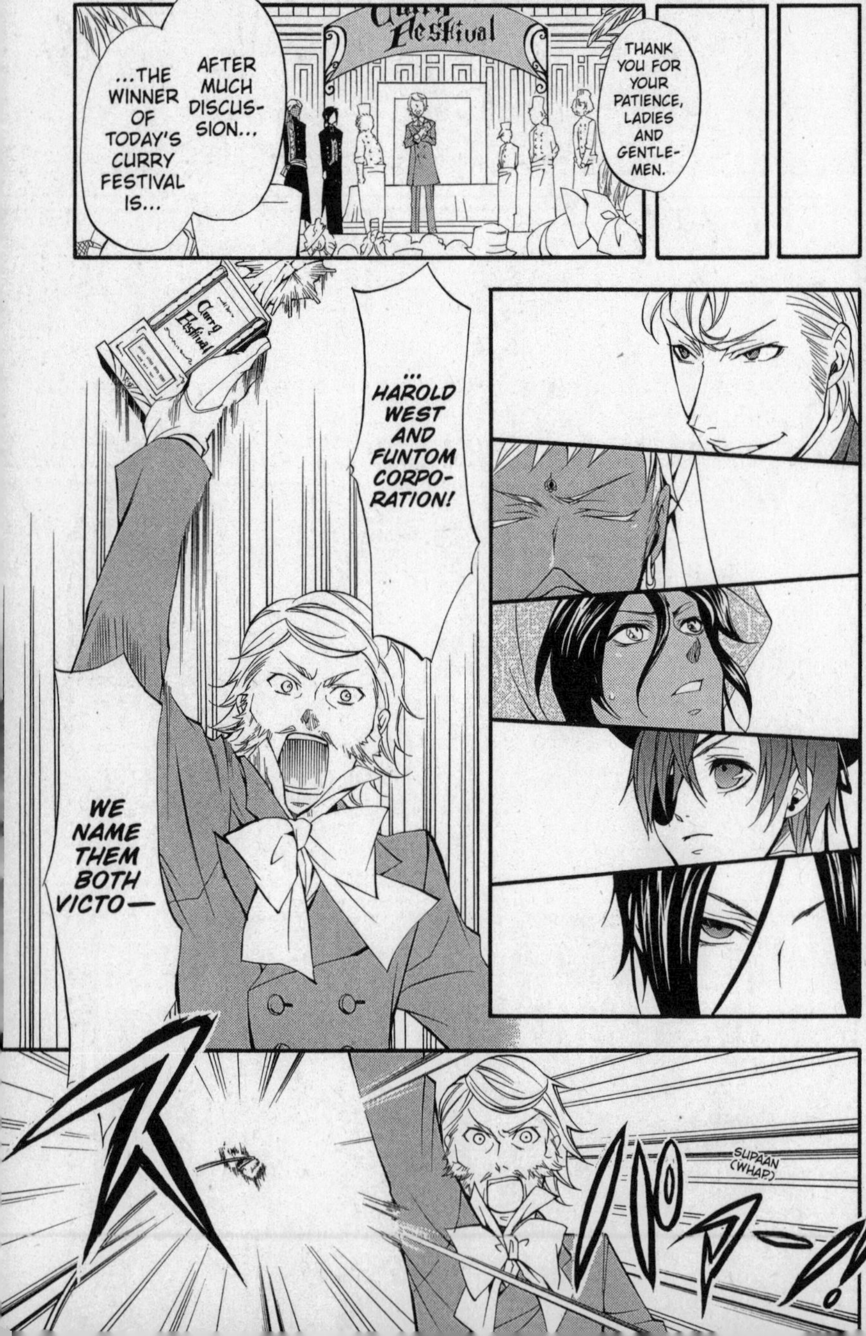
THANK YOU FOR YOUR PATIENCE, LADIES AND GENTLE-MEN.
AFTER MUCH DISCUS-SION...
...THE WINNER OF TODAY'S CURRY FESTIVAL IS...
...HAROLD WEST AND FUNTOM CORPO-RATION!
WE NAME THEM BOTH VICTO—
SUPAAN (WHAP)

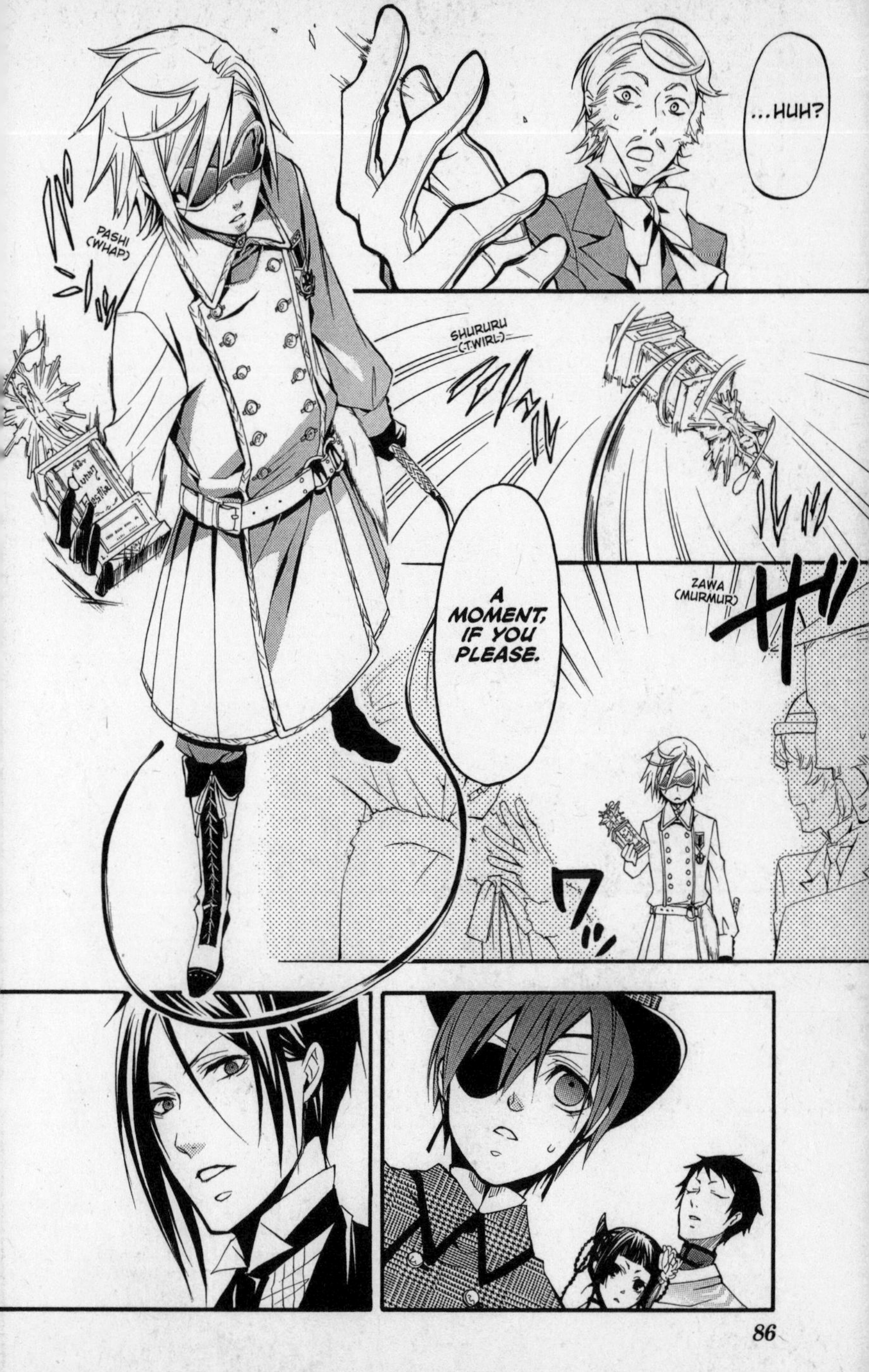
...HUH?
SHURURU (TWIRL)
ZAWA (MURMUR)
A MOMENT, IF YOU PLEASE.
ワッ
PASHI (WHAP)

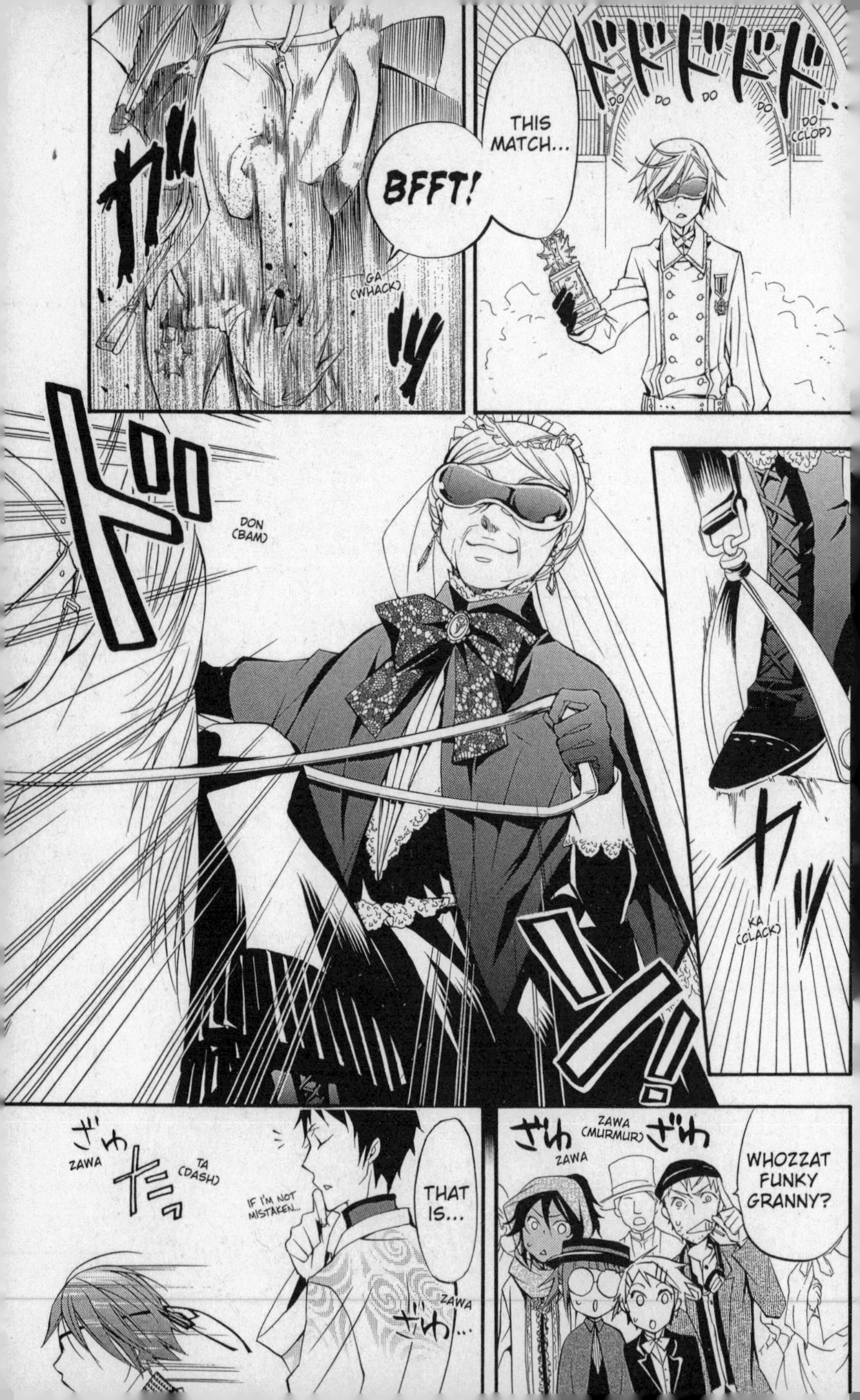
DO DO DO DO DO (CLOP)
THIS MATCH...
BFFT!
GA (WHACK)
KA (CLACK)
DON (BAM)
ZAWA (MURMUR)
ZAWA
WHOZZAT FUNKY GRANNY?
THAT IS...
IF I'M NOT MISTAKEN...
ZAWA
TA (DASH)
ZAWA

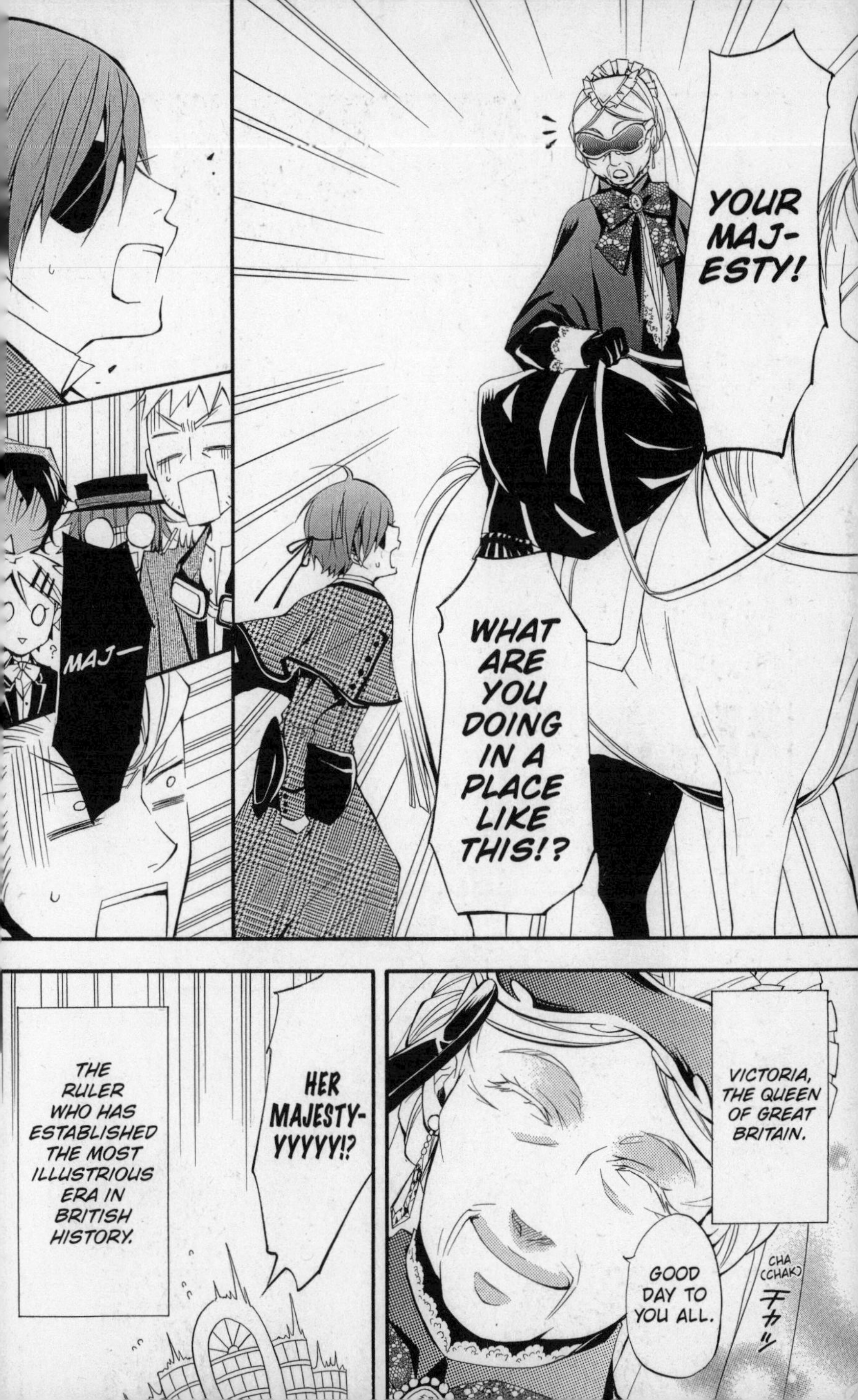

YOUR MAJ-ESTY!
WHAT ARE YOU DOING IN A PLACE LIKE THIS!?
MAJ—
VICTORIA, THE QUEEN OF GREAT BRITAIN.
GOOD DAY TO YOU ALL.
CHA (CHAK)
チャッ
HER MAJESTY-YYYYY!?
THE RULER WHO HAS ESTABLISHED THE MOST ILLUSTRIOUS ERA IN BRITISH HISTORY.

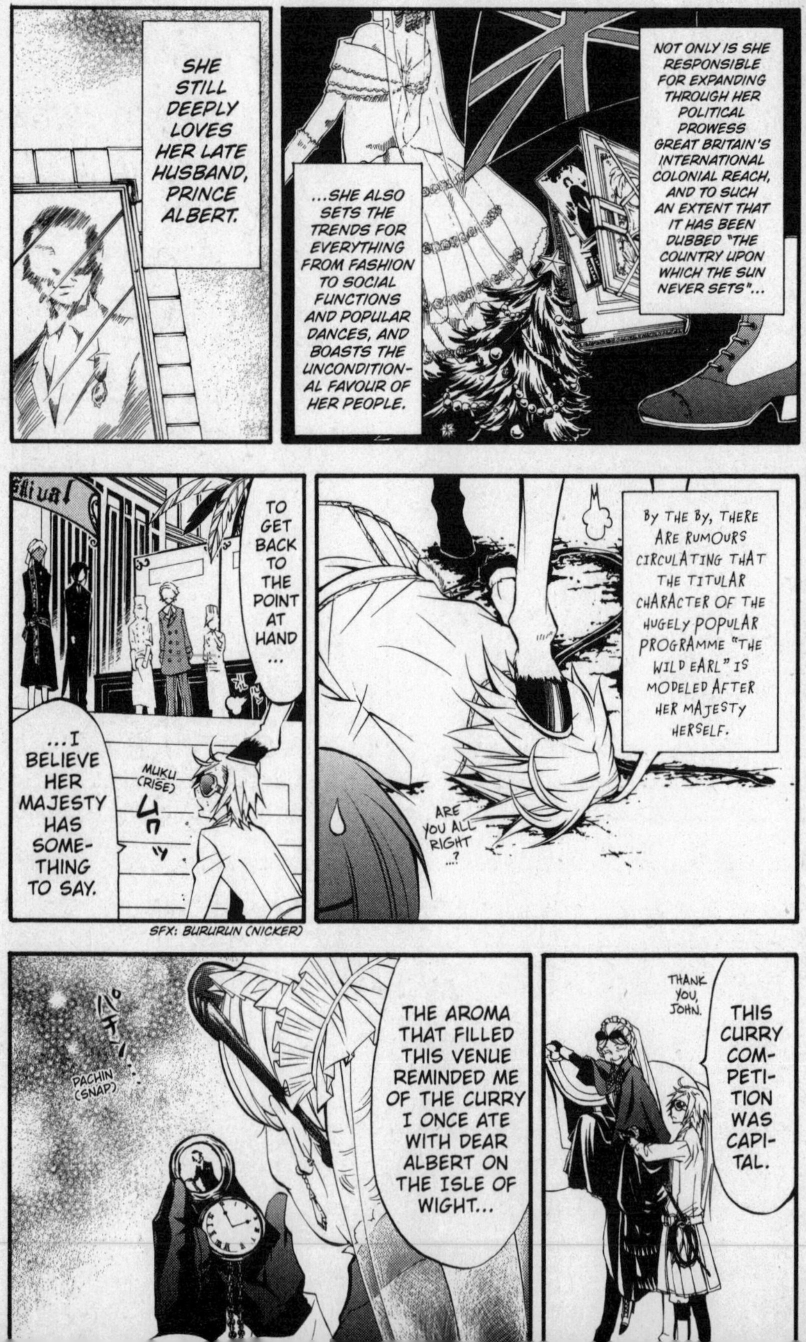
NOT ONLY IS SHE RESPONSIBLE FOR EXPANDING THROUGH HER POLITICAL PROWESS GREAT BRITAIN'S INTERNATIONAL COLONIAL REACH, AND TO SUCH AN EXTENT THAT IT HAS BEEN DUBBED "THE COUNTRY UPON WHICH THE SUN NEVER SETS"...
...SHE ALSO SETS THE TRENDS FOR EVERYTHING FROM FASHION TO SOCIAL FUNCTIONS AND POPULAR DANCES, AND BOASTS THE UNCONDITIONAL FAVOUR OF HER PEOPLE.
SHE STILL DEEPLY LOVES HER LATE HUSBAND, PRINCE ALBERT.
By THE By, THERE ARE RUMOURS CIRCULATING THAT THE TITULAR CHARACTER OF THE HUGELY POPULAR PROGRAMME "THE WILD EARL" IS MODELED AFTER HER MAJESTY HERSELF.
ARE YOU ALL RIGHT...?
TO GET BACK TO THE POINT AT HAND...
...I BELIEVE HER MAJESTY HAS SOMETHING TO SAY.
MUKU (RISE)
SFX: BURURUN (NICKER)
THANK YOU, JOHN.
THIS CURRY COMPETITION WAS CAPITAL.
THE AROMA THAT FILLED THIS VENUE REMINDED ME OF THE CURRY I ONCE ATE WITH DEAR ALBERT ON THE ISLE OF WIGHT...
PACHIN (SNAP)

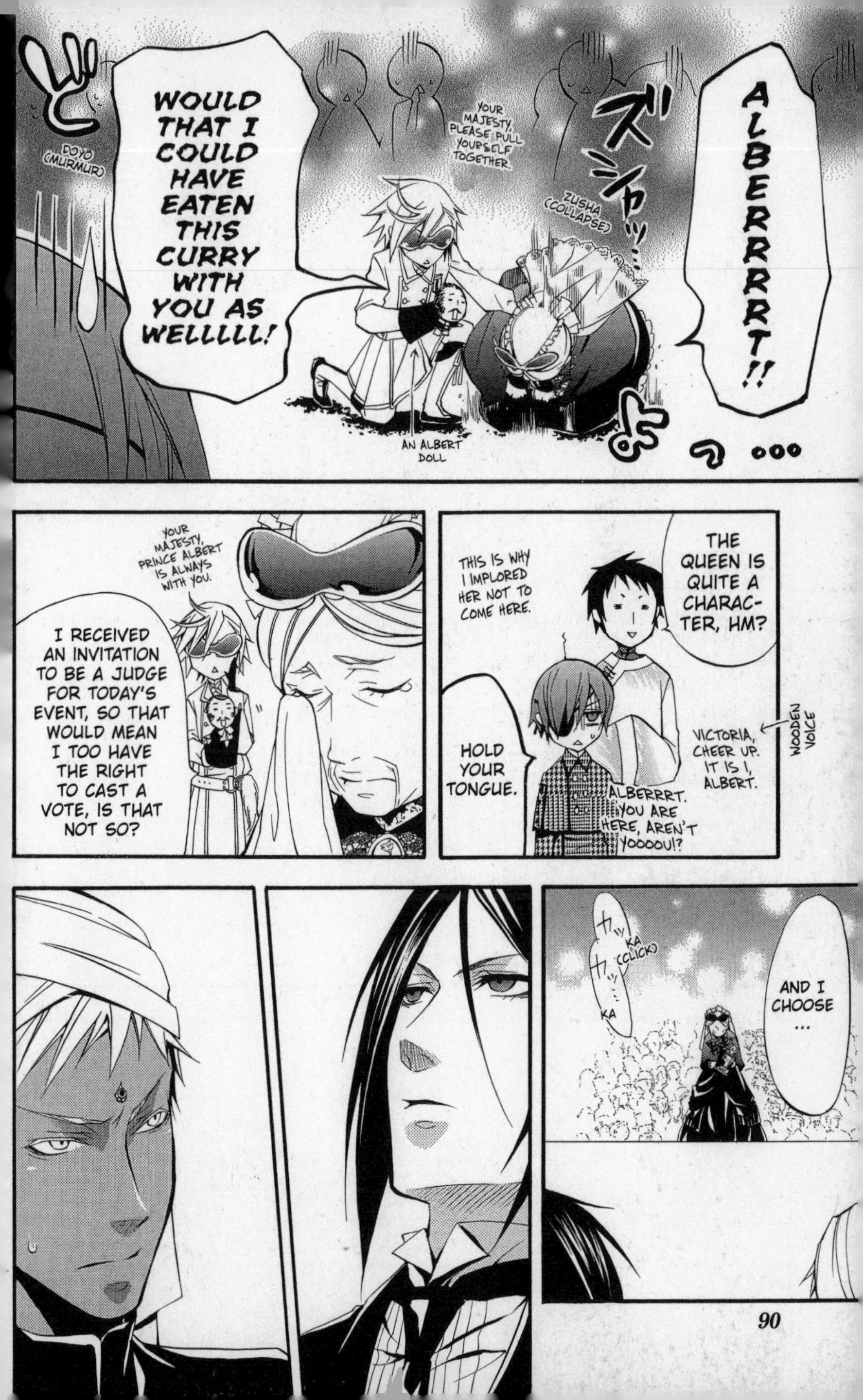
ALBERRRRT!!
ZUSHA (COLLAPSE)
YOUR MAJESTY, PLEASE PULL YOURSELF TOGETHER.
WOULD THAT I COULD HAVE EATEN THIS CURRY WITH YOU AS WELLLLL!
DOYO (MURMUR)
AN ALBERT DOLL
THE QUEEN IS QUITE A CHARACTER, HM?
THIS IS WHY I IMPLORED HER NOT TO COME HERE.
WOODEN VOICE
VICTORIA, CHEER UP. IT IS I, ALBERT.
ALBERRRT. YOU ARE HERE, AREN'T YOOOOU!?
HOLD YOUR TONGUE.
YOUR MAJESTY, PRINCE ALBERT IS ALWAYS WITH YOU.
I RECEIVED AN INVITATION TO BE A JUDGE FOR TODAY'S EVENT, SO THAT WOULD MEAN I TOO HAVE THE RIGHT TO CAST A VOTE, IS THAT NOT SO?
AND I CHOOSE ...
KA (CLICK)
KA

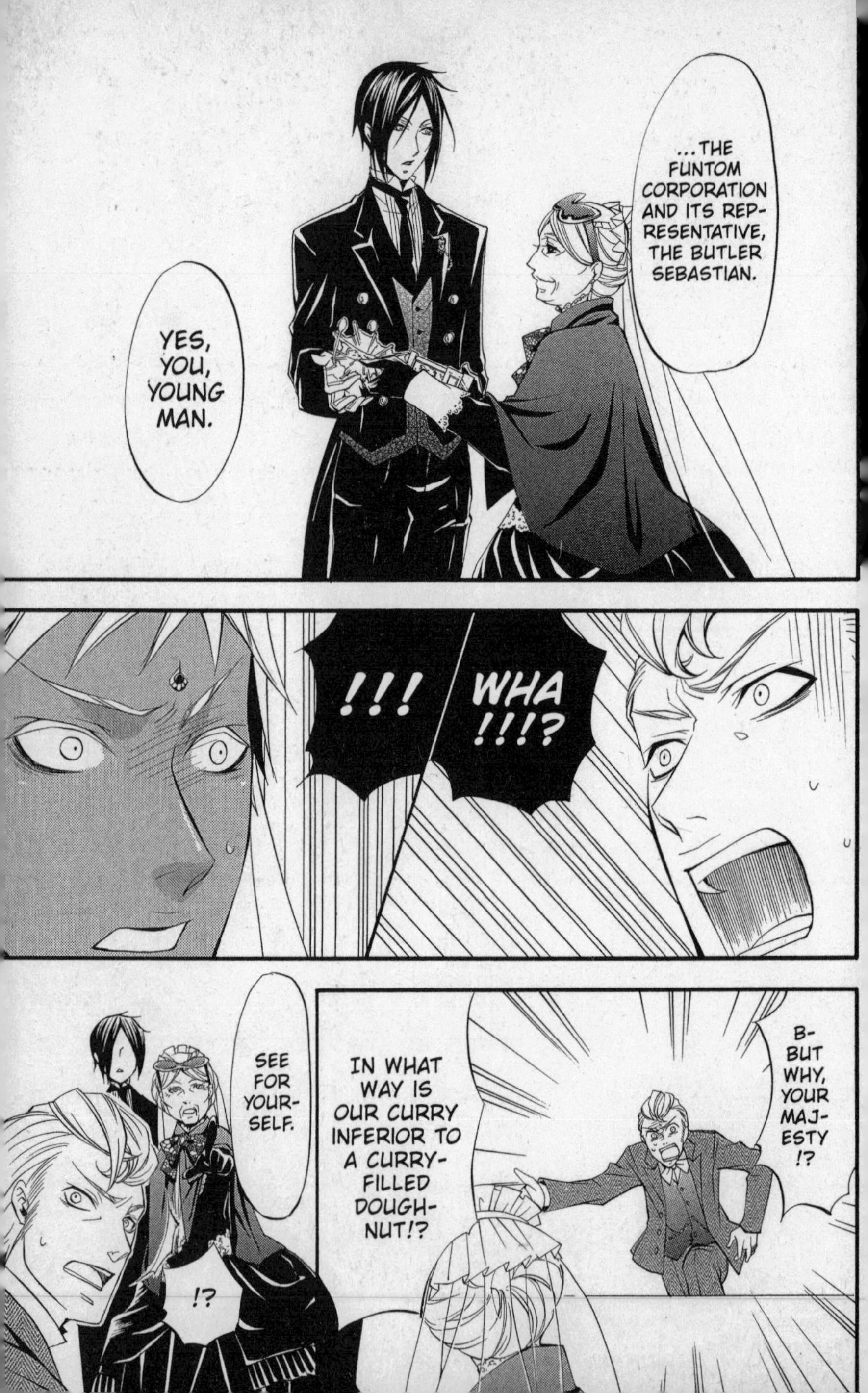
...THE FUNTOM CORPORATION AND ITS REPRESENTATIVE, THE BUTLER SEBASTIAN.
YES, YOU, YOUNG MAN.
WHA !!!?
!!!
B-BUT WHY, YOUR MAJESTY!?
IN WHAT WAY IS OUR CURRY INFERIOR TO A CURRY-FILLED DOUGHNUT!?
SEE FOR YOURSELF.
!?

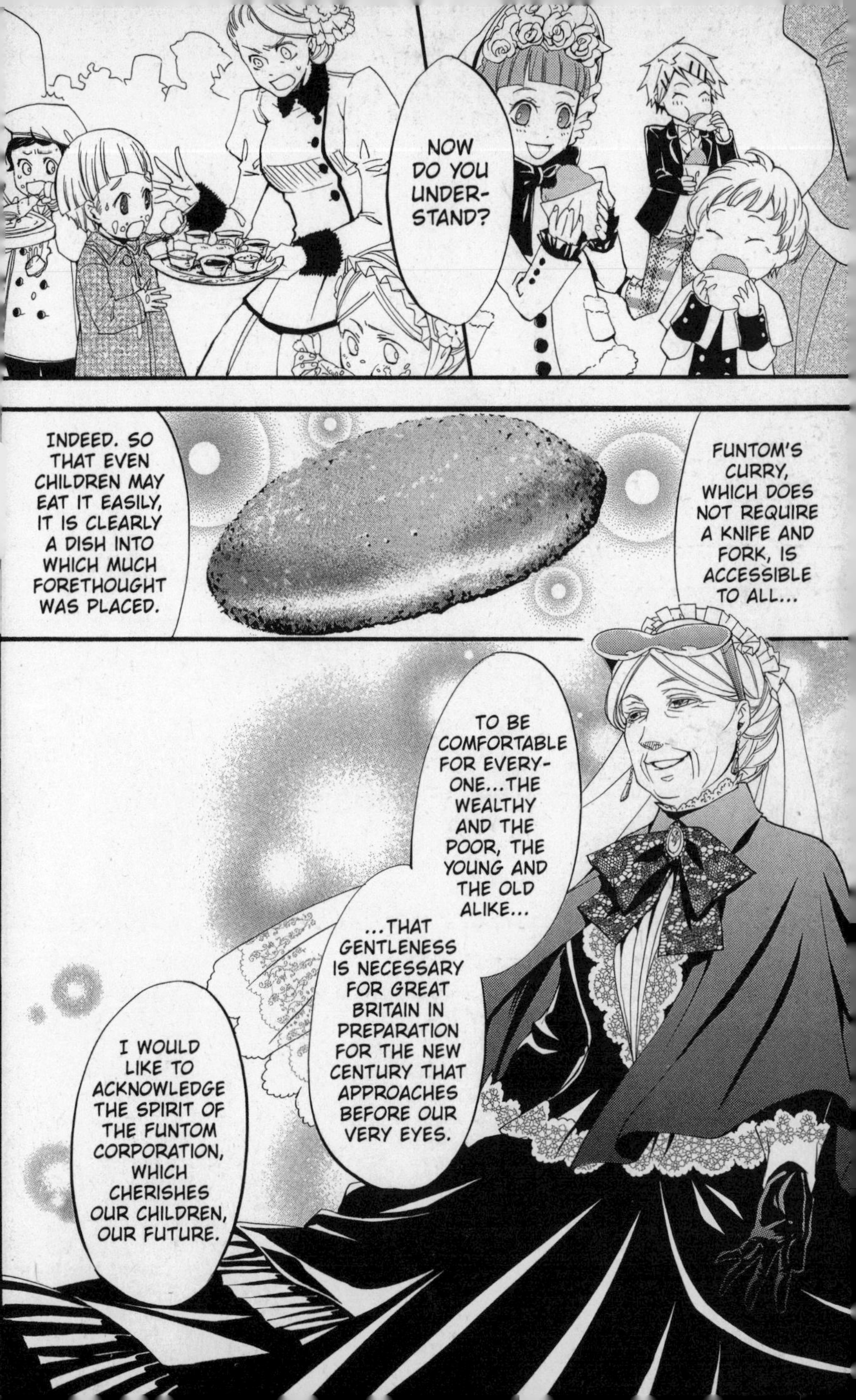
NOW DO YOU UNDERSTAND?
FUNTOM'S CURRY, WHICH DOES NOT REQUIRE A KNIFE AND FORK, IS ACCESSIBLE TO ALL...
INDEED. SO THAT EVEN CHILDREN MAY EAT IT EASILY, IT IS CLEARLY A DISH INTO WHICH MUCH FORETHOUGHT WAS PLACED.
TO BE COMFORTABLE FOR EVERYONE...THE WEALTHY AND THE POOR, THE YOUNG AND THE OLD ALIKE...
...THAT GENTLENESS IS NECESSARY FOR GREAT BRITAIN IN PREPARATION FOR THE NEW CENTURY THAT APPROACHES BEFORE OUR VERY EYES.
I WOULD LIKE TO ACKNOWLEDGE THE SPIRIT OF THE FUNTOM CORPORATION, WHICH CHERISHES OUR CHILDREN, OUR FUTURE.

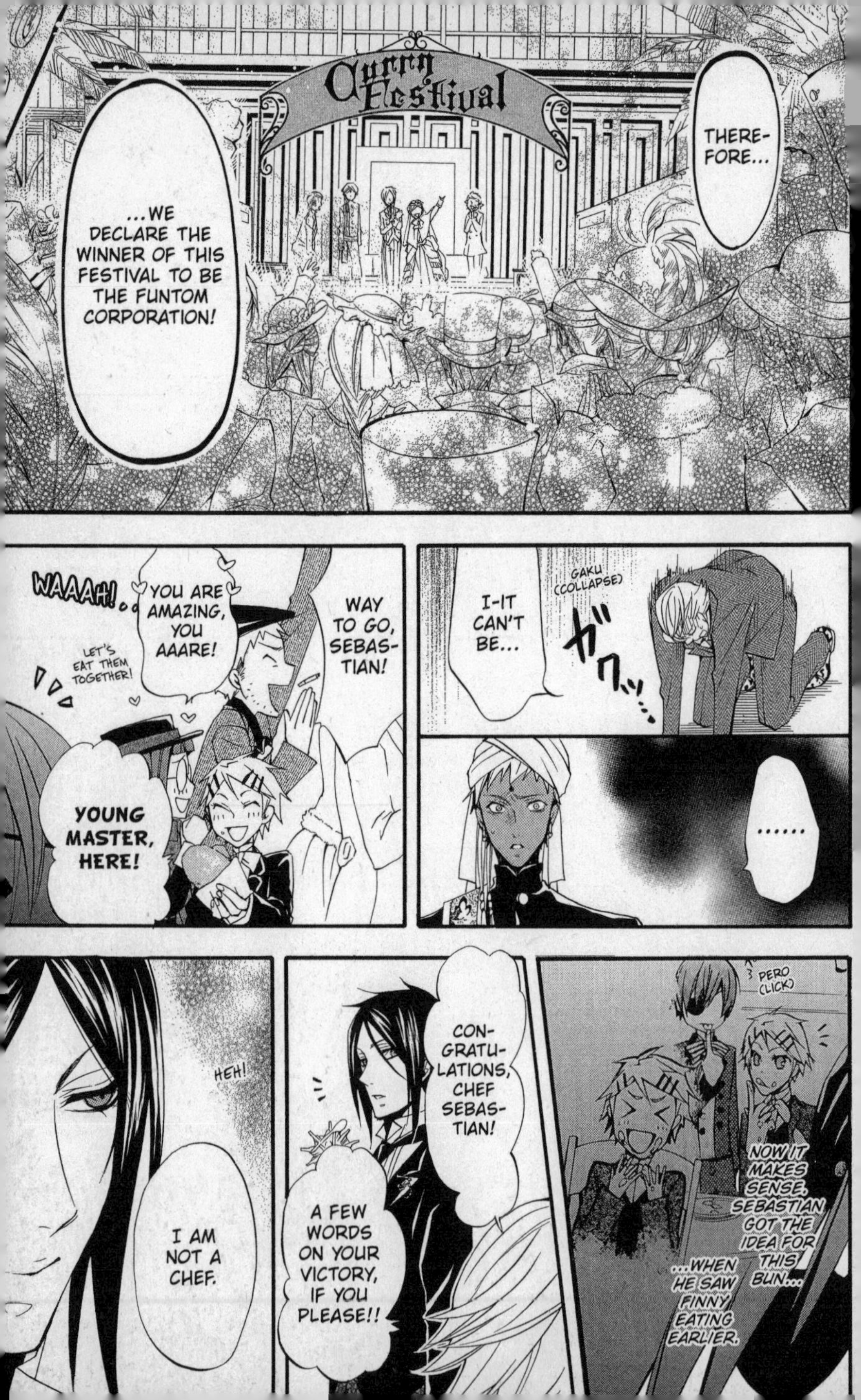
Curry Festival
THERE-FORE...
...WE DECLARE THE WINNER OF THIS FESTIVAL TO BE THE FUNTOM CORPORATION!
GAKU (COLLAPSE)
I-IT CAN'T BE...
......
WAY TO GO, SEBASTIAN!
YOU ARE AMAZING, YOU AAARE!
WAAAH!
LET'S EAT THEM TOGETHER!
YOUNG MASTER, HERE!
PERO (LICK)
NOW IT MAKES SENSE. SEBASTIAN GOT THE IDEA FOR THIS BUN...
...WHEN HE SAW FINNY EATING EARLIER.
CONGRATULATIONS, CHEF SEBASTIAN!
A FEW WORDS ON YOUR VICTORY, IF YOU PLEASE!!
HEH!
I AM NOT A CHEF.

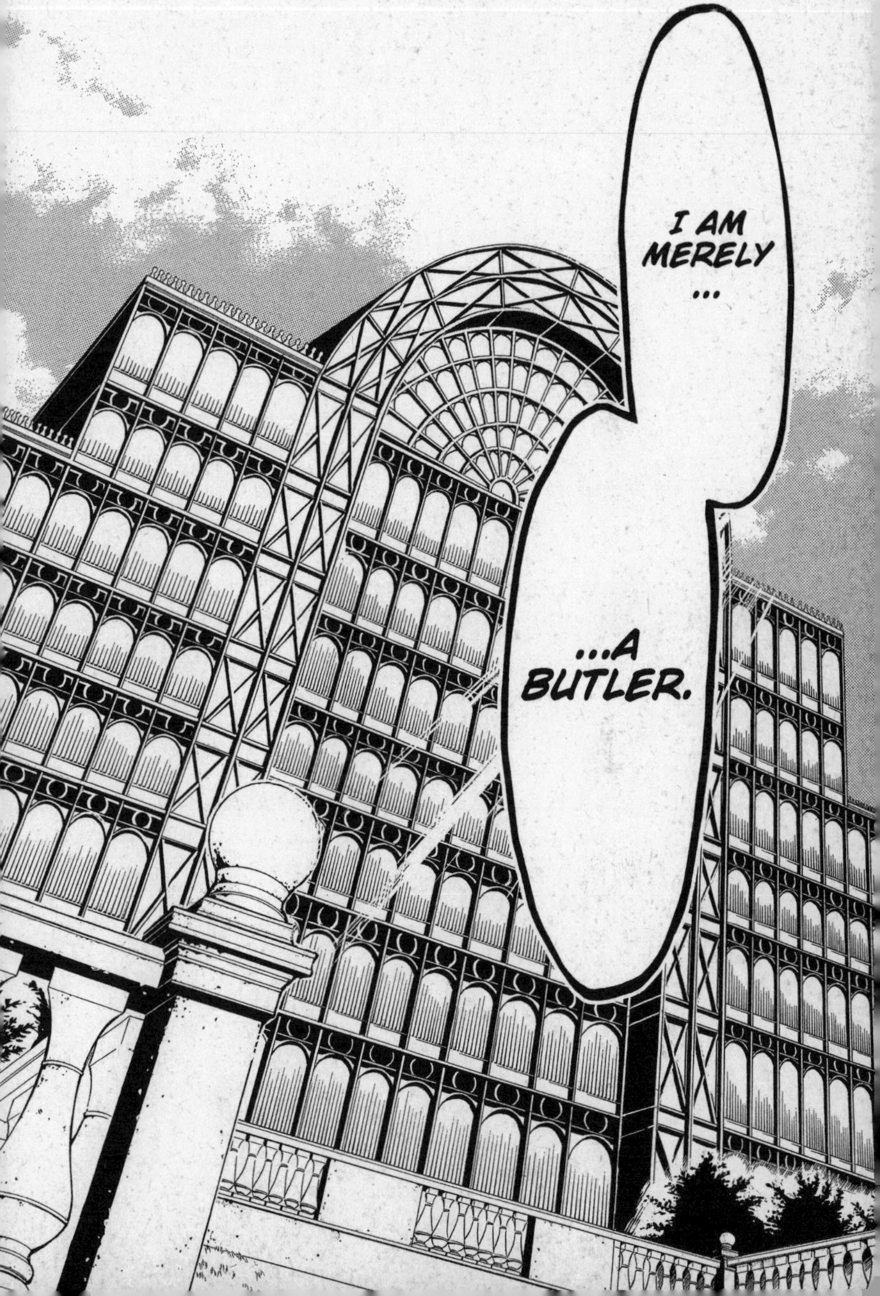
I AM MERELY ...
...A BUTLER.

Black Butler

Chapter 22

At night : The Butler, Victorious

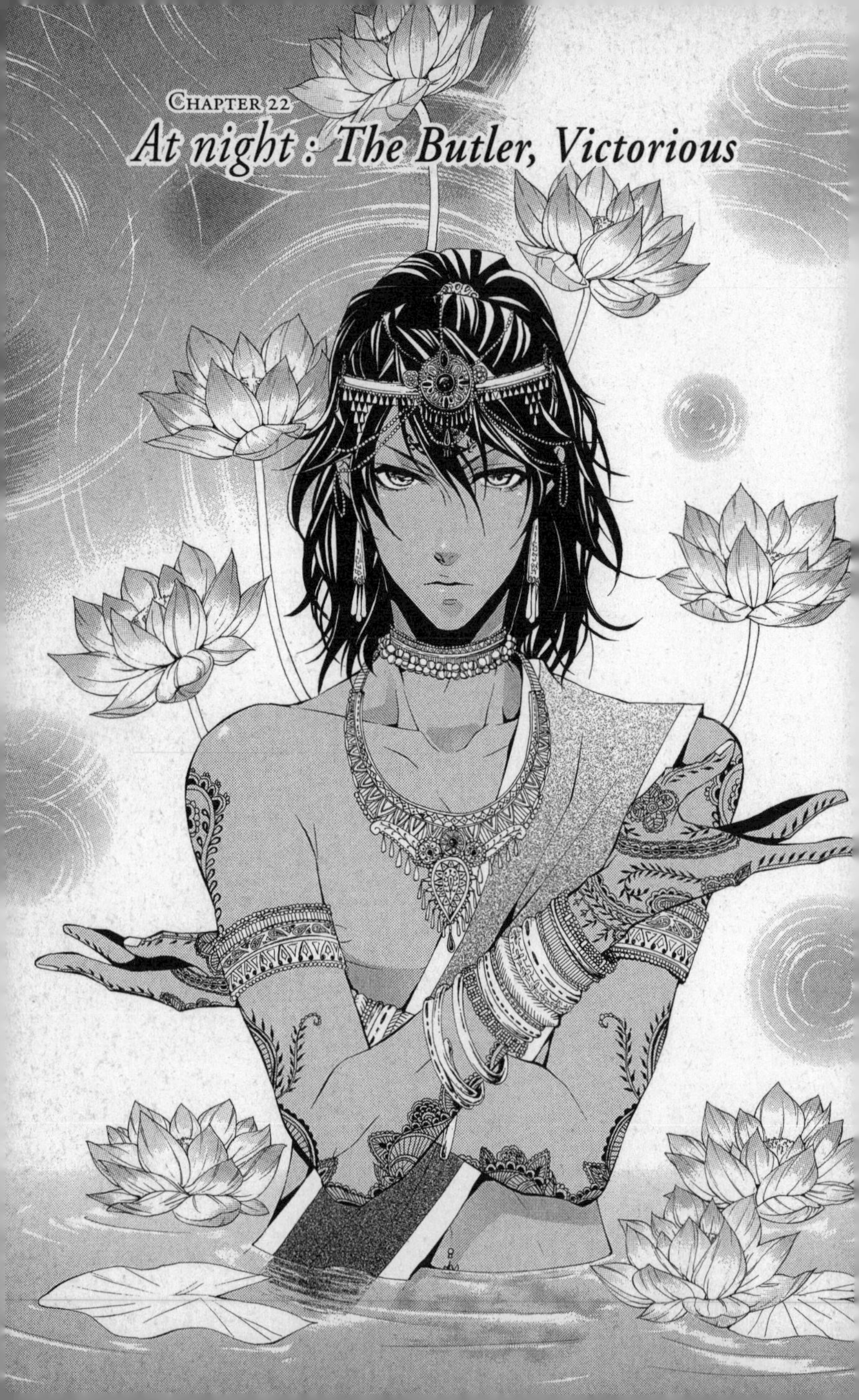

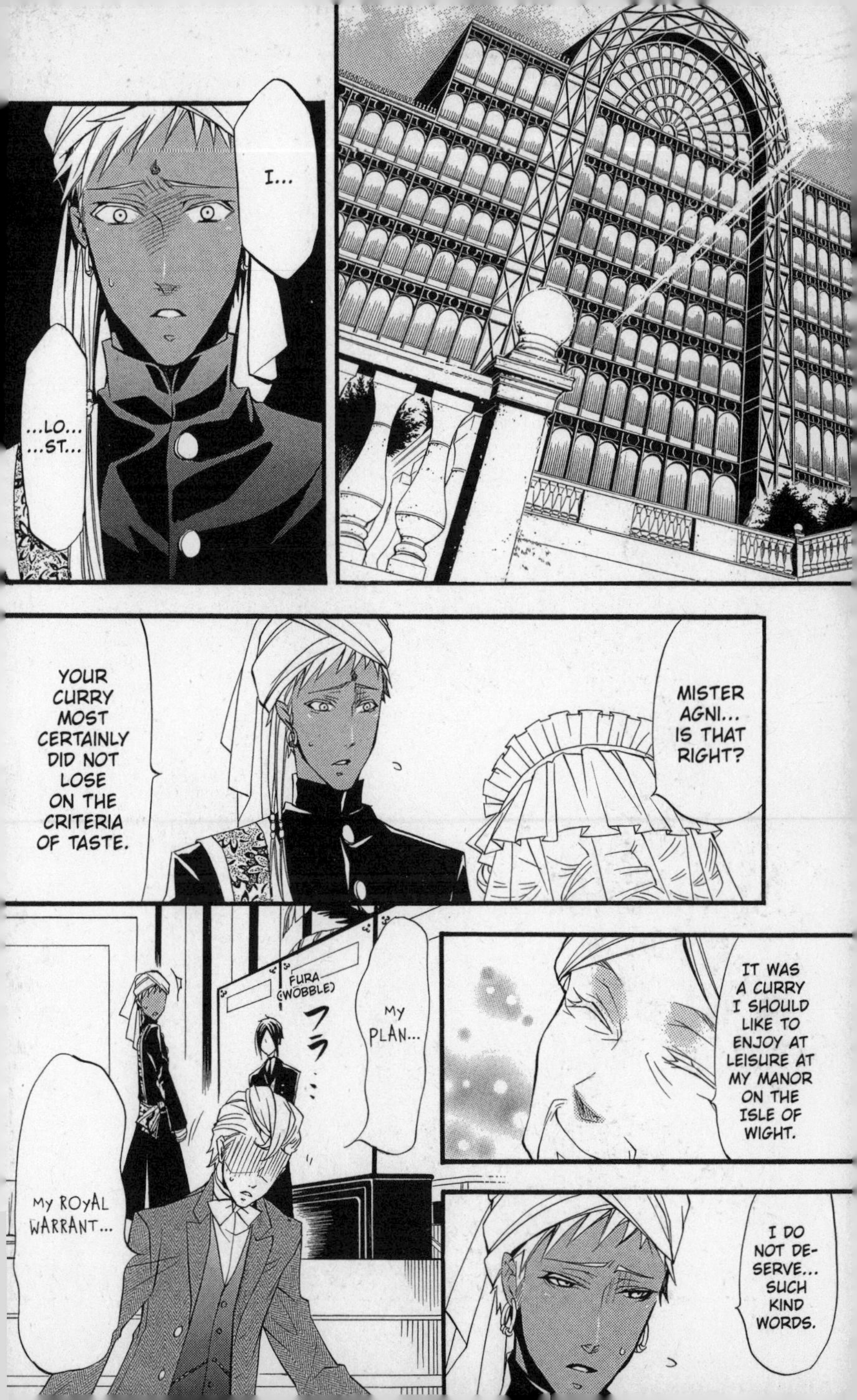
I...
...LO... ...ST...
MISTER AGNI... IS THAT RIGHT?
YOUR CURRY MOST CERTAINLY DID NOT LOSE ON THE CRITERIA OF TASTE.
IT WAS A CURRY I SHOULD LIKE TO ENJOY AT LEISURE AT MY MANOR ON THE ISLE OF WIGHT.
I DO NOT DE-SERVE... SUCH KIND WORDS.
My PLAN...
FURA (WOBBLE)
フラ
My ROYAL WARRANT...

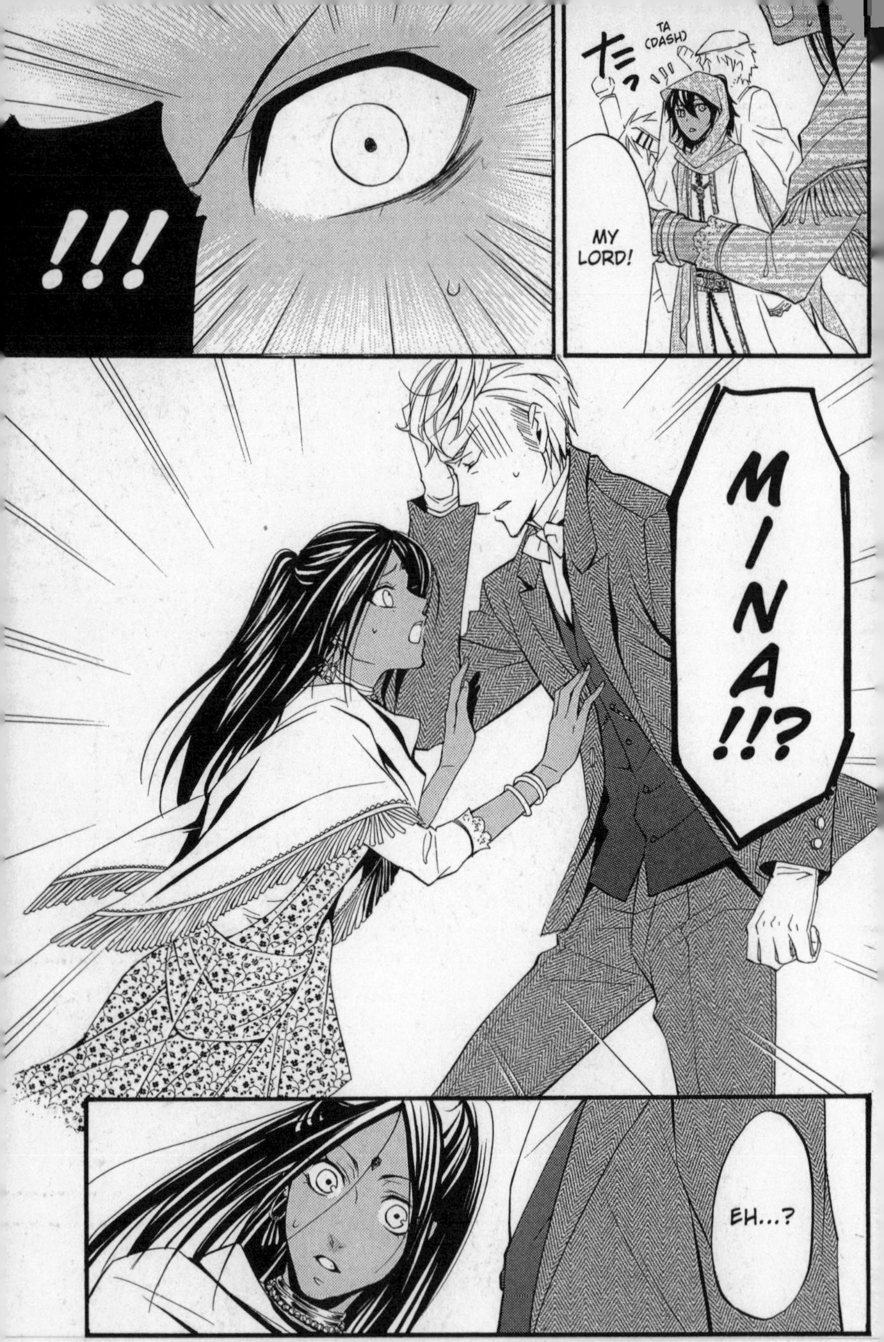
TA (DASH)
MY LORD!
!!!
MINA!!?
EH...?

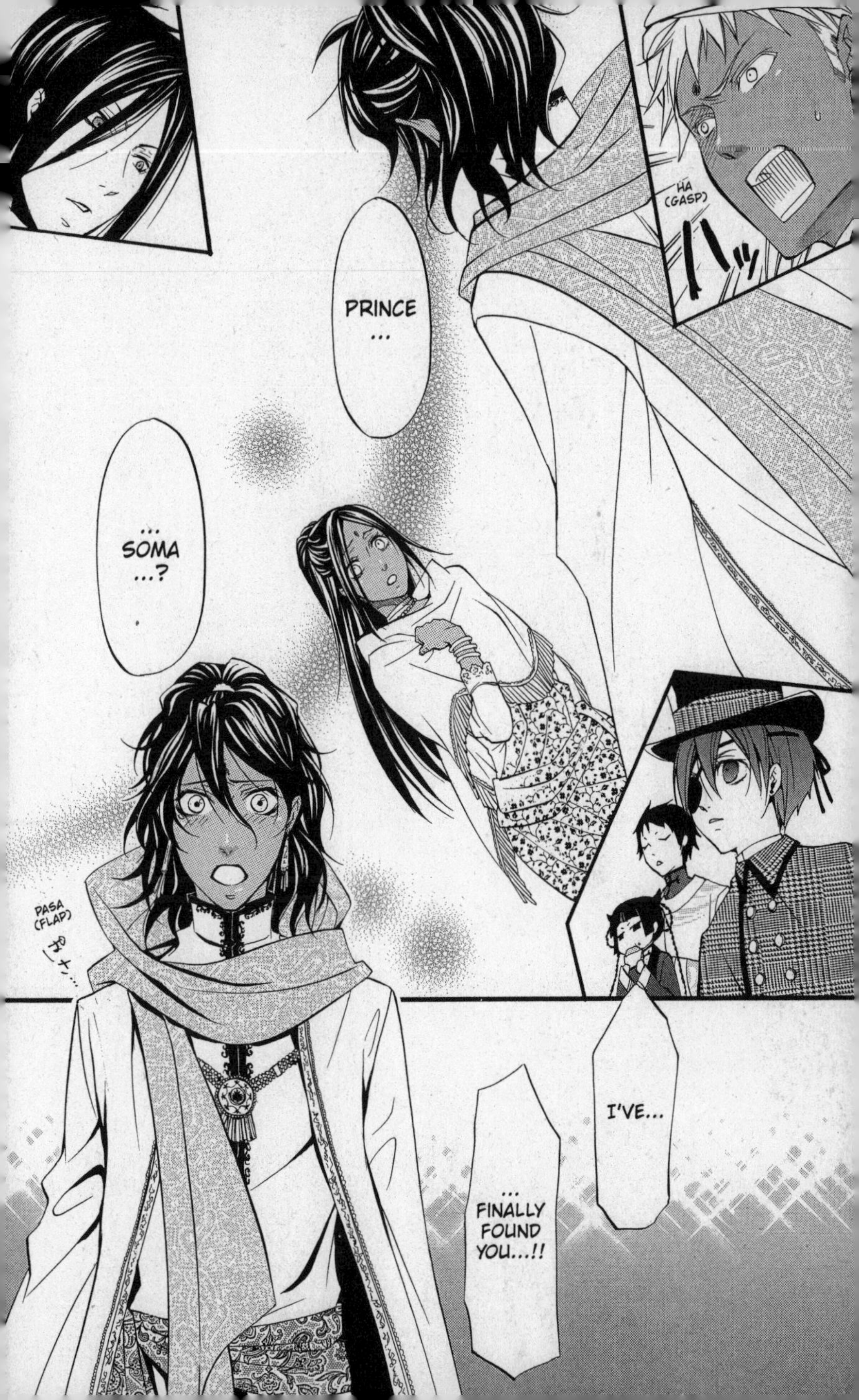
HA (GASP)
ハッ
PRINCE...
...SOMA...?
PASA (FLAP)
ぱさ…
I'VE...
...FINALLY FOUND YOU...!!

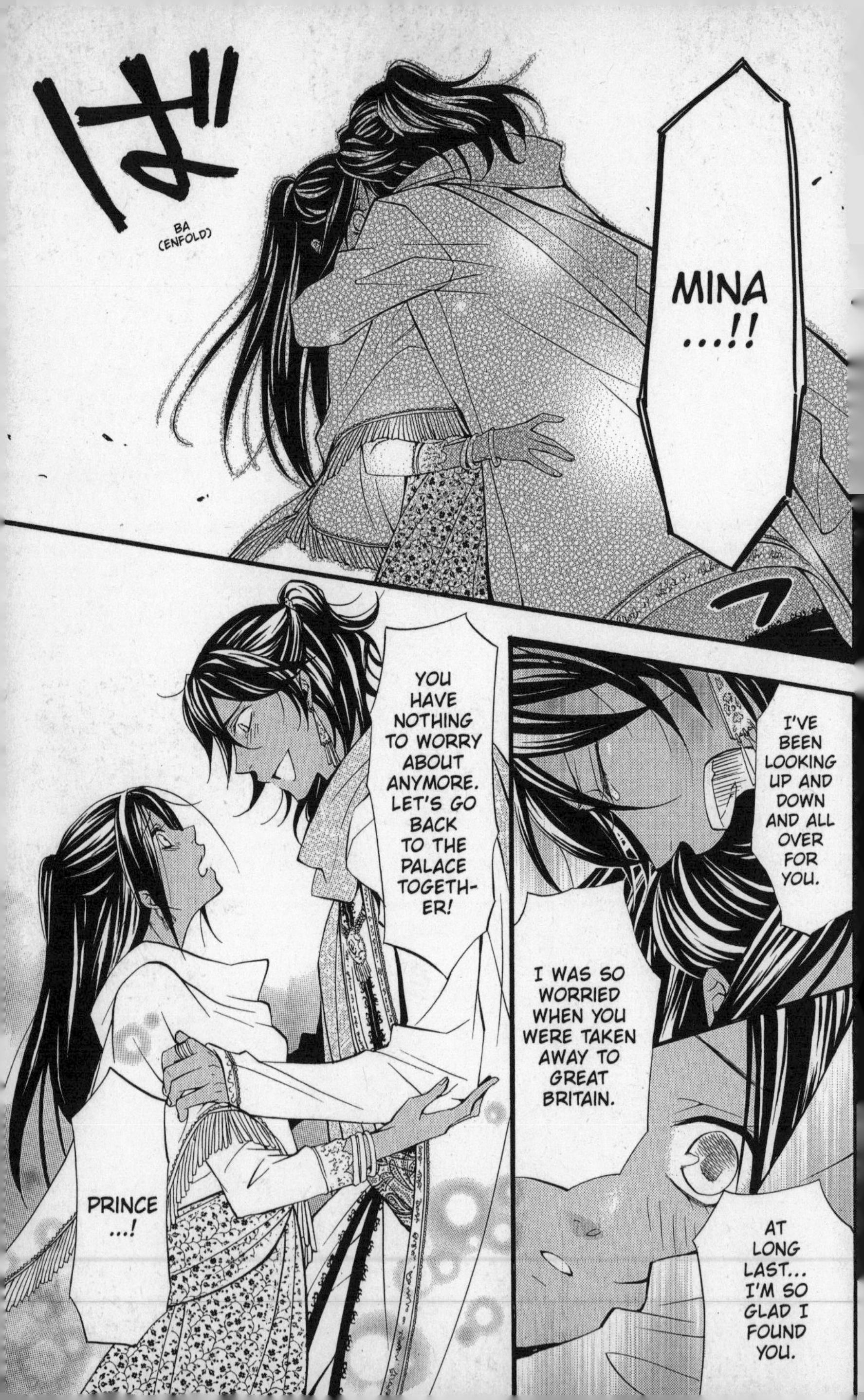

MINA ...!!
ば
BA (ENFOLD)
I'VE BEEN LOOKING UP AND DOWN AND ALL OVER FOR YOU.
I WAS SO WORRIED WHEN YOU WERE TAKEN AWAY TO GREAT BRITAIN.
AT LONG LAST... I'M SO GLAD I FOUND YOU.
YOU HAVE NOTHING TO WORRY ABOUT ANYMORE. LET'S GO BACK TO THE PALACE TOGETHER!
PRINCE ...!

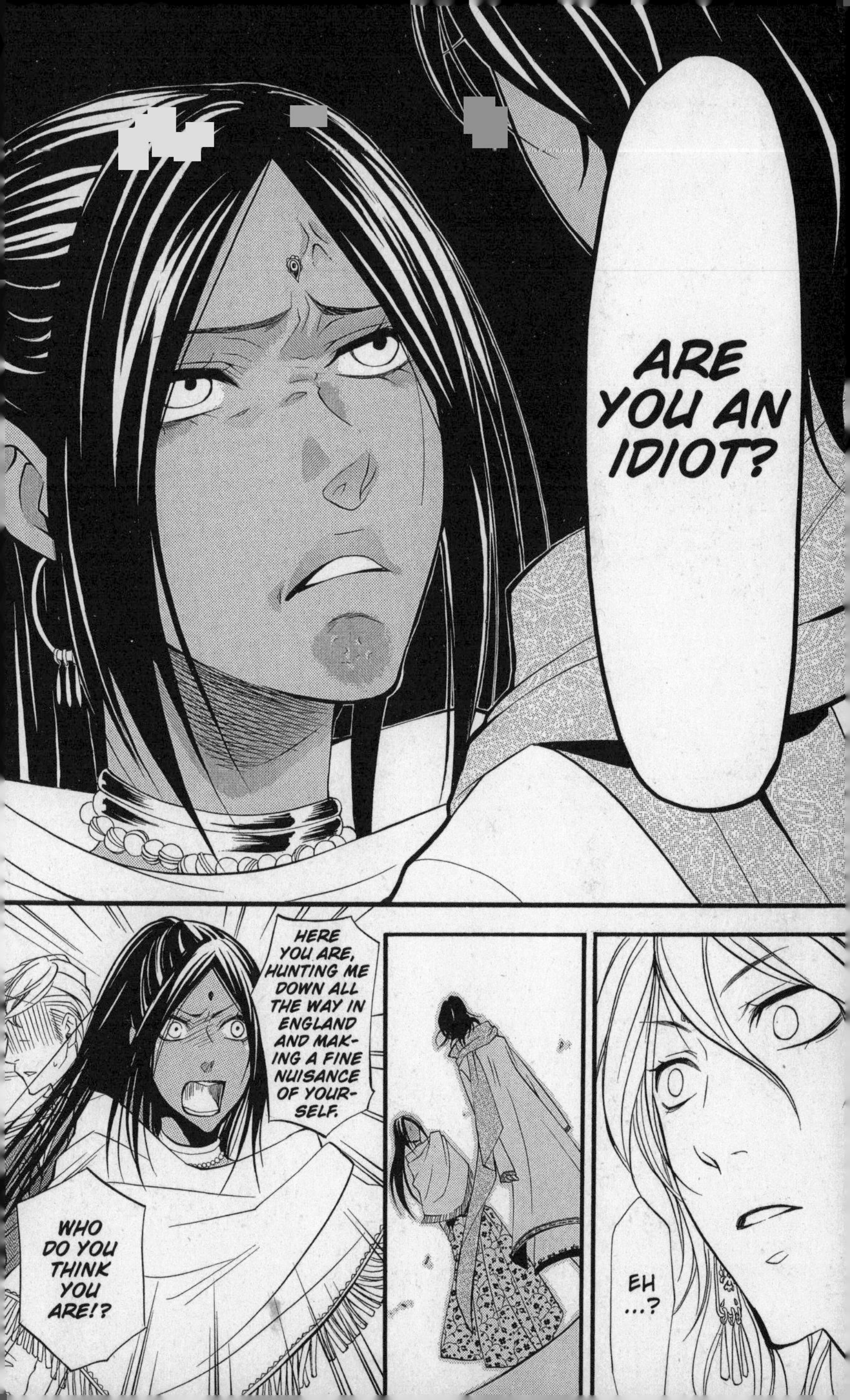
ARE YOU AN IDIOT?
EH ...?
HERE YOU ARE, HUNTING ME DOWN ALL THE WAY IN ENGLAND AND MAKING A FINE NUISANCE OF YOURSELF.
WHO DO YOU THINK YOU ARE!?

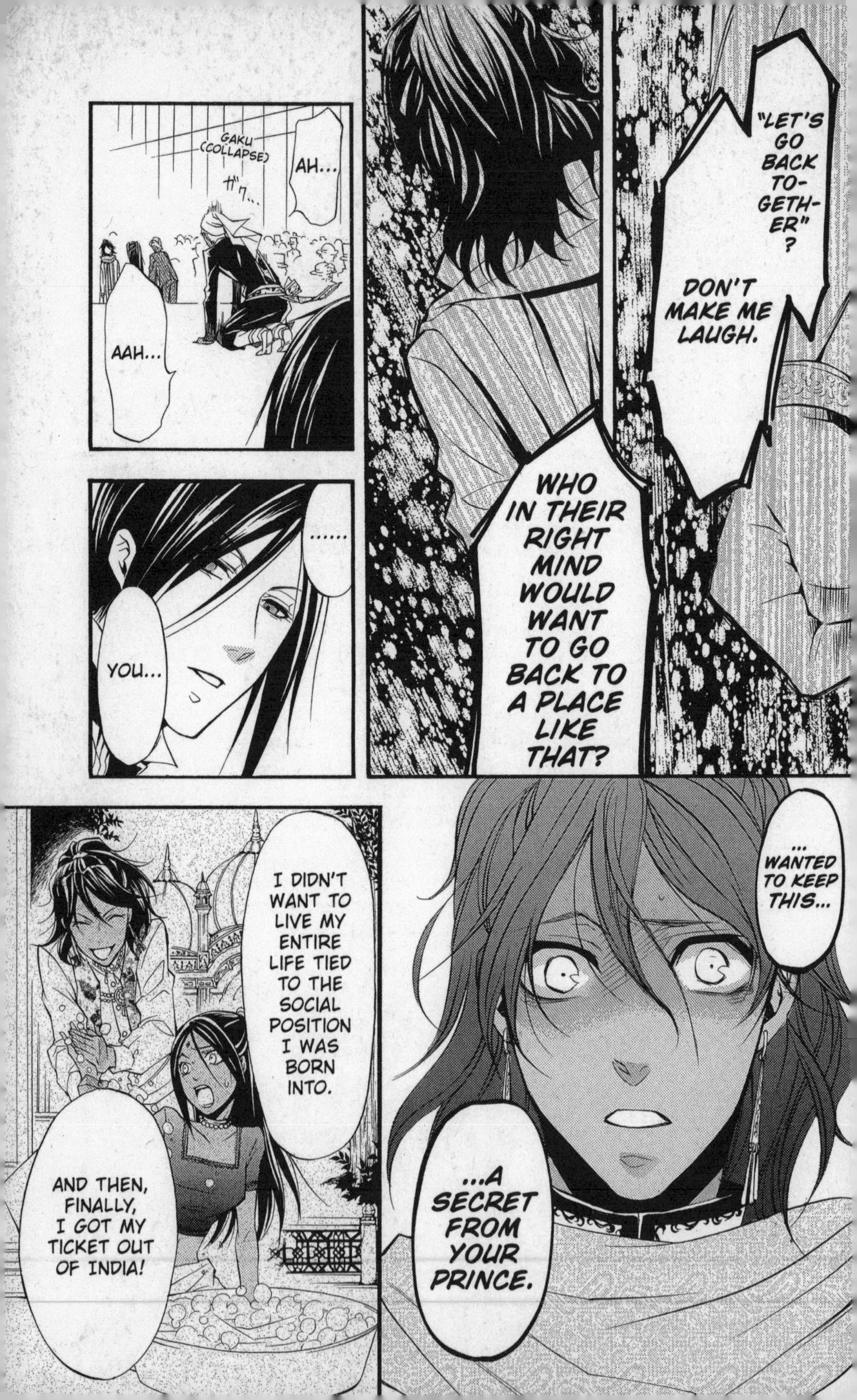
"LET'S GO BACK TO-GETH-ER"?
DON'T MAKE ME LAUGH.
WHO IN THEIR RIGHT MIND WOULD WANT TO GO BACK TO A PLACE LIKE THAT?
AH...
GAKU (COLLAPSE)
ガク...
AAH...
......
YOU...
...WANTED TO KEEP THIS...
...A SECRET FROM YOUR PRINCE.
I DIDN'T WANT TO LIVE MY ENTIRE LIFE TIED TO THE SOCIAL POSITION I WAS BORN INTO.
AND THEN, FINALLY, I GOT MY TICKET OUT OF INDIA!

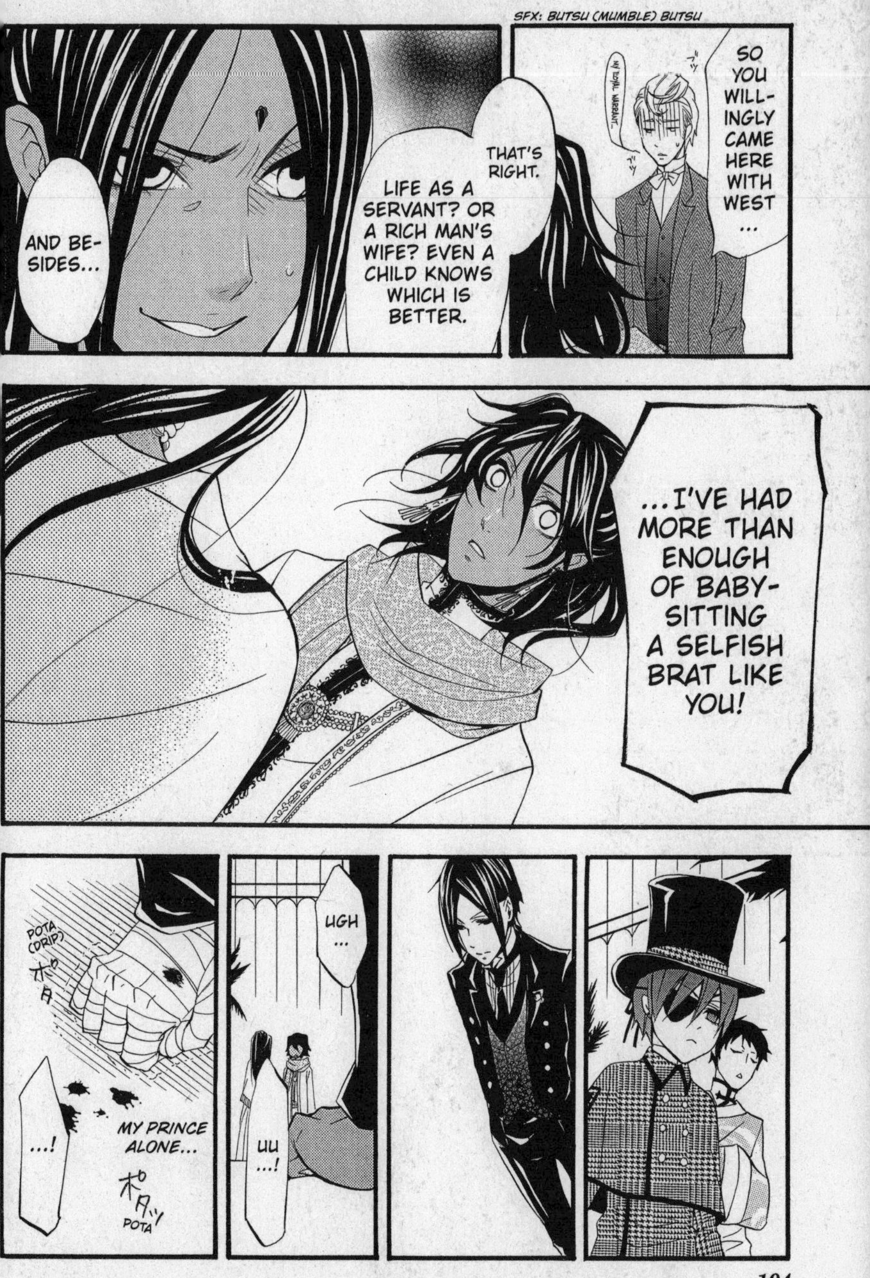
SFX: BUTSU (MUMBLE) BUTSU
SO YOU WILLINGLY CAME HERE WITH WEST...
MY ROYAL WARRANT...
THAT'S RIGHT.
LIFE AS A SERVANT? OR A RICH MAN'S WIFE? EVEN A CHILD KNOWS WHICH IS BETTER.
AND BESIDES...
...I'VE HAD MORE THAN ENOUGH OF BABYSITTING A SELFISH BRAT LIKE YOU!
UGH...
UU...!
POTA (DRIP)
MY PRINCE ALONE...
...!
POTA

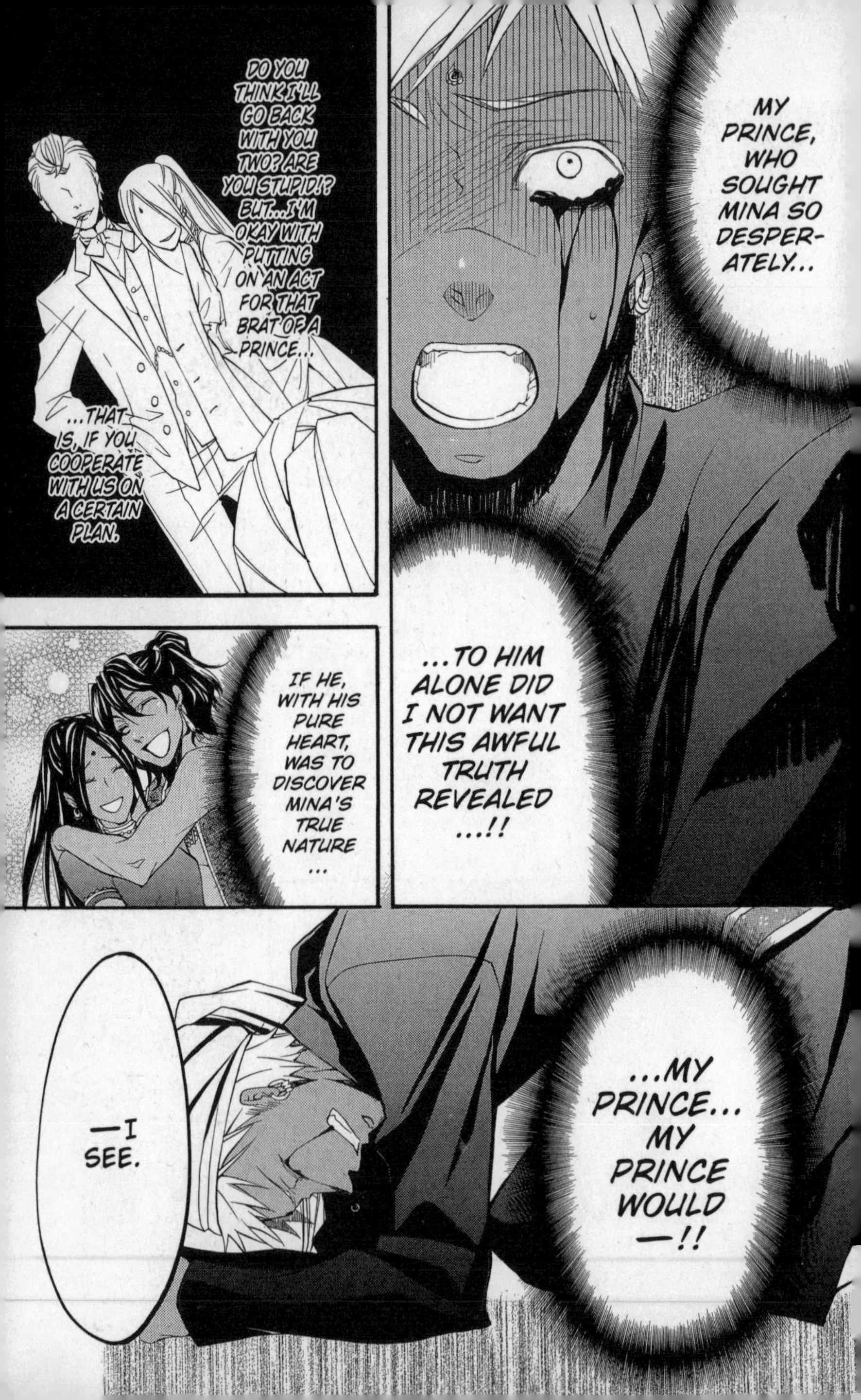

MY PRINCE, WHO SOUGHT MINA SO DESPER-ATELY...
...TO HIM ALONE DID I NOT WANT THIS AWFUL TRUTH REVEALED ...!!
DO YOU THINK I'LL GO BACK WITH YOU TWO? ARE YOU STUPID!? BUT...I'M OKAY WITH PUTTING ON AN ACT FOR THAT BRAT OF A PRINCE...
...THAT IS, IF YOU COOPERATE WITH US ON A CERTAIN PLAN.
IF HE, WITH HIS PURE HEART, WAS TO DISCOVER MINA'S TRUE NATURE ...
...MY PRINCE... MY PRINCE WOULD —!!
—I SEE.

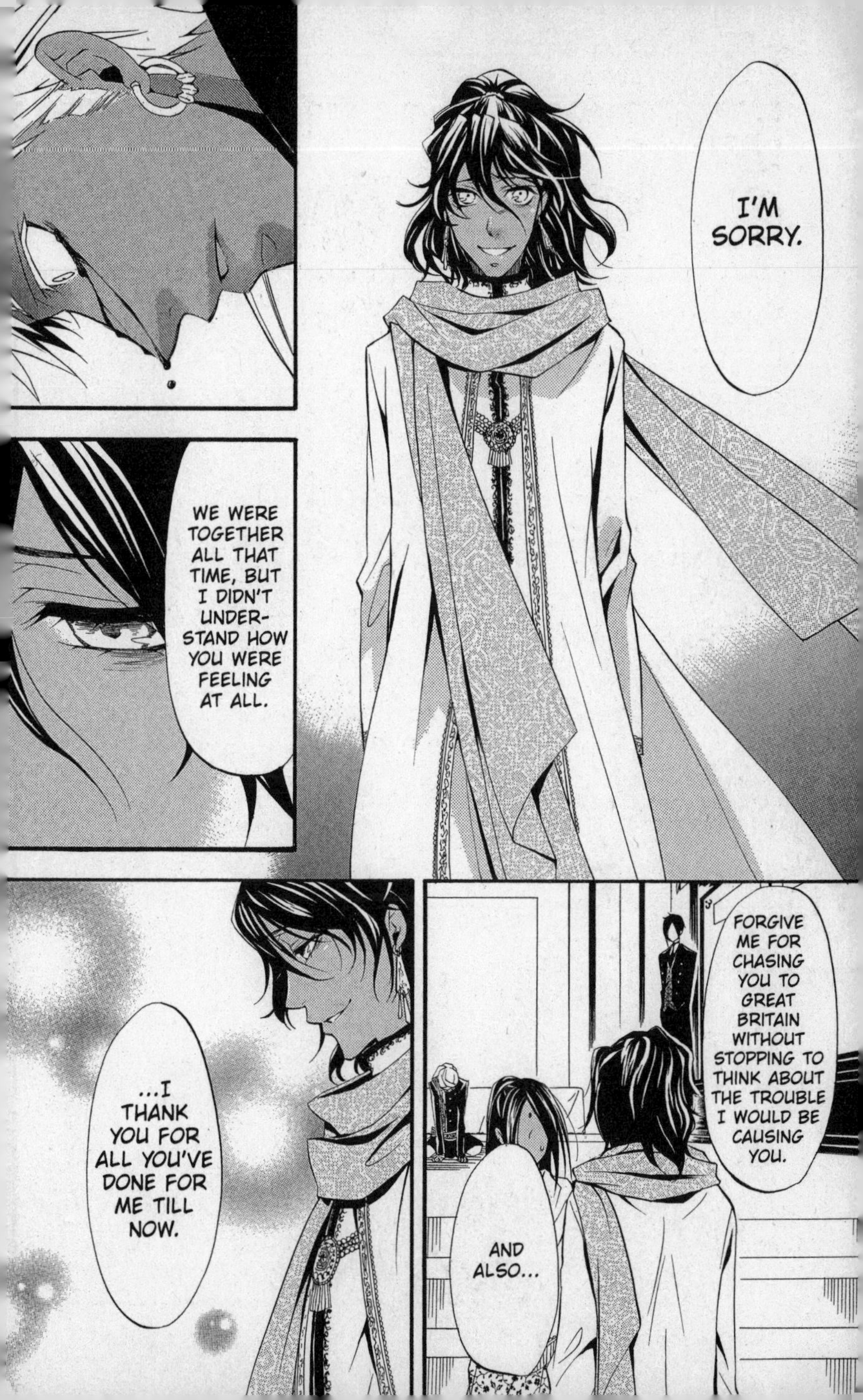
I'M SORRY.
WE WERE TOGETHER ALL THAT TIME, BUT I DIDN'T UNDER-STAND HOW YOU WERE FEELING AT ALL.
FORGIVE ME FOR CHASING YOU TO GREAT BRITAIN WITHOUT STOPPING TO THINK ABOUT THE TROUBLE I WOULD BE CAUSING YOU.
AND ALSO...
...I THANK YOU FOR ALL YOU'VE DONE FOR ME TILL NOW.

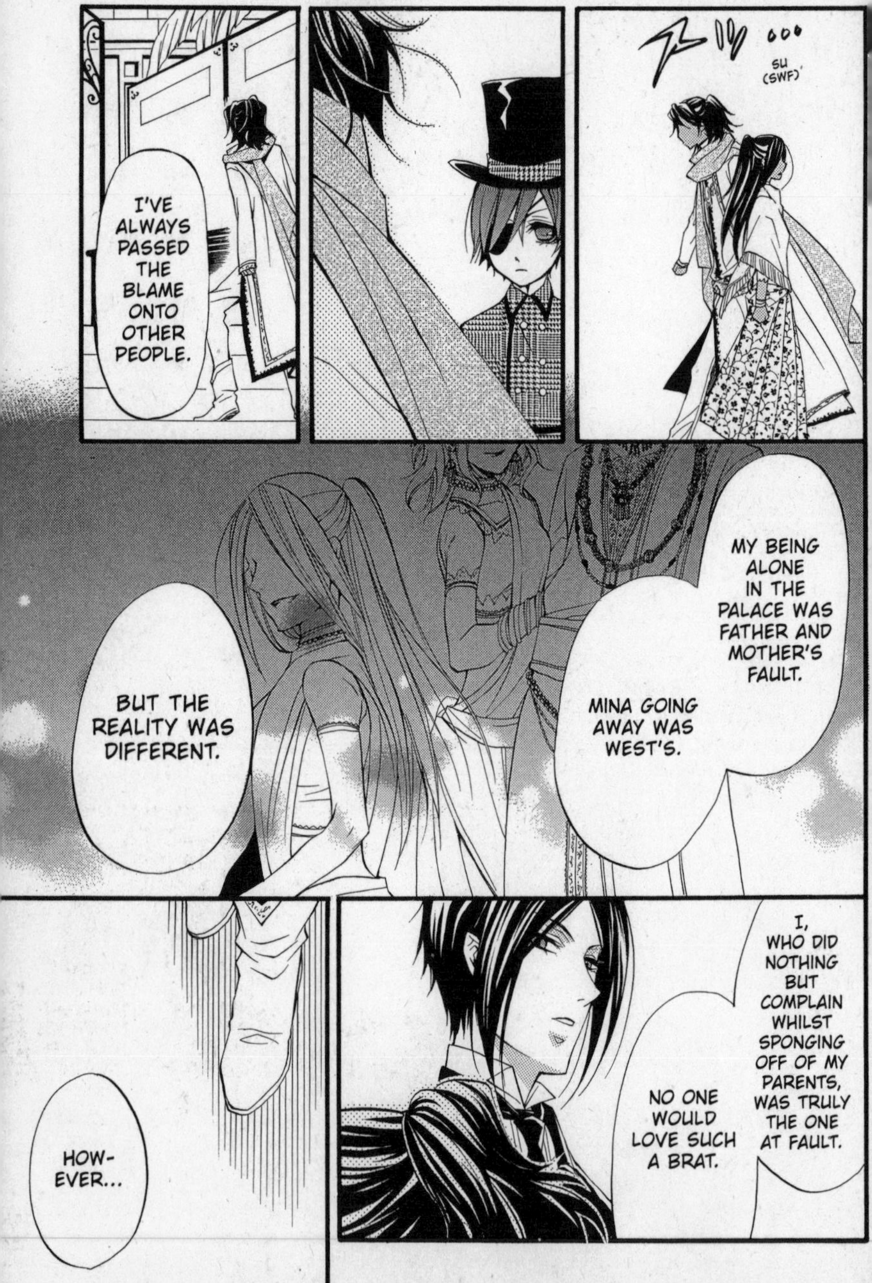
SU (SWF)
I'VE ALWAYS PASSED THE BLAME ONTO OTHER PEOPLE.
MY BEING ALONE IN THE PALACE WAS FATHER AND MOTHER'S FAULT.
MINA GOING AWAY WAS WEST'S.
BUT THE REALITY WAS DIFFERENT.
I, WHO DID NOTHING BUT COMPLAIN WHILST SPONGING OFF OF MY PARENTS, WAS TRULY THE ONE AT FAULT.
NO ONE WOULD LOVE SUCH A BRAT.
HOW-EVER...

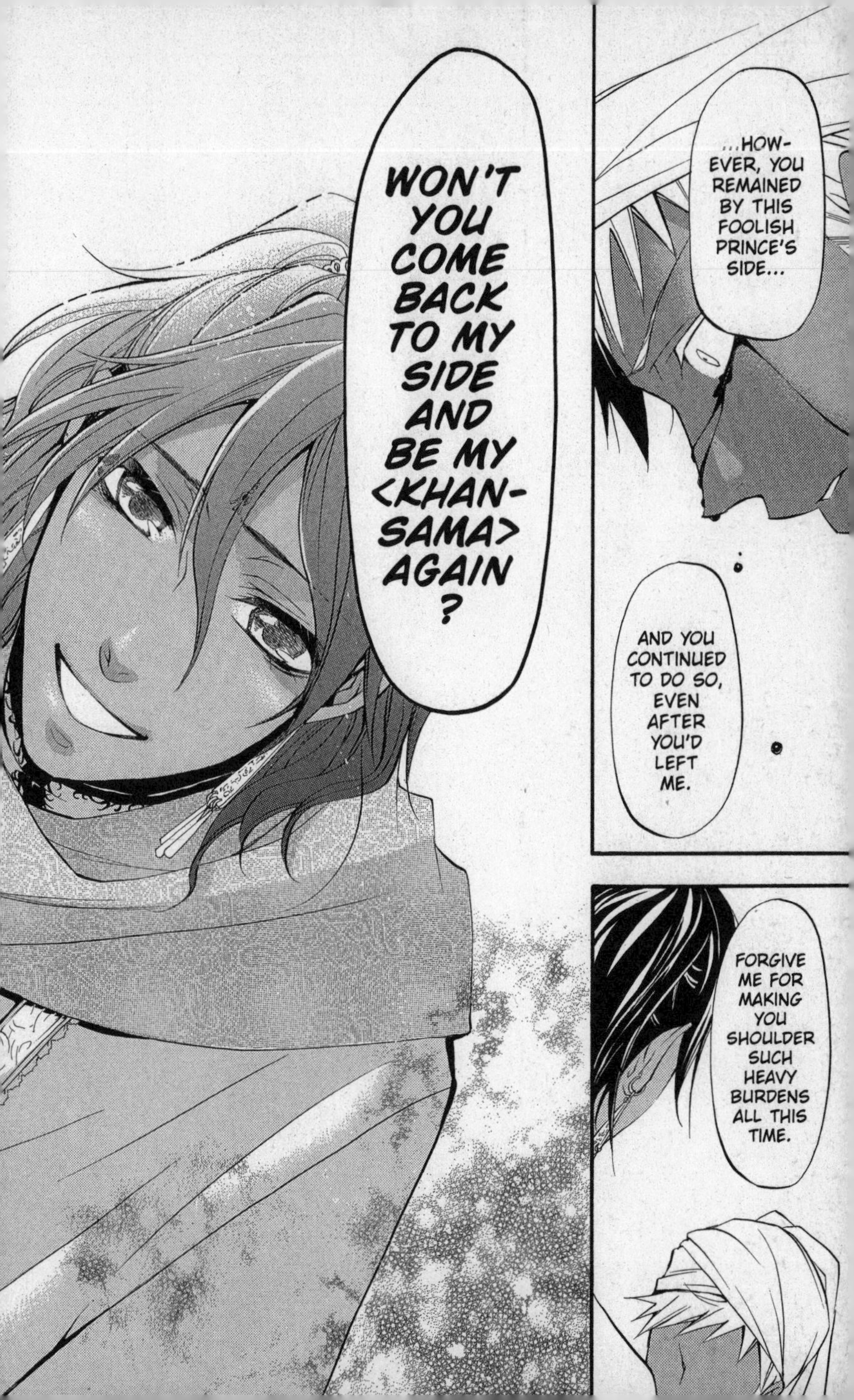
...HOWEVER, YOU REMAINED BY THIS FOOLISH PRINCE'S SIDE...
AND YOU CONTINUED TO DO SO, EVEN AFTER YOU'D LEFT ME.
FORGIVE ME FOR MAKING YOU SHOULDER SUCH HEAVY BURDENS ALL THIS TIME.
WON'T YOU COME BACK TO MY SIDE AND BE MY <KHAN-SAMA> AGAIN?

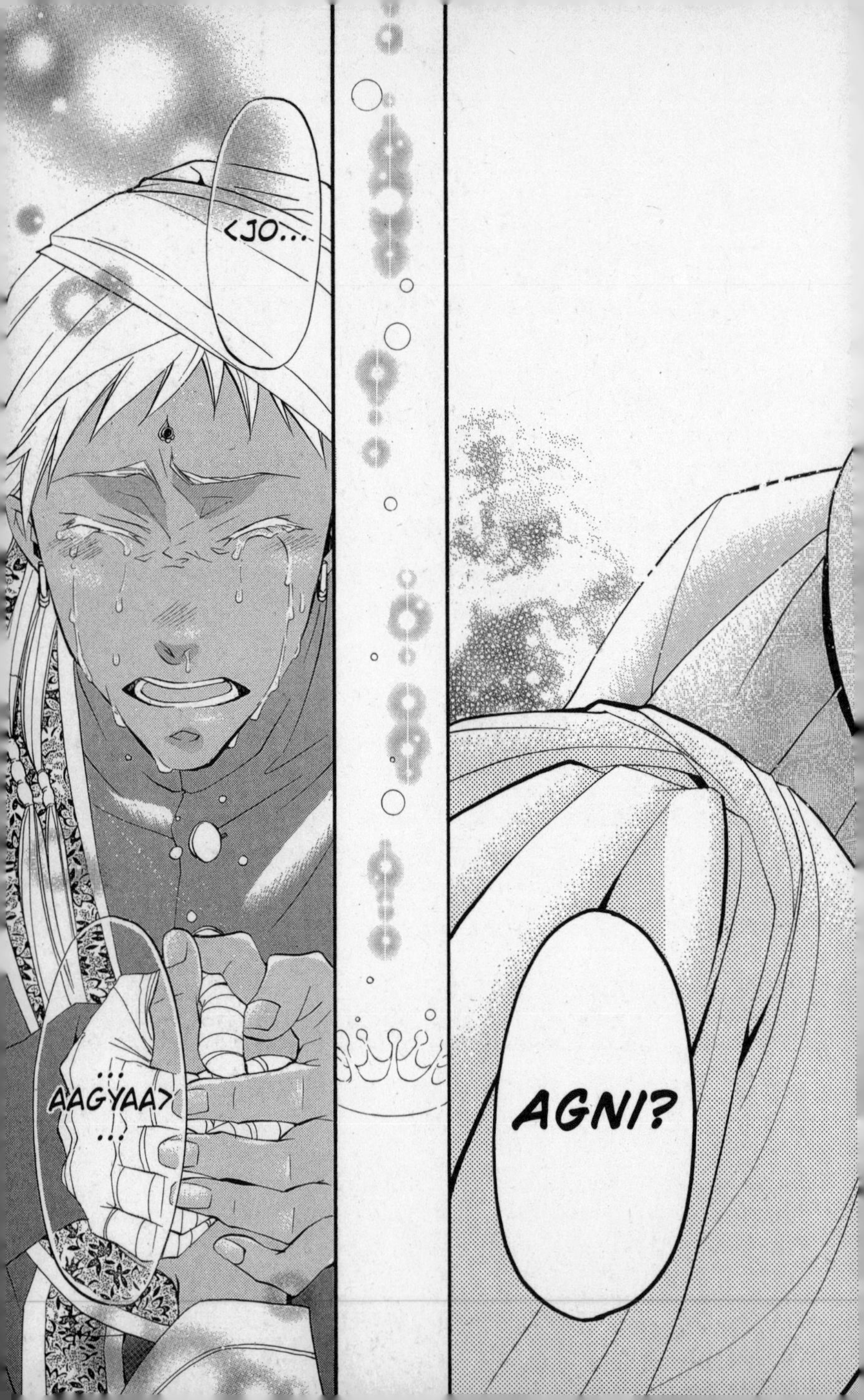
AGNI?
<JO...
... AAGYAA> ...

SFX: MORI (MUNCH) MORI

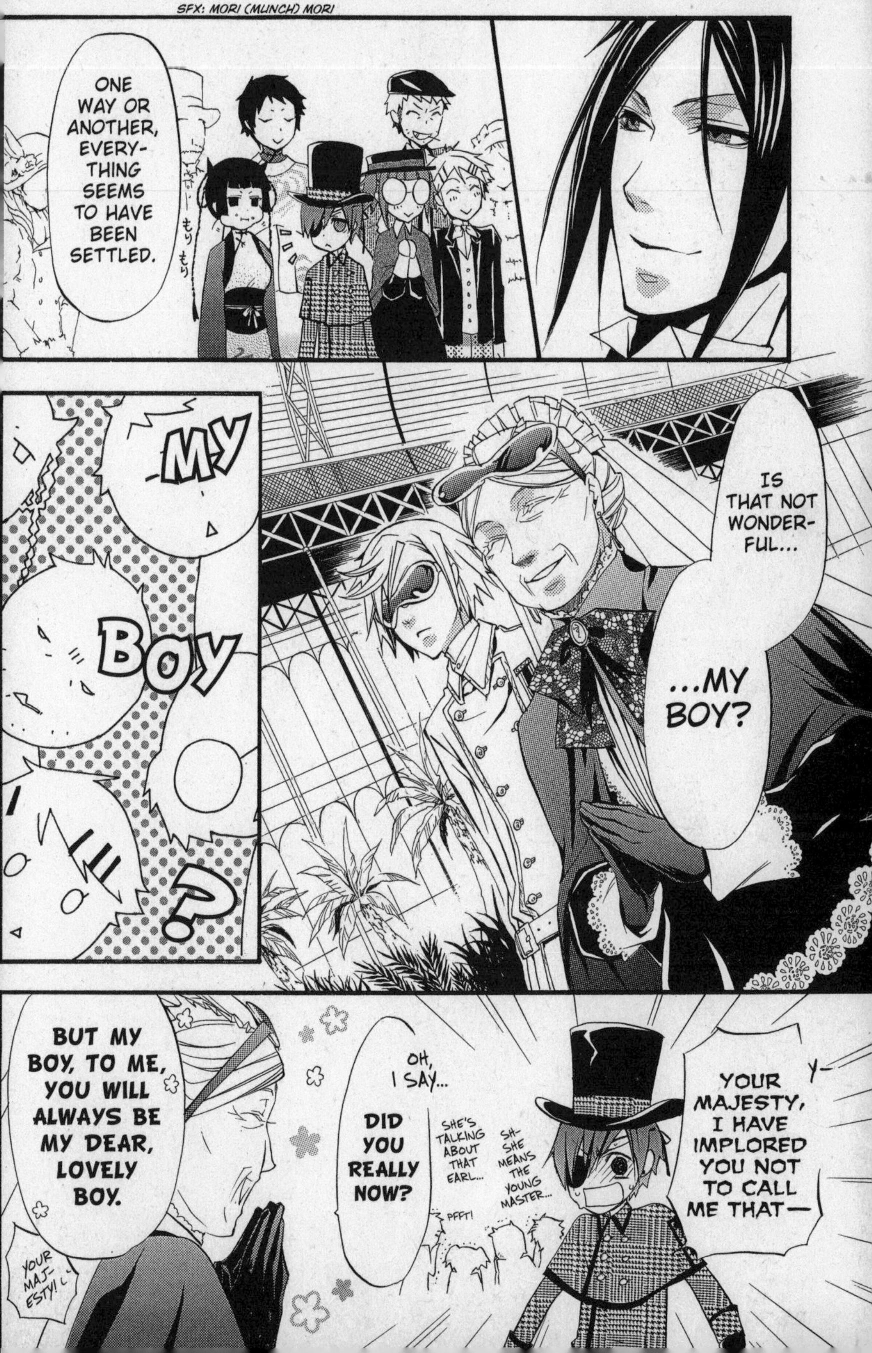
ONE WAY OR ANOTHER, EVERYTHING SEEMS TO HAVE BEEN SETTLED.
もり もり
IS THAT NOT WONDERFUL...
...MY BOY?
MY BOY ?
Y—
YOUR MAJESTY, I HAVE IMPLORED YOU NOT TO CALL ME THAT—
SH-SHE MEANS THE YOUNG MASTER...
SHE'S TALKING ABOUT THAT EARL...
PFFT!
OH, I SAY...
DID YOU REALLY NOW?
BUT MY BOY, TO ME, YOU WILL ALWAYS BE MY DEAR, LOVELY BOY.
YOUR MAJESTY!

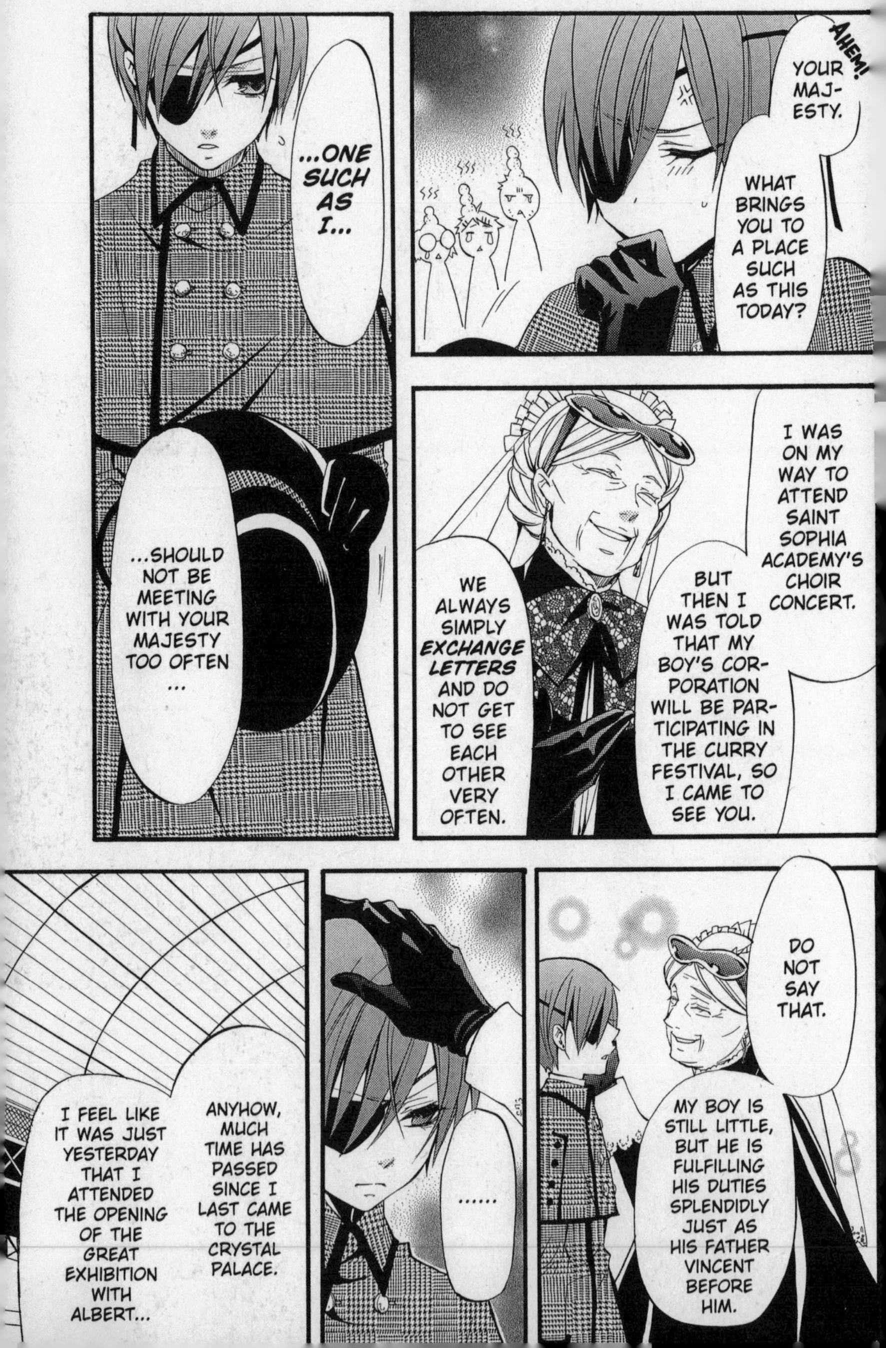
AHEM!
YOUR MAJ-ESTY.
WHAT BRINGS YOU TO A PLACE SUCH AS THIS TODAY?
I WAS ON MY WAY TO ATTEND SAINT SOPHIA ACADEMY'S CHOIR CONCERT.
BUT THEN I WAS TOLD THAT MY BOY'S COR-PORATION WILL BE PAR-TICIPATING IN THE CURRY FESTIVAL, SO I CAME TO SEE YOU.
WE ALWAYS SIMPLY *EXCHANGE LETTERS* AND DO NOT GET TO SEE EACH OTHER VERY OFTEN.
...ONE SUCH AS I...
...SHOULD NOT BE MEETING WITH YOUR MAJESTY TOO OFTEN ...
DO NOT SAY THAT.
MY BOY IS STILL LITTLE, BUT HE IS FULFILLING HIS DUTIES SPLENDIDLY JUST AS HIS FATHER VINCENT BEFORE HIM.
......
ANYHOW, MUCH TIME HAS PASSED SINCE I LAST CAME TO THE CRYSTAL PALACE.
I FEEL LIKE IT WAS JUST YESTERDAY THAT I ATTENDED THE OPENING OF THE GREAT EXHIBITION WITH ALBERT...

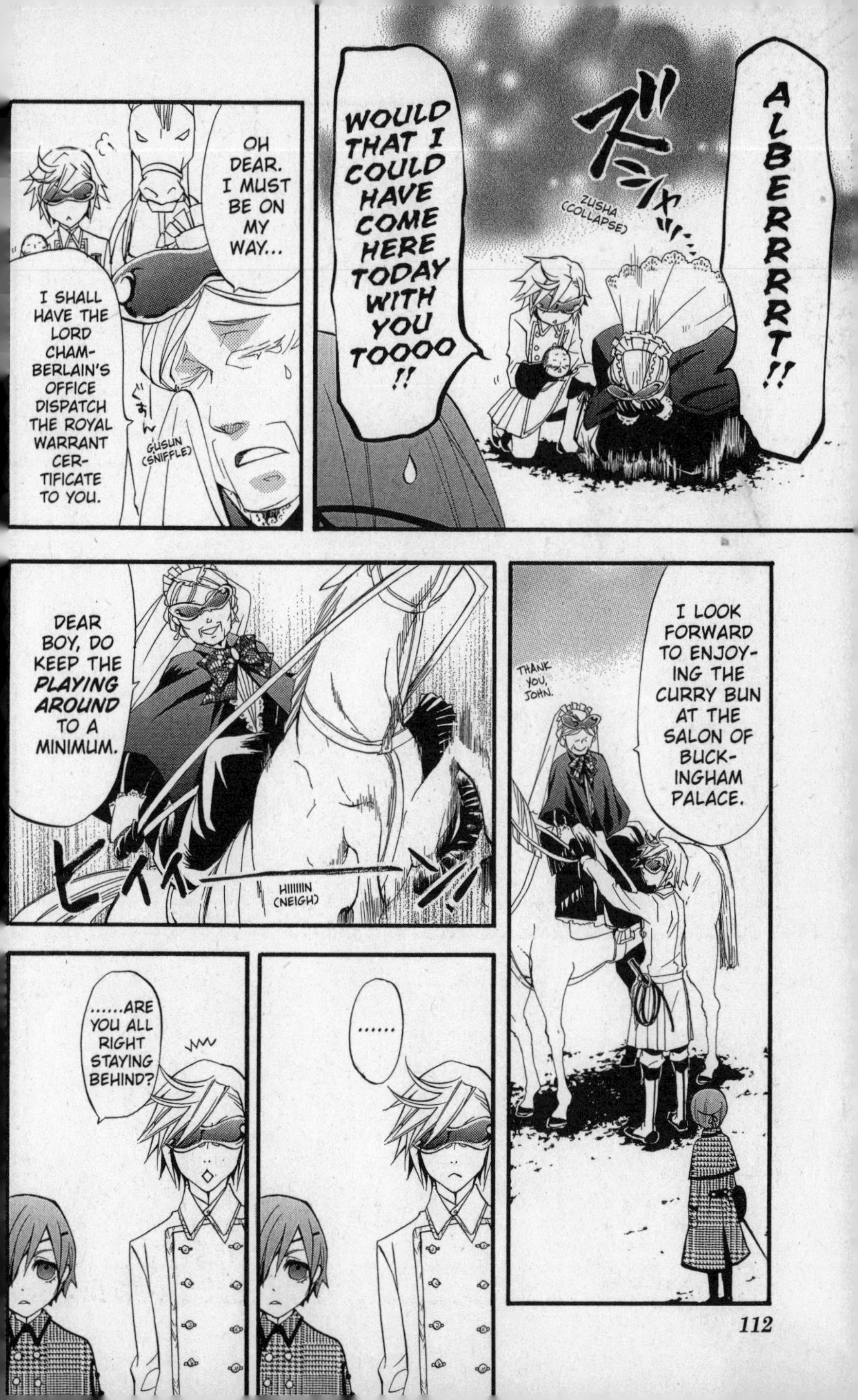
ALBERRRRT!!
ZUSHA (COLLAPSE)
WOULD THAT I COULD HAVE COME HERE TODAY WITH YOU TOOOO!!
OH DEAR. I MUST BE ON MY WAY...
I SHALL HAVE THE LORD CHAMBERLAIN'S OFFICE DISPATCH THE ROYAL WARRANT CERTIFICATE TO YOU.
GUSUN (SNIFFLE)
I LOOK FORWARD TO ENJOYING THE CURRY BUN AT THE SALON OF BUCKINGHAM PALACE.
THANK YOU, JOHN.
DEAR BOY, DO KEEP THE *PLAYING AROUND* TO A MINIMUM.
HIIIIIN (NEIGH)
......
......ARE YOU ALL RIGHT STAYING BEHIND?

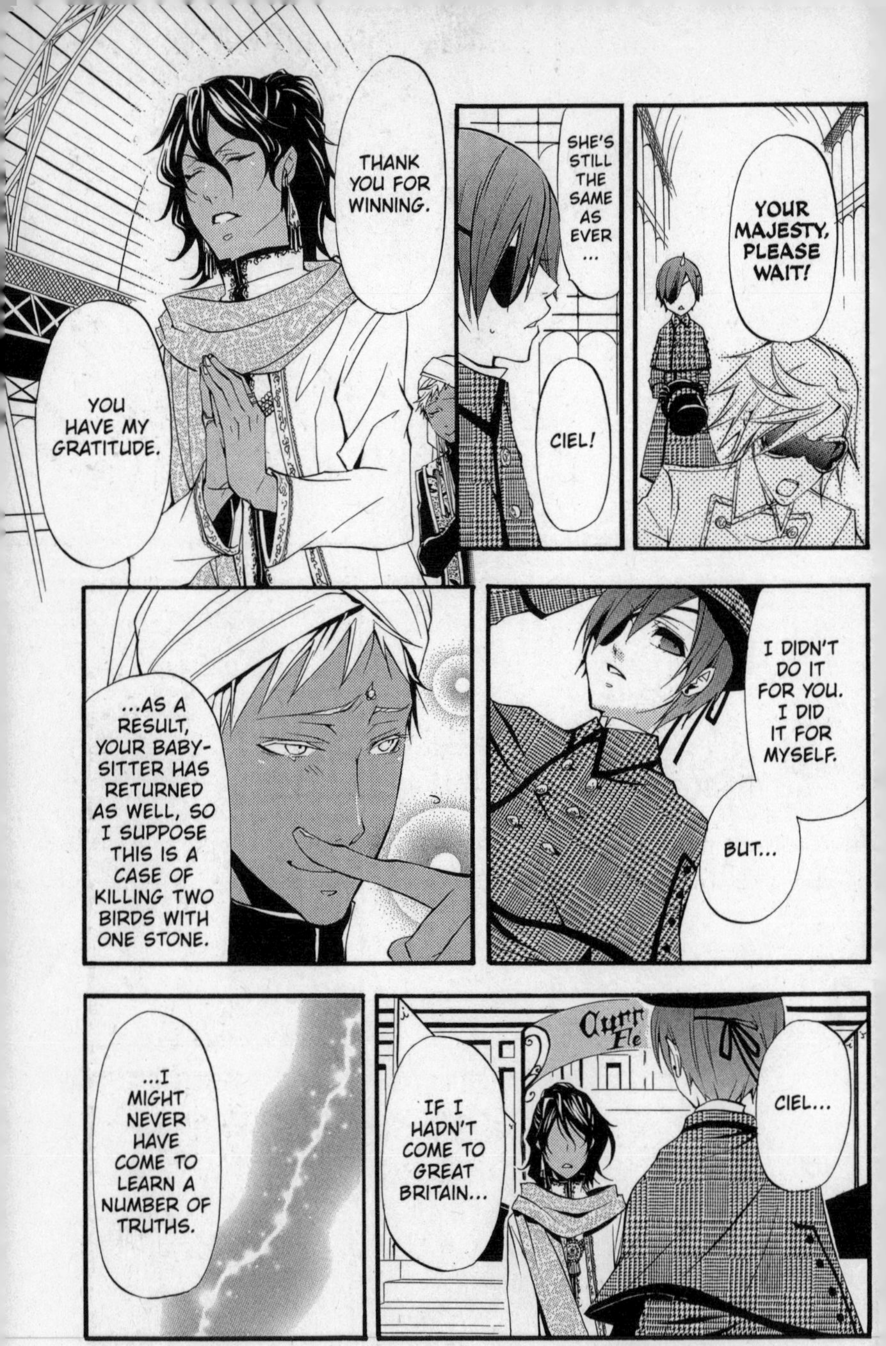
YOUR MAJESTY, PLEASE WAIT!
SHE'S STILL THE SAME AS EVER...
CIEL!
THANK YOU FOR WINNING.
YOU HAVE MY GRATITUDE.
I DIDN'T DO IT FOR YOU. I DID IT FOR MYSELF.
BUT...
...AS A RESULT, YOUR BABY-SITTER HAS RETURNED AS WELL, SO I SUPPOSE THIS IS A CASE OF KILLING TWO BIRDS WITH ONE STONE.
CIEL...
IF I HADN'T COME TO GREAT BRITAIN...
...I MIGHT NEVER HAVE COME TO LEARN A NUMBER OF TRUTHS.

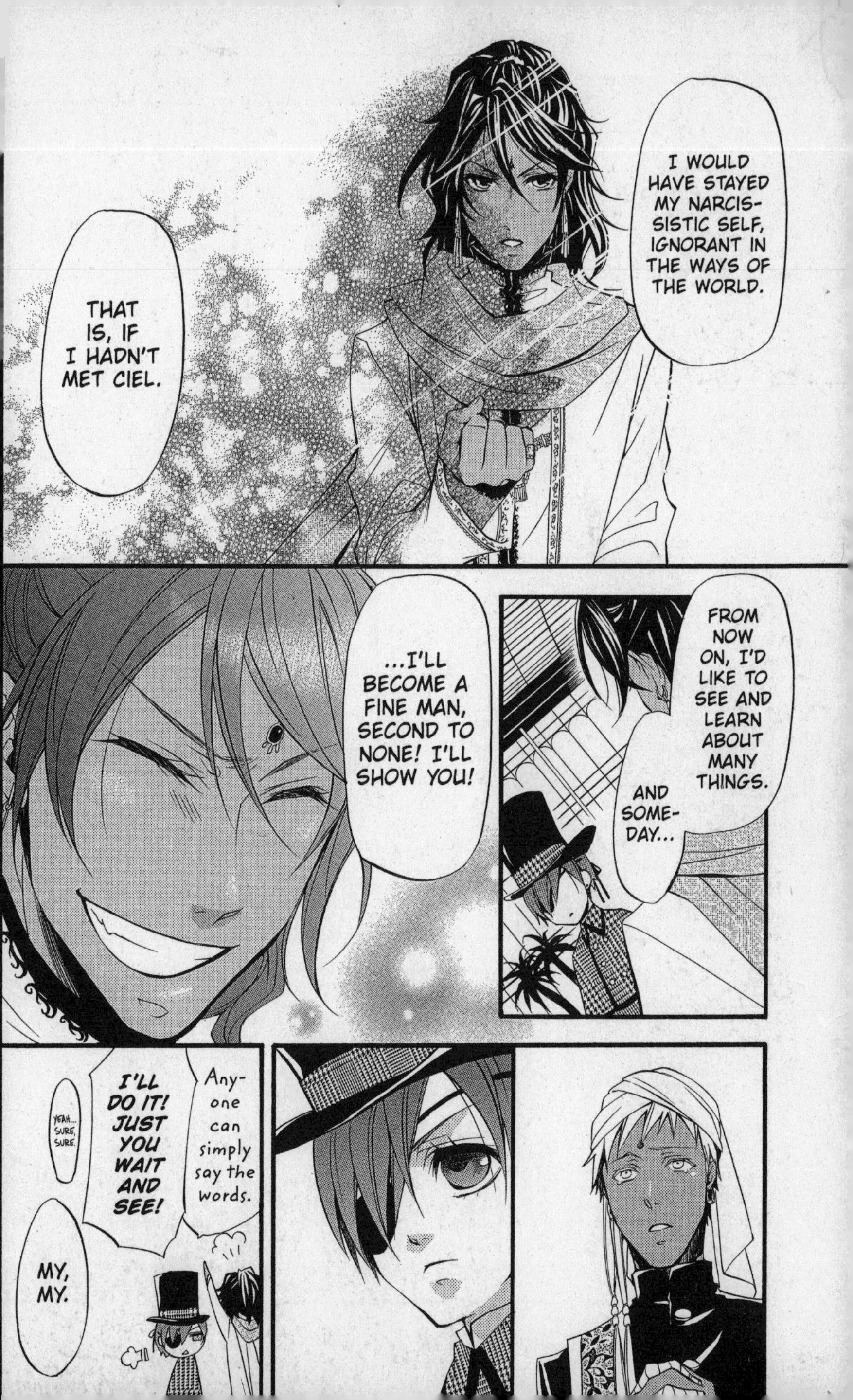
I WOULD HAVE STAYED MY NARCIS-SISTIC SELF, IGNORANT IN THE WAYS OF THE WORLD.
THAT IS, IF I HADN'T MET CIEL.
FROM NOW ON, I'D LIKE TO SEE AND LEARN ABOUT MANY THINGS.
AND SOME-DAY...
...I'LL BECOME A FINE MAN, SECOND TO NONE! I'LL SHOW YOU!
Any-one can simply say the words.
I'LL DO IT! JUST YOU WAIT AND SEE!
YEAH... SURE, SURE.
MY, MY.

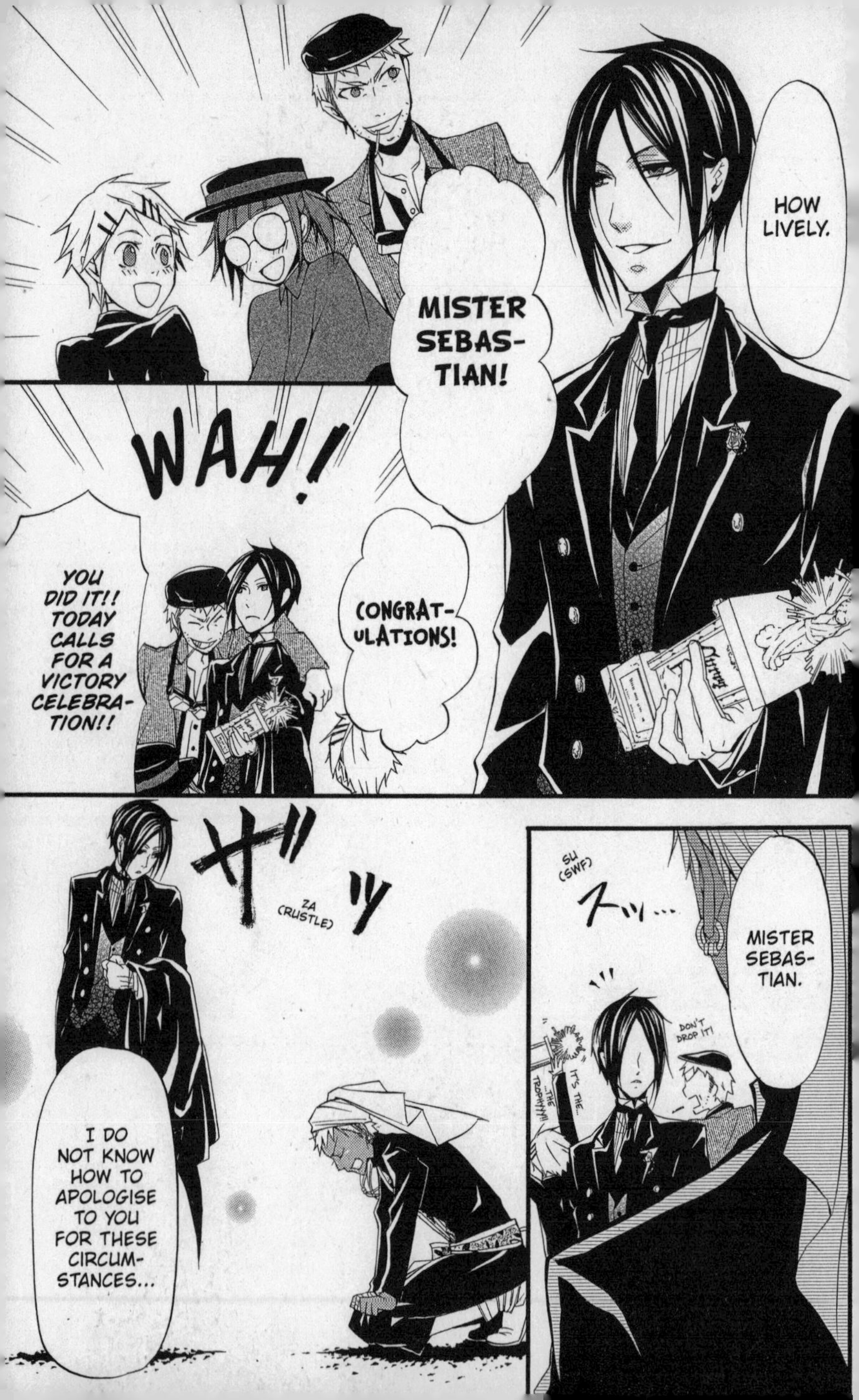
HOW LIVELY.
MISTER SEBAS-TIAN!
WAH!
CONGRAT-ULATIONS!
YOU DID IT!! TODAY CALLS FOR A VICTORY CELEBRA-TION!!
スッ…
SU (SWF)
MISTER SEBAS-TIAN.
DON'T DROP IT!
IT'S THE... ...THE TROPHY!!!
ザッ
ZA (RUSTLE)
I DO NOT KNOW HOW TO APOLOGISE TO YOU FOR THESE CIRCUM-STANCES...

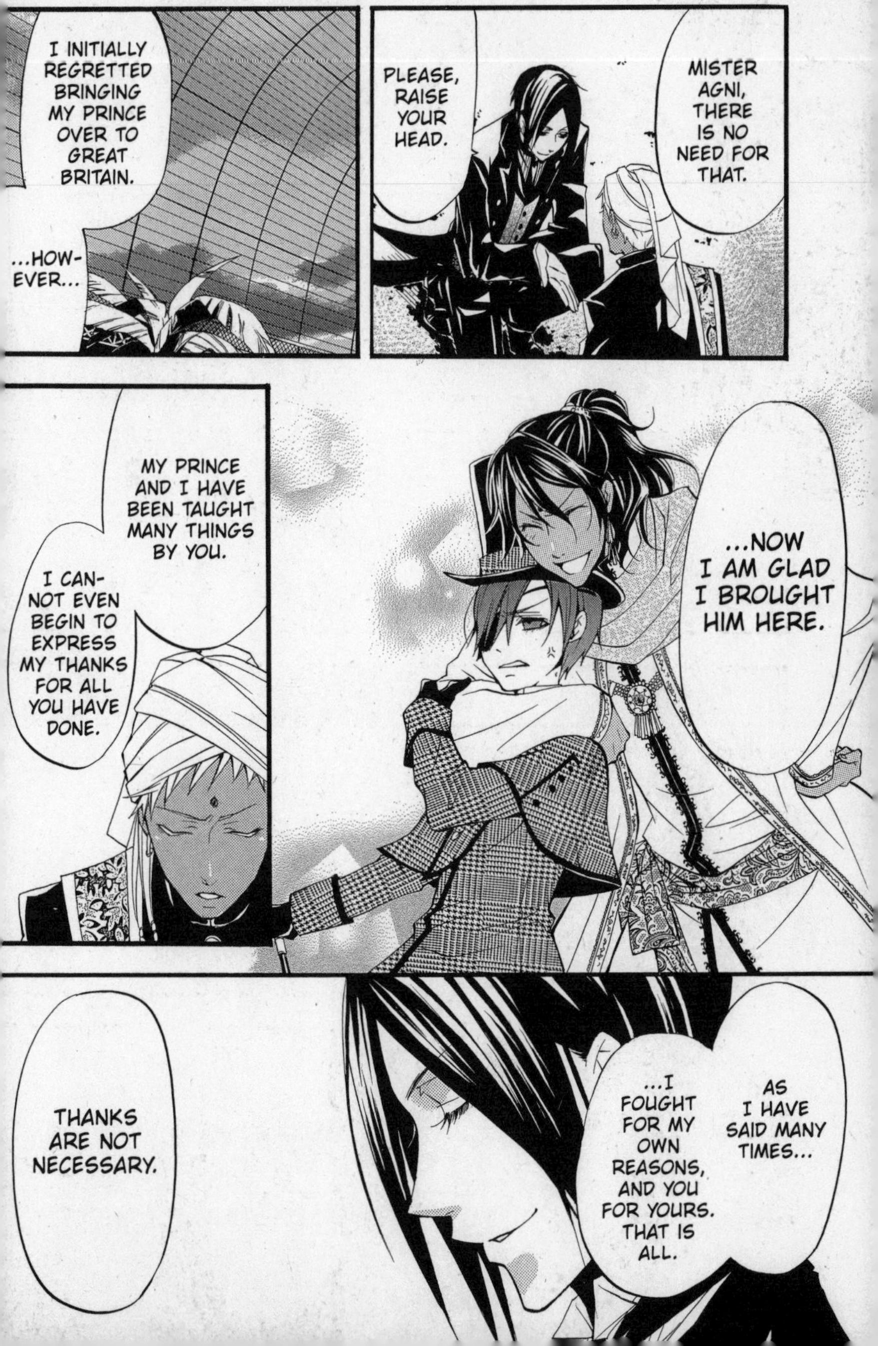
MISTER AGNI, THERE IS NO NEED FOR THAT.
PLEASE, RAISE YOUR HEAD.
I INITIALLY REGRETTED BRINGING MY PRINCE OVER TO GREAT BRITAIN.
...HOW-EVER...
...NOW I AM GLAD I BROUGHT HIM HERE.
MY PRINCE AND I HAVE BEEN TAUGHT MANY THINGS BY YOU.
I CAN-NOT EVEN BEGIN TO EXPRESS MY THANKS FOR ALL YOU HAVE DONE.
AS I HAVE SAID MANY TIMES...
...I FOUGHT FOR MY OWN REASONS, AND YOU FOR YOURS. THAT IS ALL.
THANKS ARE NOT NECESSARY.

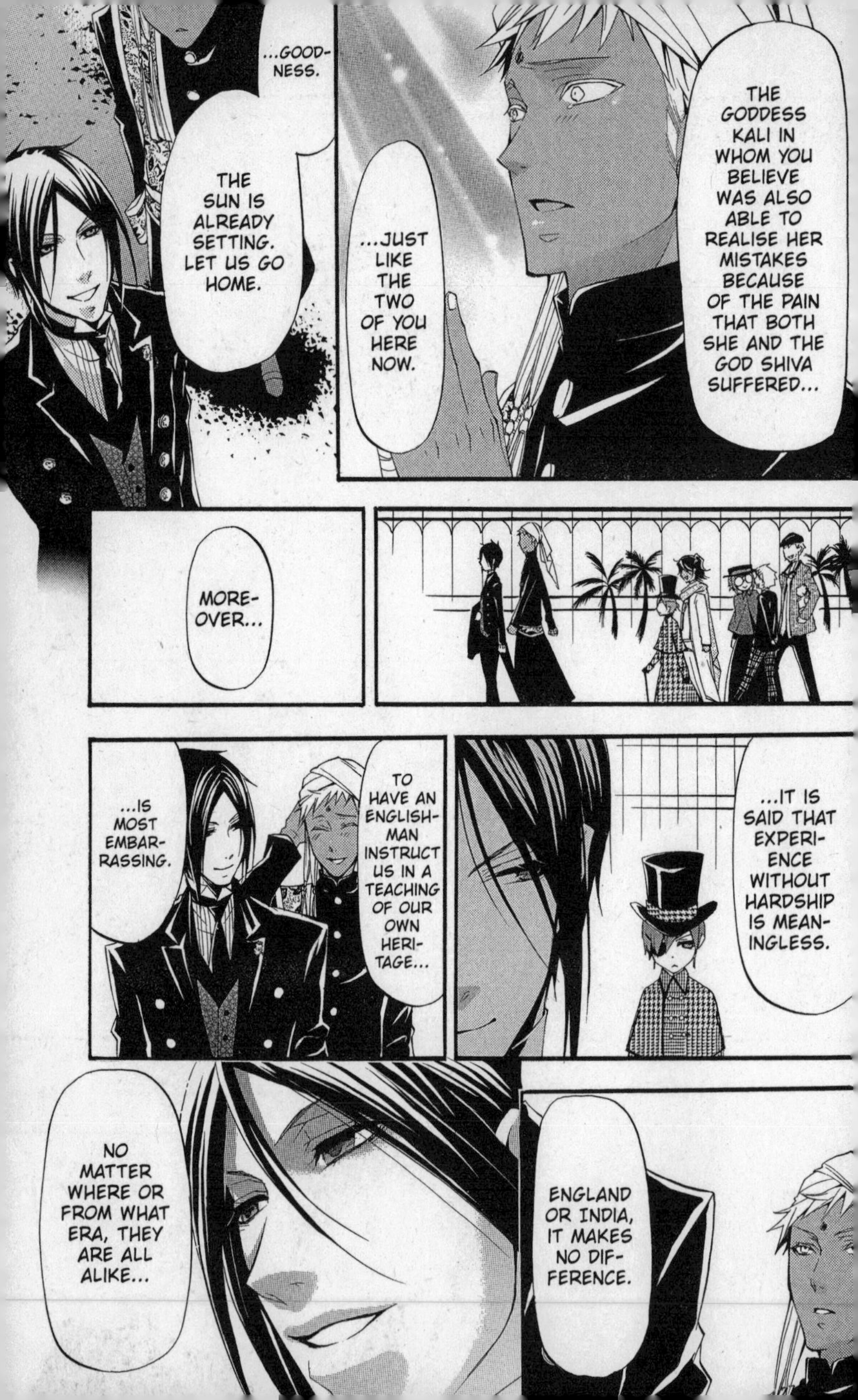
THE GODDESS KALI IN WHOM YOU BELIEVE WAS ALSO ABLE TO REALISE HER MISTAKES BECAUSE OF THE PAIN THAT BOTH SHE AND THE GOD SHIVA SUFFERED...
...JUST LIKE THE TWO OF YOU HERE NOW.
...GOODNESS.
THE SUN IS ALREADY SETTING. LET US GO HOME.
MOREOVER...
...IT IS SAID THAT EXPERIENCE WITHOUT HARDSHIP IS MEANINGLESS.
TO HAVE AN ENGLISHMAN INSTRUCT US IN A TEACHING OF OUR OWN HERITAGE...
...IS MOST EMBARRASSING.
ENGLAND OR INDIA, IT MAKES NO DIFFERENCE.
NO MATTER WHERE OR FROM WHAT ERA, THEY ARE ALL ALIKE...

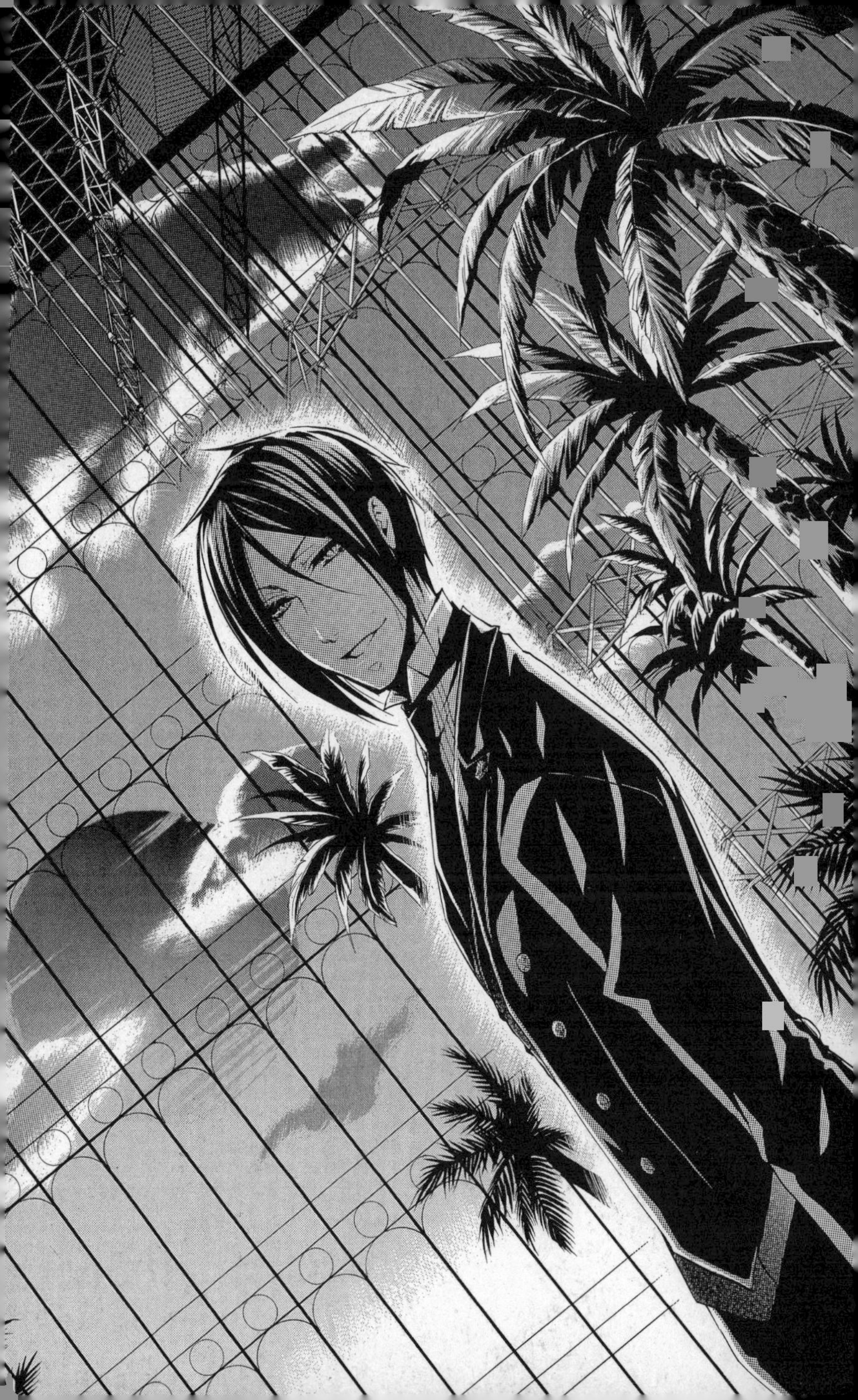

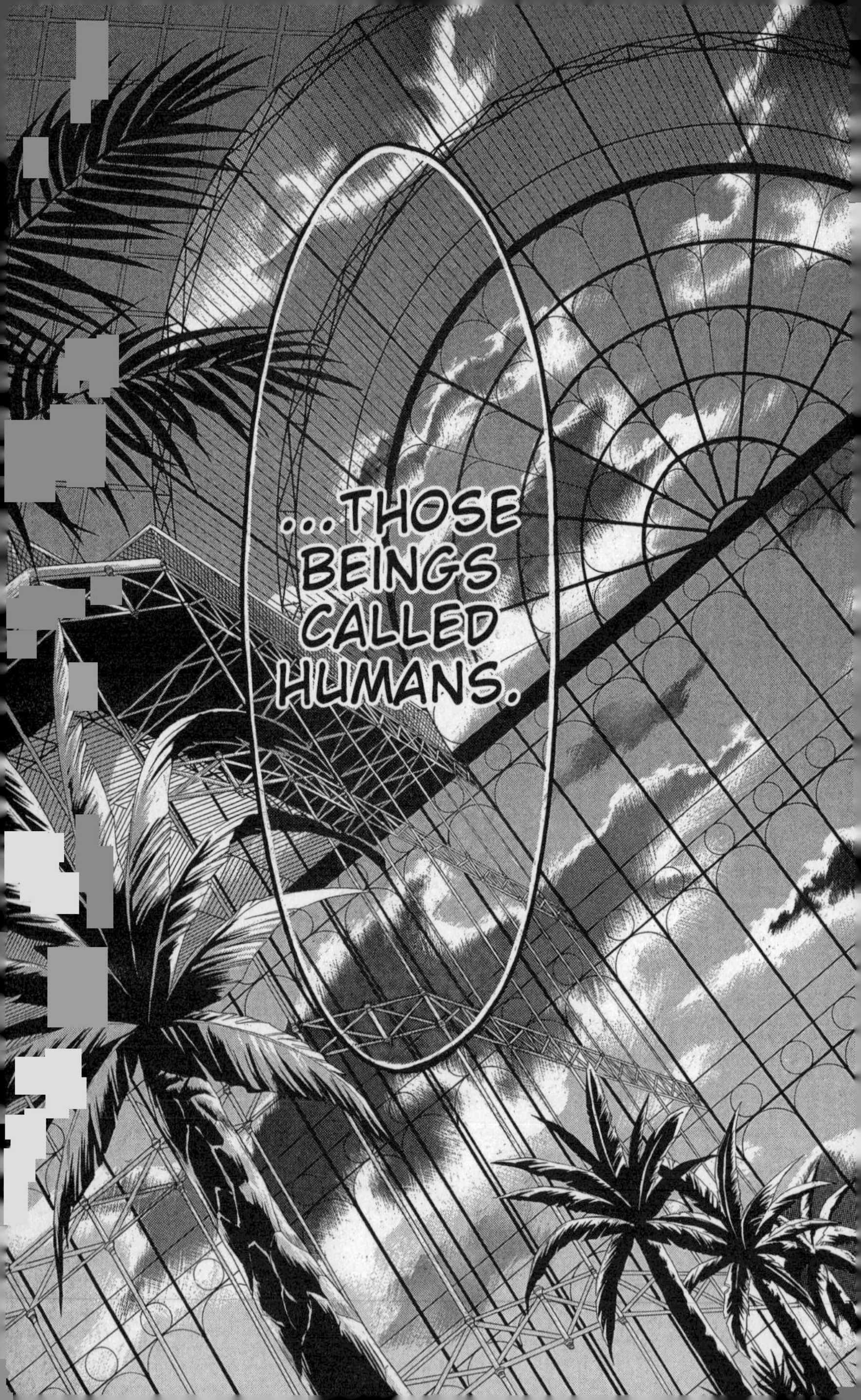
...THOSE BEINGS CALLED HUMANS.

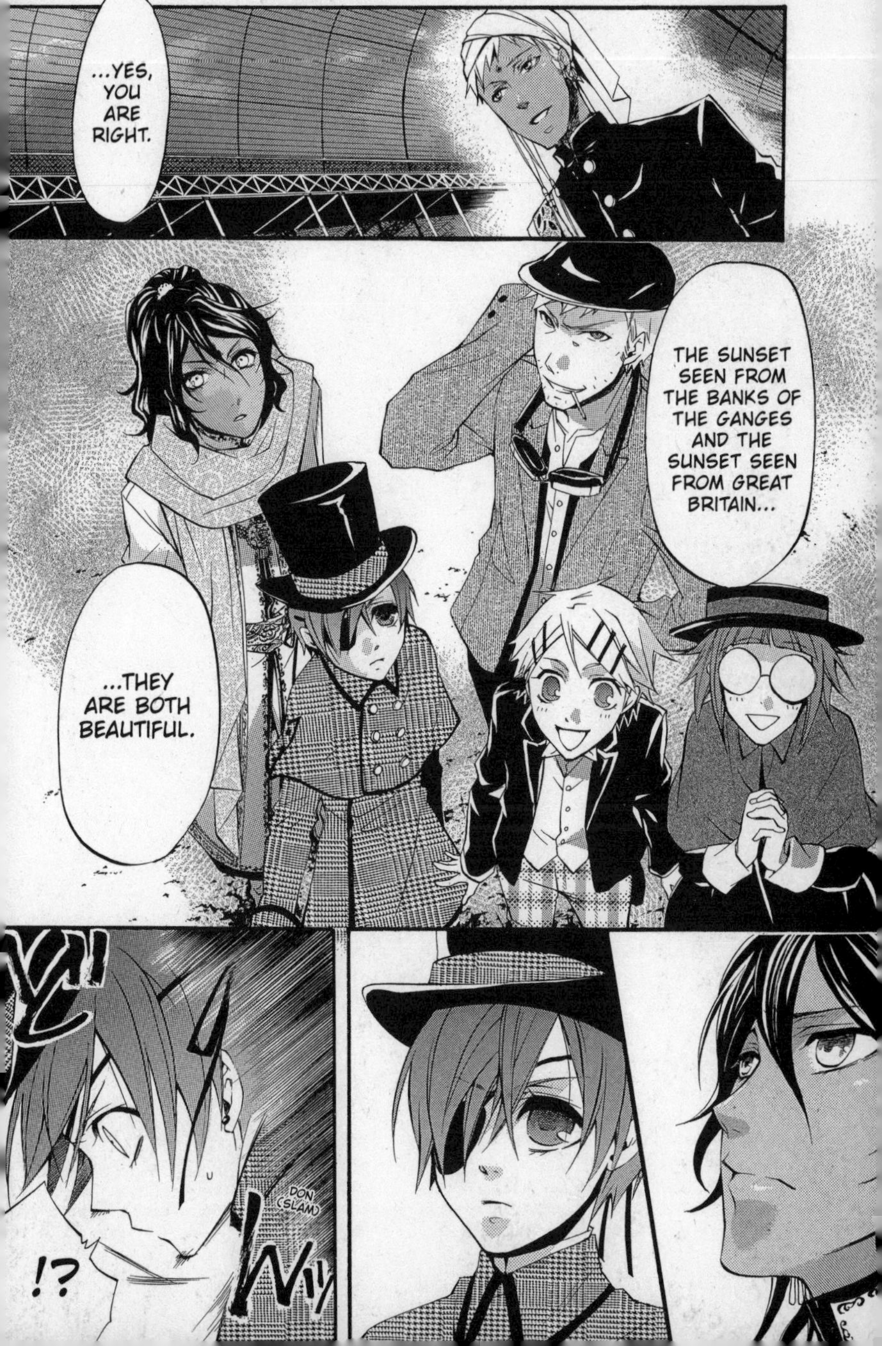
...YES, YOU ARE RIGHT.
THE SUNSET SEEN FROM THE BANKS OF THE GANGES AND THE SUNSET SEEN FROM GREAT BRITAIN...
...THEY ARE BOTH BEAUTIFUL.
DON (SLAM)
!?

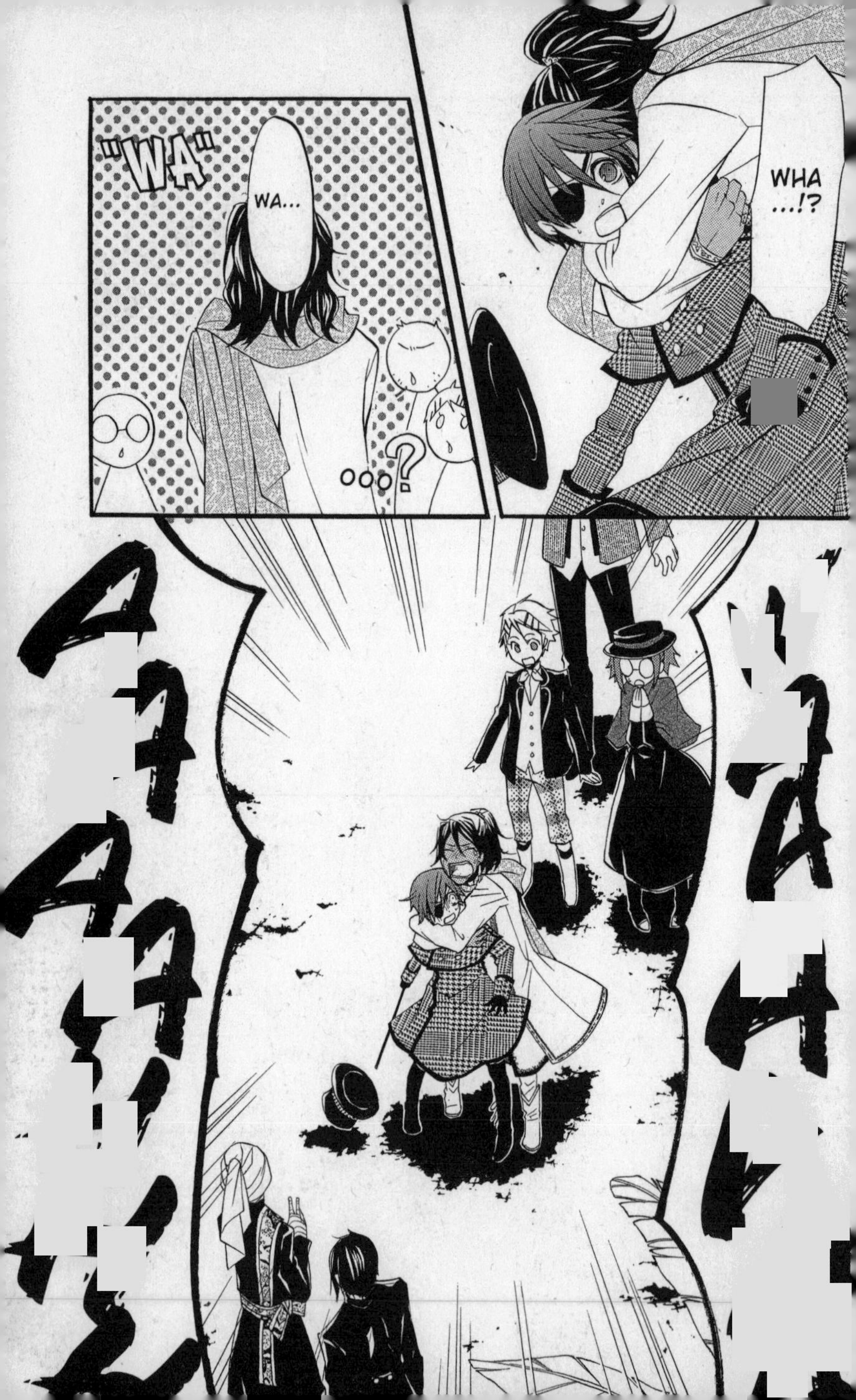
WHA ...!?
WA...
"WA"
ooo?

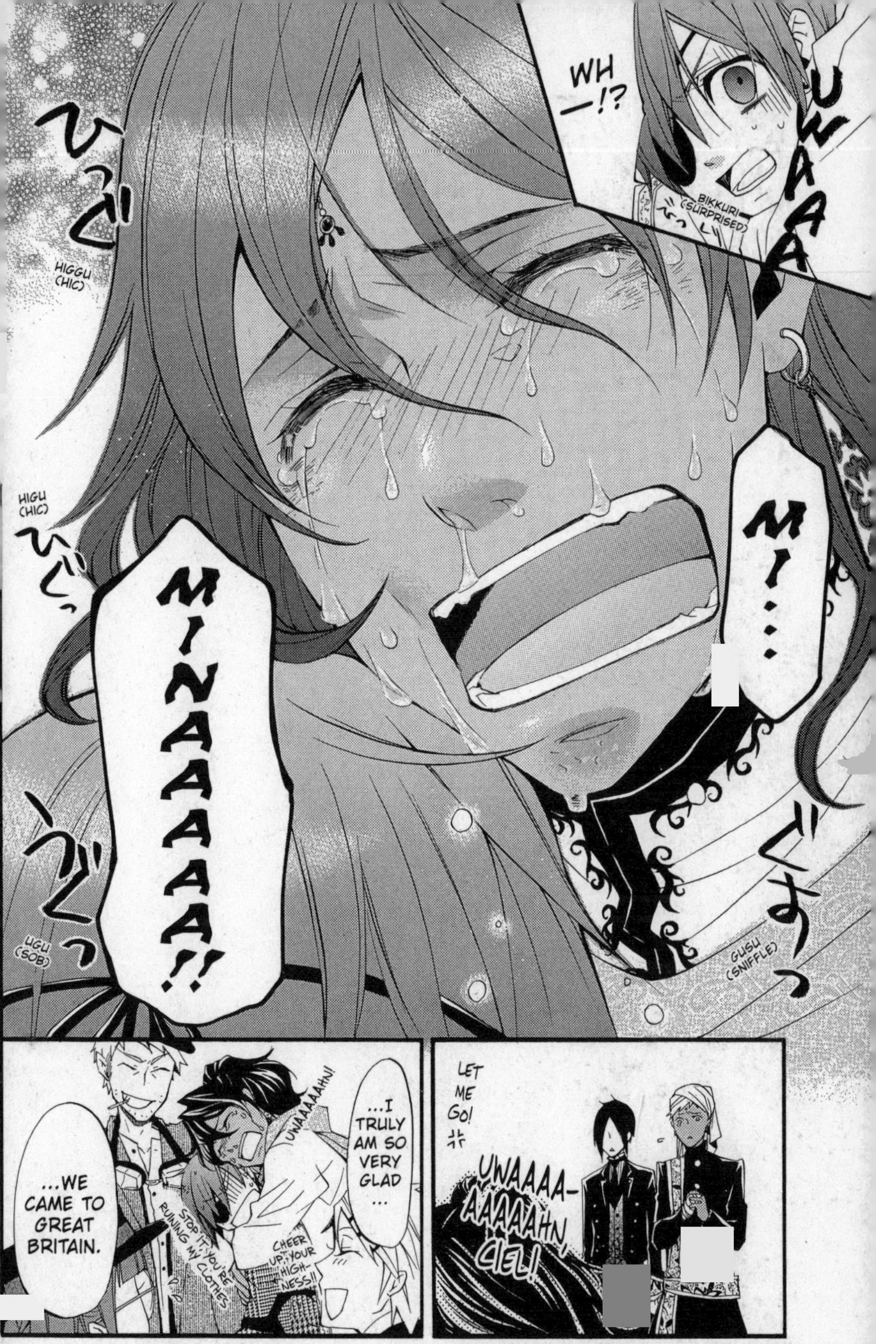
WH—!?
UWAAAA
びっくり
BIKKURI (SURPRISED)
MI...
MINAAAAAA!!
ぐすっ
GUSU (SNIFFLE)
ひっぐ
HIGGU (HIC)
ひぐっ
HIGU (HIC)
うぐっ
UGU (SOB)
LET ME GO!
UWAAAA-AAAAAHN, CIEL!
...I TRULY AM SO VERY GLAD...
UWAAAAAHN!
...WE CAME TO GREAT BRITAIN.
CHEER UP, YOUR HIGHNESS!!
STOP IT, YOU'RE RUINING MY CLOTHES

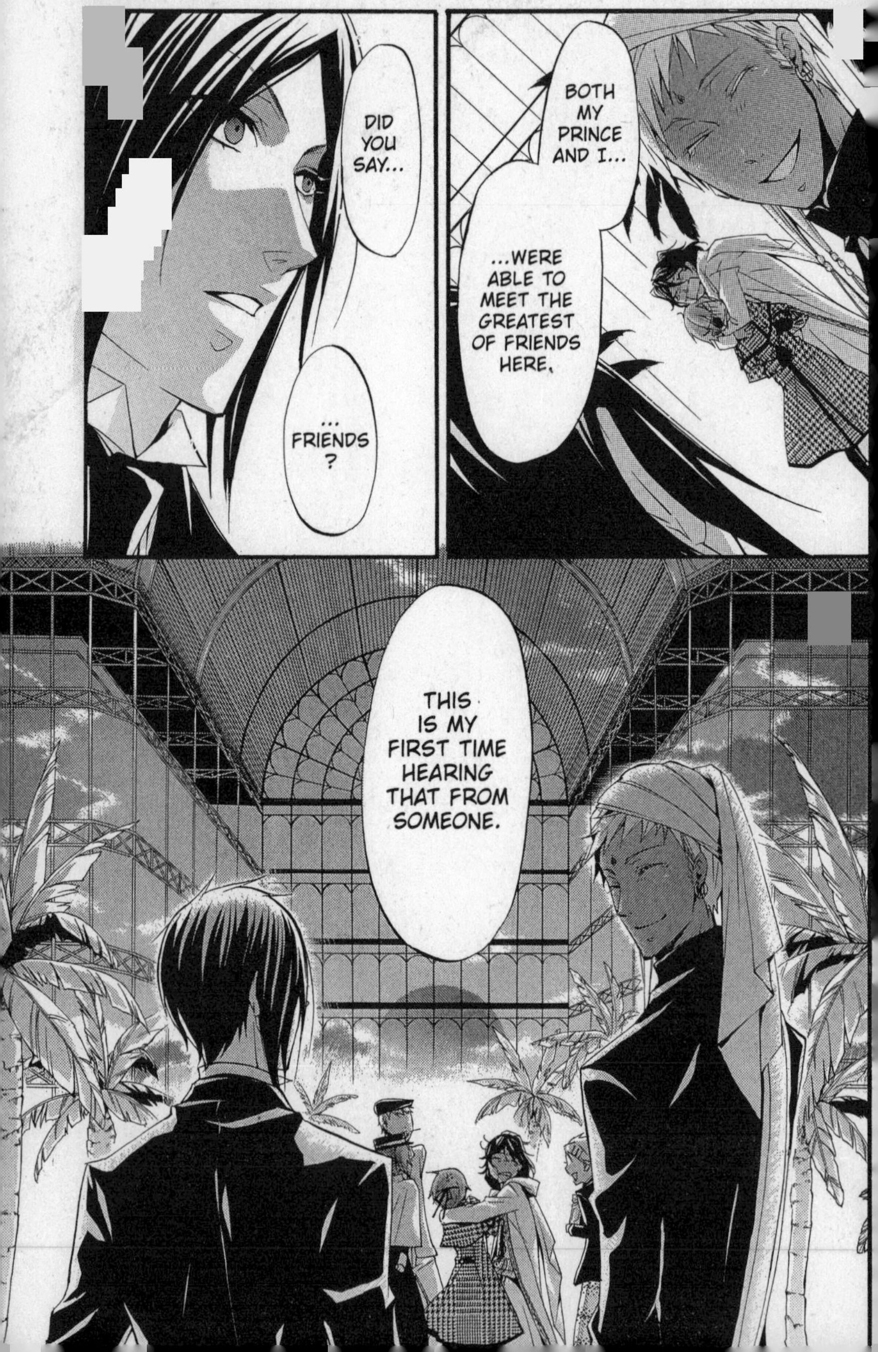
BOTH MY PRINCE AND I...
...WERE ABLE TO MEET THE GREATEST OF FRIENDS HERE.
DID YOU SAY...
...FRIENDS?
THIS IS MY FIRST TIME HEARING THAT FROM SOMEONE.

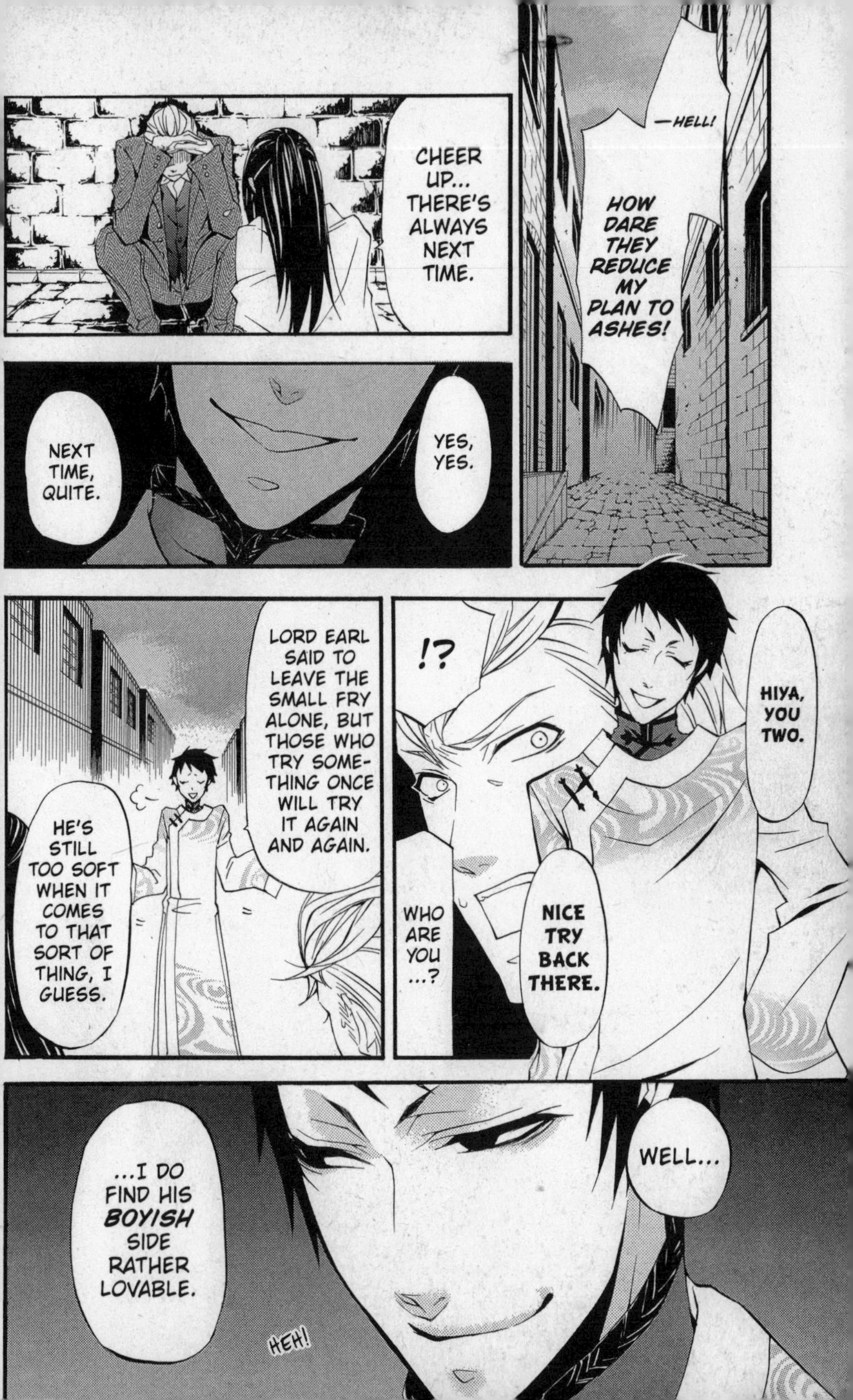
—HELL!
HOW DARE THEY REDUCE MY PLAN TO ASHES!
CHEER UP... THERE'S ALWAYS NEXT TIME.
YES, YES.
NEXT TIME, QUITE.
HIYA, YOU TWO.
!?
NICE TRY BACK THERE.
WHO ARE YOU ...?
LORD EARL SAID TO LEAVE THE SMALL FRY ALONE, BUT THOSE WHO TRY SOME-THING ONCE WILL TRY IT AGAIN AND AGAIN.
HE'S STILL TOO SOFT WHEN IT COMES TO THAT SORT OF THING, I GUESS.
WELL...
...I DO FIND HIS BOYISH SIDE RATHER LOVABLE.
HEH!

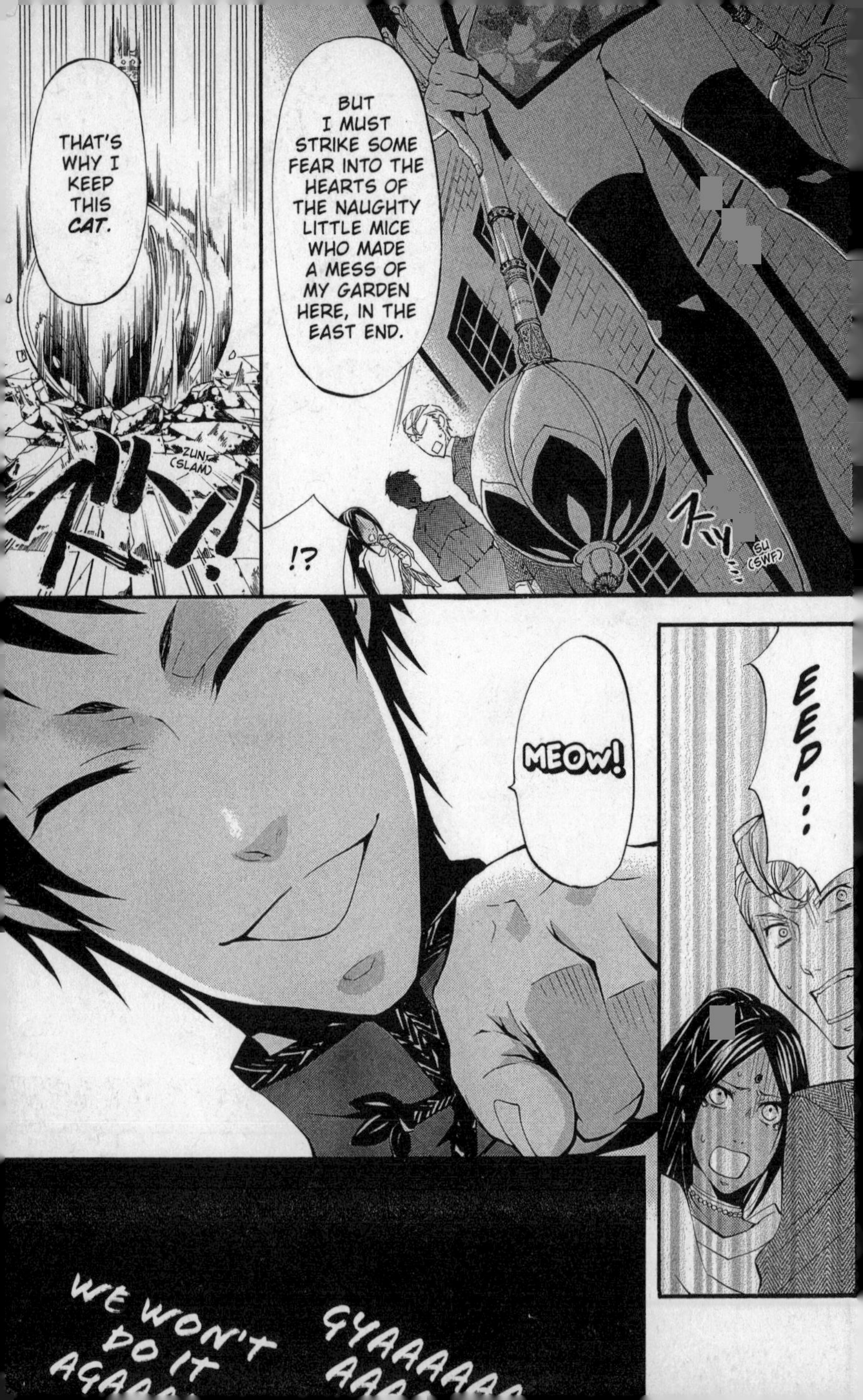

BUT I MUST STRIKE SOME FEAR INTO THE HEARTS OF THE NAUGHTY LITTLE MICE WHO MADE A MESS OF MY GARDEN HERE, IN THE EAST END.
SU (SWF)
!?
THAT'S WHY I KEEP THIS CAT.
ZUN (SLAM)
EEP...
MEOW!
GYAAAAAAA AAAAA
WE WON'T DO IT AGAAA

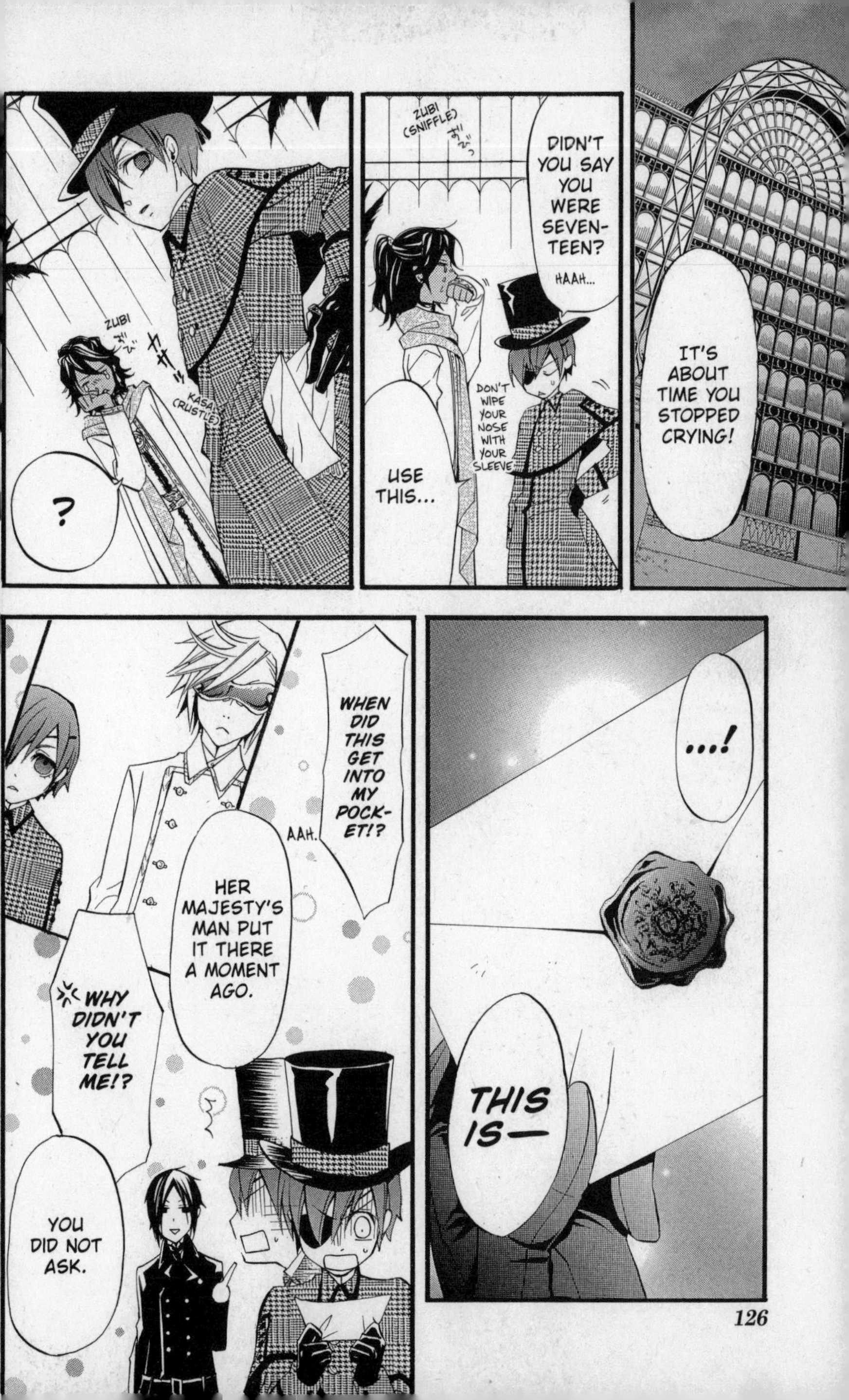
IT'S ABOUT TIME YOU STOPPED CRYING!
DIDN'T YOU SAY YOU WERE SEVENTEEN?
ZUBI (SNIFFLE)
HAAH...
DON'T WIPE YOUR NOSE WITH YOUR SLEEVE
USE THIS...
ZUBI
KASA (RUSTLE)
?
...!
THIS IS—
WHEN DID THIS GET INTO MY POCKET!?
AAH.
HER MAJESTY'S MAN PUT IT THERE A MOMENT AGO.
WHY DIDN'T YOU TELL ME!?
YOU DID NOT ASK.

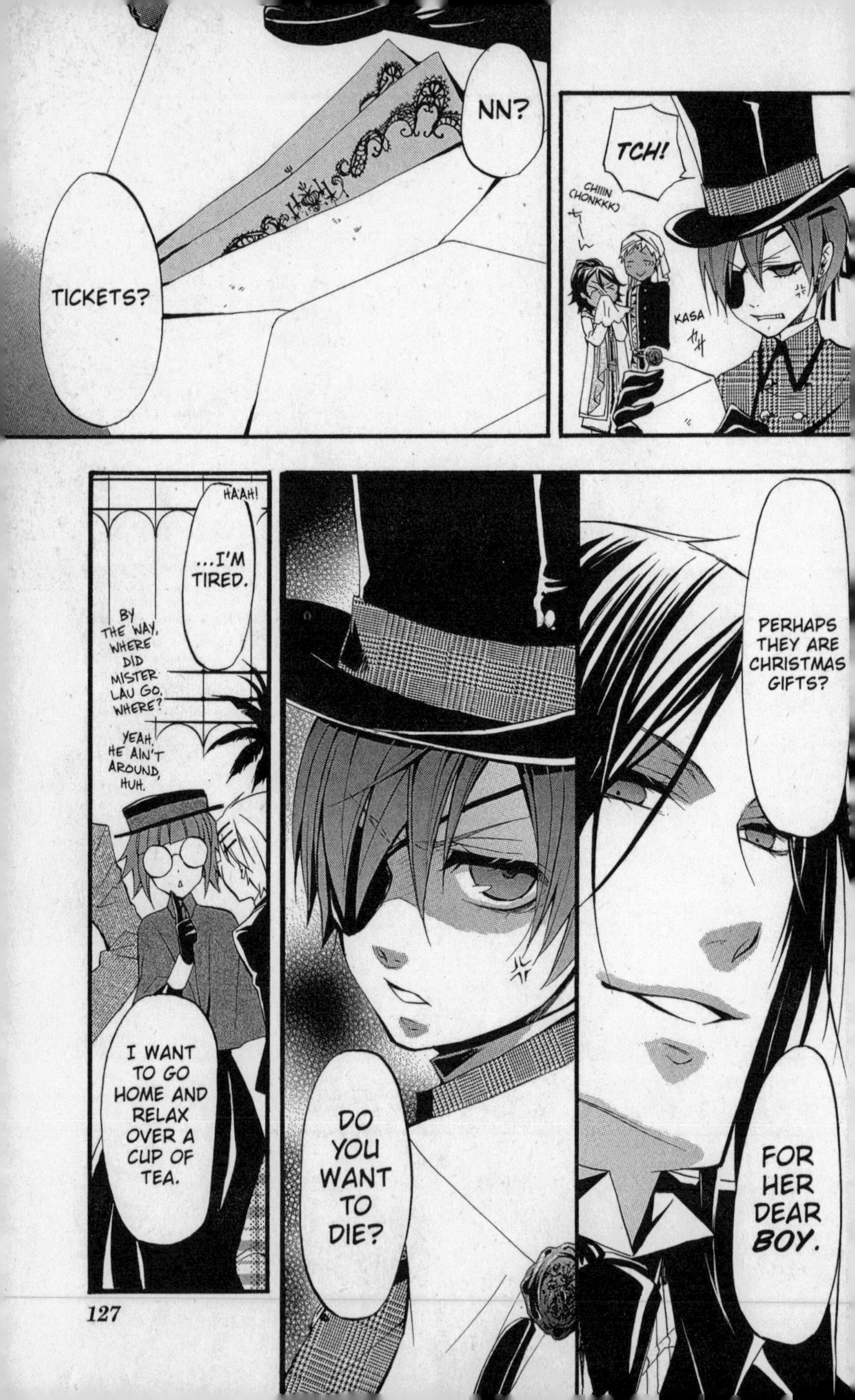
TCH!
CHIIIN (HONKKK)
KASA
NN?
TICKETS?
PERHAPS THEY ARE CHRISTMAS GIFTS?
FOR HER DEAR BOY.
DO YOU WANT TO DIE?
HA'AH!
...I'M TIRED.
BY THE WAY, WHERE DID MISTER LAU GO, WHERE?
YEAH, HE AIN'T AROUND, HUH.
I WANT TO GO HOME AND RELAX OVER A CUP OF TEA.

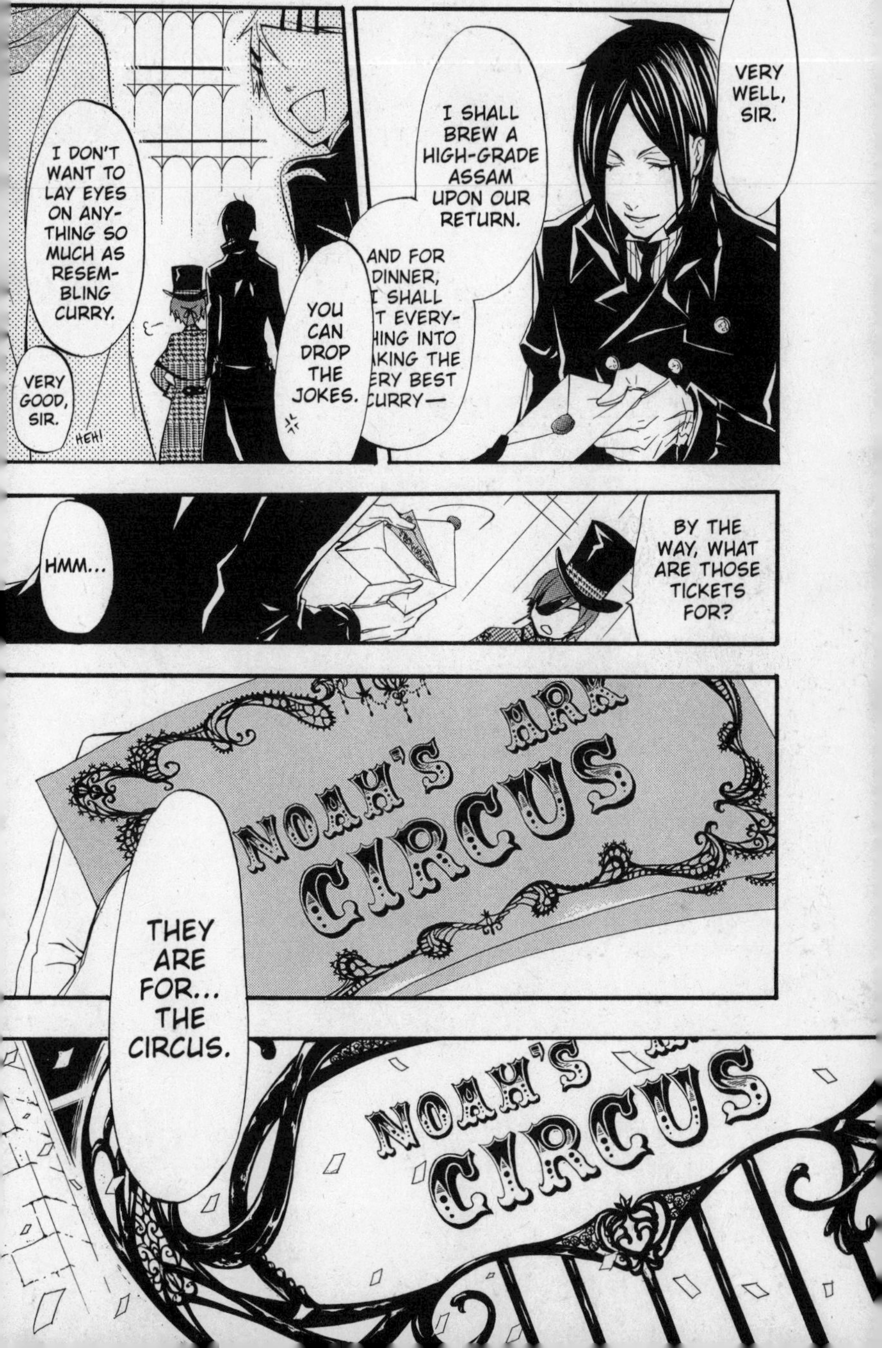
VERY WELL, SIR.
I SHALL BREW A HIGH-GRADE ASSAM UPON OUR RETURN.
AND FOR DINNER, I SHALL T EVERY-HING INTO AKING THE ERY BEST CURRY—
YOU CAN DROP THE JOKES.
I DON'T WANT TO LAY EYES ON ANY-THING SO MUCH AS RESEM-BLING CURRY.
VERY GOOD, SIR.
HEH!
BY THE WAY, WHAT ARE THOSE TICKETS FOR?
HMM...
NOAH'S ARK CIRCUS
THEY ARE FOR... THE CIRCUS.
NOAH'S CIRCUS

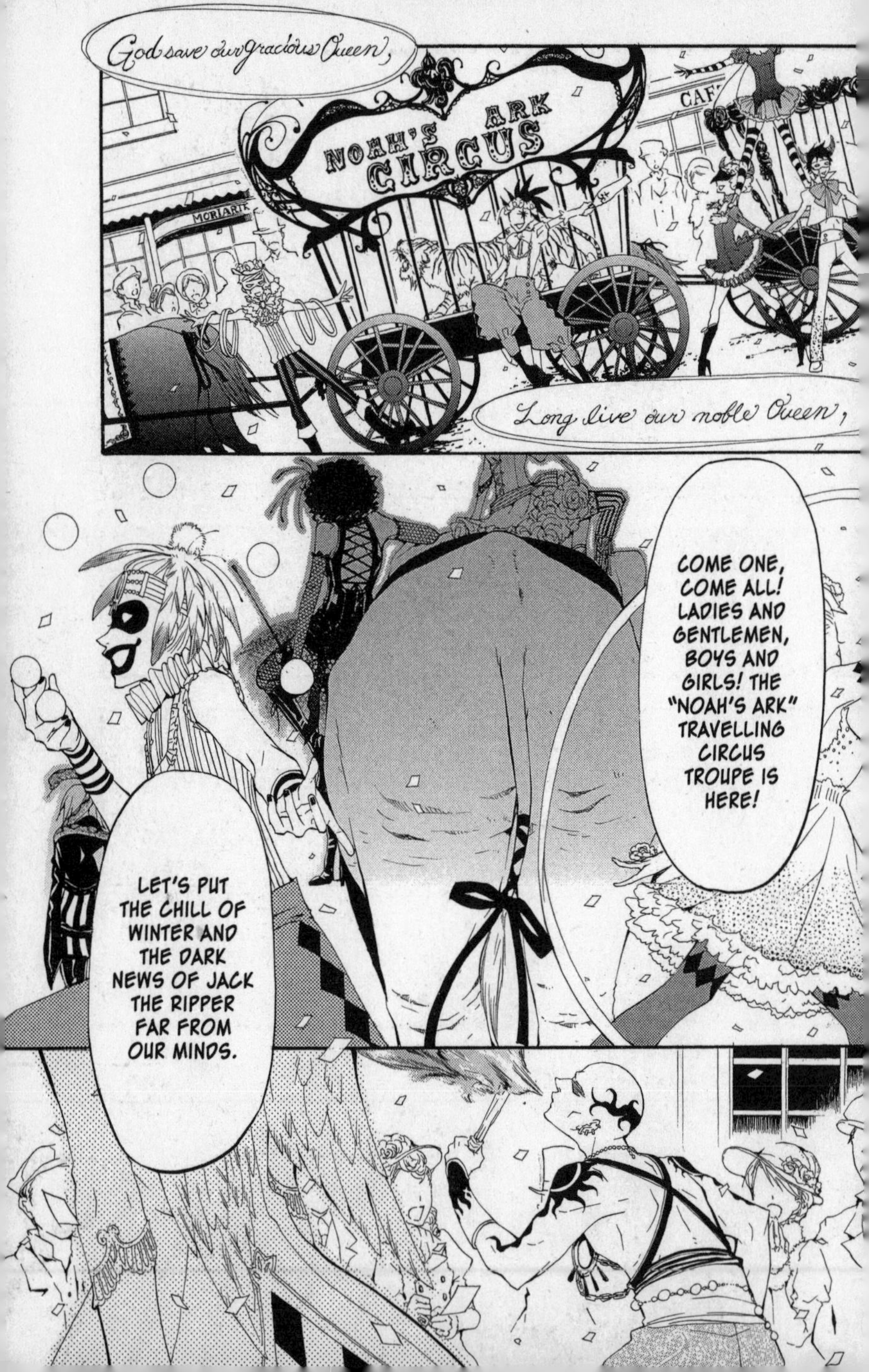

God save our gracious Queen,
NOAH'S ARK CIRCUS
Long live our noble Queen,
COME ONE, COME ALL! LADIES AND GENTLEMEN, BOYS AND GIRLS! THE "NOAH'S ARK" TRAVELLING CIRCUS TROUPE IS HERE!
LET'S PUT THE CHILL OF WINTER AND THE DARK NEWS OF JACK THE RIPPER FAR FROM OUR MINDS.

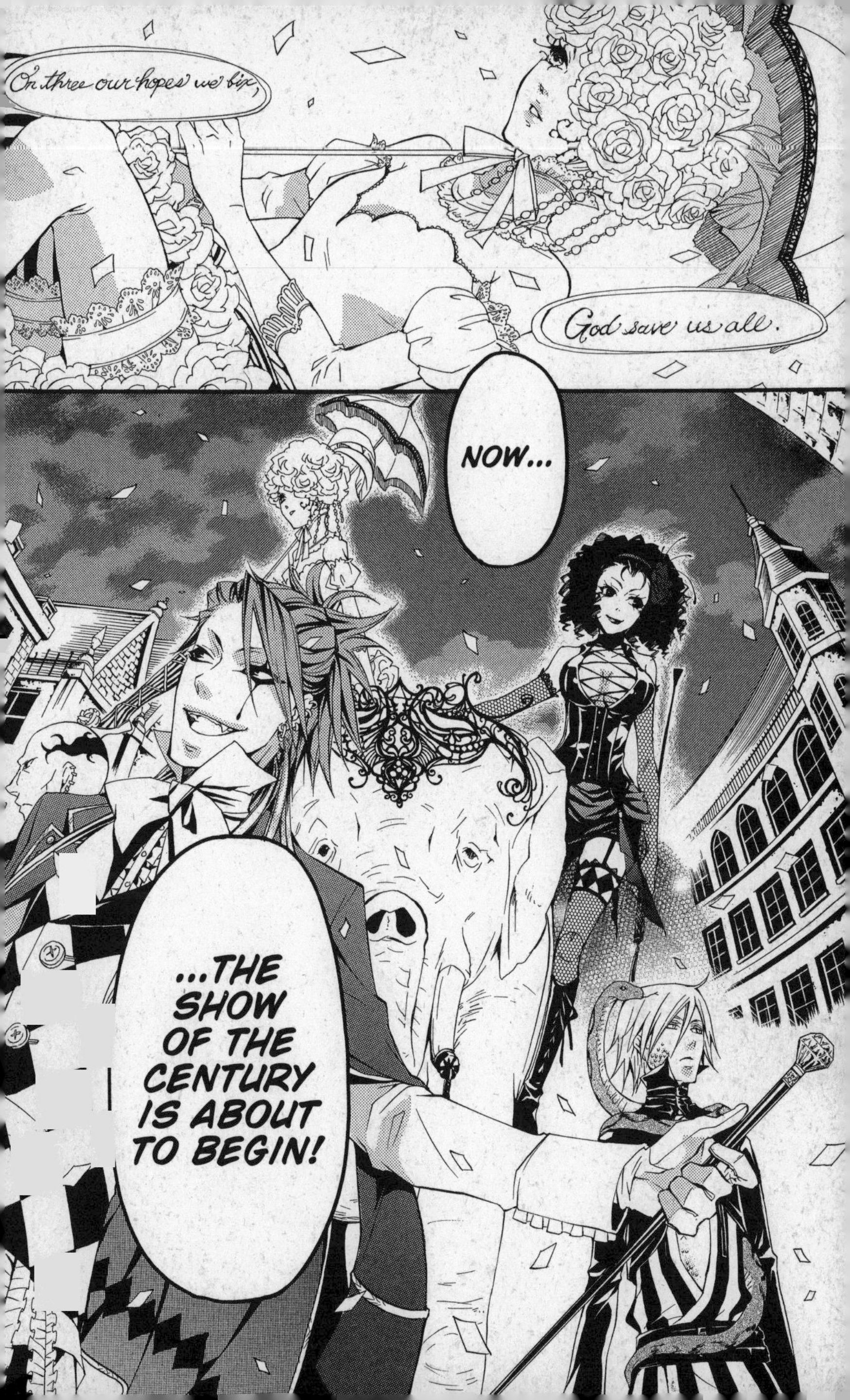
On three our hopes we fix,
God save us all.
NOW...
...THE SHOW OF THE CENTURY IS ABOUT TO BEGIN!

Black Butler

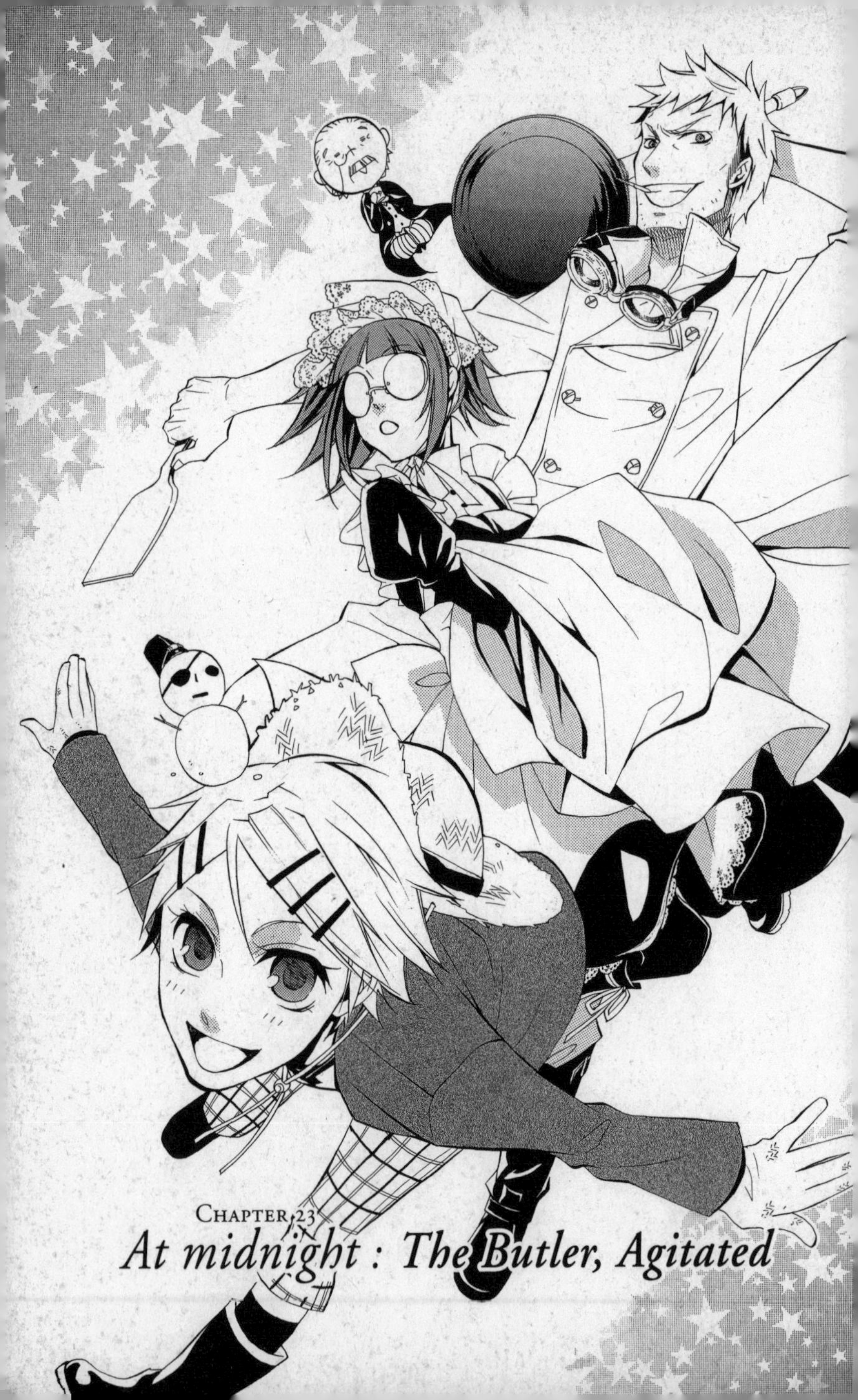

CHAPTER 23

At midnight : The Butler, Agitated

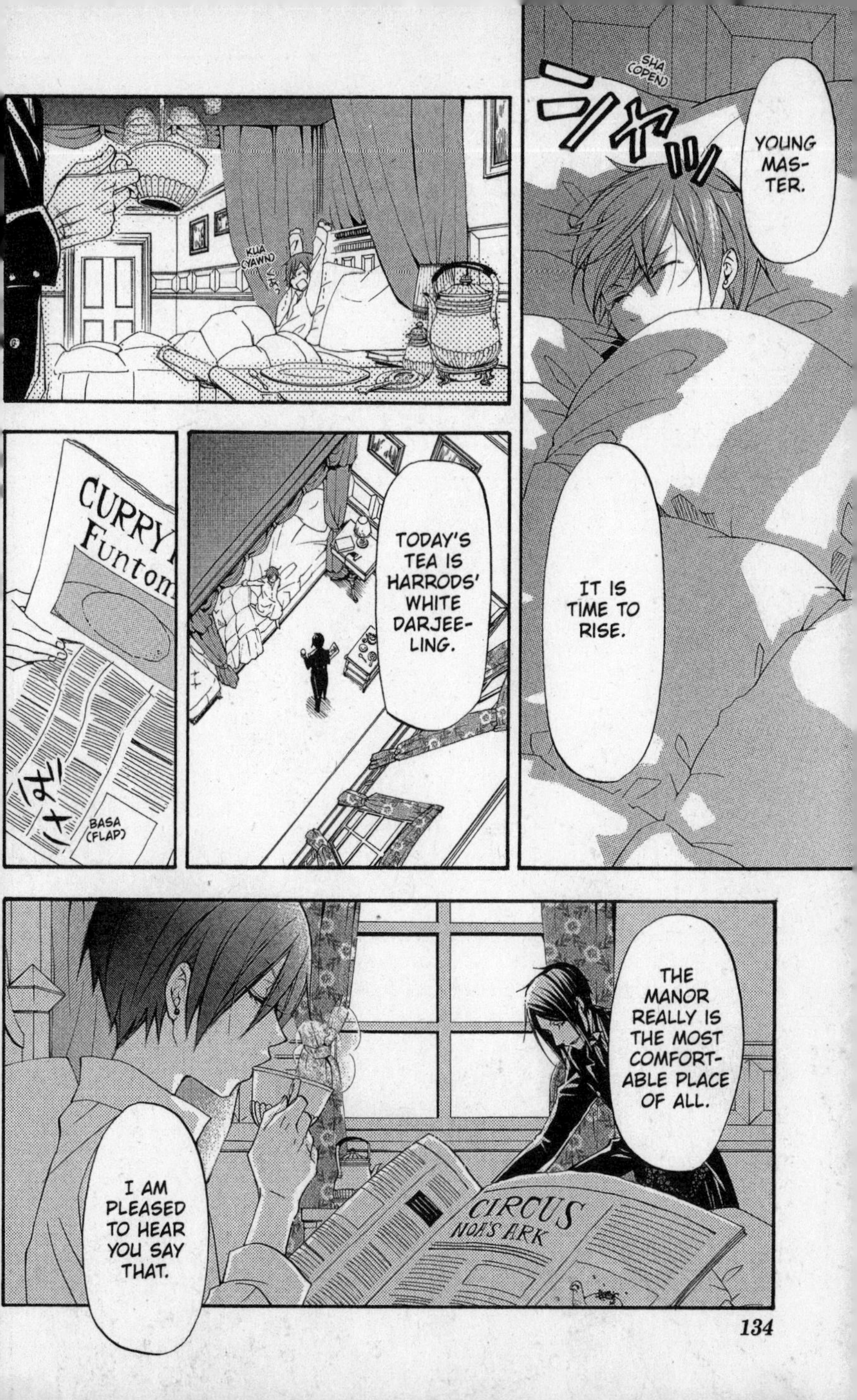
SHA (OPEN)
YOUNG MASTER.
IT IS TIME TO RISE.
KUA (YAWN)
TODAY'S TEA IS HARRODS' WHITE DARJEELING.
CURRY
Funtom
BASA (FLAP)
THE MANOR REALLY IS THE MOST COMFORTABLE PLACE OF ALL.
I AM PLEASED TO HEAR YOU SAY THAT.
CIRCUS
NOA'S ARK

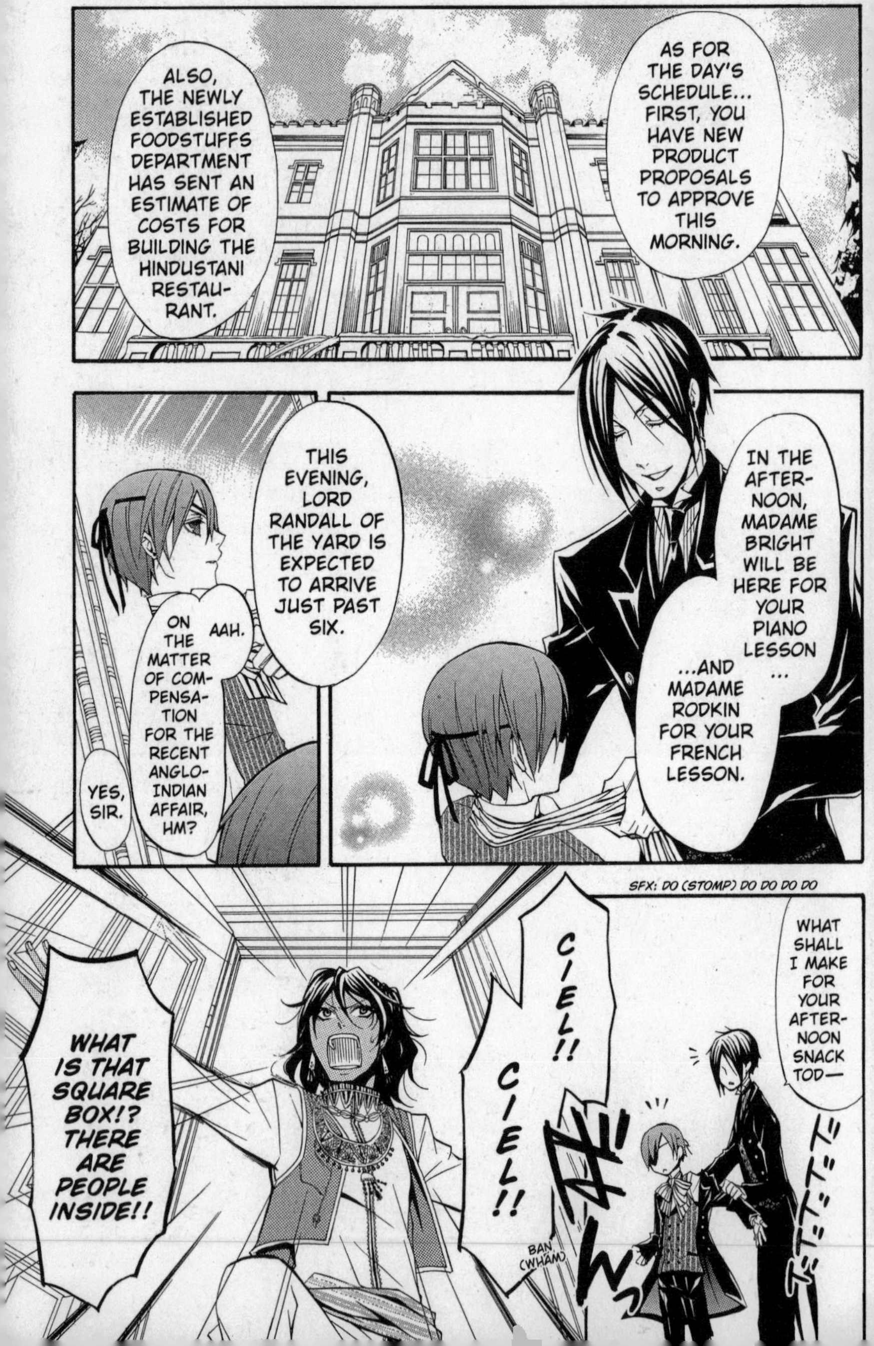
AS FOR THE DAY'S SCHEDULE... FIRST, YOU HAVE NEW PRODUCT PROPOSALS TO APPROVE THIS MORNING.
ALSO, THE NEWLY ESTABLISHED FOODSTUFFS DEPARTMENT HAS SENT AN ESTIMATE OF COSTS FOR BUILDING THE HINDUSTANI RESTAU-RANT.
IN THE AFTER-NOON, MADAME BRIGHT WILL BE HERE FOR YOUR PIANO LESSON...
...AND MADAME RODKIN FOR YOUR FRENCH LESSON.
THIS EVENING, LORD RANDALL OF THE YARD IS EXPECTED TO ARRIVE JUST PAST SIX.
AAH.
ON THE MATTER OF COM-PENSA-TION FOR THE RECENT ANGLO-INDIAN AFFAIR, HM?
YES, SIR.
SFX: DO (STOMP) DO DO DO DO
WHAT SHALL I MAKE FOR YOUR AFTER-NOON SNACK TOD—
BAN (WHAM)
CIEL!!
CIEL!!
WHAT IS THAT SQUARE BOX!? THERE ARE PEOPLE INSIDE!!

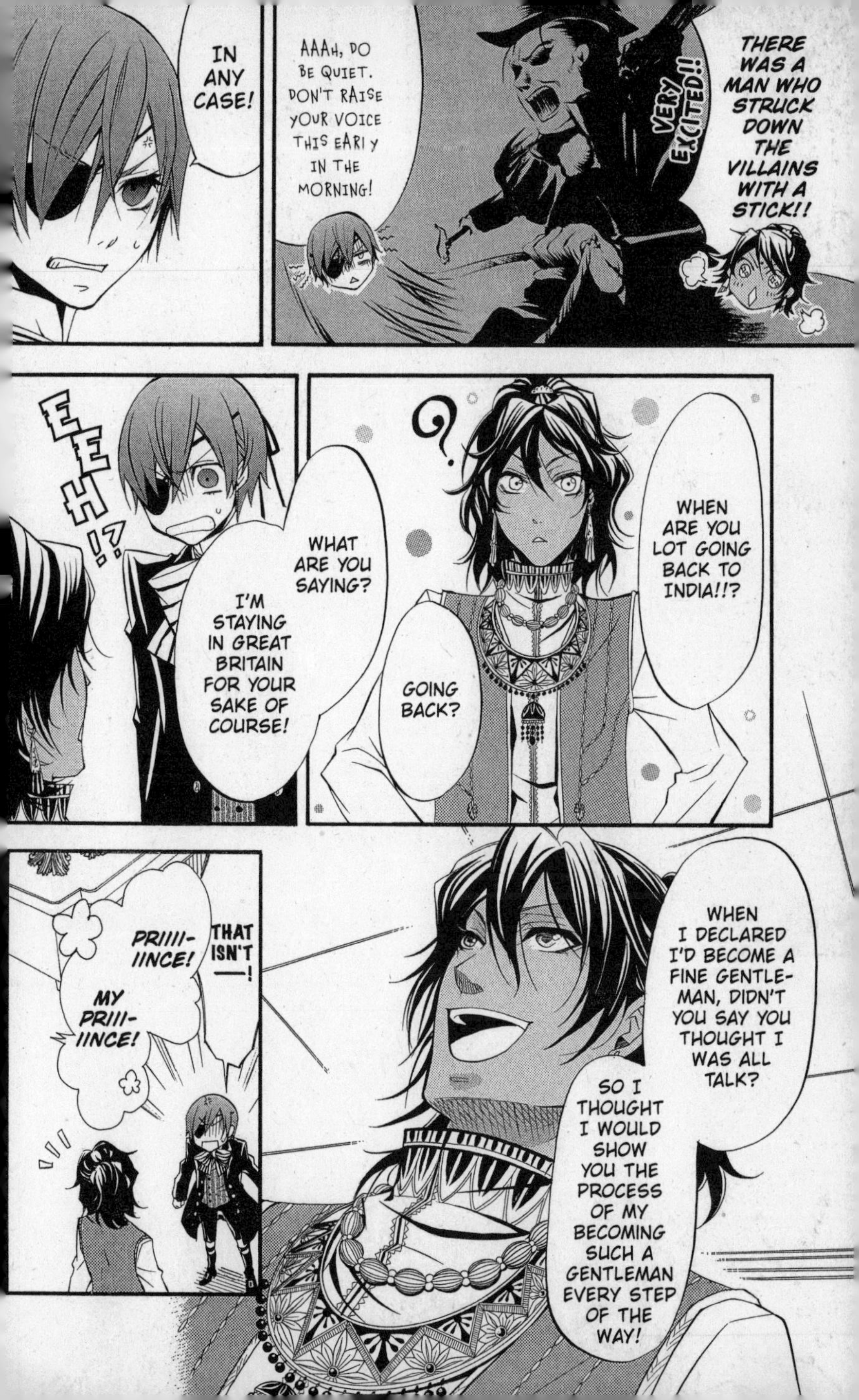

THERE WAS A MAN WHO STRUCK DOWN THE VILLAINS WITH A STICK!!
VERY EXCITED!!
AAAH, DO BE QUIET. DON'T RAISE YOUR VOICE THIS EARLY IN THE MORNING!
IN ANY CASE!
WHEN ARE YOU LOT GOING BACK TO INDIA!!?
?
GOING BACK?
EEH!?
WHAT ARE YOU SAYING?
I'M STAYING IN GREAT BRITAIN FOR YOUR SAKE OF COURSE!
WHEN I DECLARED I'D BECOME A FINE GENTLE-MAN, DIDN'T YOU SAY YOU THOUGHT I WAS ALL TALK?
SO I THOUGHT I WOULD SHOW YOU THE PROCESS OF MY BECOMING SUCH A GENTLEMAN EVERY STEP OF THE WAY!
THAT ISN'T—!
PRIIII-IINCE!
MY PRIIII-IINCE!

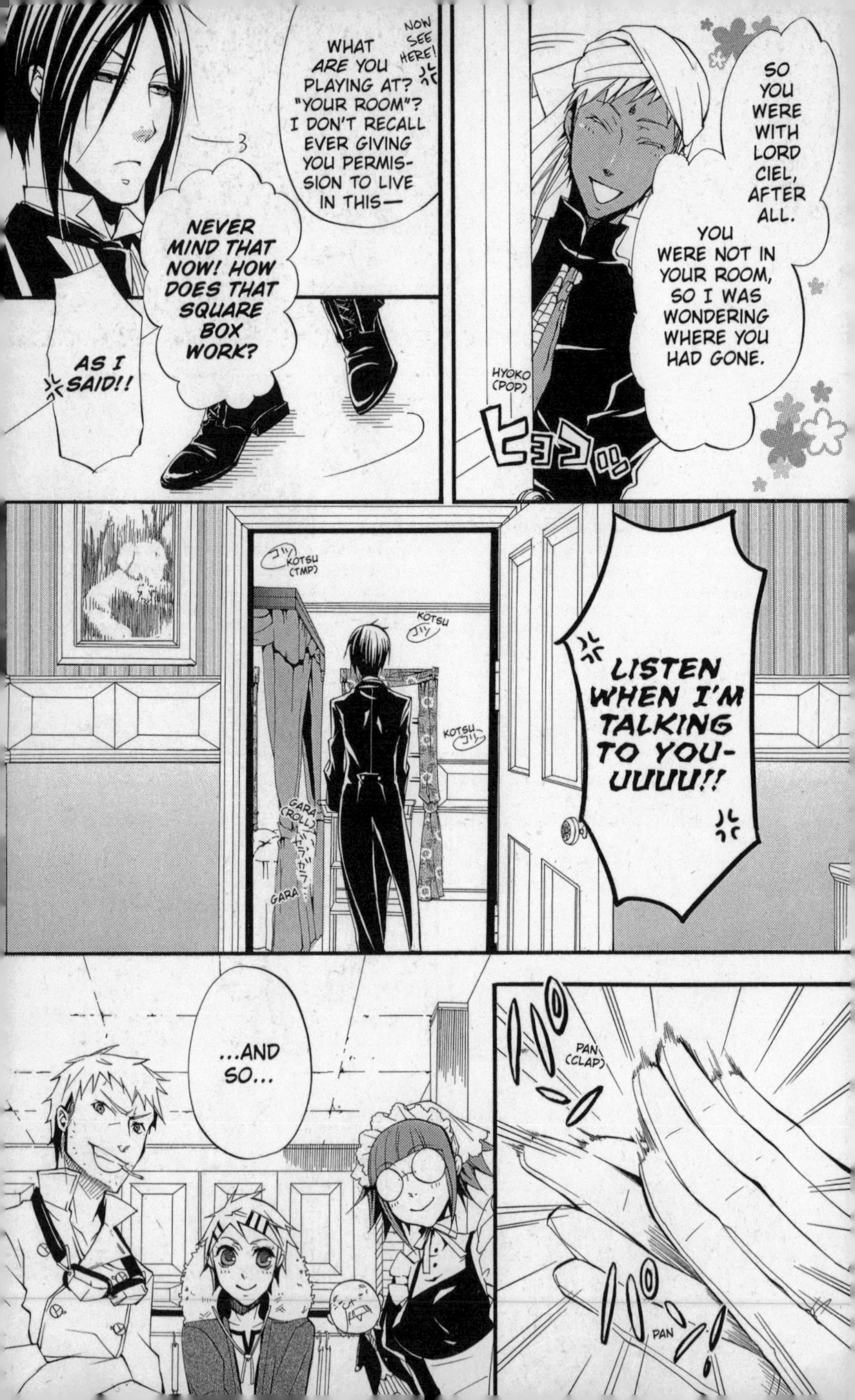
SO YOU WERE WITH LORD CIEL, AFTER ALL.
YOU WERE NOT IN YOUR ROOM, SO I WAS WONDERING WHERE YOU HAD GONE.
HYOKO (POP)
WHAT ARE YOU PLAYING AT? "YOUR ROOM"? I DON'T RECALL EVER GIVING YOU PERMISSION TO LIVE IN THIS—
NOW SEE HERE!
NEVER MIND THAT NOW! HOW DOES THAT SQUARE BOX WORK?
AS I SAID!!
LISTEN WHEN I'M TALKING TO YOU-UUUU!!
KOTSU (TMP)
KOTSU
KOTSU
GARA (ROLL)
GARA
PAN (CLAP)
PAN
...AND SO...

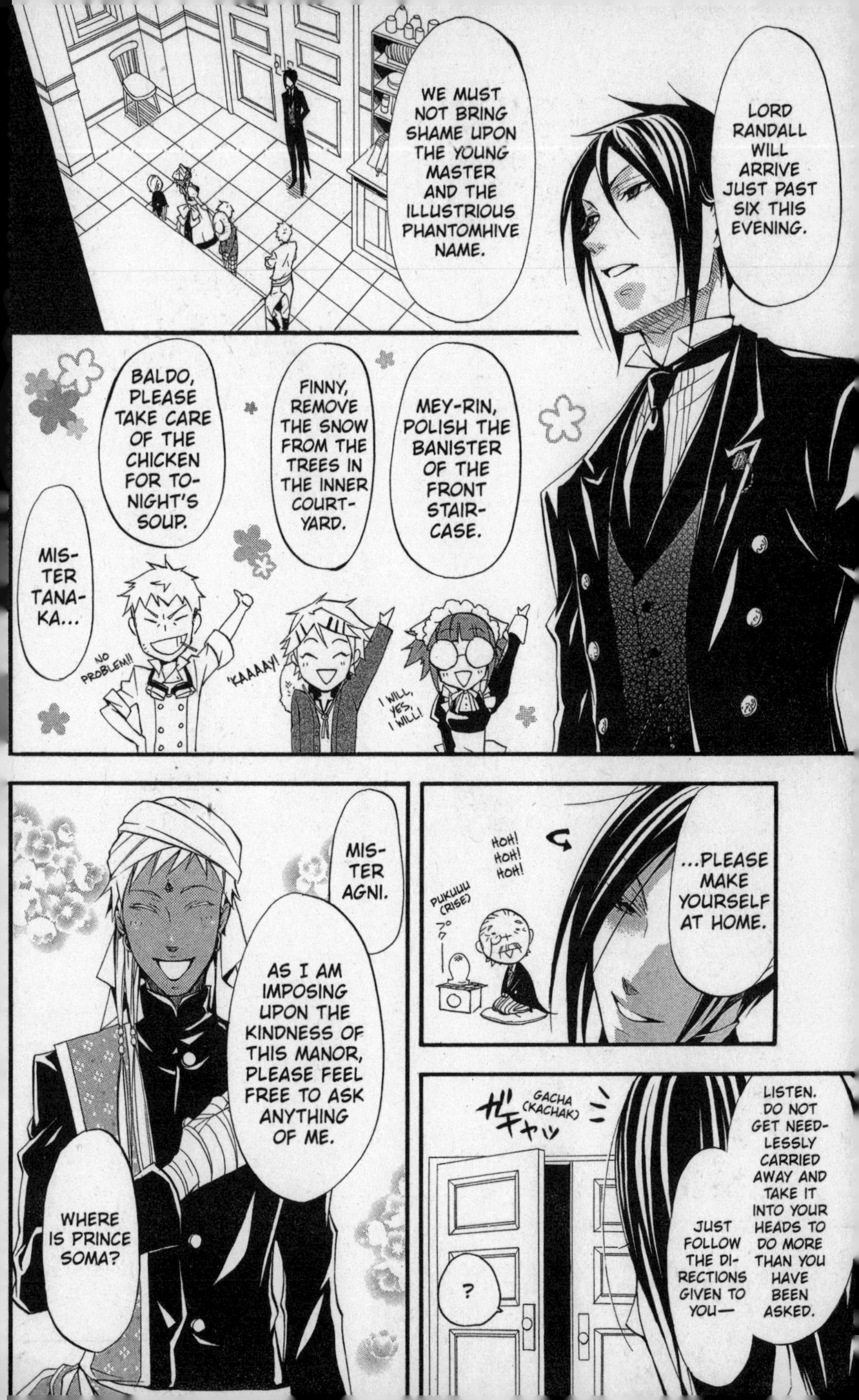

LORD RANDALL WILL ARRIVE JUST PAST SIX THIS EVENING.
WE MUST NOT BRING SHAME UPON THE YOUNG MASTER AND THE ILLUSTRIOUS PHANTOMHIVE NAME.
MEY-RIN, POLISH THE BANISTER OF THE FRONT STAIR-CASE.
FINNY, REMOVE THE SNOW FROM THE TREES IN THE INNER COURT-YARD.
BALDO, PLEASE TAKE CARE OF THE CHICKEN FOR TO-NIGHT'S SOUP.
MIS-TER TANA-KA...
I WILL, YES, I WILL!
'KAAAAY!
NO PROBLEM!!
...PLEASE MAKE YOURSELF AT HOME.
HOH! HOH! HOH!
PUKUUU (RISE)
GACHA (KACHAK)
LISTEN. DO NOT GET NEED-LESSLY CARRIED AWAY AND TAKE IT INTO YOUR HEADS TO DO MORE THAN YOU HAVE BEEN ASKED.
JUST FOLLOW THE DI-RECTIONS GIVEN TO YOU—
?
MIS-TER AGNI.
AS I AM IMPOSING UPON THE KINDNESS OF THIS MANOR, PLEASE FEEL FREE TO ASK ANYTHING OF ME.
WHERE IS PRINCE SOMA?

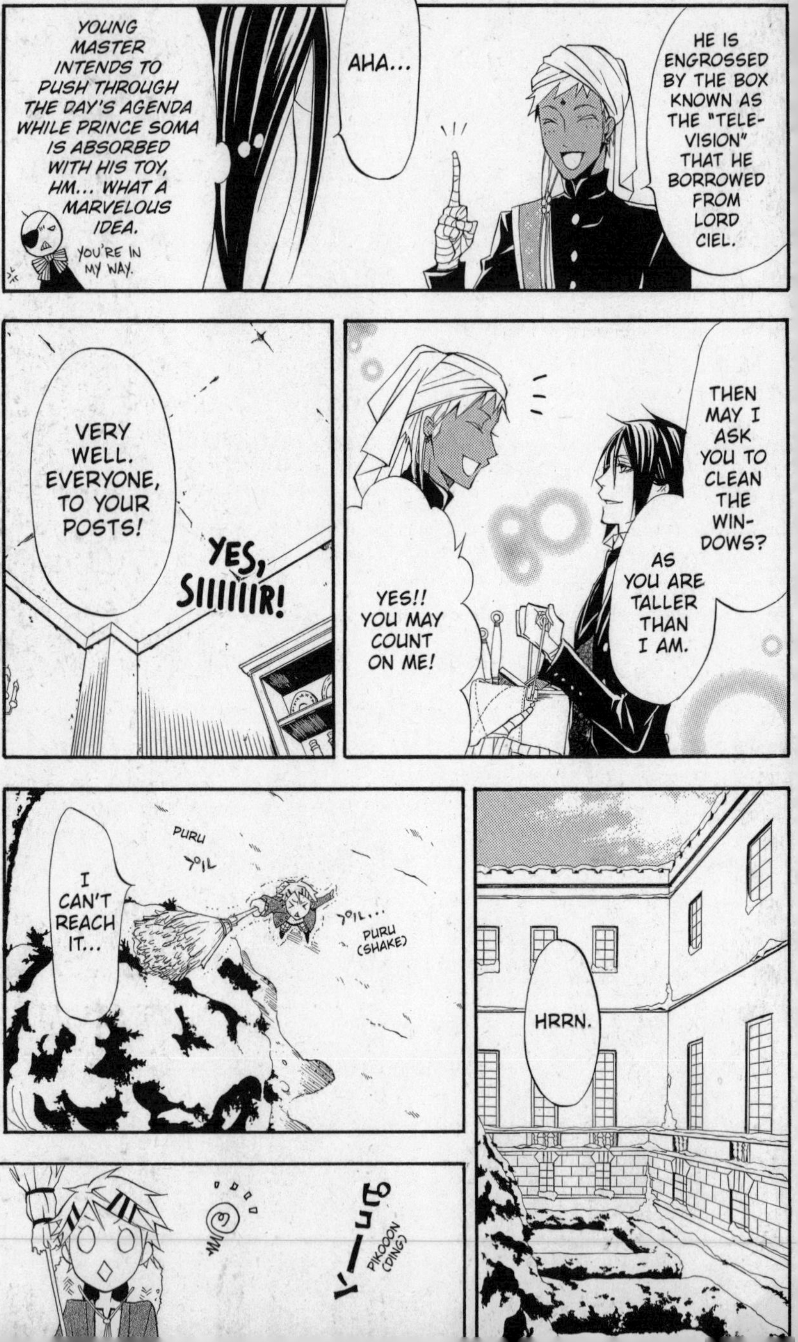
HE IS ENGROSSED BY THE BOX KNOWN AS THE "TELE-VISION" THAT HE BORROWED FROM LORD CIEL.
AHA...
YOUNG MASTER INTENDS TO PUSH THROUGH THE DAY'S AGENDA WHILE PRINCE SOMA IS ABSORBED WITH HIS TOY, HM... WHAT A MARVELOUS IDEA.
YOU'RE IN MY WAY.
THEN MAY I ASK YOU TO CLEAN THE WIN-DOWS?
AS YOU ARE TALLER THAN I AM.
YES!! YOU MAY COUNT ON ME!
VERY WELL. EVERYONE, TO YOUR POSTS!
YES, SIIIIIIR!
HRRN.
I CAN'T REACH IT...
PURU
プル
プル...
PURU (SHAKE)
ピコーン
PIKOOON (DING)

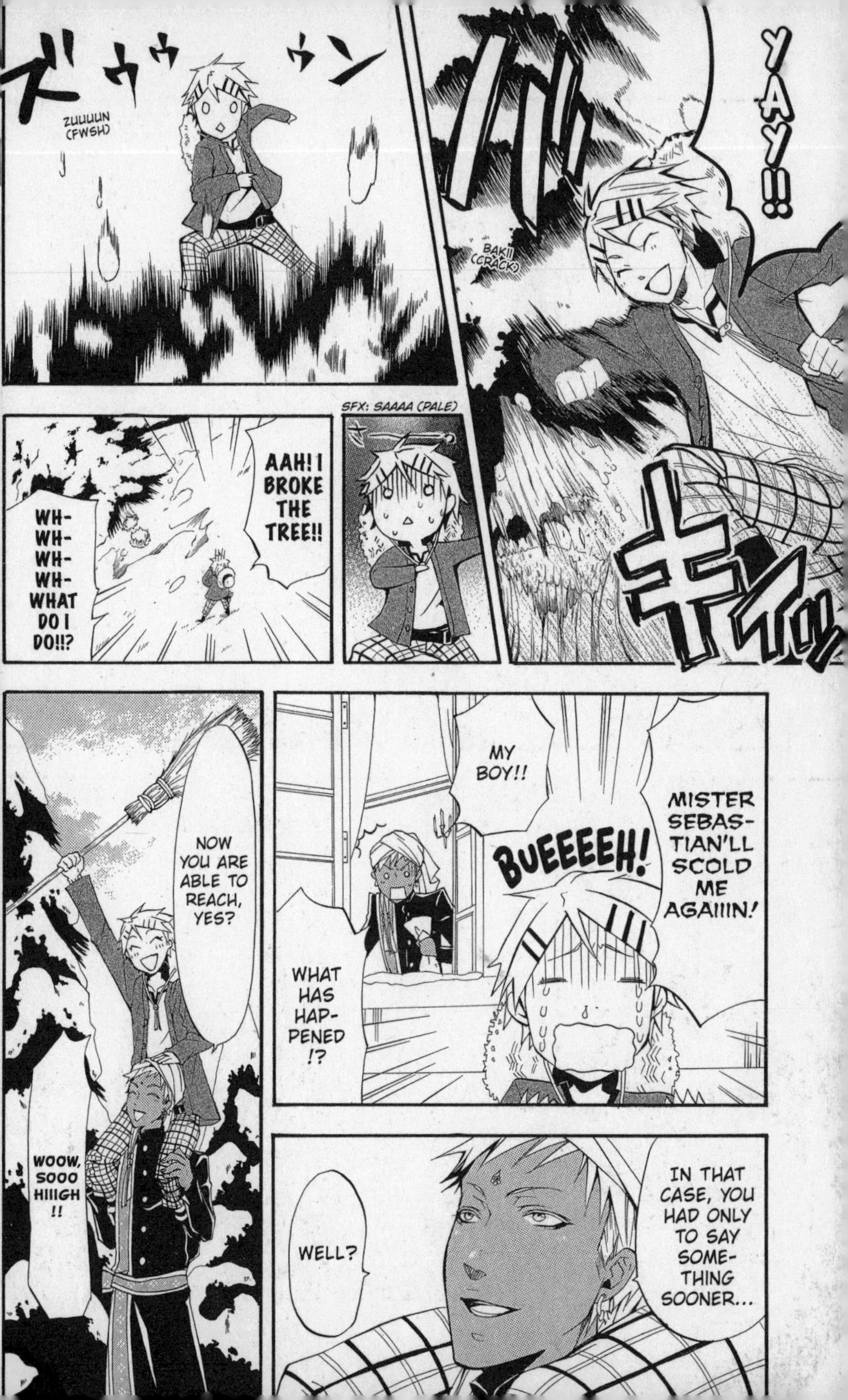
YAY!!
BAKI! (CRACK)
ズゥゥウン
ZUUUUN (FWSH)
SFX: SAAAA (PALE)
AAH! I BROKE THE TREE!!
WH-WH-WH-WH-WHAT DO I DO!!?
MISTER SEBASTIAN'LL SCOLD ME AGAIIIN!
BUEEEEH!
MY BOY!!
WHAT HAS HAPPENED!?
IN THAT CASE, YOU HAD ONLY TO SAY SOMETHING SOONER...
WELL?
NOW YOU ARE ABLE TO REACH, YES?
WOOW, SOOO HIIIGH!!

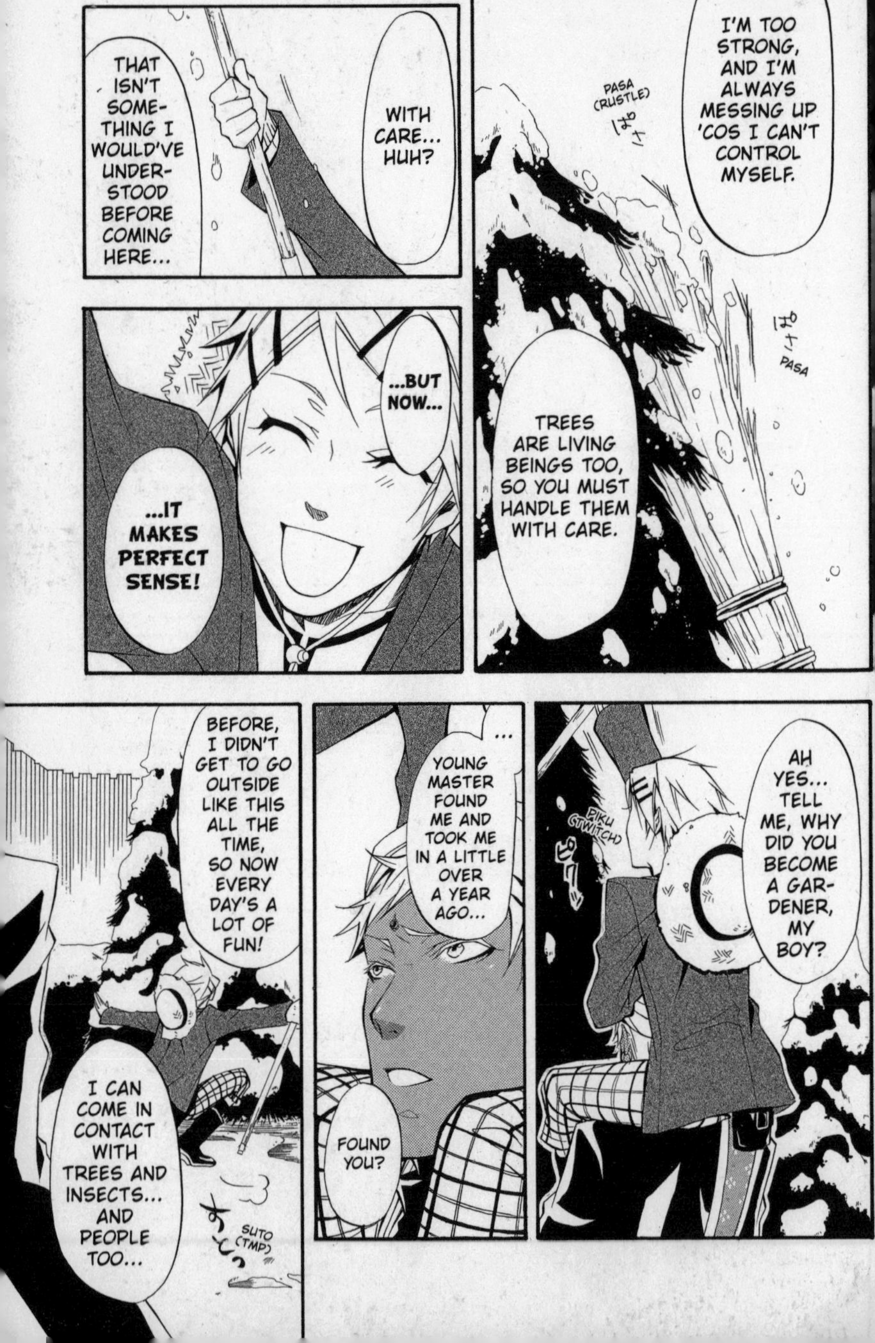

I'M TOO STRONG, AND I'M ALWAYS MESSING UP 'COS I CAN'T CONTROL MYSELF.
PASA (RUSTLE)
TREES ARE LIVING BEINGS TOO, SO YOU MUST HANDLE THEM WITH CARE.
PASA
WITH CARE... HUH?
THAT ISN'T SOME-THING I WOULD'VE UNDER-STOOD BEFORE COMING HERE...
...BUT NOW...
...IT MAKES PERFECT SENSE!
AH YES... TELL ME, WHY DID YOU BECOME A GAR-DENER, MY BOY?
PIKU (TWITCH)
...
YOUNG MASTER FOUND ME AND TOOK ME IN A LITTLE OVER A YEAR AGO...
FOUND YOU?
BEFORE, I DIDN'T GET TO GO OUTSIDE LIKE THIS ALL THE TIME, SO NOW EVERY DAY'S A LOT OF FUN!
I CAN COME IN CONTACT WITH TREES AND INSECTS... AND PEOPLE TOO...
SUTO (TMP)

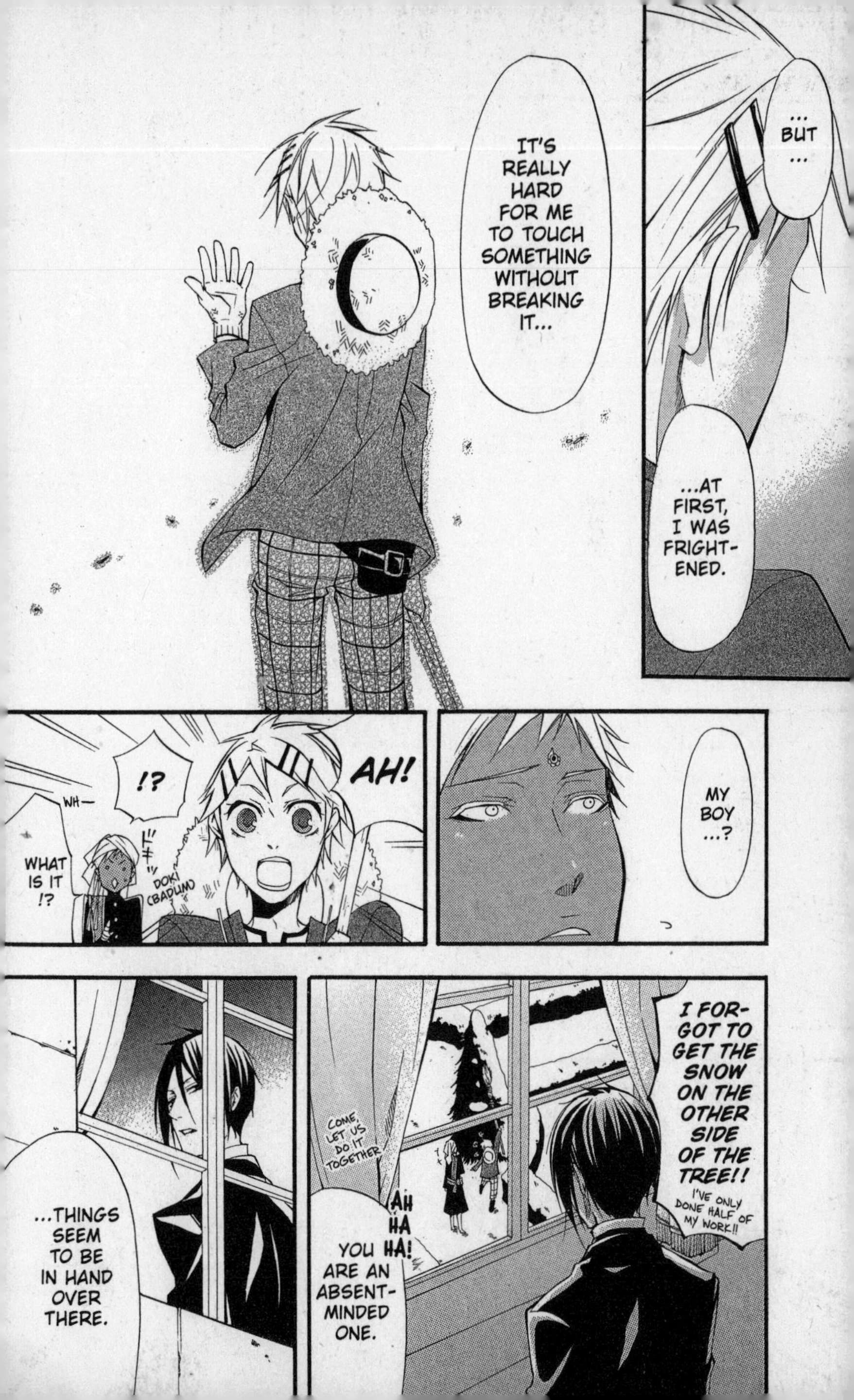
...BUT...
...AT FIRST, I WAS FRIGHTENED.
IT'S REALLY HARD FOR ME TO TOUCH SOMETHING WITHOUT BREAKING IT...
MY BOY...?
AH!
!?
DOKI (BADUM)
WH—
WHAT IS IT!?
I FORGOT TO GET THE SNOW ON THE OTHER SIDE OF THE TREE!!
I'VE ONLY DONE HALF OF MY WORK!!
AH HA HA!
YOU ARE AN ABSENT-MINDED ONE.
COME, LET US DO IT TOGETHER
...THINGS SEEM TO BE IN HAND OVER THERE.

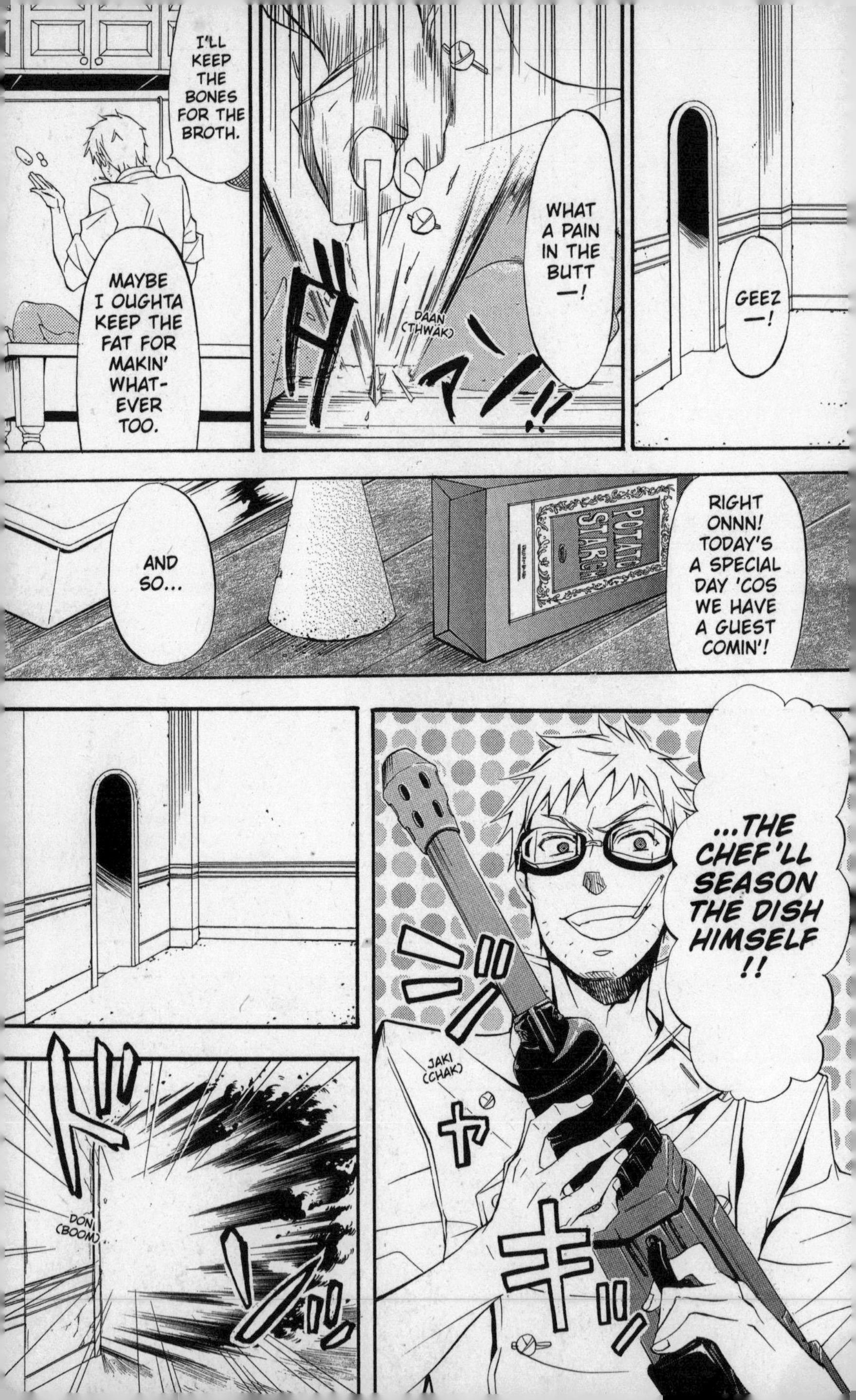
GEEZ—!
WHAT A PAIN IN THE BUTT—!
DAAN (THWAK)
I'LL KEEP THE BONES FOR THE BROTH.
MAYBE I OUGHTA KEEP THE FAT FOR MAKIN' WHAT-EVER TOO.
RIGHT ONNN! TODAY'S A SPECIAL DAY 'COS WE HAVE A GUEST COMIN'!
POTATO STARCH
AND SO...
...THE CHEF'LL SEASON THE DISH HIMSELF!!
JAKI (CHAK)
DON (BOOM)

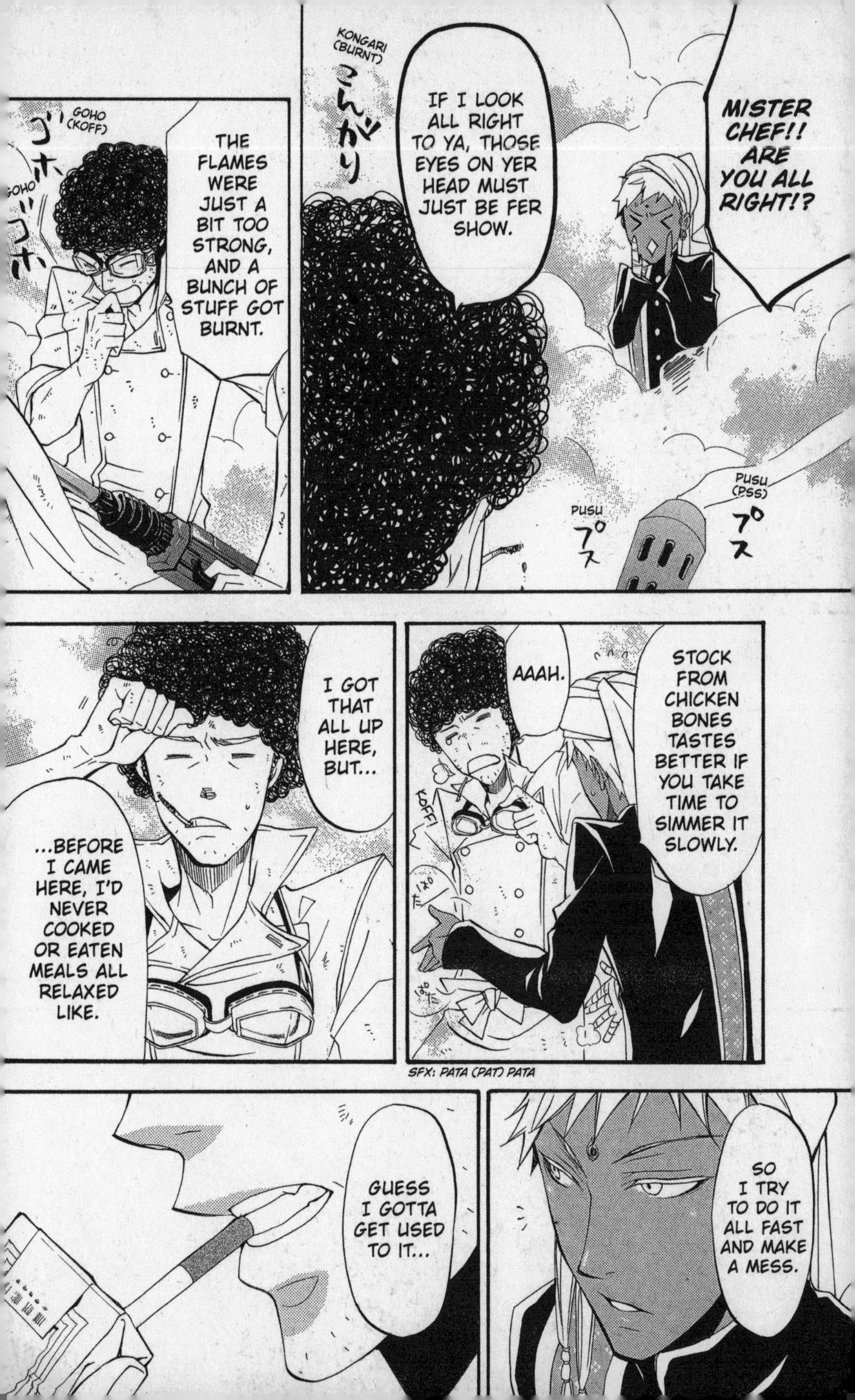
MISTER CHEF!! ARE YOU ALL RIGHT!?
KONGARI (BURNT)
こんがり
IF I LOOK ALL RIGHT TO YA, THOSE EYES ON YER HEAD MUST JUST BE FER SHOW.
PUSU (PSS)
プス
PUSU
プス
GOHO (KOFF)
ゴホ
GOHO
ゴホ
THE FLAMES WERE JUST A BIT TOO STRONG, AND A BUNCH OF STUFF GOT BURNT.
STOCK FROM CHICKEN BONES TASTES BETTER IF YOU TAKE TIME TO SIMMER IT SLOWLY.
AAAH.
KOFF!
SFX: PATA (PAT) PATA
I GOT THAT ALL UP HERE, BUT...
...BEFORE I CAME HERE, I'D NEVER COOKED OR EATEN MEALS ALL RELAXED LIKE.
SO I TRY TO DO IT ALL FAST AND MAKE A MESS.
GUESS I GOTTA GET USED TO IT...

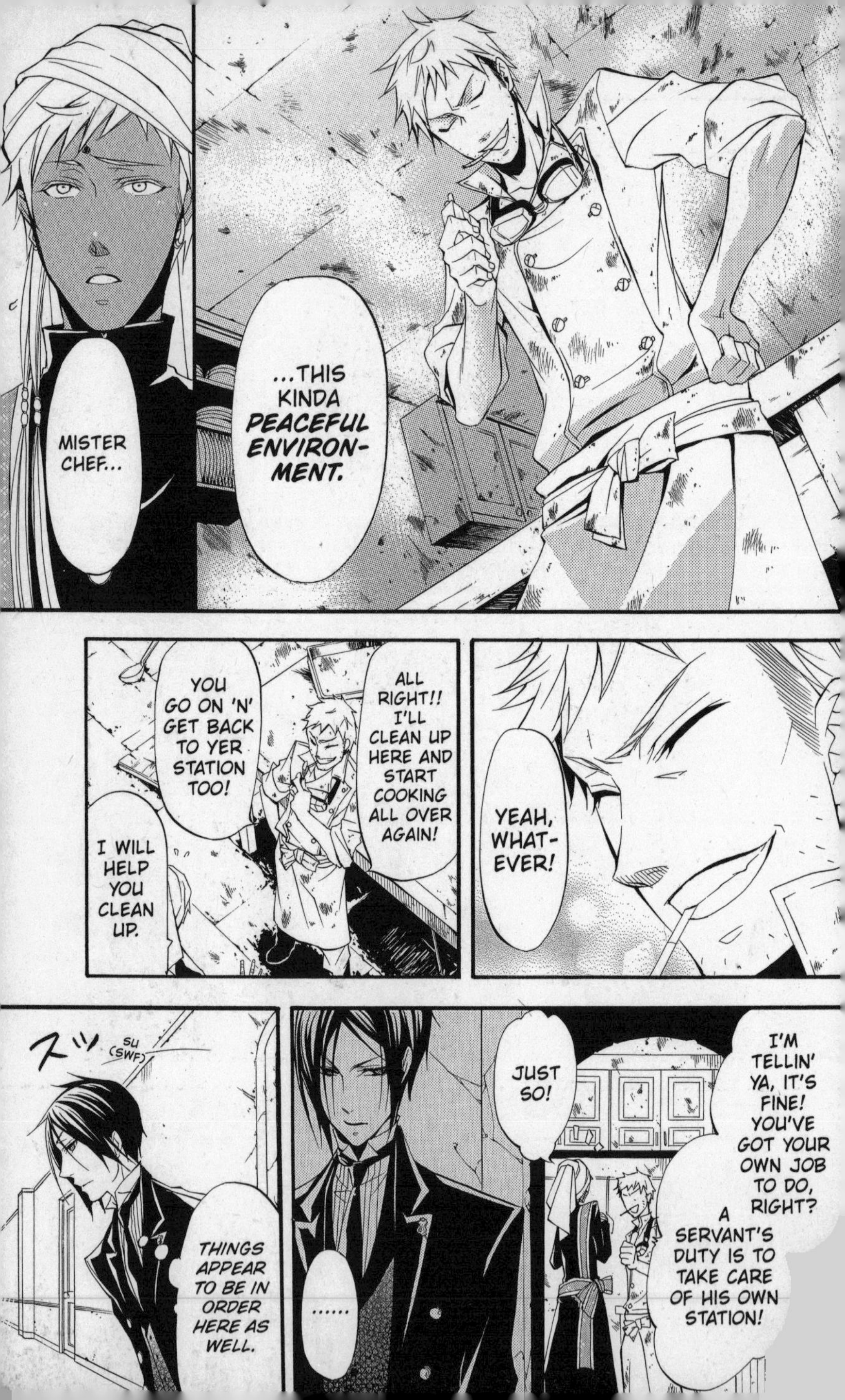
...THIS KINDA PEACEFUL ENVIRONMENT.
MISTER CHEF...
YEAH, WHATEVER!
ALL RIGHT!! I'LL CLEAN UP HERE AND START COOKING ALL OVER AGAIN!
YOU GO ON 'N' GET BACK TO YER STATION TOO!
I WILL HELP YOU CLEAN UP.
I'M TELLIN' YA, IT'S FINE! YOU'VE GOT YOUR OWN JOB TO DO, RIGHT?
A SERVANT'S DUTY IS TO TAKE CARE OF HIS OWN STATION!
JUST SO!
......
THINGS APPEAR TO BE IN ORDER HERE AS WELL.
スッ
SU (SWF)

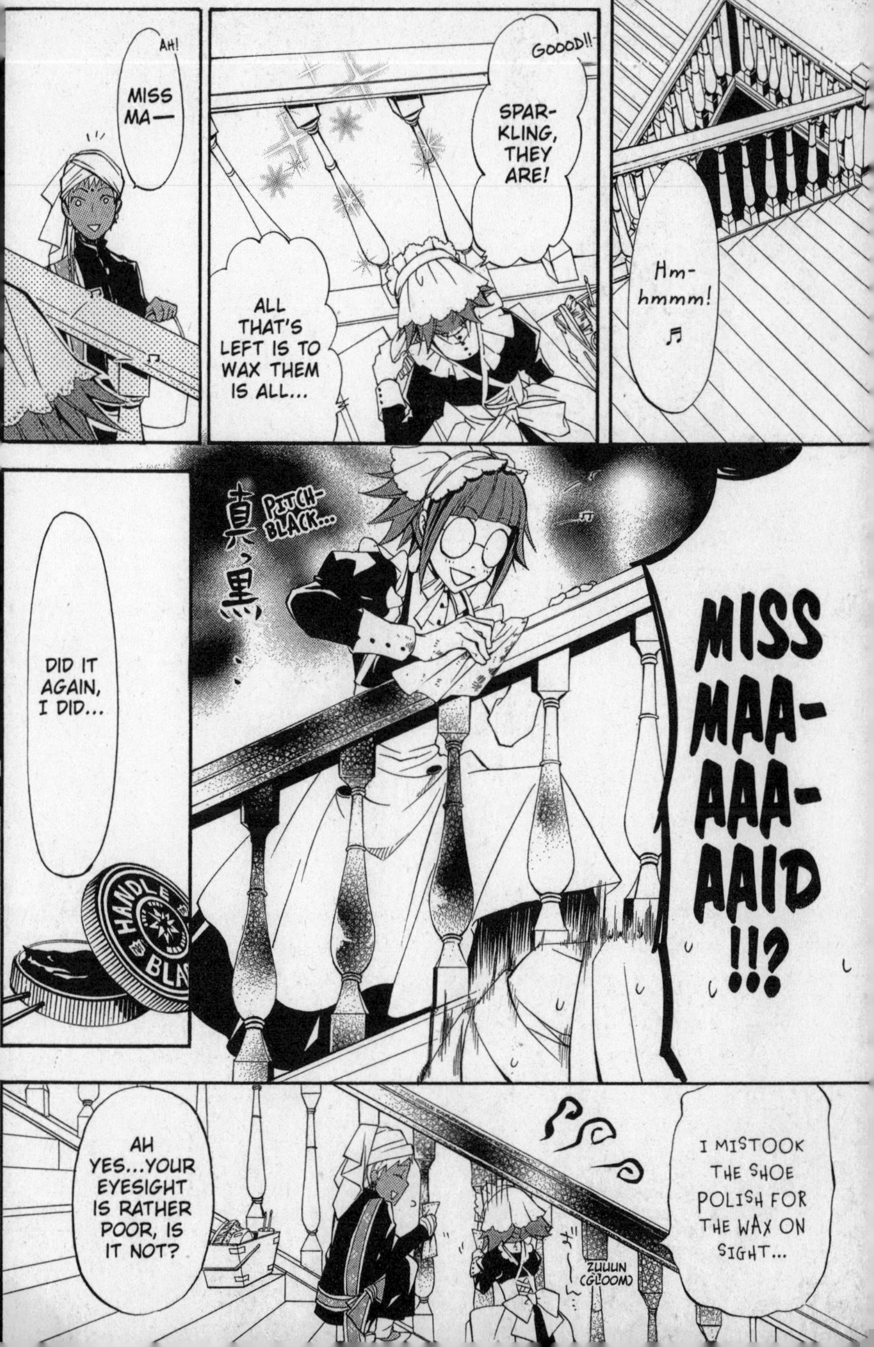
Hm-hmmm! ♬
GOOOD!!
SPARKLING, THEY ARE!
ALL THAT'S LEFT IS TO WAX THEM IS ALL...
AH!
MISS MA—
MISS MAAAAAAAAID!!?
真っ黒
PITCH-BLACK...
DID IT AGAIN, I DID...
I MISTOOK THE SHOE POLISH FOR THE WAX ON SIGHT...
ZUUUN (GLOOM)
AH YES...YOUR EYESIGHT IS RATHER POOR, IS IT NOT?

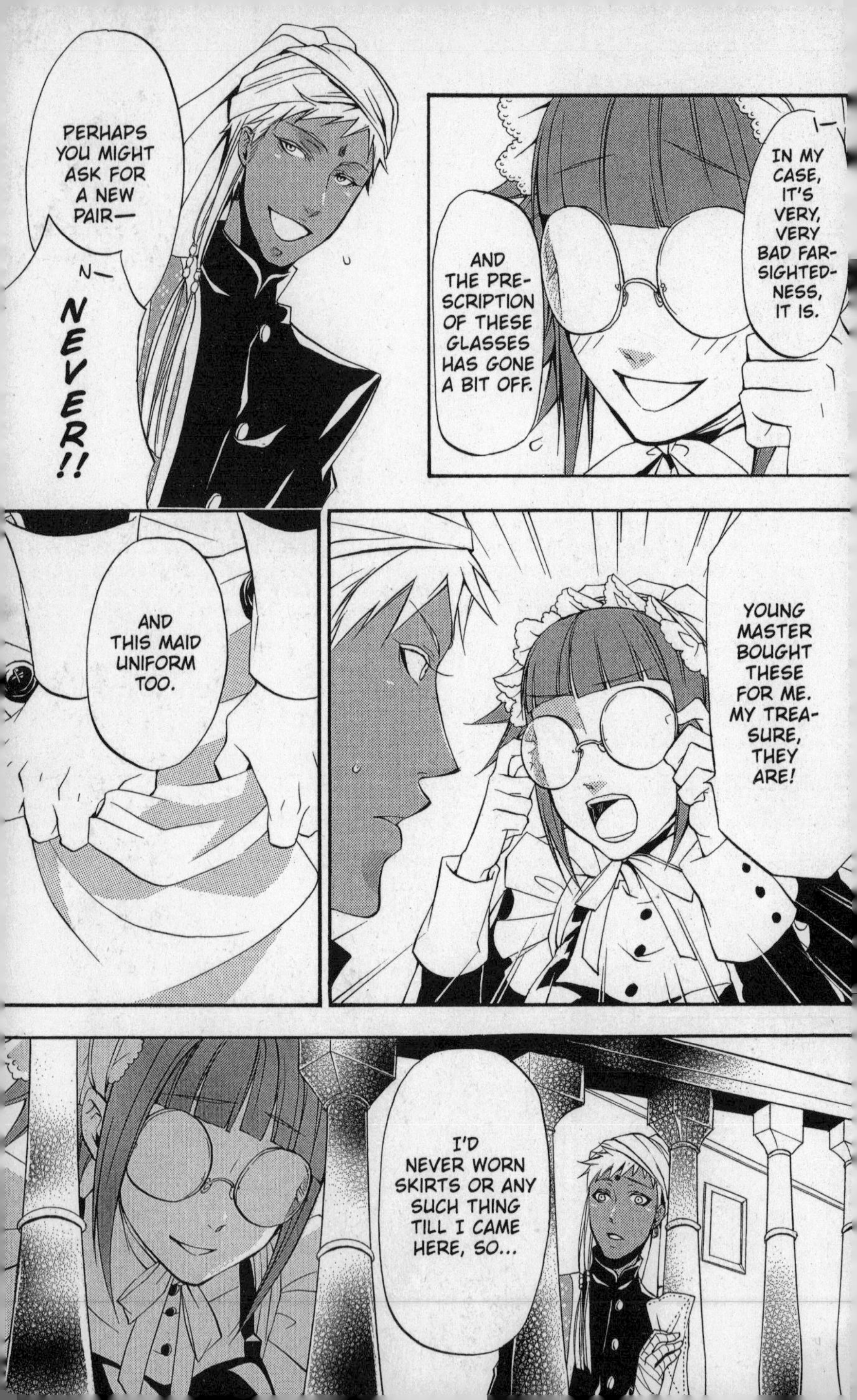
I—
IN MY CASE, IT'S VERY, VERY BAD FAR-SIGHTEDNESS, IT IS.
AND THE PRESCRIPTION OF THESE GLASSES HAS GONE A BIT OFF.
PERHAPS YOU MIGHT ASK FOR A NEW PAIR—
N—
NEVER!!
YOUNG MASTER BOUGHT THESE FOR ME. MY TREASURE, THEY ARE!
AND THIS MAID UNIFORM TOO.
I'D NEVER WORN SKIRTS OR ANY SUCH THING TILL I CAME HERE, SO...

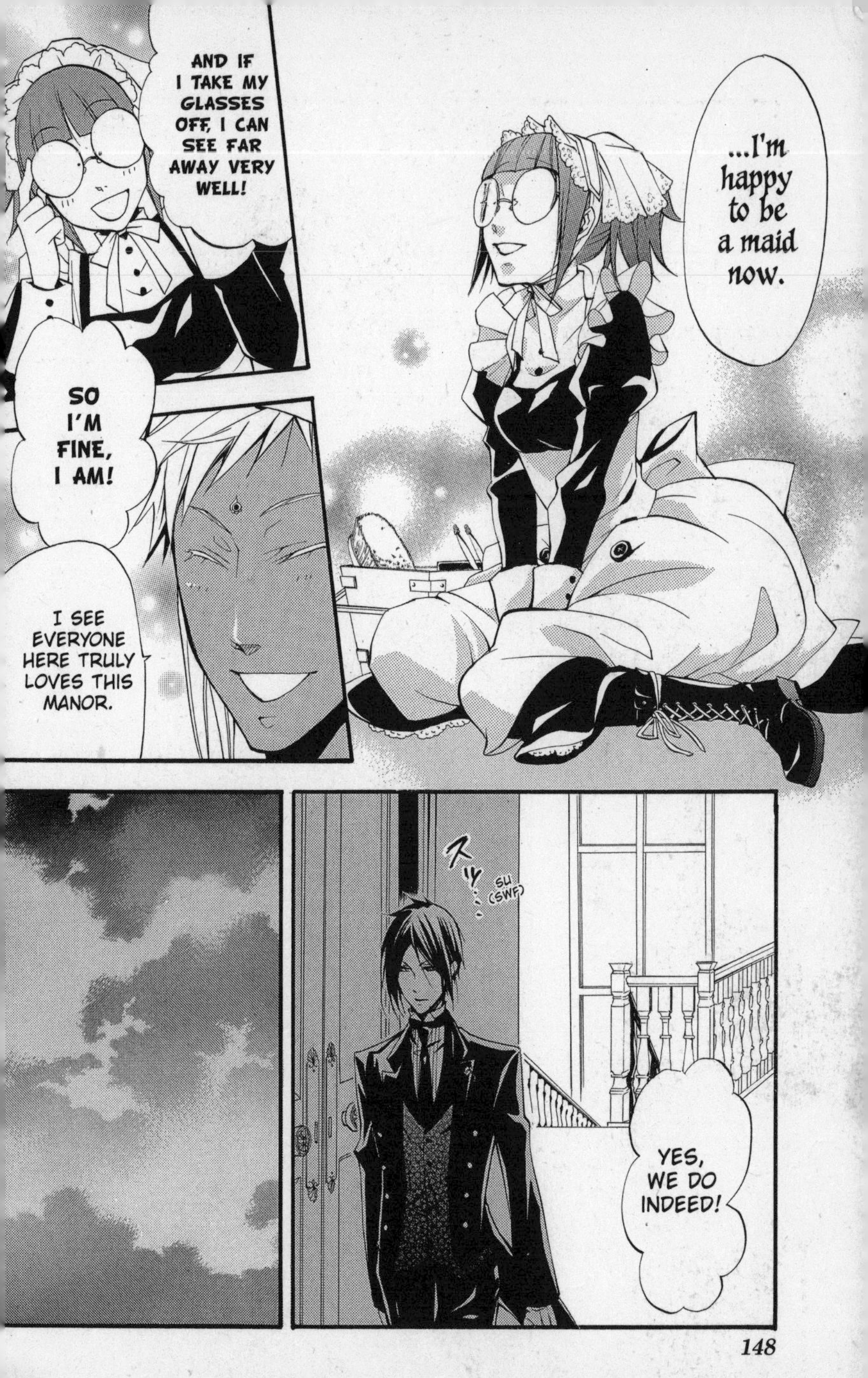
...I'm happy to be a maid now.
AND IF I TAKE MY GLASSES OFF, I CAN SEE FAR AWAY VERY WELL!
SO I'M FINE, I AM!
I SEE EVERYONE HERE TRULY LOVES THIS MANOR.
スッ
SU (SWF)
YES, WE DO INDEED!

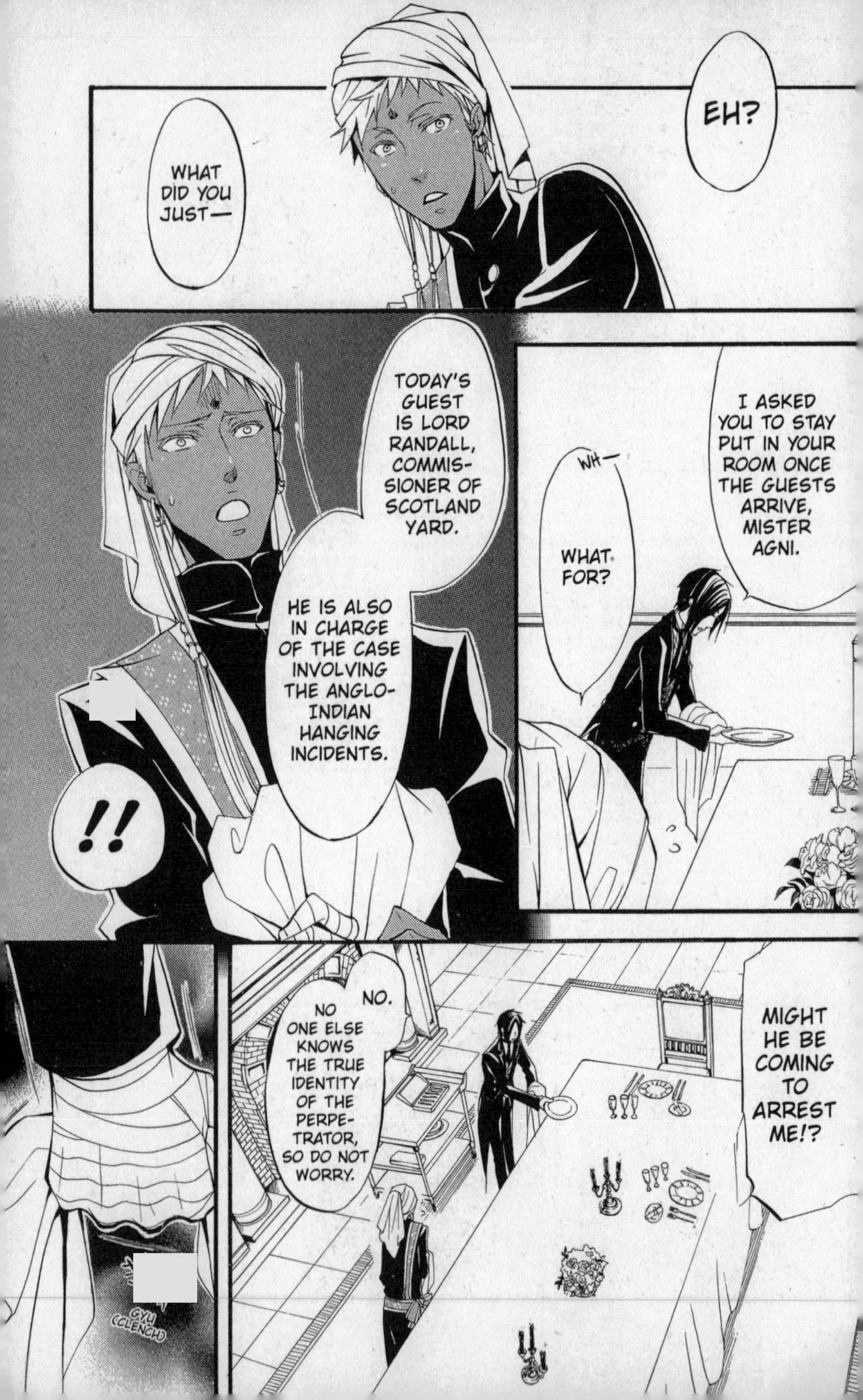
EH?
WHAT DID YOU JUST—
I ASKED YOU TO STAY PUT IN YOUR ROOM ONCE THE GUESTS ARRIVE, MISTER AGNI.
WH—
WHAT FOR?
TODAY'S GUEST IS LORD RANDALL, COMMIS-SIONER OF SCOTLAND YARD.
HE IS ALSO IN CHARGE OF THE CASE INVOLVING THE ANGLO-INDIAN HANGING INCIDENTS.
!!
MIGHT HE BE COMING TO ARREST ME!?
NO.
NO ONE ELSE KNOWS THE TRUE IDENTITY OF THE PERPE-TRATOR, SO DO NOT WORRY.
GYU (CLENCH)

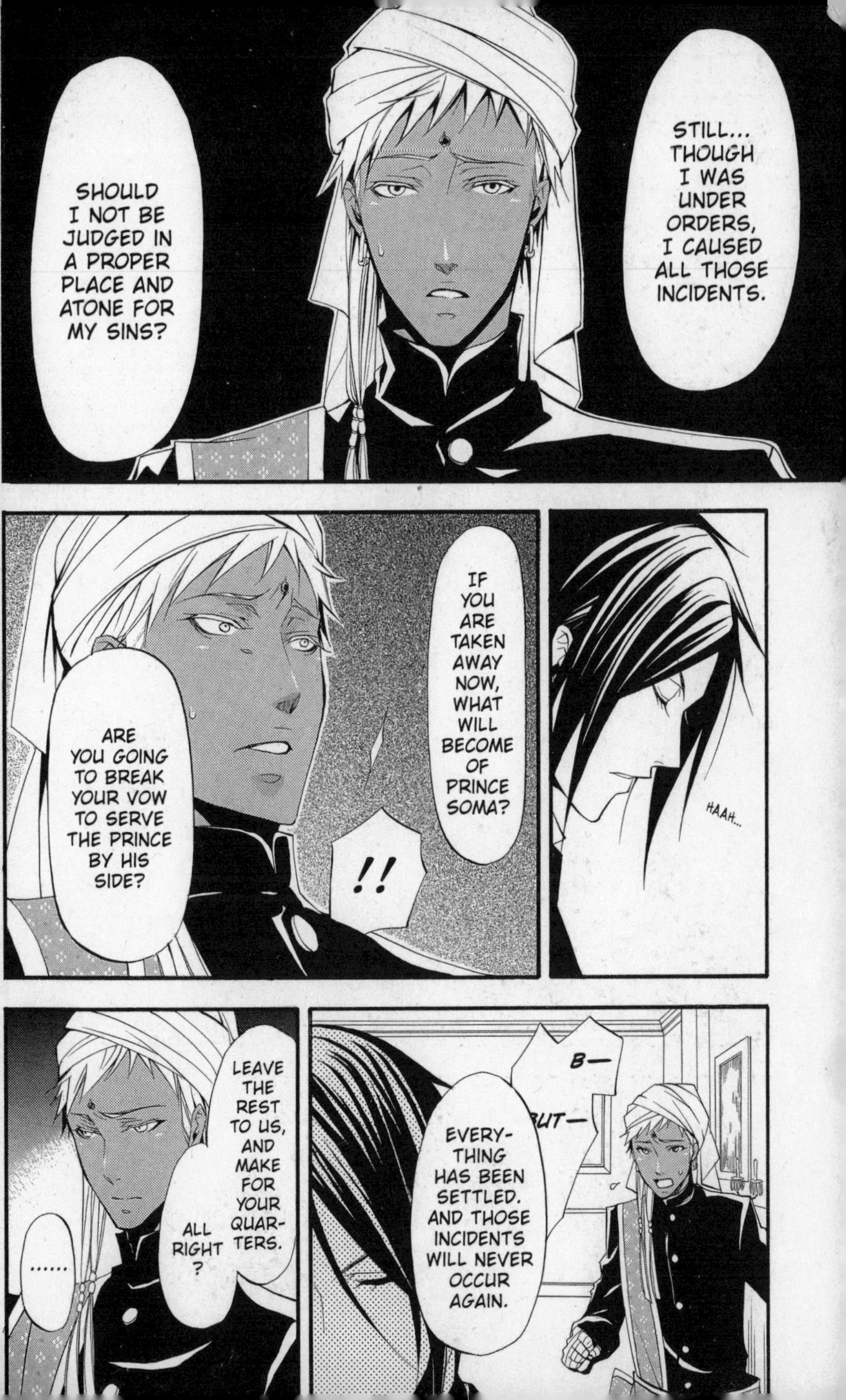
STILL... THOUGH I WAS UNDER ORDERS, I CAUSED ALL THOSE INCIDENTS.
SHOULD I NOT BE JUDGED IN A PROPER PLACE AND ATONE FOR MY SINS?
HAAH...
IF YOU ARE TAKEN AWAY NOW, WHAT WILL BECOME OF PRINCE SOMA?
!!
ARE YOU GOING TO BREAK YOUR VOW TO SERVE THE PRINCE BY HIS SIDE?
B—
BUT—
EVERY-THING HAS BEEN SETTLED. AND THOSE INCIDENTS WILL NEVER OCCUR AGAIN.
LEAVE THE REST TO US, AND MAKE FOR YOUR QUAR-TERS.
ALL RIGHT?
......

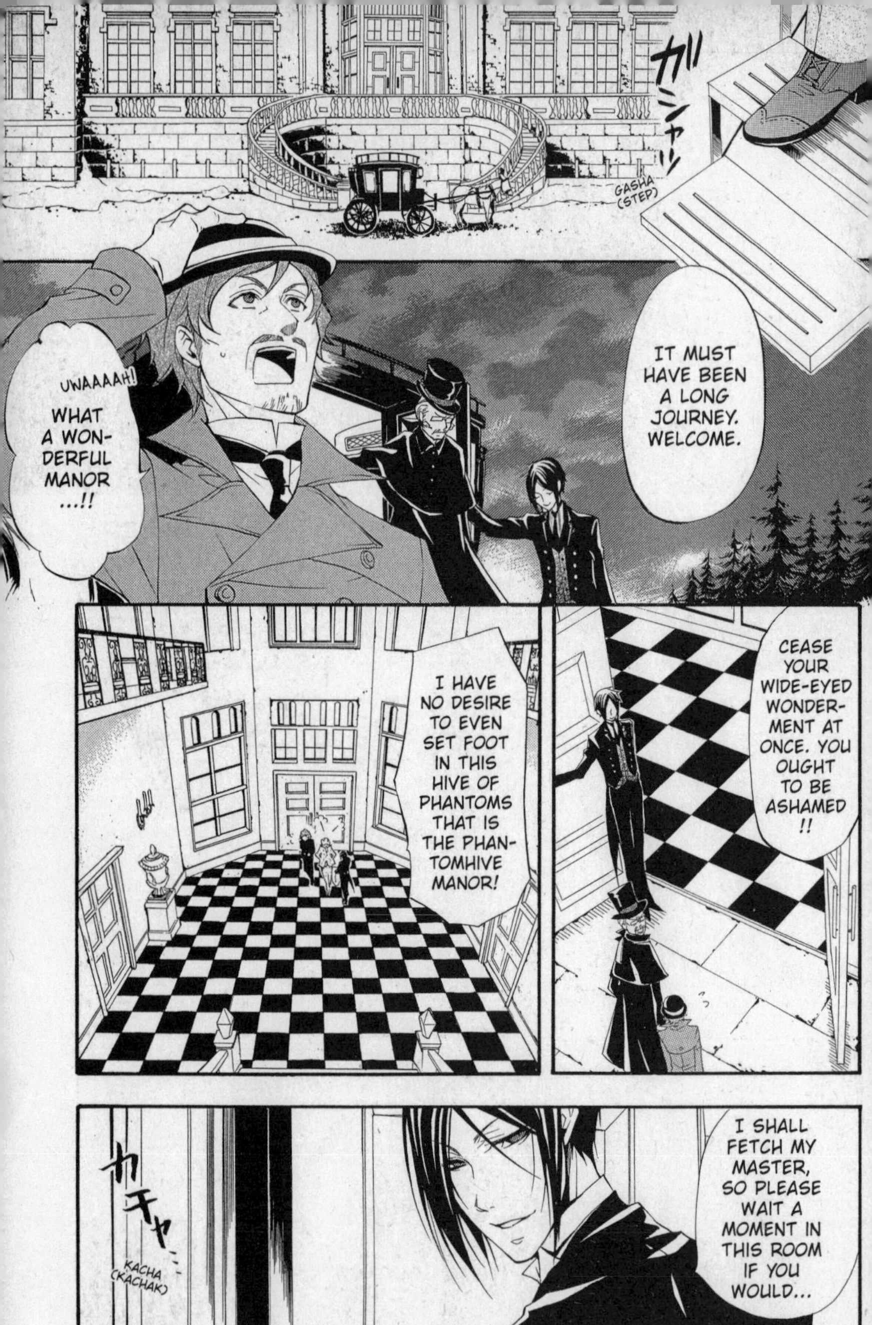
ガシャッ
GASHA (STEP)
IT MUST HAVE BEEN A LONG JOURNEY. WELCOME.
UWAAAAH!
WHAT A WON-DERFUL MANOR ...!!
CEASE YOUR WIDE-EYED WONDER-MENT AT ONCE. YOU OUGHT TO BE ASHAMED !!
I HAVE NO DESIRE TO EVEN SET FOOT IN THIS HIVE OF PHANTOMS THAT IS THE PHAN-TOMHIVE MANOR!
I SHALL FETCH MY MASTER, SO PLEASE WAIT A MOMENT IN THIS ROOM IF YOU WOULD...
カチャ
KACHA (KACHAK)

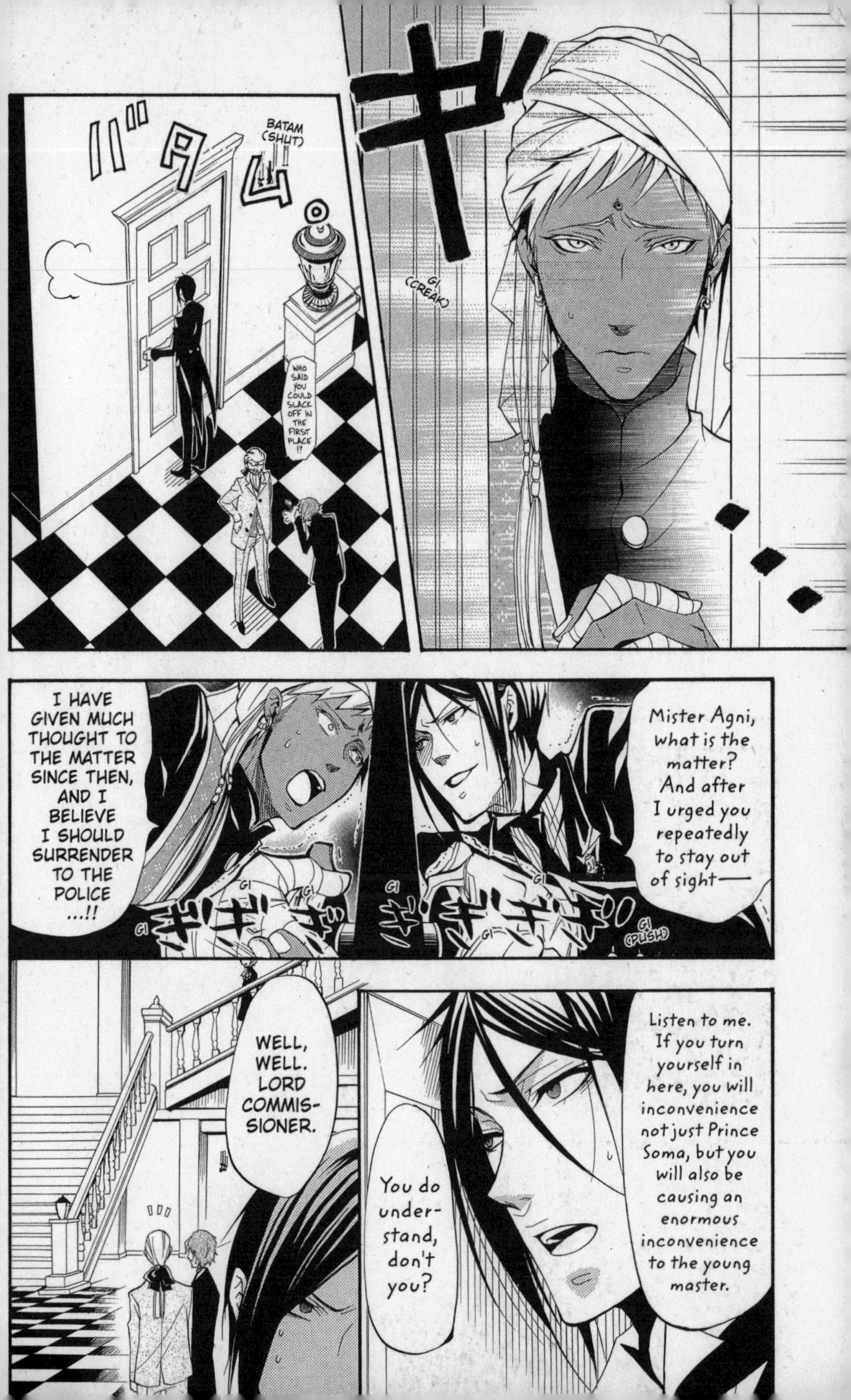

ギ
GI (CREAK)
...
バタム
BATAM (SHUT)
WHO SAID YOU COULD SLACK OFF IN THE FIRST PLACE!?
Mister Agni, what is the matter? And after I urged you repeatedly to stay out of sight—
GI GI GI (PUSH)
I HAVE GIVEN MUCH THOUGHT TO THE MATTER SINCE THEN, AND I BELIEVE I SHOULD SURRENDER TO THE POLICE ...!!
GI GI
Listen to me. If you turn yourself in here, you will inconvenience not just Prince Soma, but you will also be causing an enormous inconvenience to the young master.
You do under-stand, don't you?
WELL, WELL. LORD COMMIS-SIONER.

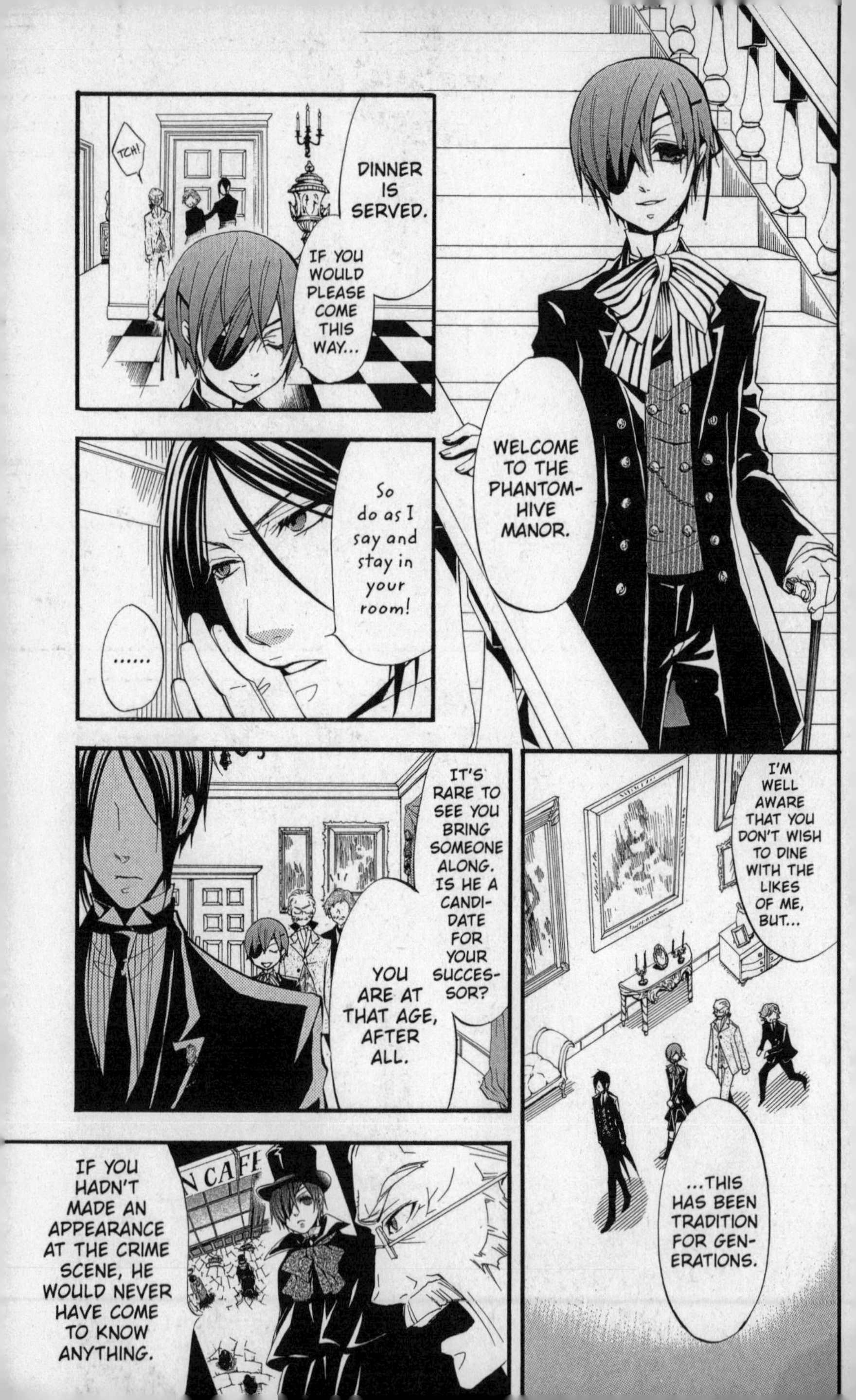
WELCOME TO THE PHANTOM-HIVE MANOR.
TCH!
DINNER IS SERVED.
IF YOU WOULD PLEASE COME THIS WAY...
So do as I say and stay in your room!
......
I'M WELL AWARE THAT YOU DON'T WISH TO DINE WITH THE LIKES OF ME, BUT...
...THIS HAS BEEN TRADITION FOR GEN-ERATIONS.
IT'S RARE TO SEE YOU BRING SOMEONE ALONG. IS HE A CANDI-DATE FOR YOUR SUCCES-SOR?
YOU ARE AT THAT AGE, AFTER ALL.
IF YOU HADN'T MADE AN APPEARANCE AT THE CRIME SCENE, HE WOULD NEVER HAVE COME TO KNOW ANYTHING.

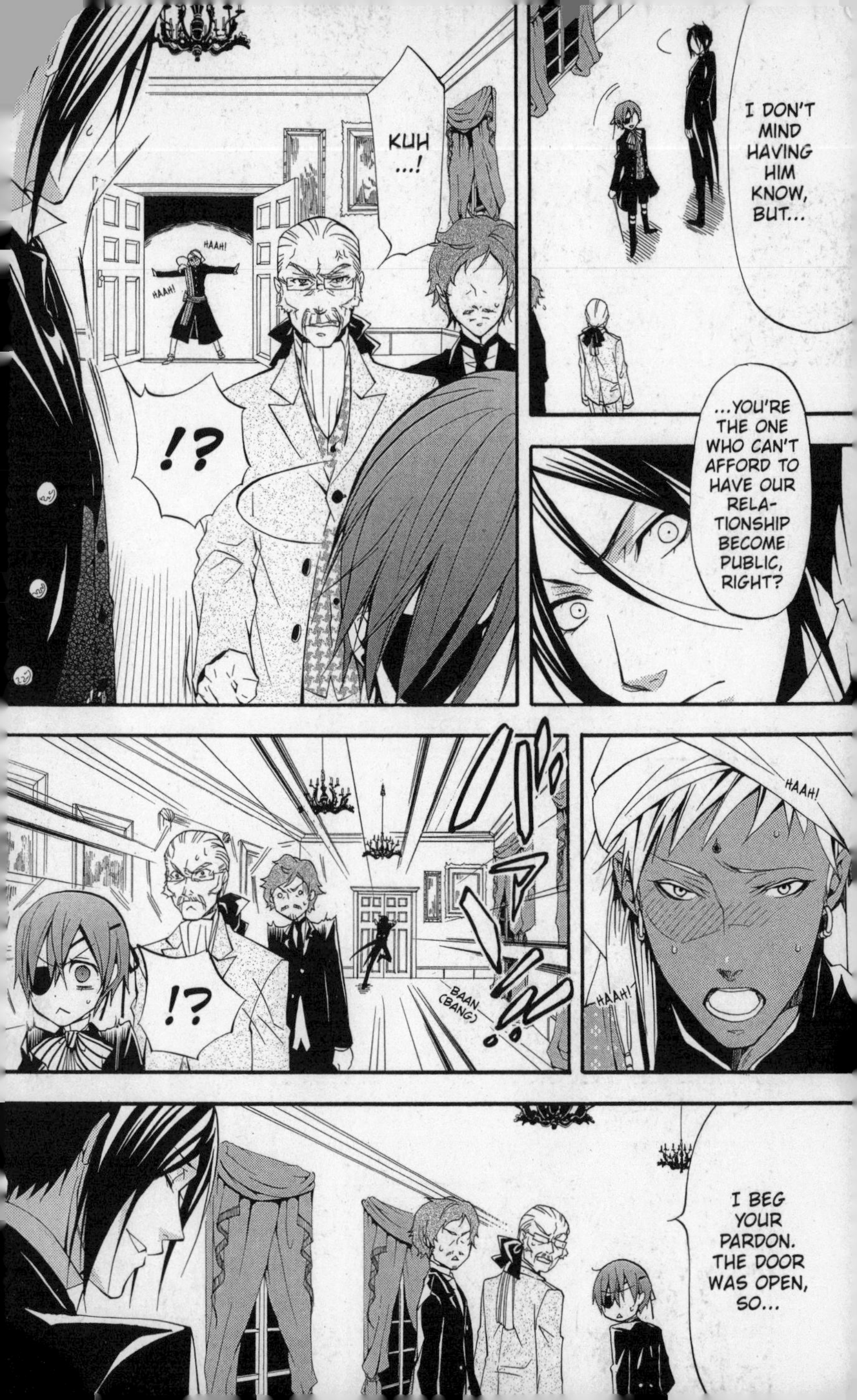
I DON'T MIND HAVING HIM KNOW, BUT...
...YOU'RE THE ONE WHO CAN'T AFFORD TO HAVE OUR RELATIONSHIP BECOME PUBLIC, RIGHT?
KUH ...!
HAAH!
HAAH!
!?
HAAH!
HAAH!
BAAN (BANG)
!?
I BEG YOUR PARDON. THE DOOR WAS OPEN, SO...

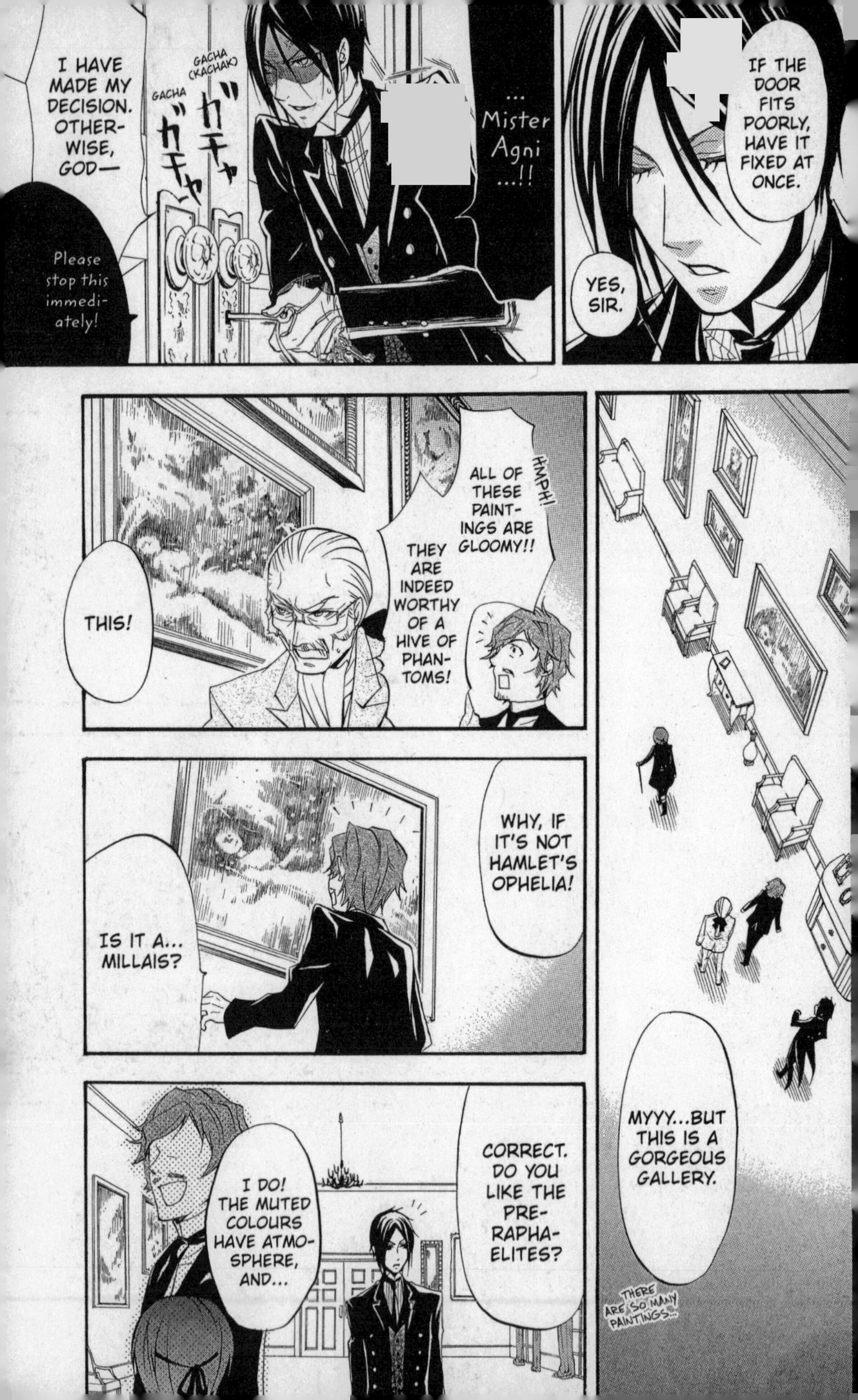
IF THE DOOR FITS POORLY, HAVE IT FIXED AT ONCE.
YES, SIR.
...Mister Agni...!!
I HAVE MADE MY DECISION. OTHERWISE, GOD—
GACHA (KACHAK)
GACHA
ガチャ
ガチャ
Please stop this immediately!
MYYY...BUT THIS IS A GORGEOUS GALLERY.
THERE ARE SO MANY PAINTINGS...
ALL OF THESE PAINTINGS ARE GLOOMY!!
HMPH!
THEY ARE INDEED WORTHY OF A HIVE OF PHANTOMS!
THIS!
WHY, IF IT'S NOT HAMLET'S OPHELIA!
IS IT A... MILLAIS?
CORRECT. DO YOU LIKE THE PRE-RAPHAELITES?
I DO! THE MUTED COLOURS HAVE ATMOSPHERE, AND...

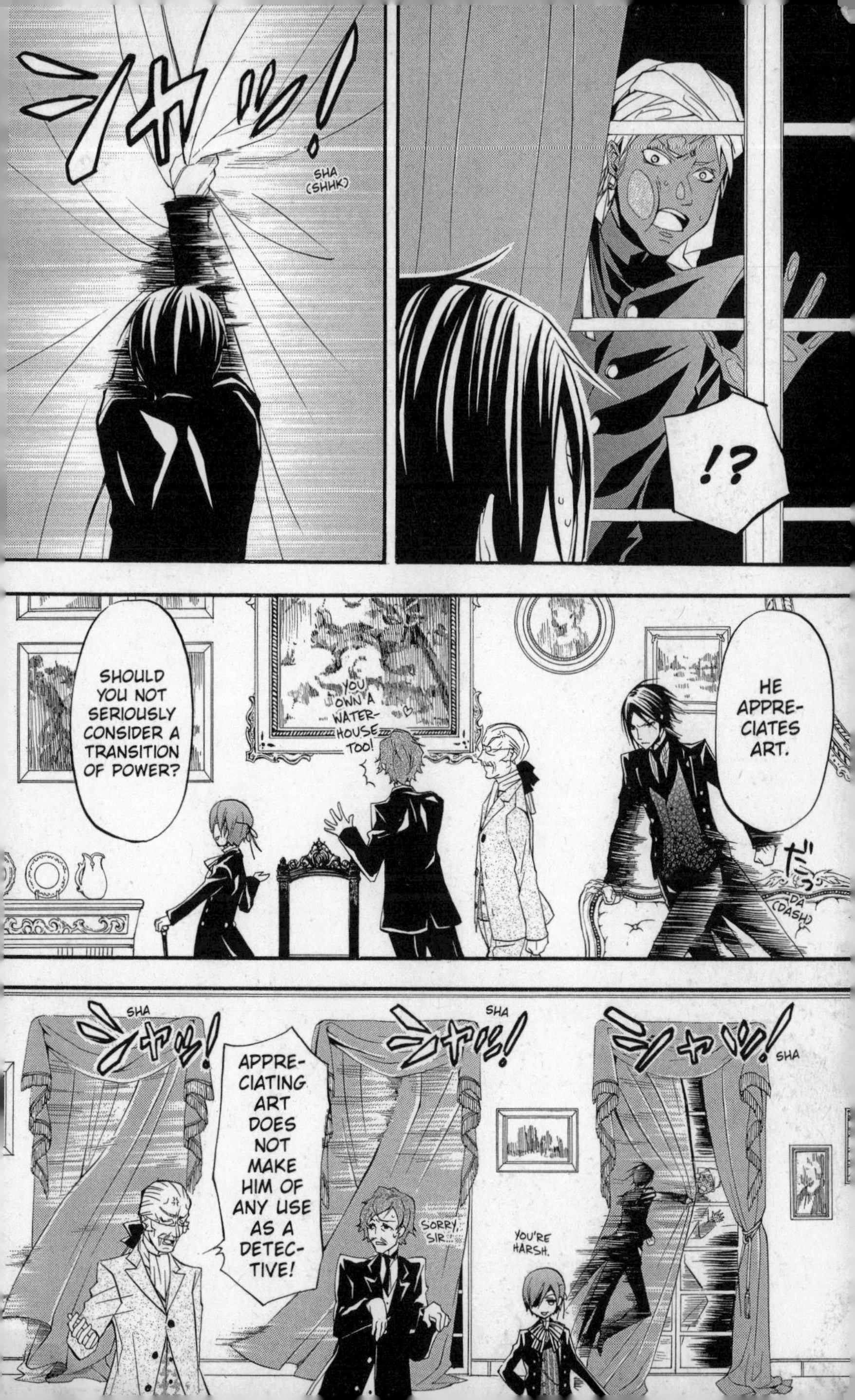
!?
SHA (SHHK)
HE APPRE-CIATES ART.
DA (DASH)
YOU OWN A WATER-HOUSE TOO!
SHOULD YOU NOT SERIOUSLY CONSIDER A TRANSITION OF POWER?
SHA
YOU'RE HARSH.
SORRY, SIR...
SHA
APPRE-CIATING ART DOES NOT MAKE HIM OF ANY USE AS A DETEC-TIVE!
SHA

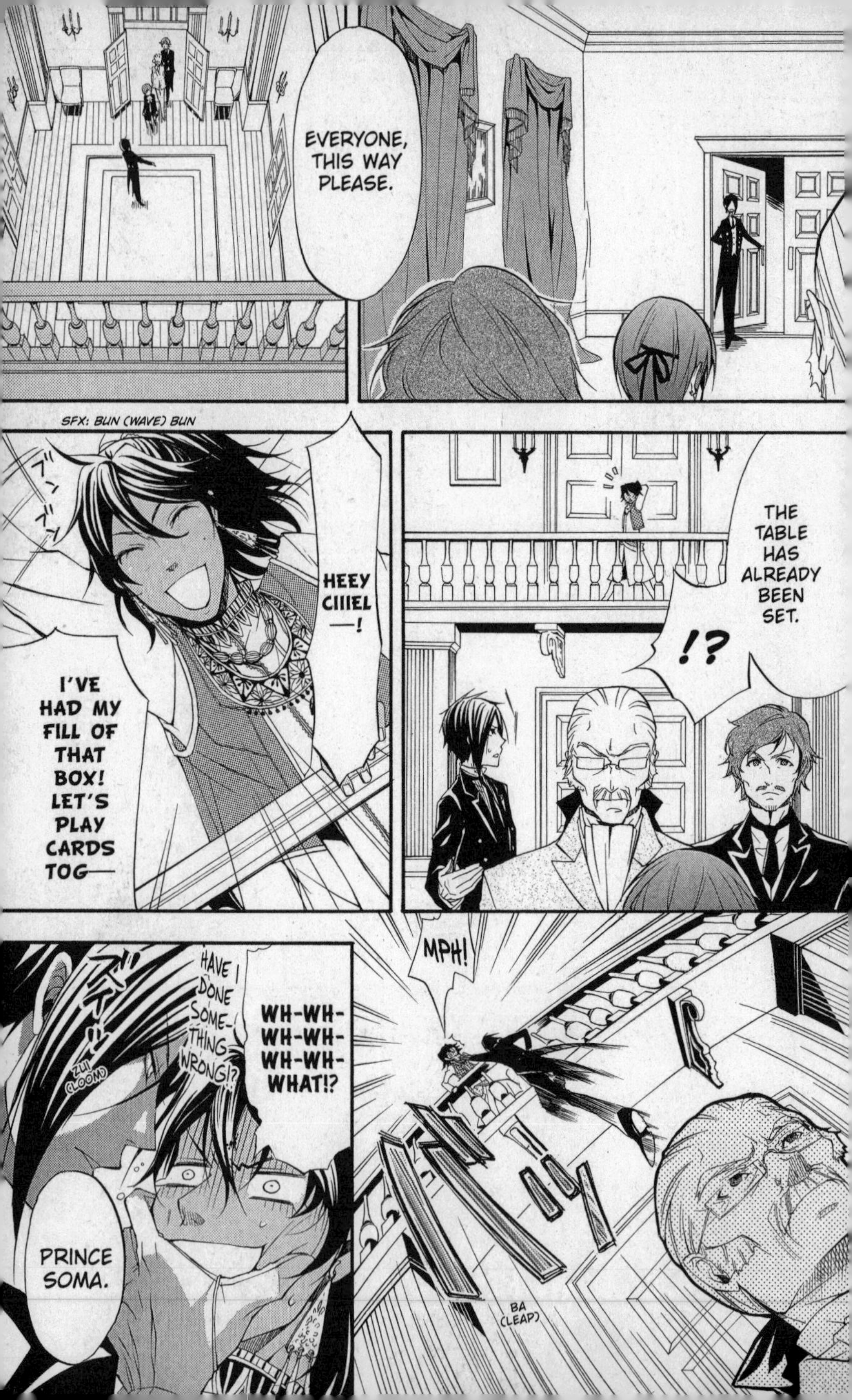
EVERYONE, THIS WAY PLEASE.
SFX: BUN (WAVE) BUN
THE TABLE HAS ALREADY BEEN SET.
!?
HEEY CIIIEL—!
I'VE HAD MY FILL OF THAT BOX! LET'S PLAY CARDS TOG—
MPH!
BA (LEAP)
WH-WH-WH-WH-WH-WH-WHAT!?
HAVE I DONE SOME-THING WRONG!?
ZUI (GLOOM)
PRINCE SOMA.

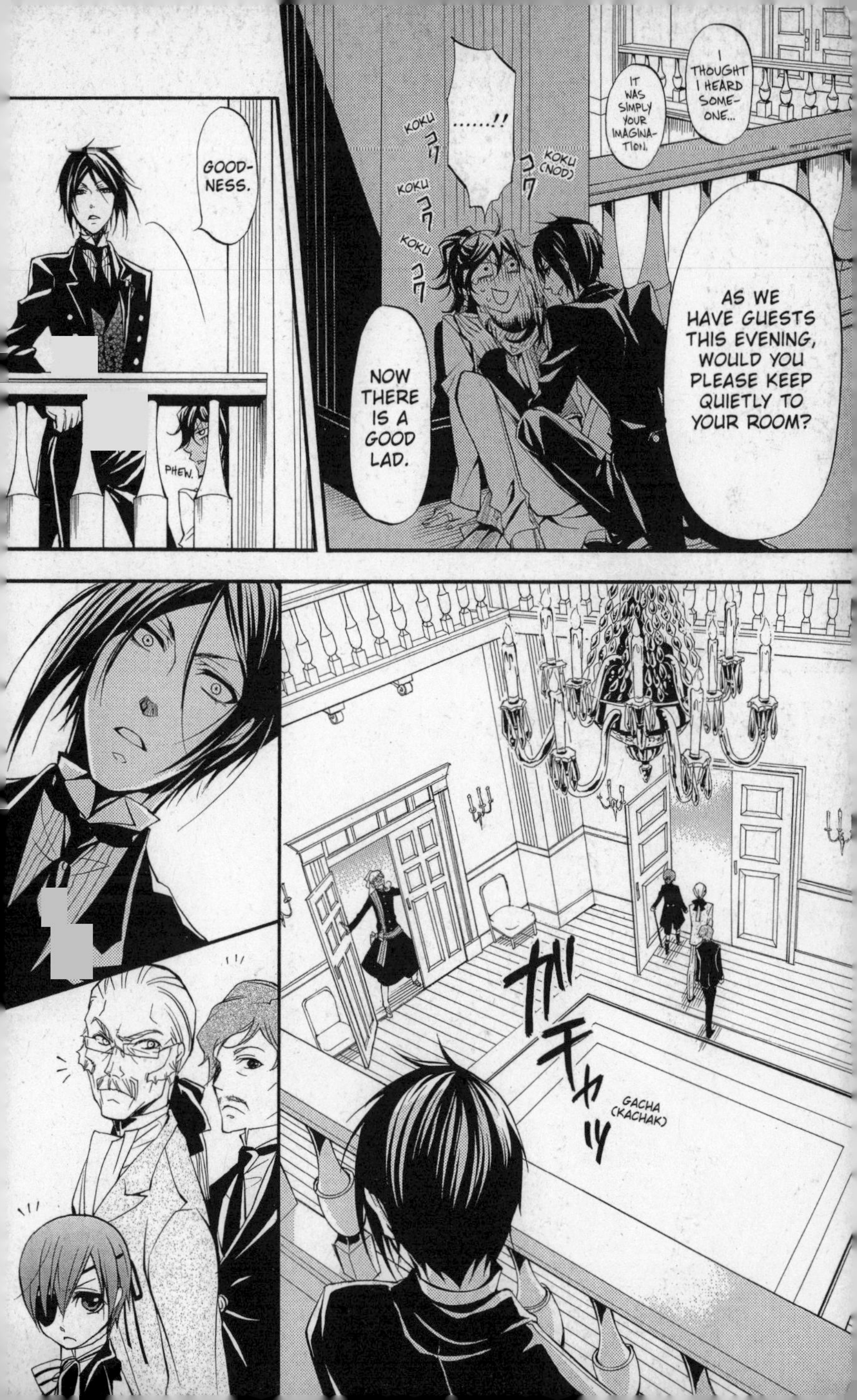

I THOUGHT I HEARD SOME-ONE...
IT WAS SIMPLY YOUR IMAGINA-TION.
AS WE HAVE GUESTS THIS EVENING, WOULD YOU PLEASE KEEP QUIETLY TO YOUR ROOM?
KOKU (NOD)
......!!
KOKU
KOKU
KOKU
NOW THERE IS A GOOD LAD.
GOOD-NESS.
PHEW.
GACHA (KACHAK)

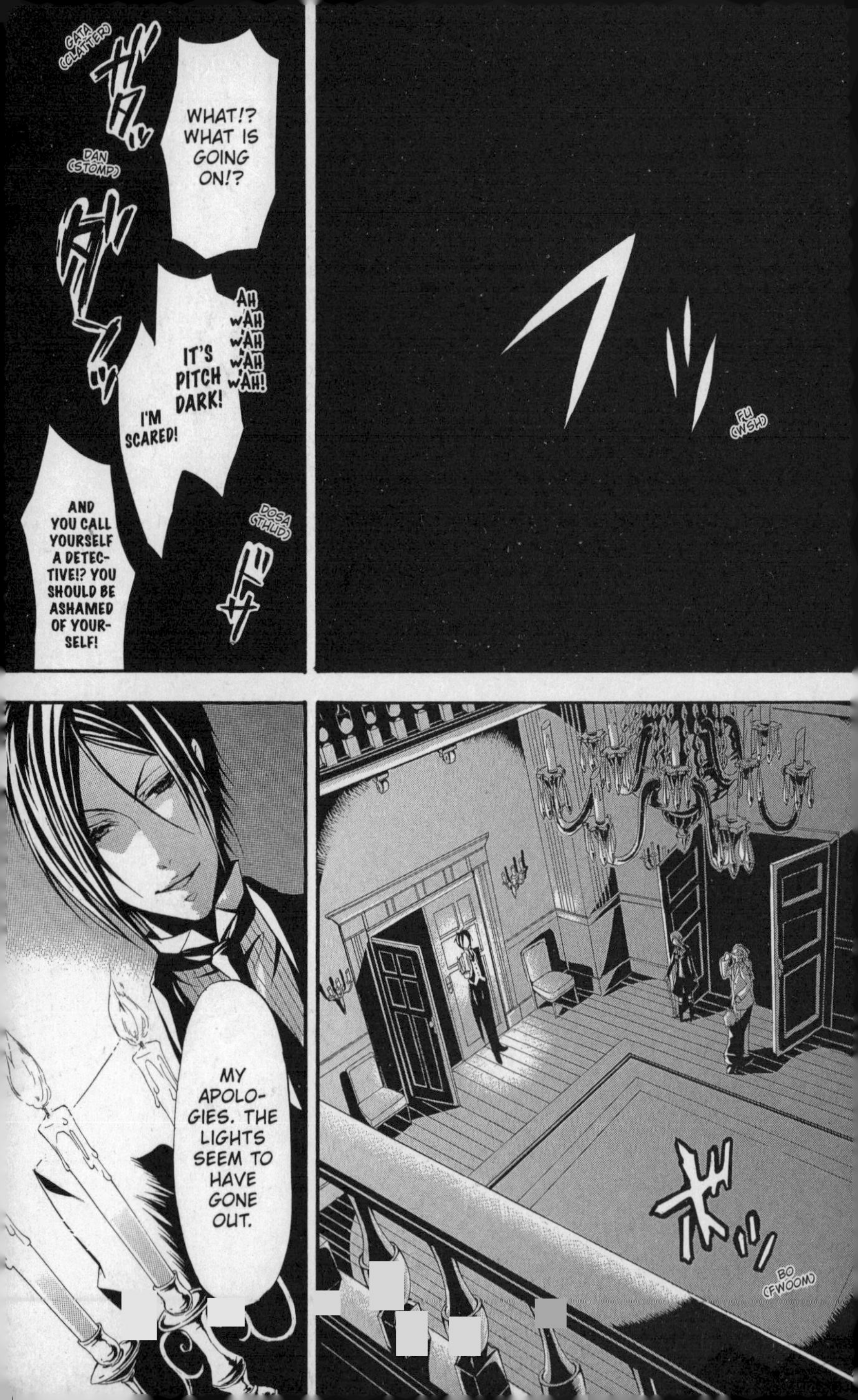
FU (WSH)
WHAT!? WHAT IS GOING ON!?
GATA (CLATTER)
DAN (STOMP)
AH WAH WAH WAH WAH!
IT'S PITCH DARK!
I'M SCARED!
DOSA (THUD)
AND YOU CALL YOURSELF A DETECTIVE!? YOU SHOULD BE ASHAMED OF YOURSELF!
BO (FWOOM)
MY APOLOGIES. THE LIGHTS SEEM TO HAVE GONE OUT.

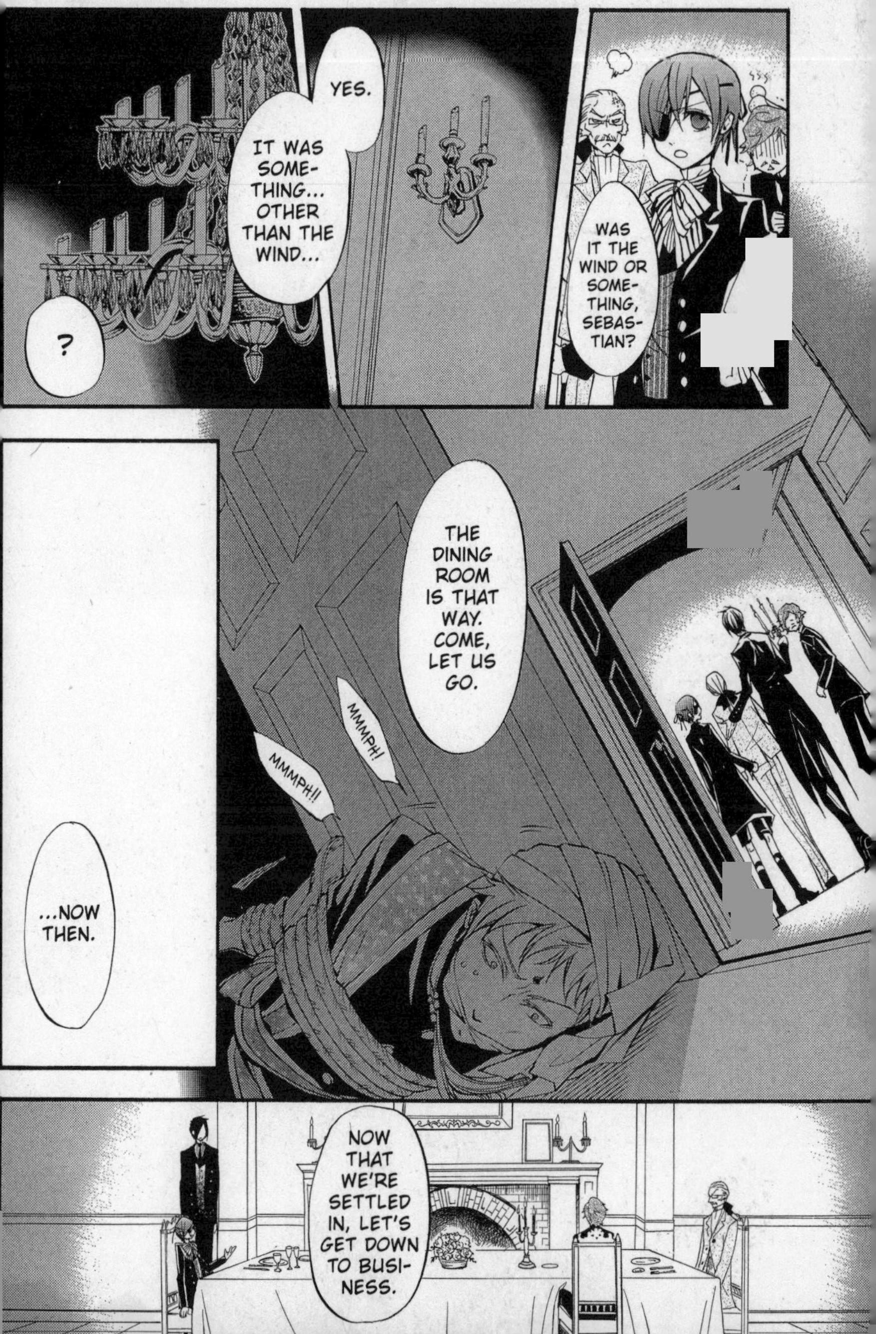
WAS IT THE WIND OR SOMETHING, SEBASTIAN?
YES.
IT WAS SOMETHING... OTHER THAN THE WIND...
?
THE DINING ROOM IS THAT WAY. COME, LET US GO.
MMMPH!
MMMPH!!
...NOW THEN.
NOW THAT WE'RE SETTLED IN, LET'S GET DOWN TO BUSINESS.

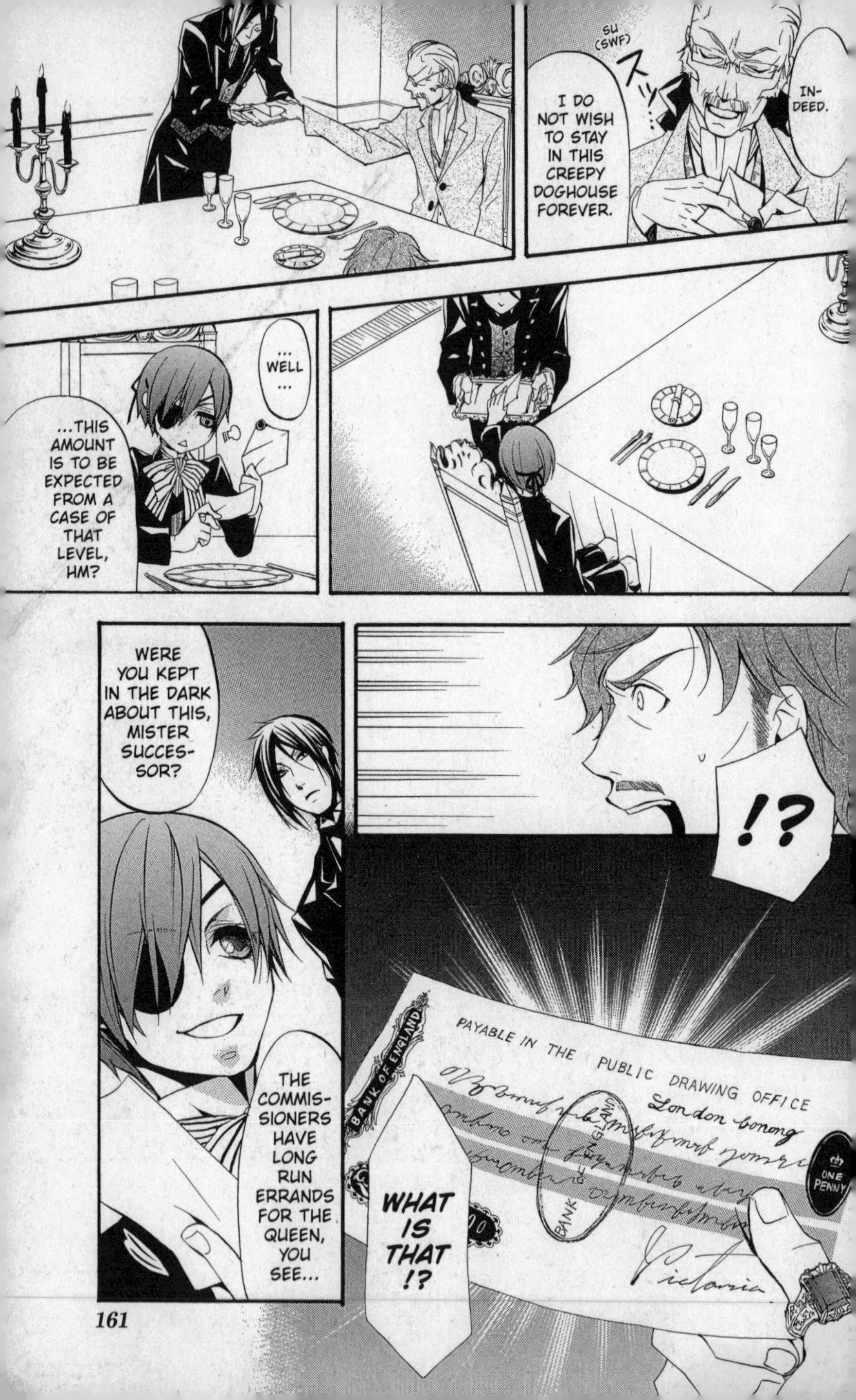

IN-DEED.
SU (SWF)
I DO NOT WISH TO STAY IN THIS CREEPY DOGHOUSE FOREVER.
...WELL...
...THIS AMOUNT IS TO BE EXPECTED FROM A CASE OF THAT LEVEL, HM?
!?
BANK OF ENGLAND
PAYABLE IN THE PUBLIC DRAWING OFFICE
ONE PENNY
Victoria
WHAT IS THAT!?
WERE YOU KEPT IN THE DARK ABOUT THIS, MISTER SUCCES-SOR?
THE COMMIS-SIONERS HAVE LONG RUN ERRANDS FOR THE QUEEN, YOU SEE...

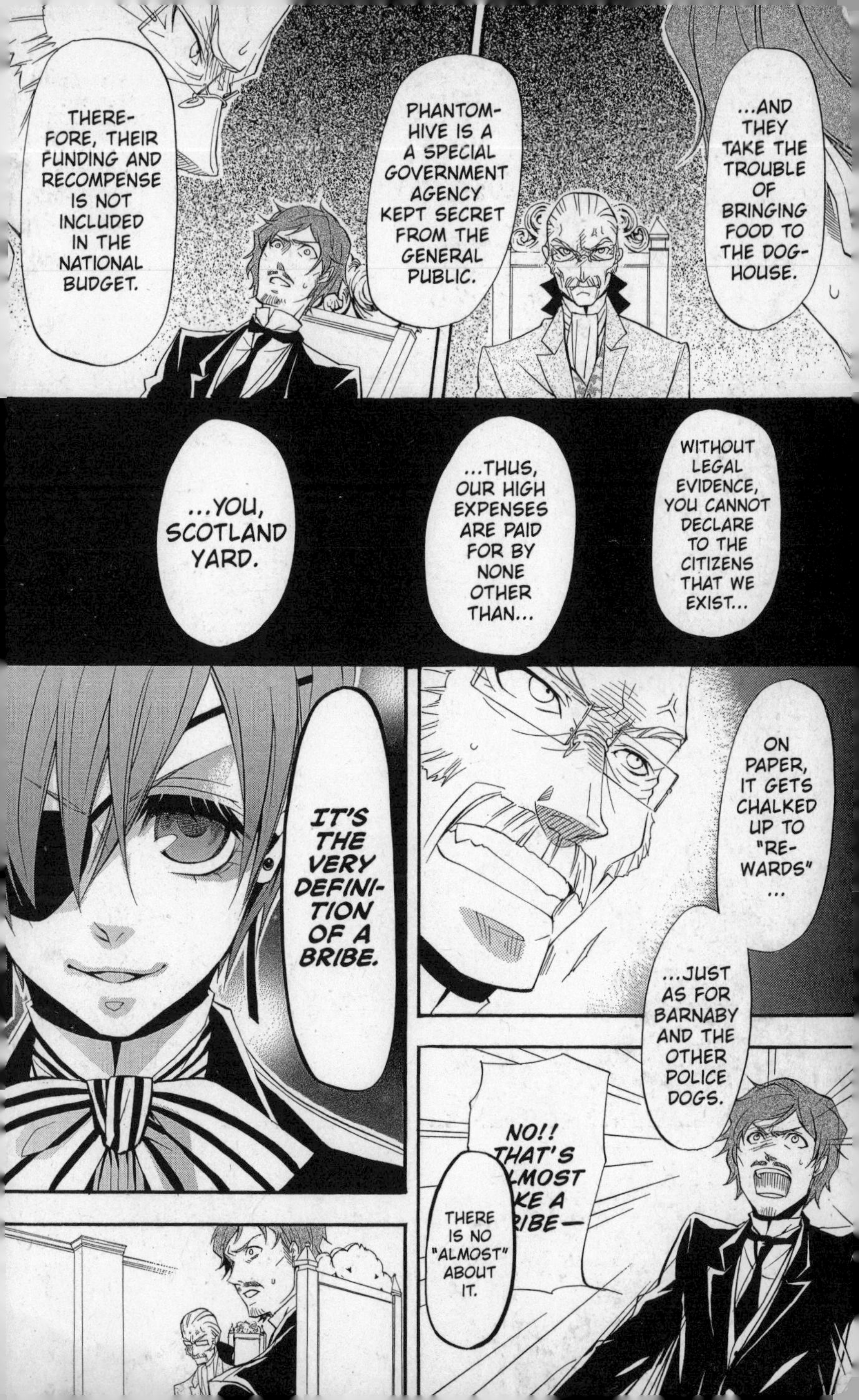

...AND THEY TAKE THE TROUBLE OF BRINGING FOOD TO THE DOG-HOUSE.
PHANTOM-HIVE IS A A SPECIAL GOVERNMENT AGENCY KEPT SECRET FROM THE GENERAL PUBLIC.
THERE-FORE, THEIR FUNDING AND RECOMPENSE IS NOT INCLUDED IN THE NATIONAL BUDGET.
WITHOUT LEGAL EVIDENCE, YOU CANNOT DECLARE TO THE CITIZENS THAT WE EXIST...
...THUS, OUR HIGH EXPENSES ARE PAID FOR BY NONE OTHER THAN...
...YOU, SCOTLAND YARD.
ON PAPER, IT GETS CHALKED UP TO "RE-WARDS"...
...JUST AS FOR BARNABY AND THE OTHER POLICE DOGS.
NO!! THAT'S LMOST KE A RIBE—
THERE IS NO "ALMOST" ABOUT IT.
IT'S THE VERY DEFINI-TION OF A BRIBE.

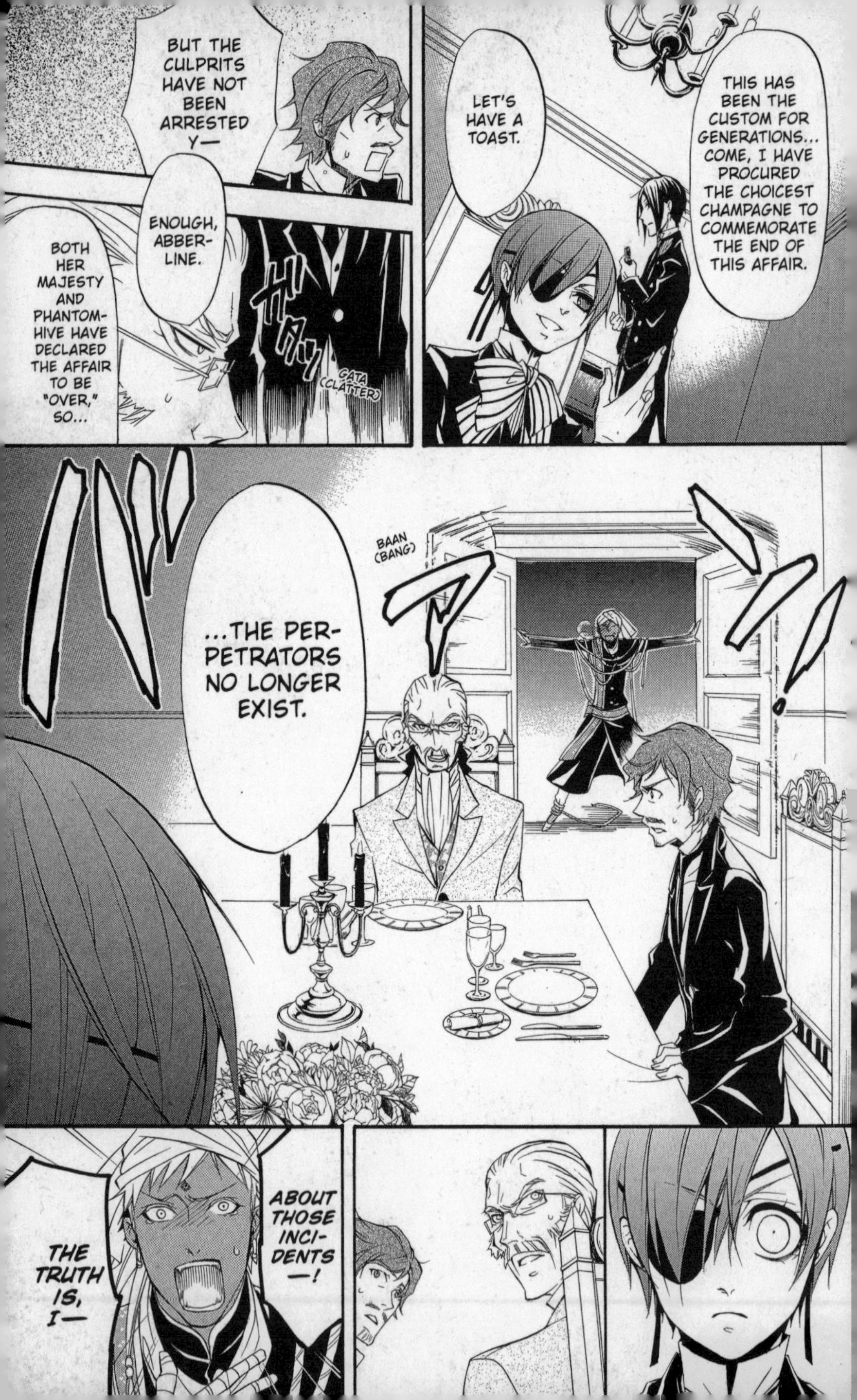
THIS HAS BEEN THE CUSTOM FOR GENERATIONS... COME, I HAVE PROCURED THE CHOICEST CHAMPAGNE TO COMMEMORATE THE END OF THIS AFFAIR.
LET'S HAVE A TOAST.
BUT THE CULPRITS HAVE NOT BEEN ARRESTED Y—
GATA (CLATTER)
ENOUGH, ABBER-LINE.
BOTH HER MAJESTY AND PHANTOM-HIVE HAVE DECLARED THE AFFAIR TO BE "OVER," SO...
BAAN (BANG)
...THE PER-PETRATORS NO LONGER EXIST.
ABOUT THOSE INCI-DENTS —!
THE TRUTH IS, I—

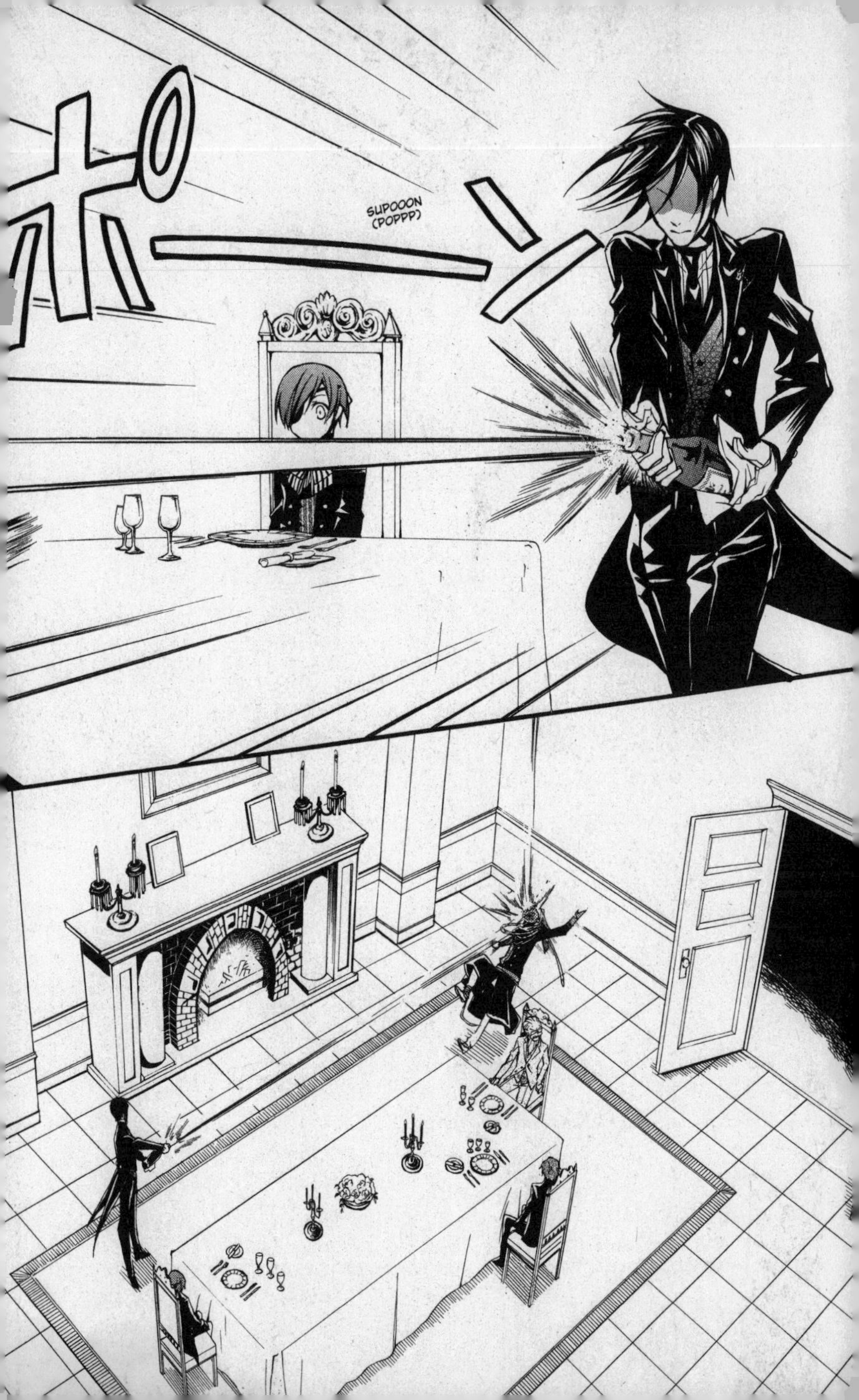
ポーン
SUPOOON
(POPPP)

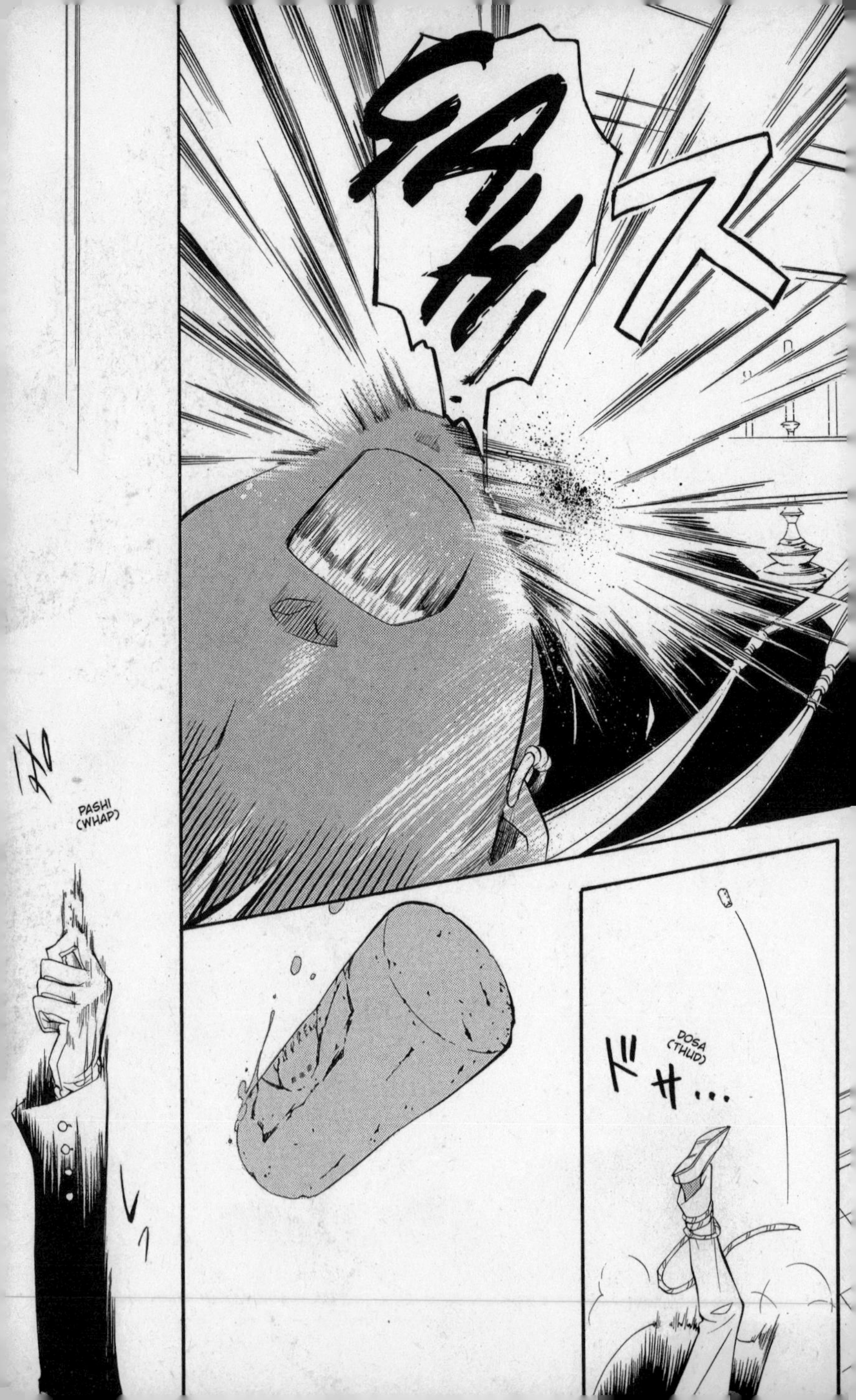
ドサ…
DOSA
(THUD)
PASHI
(WHAP)

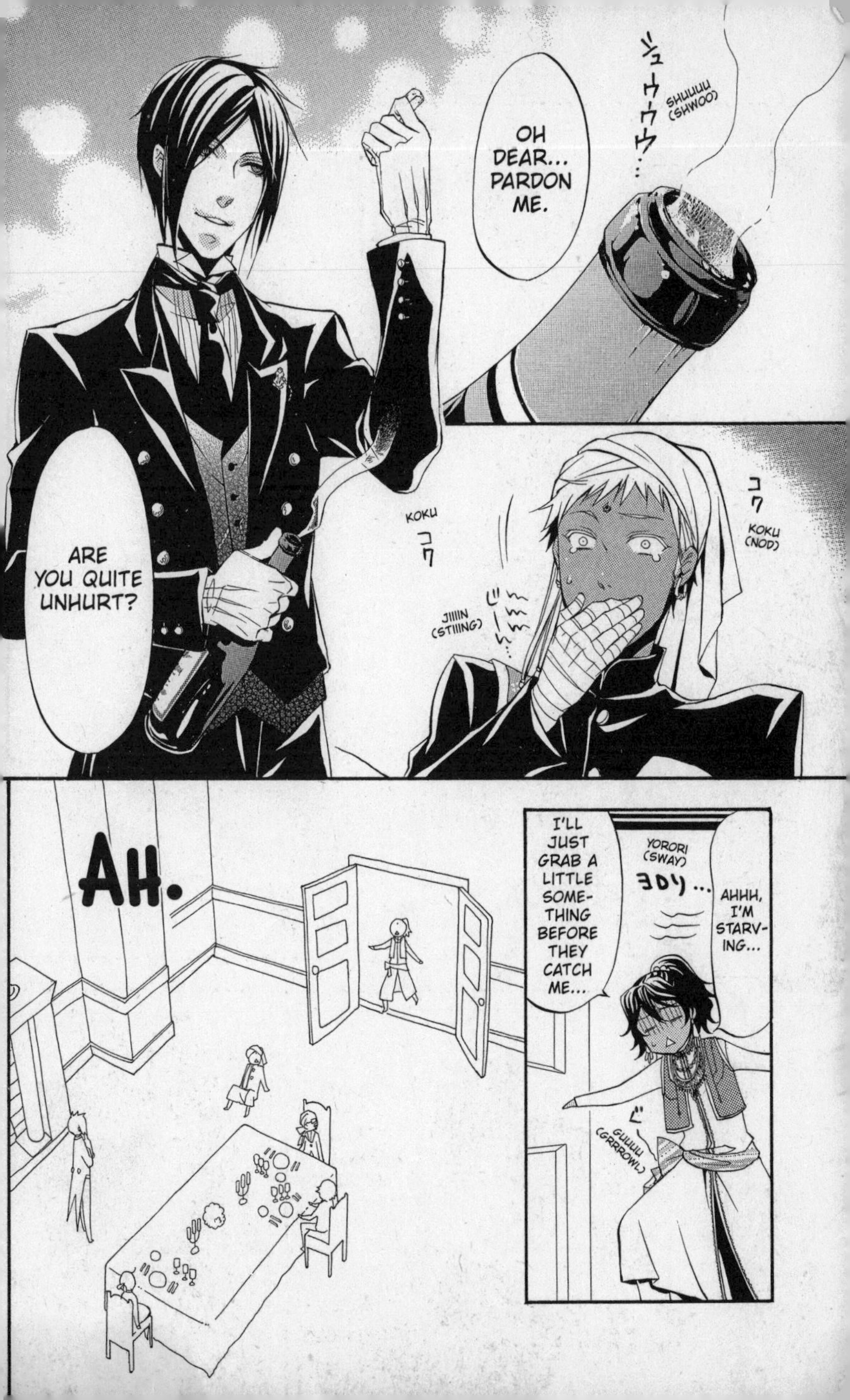
シュウウウ…
SHUUUUU (SHWOO)
OH DEAR... PARDON ME.
ARE YOU QUITE UNHURT?
コク
KOKU (NOD)
コク
KOKU
じーん…
JIIIIN (STIIING)
ヨロリ…
YORORI (SWAY)
AHHH, I'M STARV-ING...
I'LL JUST GRAB A LITTLE SOME-THING BEFORE THEY CATCH ME...
グ
GUUUU (GRRROWL)
AH.

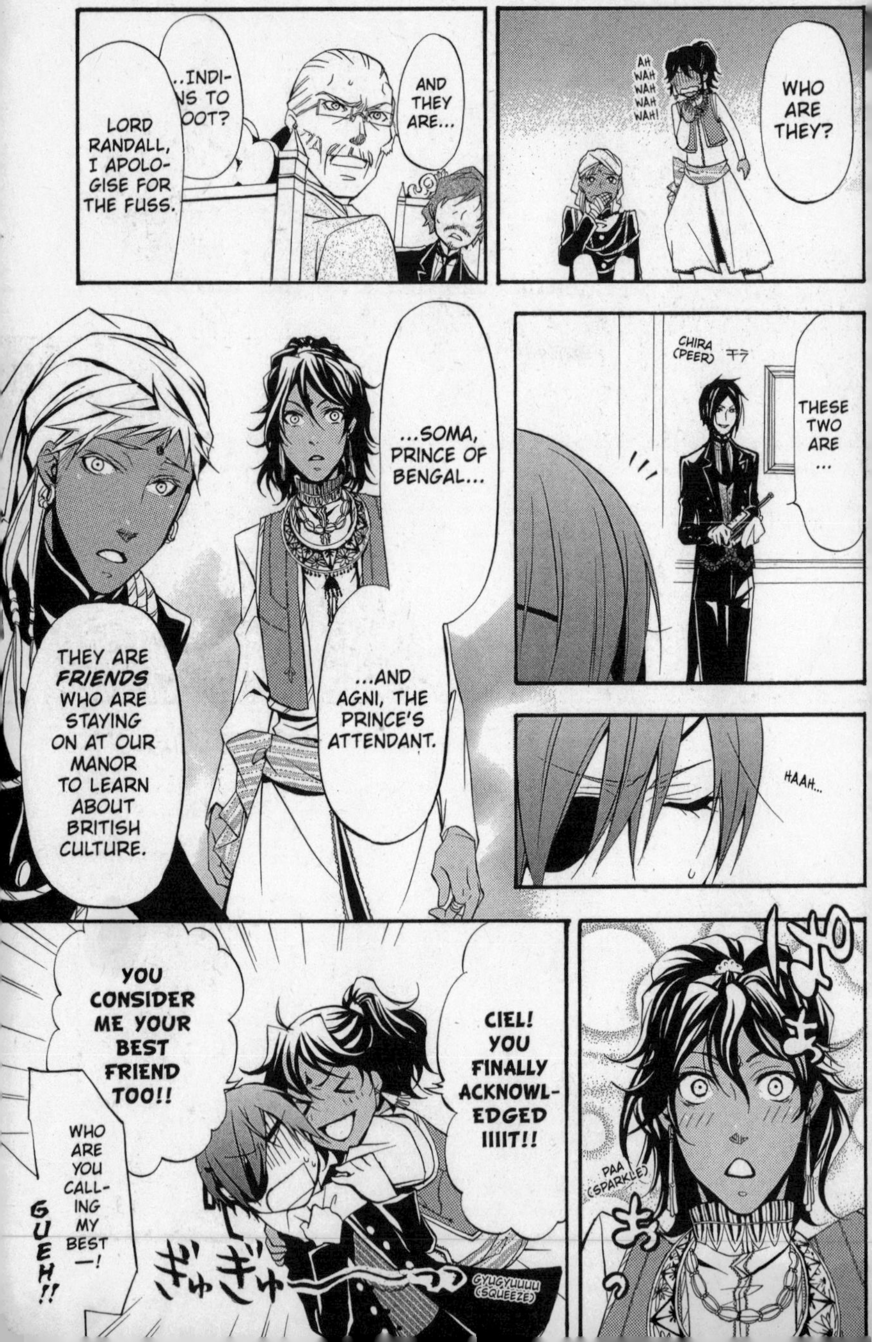
WHO ARE THEY?
AH WAH WAH WAH WAH!
AND THEY ARE...
..INDI-
NS TO
OOT?
LORD RANDALL, I APOLOGISE FOR THE FUSS.
CHIRA (PEER) チラ
THESE TWO ARE...
HAAH...
...SOMA, PRINCE OF BENGAL...
...AND AGNI, THE PRINCE'S ATTENDANT.
THEY ARE *FRIENDS* WHO ARE STAYING ON AT OUR MANOR TO LEARN ABOUT BRITISH CULTURE.
PAA (SPARKLE)
CIEL! YOU FINALLY ACKNOWL-EDGED IIIIT!!
YOU CONSIDER ME YOUR BEST FRIEND TOO!!
WHO ARE YOU CALLING MY BEST—!
GUEH!!
ぎゅぎゅ
GYUGYUUUU (SQUEEZE)

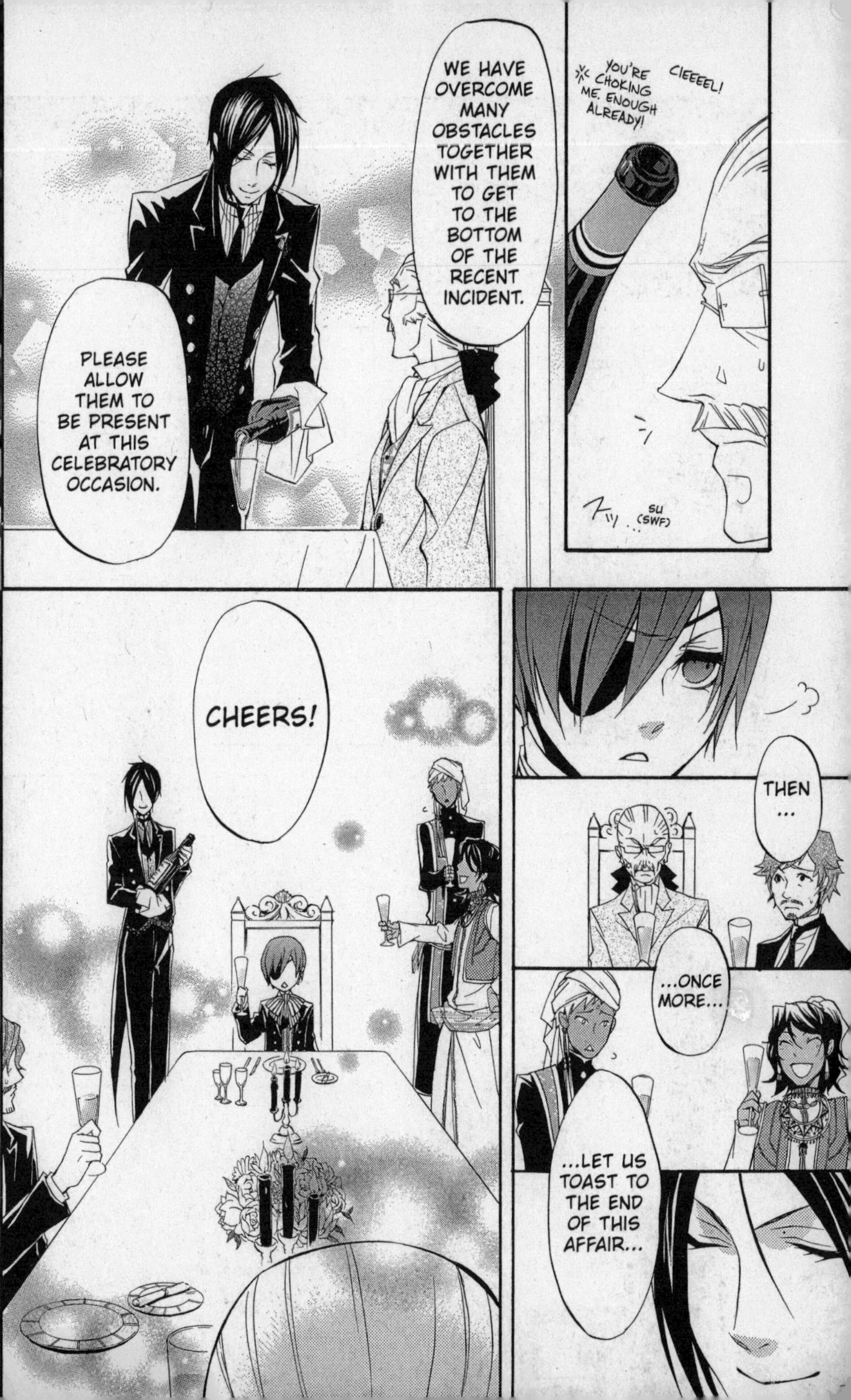

CIEEEEL!
YOU'RE CHOKING ME. ENOUGH ALREADY!
SU (SWF)
WE HAVE OVERCOME MANY OBSTACLES TOGETHER WITH THEM TO GET TO THE BOTTOM OF THE RECENT INCIDENT.
PLEASE ALLOW THEM TO BE PRESENT AT THIS CELEBRATORY OCCASION.
THEN ...
...ONCE MORE...
...LET US TOAST TO THE END OF THIS AFFAIR...
CHEERS!

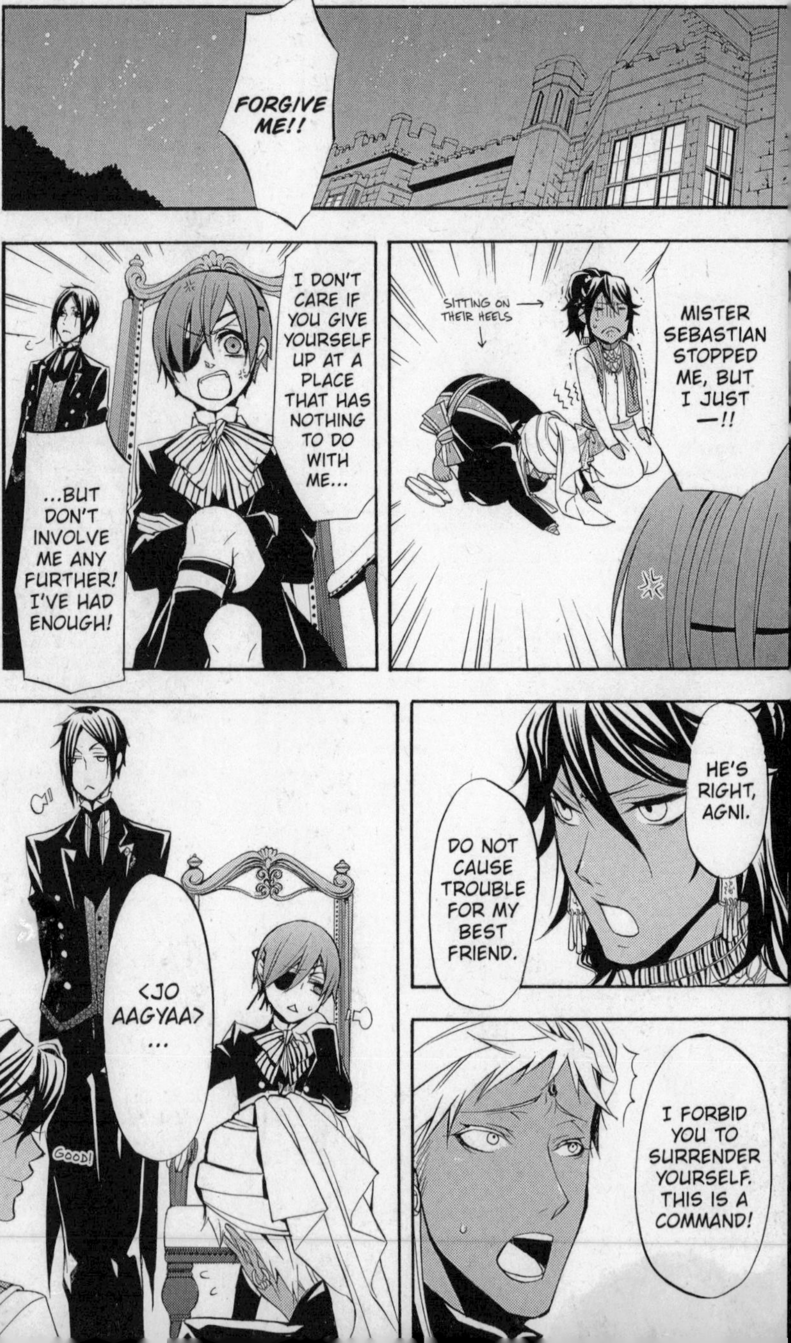
FORGIVE ME!!
MISTER SEBASTIAN STOPPED ME, BUT I JUST —!!
SITTING ON THEIR HEELS
I DON'T CARE IF YOU GIVE YOURSELF UP AT A PLACE THAT HAS NOTHING TO DO WITH ME...
...BUT DON'T INVOLVE ME ANY FURTHER! I'VE HAD ENOUGH!
HE'S RIGHT, AGNI.
DO NOT CAUSE TROUBLE FOR MY BEST FRIEND.
I FORBID YOU TO SURRENDER YOURSELF. THIS IS A COMMAND!
<JO AAGYAA>...
GOOD!

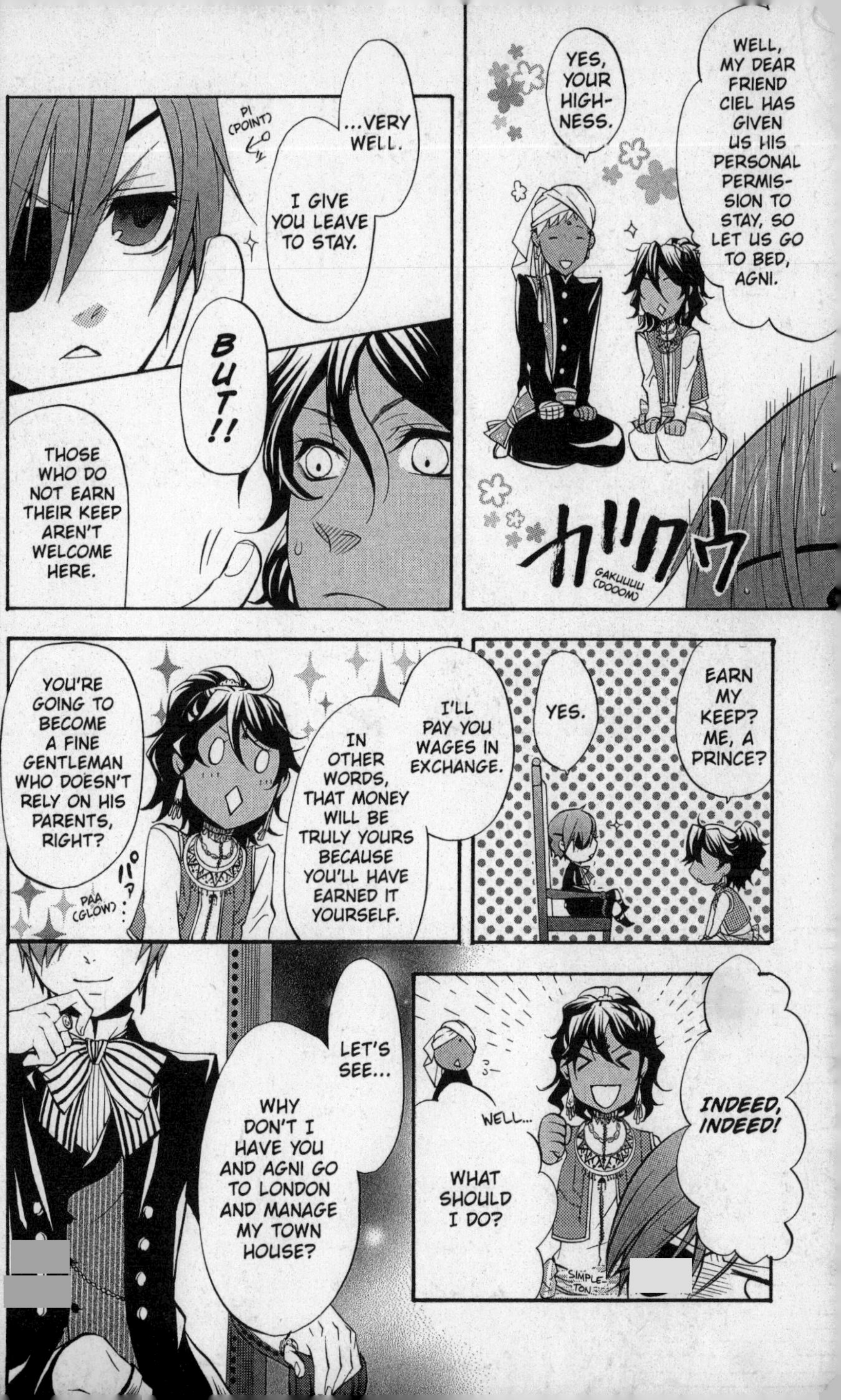
WELL, MY DEAR FRIEND CIEL HAS GIVEN US HIS PERSONAL PERMISSION TO STAY, SO LET US GO TO BED, AGNI.
YES, YOUR HIGHNESS.
GAKUUUU (DOOOM)
...VERY WELL.
PI (POINT)
I GIVE YOU LEAVE TO STAY.
BUT!!
THOSE WHO DO NOT EARN THEIR KEEP AREN'T WELCOME HERE.
EARN MY KEEP? ME, A PRINCE?
YES.
I'LL PAY YOU WAGES IN EXCHANGE.
IN OTHER WORDS, THAT MONEY WILL BE TRULY YOURS BECAUSE YOU'LL HAVE EARNED IT YOURSELF.
YOU'RE GOING TO BECOME A FINE GENTLEMAN WHO DOESN'T RELY ON HIS PARENTS, RIGHT?
PAA (GLOW)
INDEED, INDEED!
WHAT SHOULD I DO?
WELL...
SIMPLETON
LET'S SEE...
WHY DON'T I HAVE YOU AND AGNI GO TO LONDON AND MANAGE MY TOWN HOUSE?

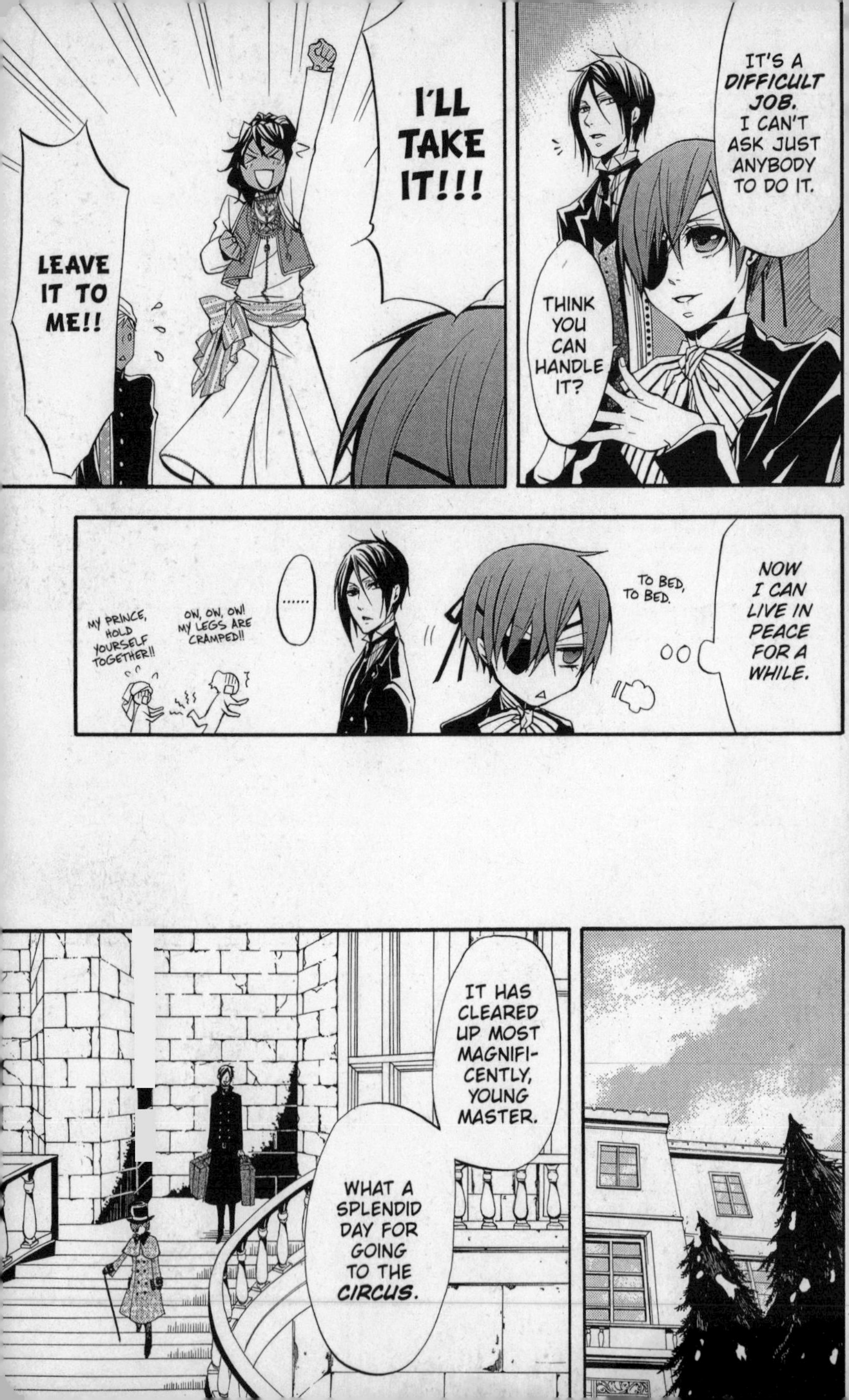
IT'S A *DIFFICULT JOB.* I CAN'T ASK JUST ANYBODY TO DO IT.
THINK YOU CAN HANDLE IT?
I'LL TAKE IT!!!
LEAVE IT TO ME!!
NOW I CAN LIVE IN PEACE FOR A WHILE.
TO BED, TO BED.
......
OW, OW, OW! MY LEGS ARE CRAMPED!!
MY PRINCE, HOLD YOURSELF TOGETHER!!
IT HAS CLEARED UP MOST MAGNIFICENTLY, YOUNG MASTER.
WHAT A SPLENDID DAY FOR GOING TO THE *CIRCUS.*

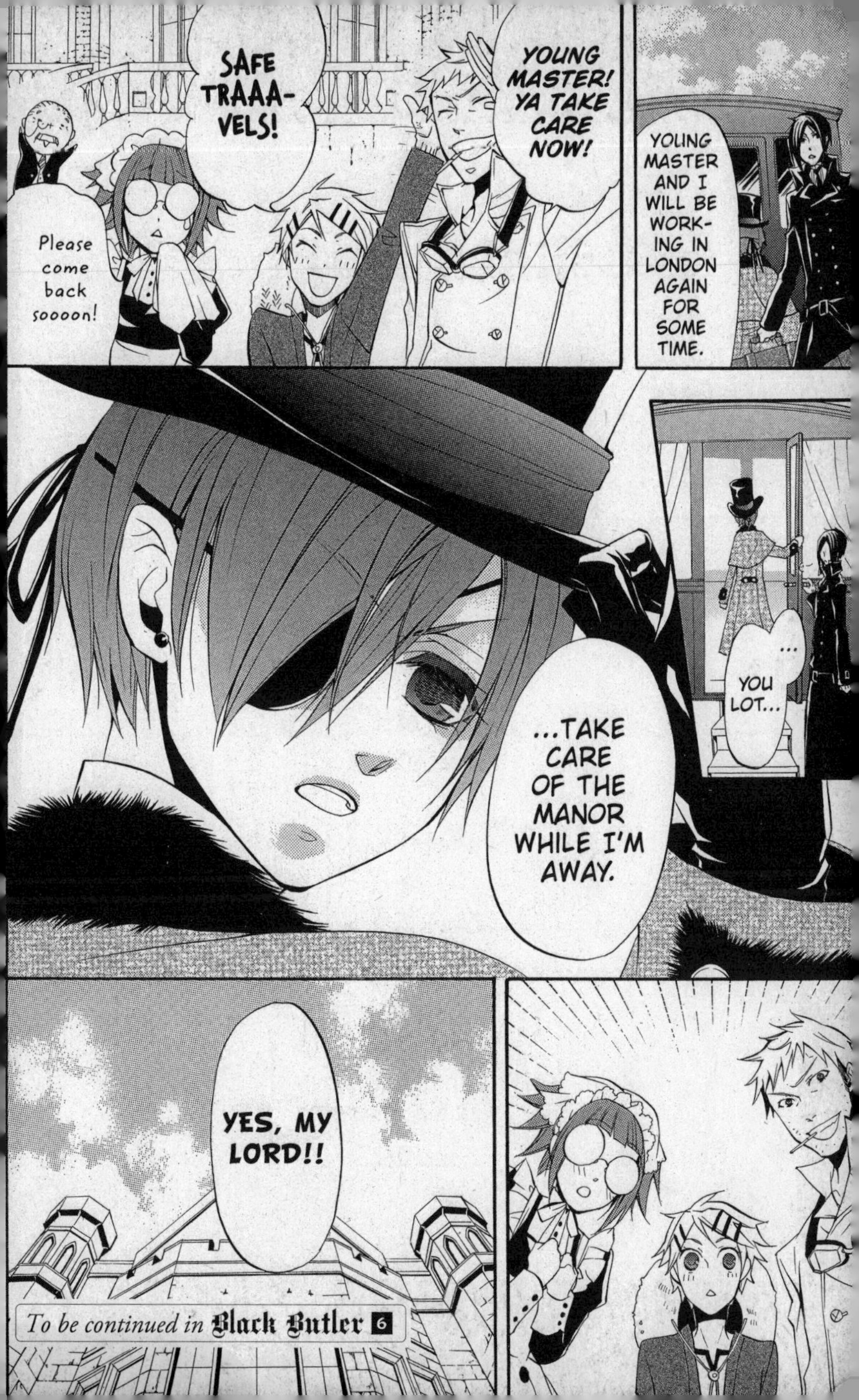
YOUNG MASTER AND I WILL BE WORKING IN LONDON AGAIN FOR SOME TIME.
YOUNG MASTER! YA TAKE CARE NOW!
SAFE TRAAA-VELS!
Please come back sooooon!
... YOU LOT...
...TAKE CARE OF THE MANOR WHILE I'M AWAY.
YES, MY LORD!!
To be continued in Black Butler 6

⇒ Black Butler ⇐
黒執事

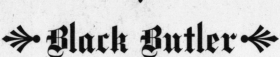

✤

Downstairs

Wakana Haduki

Akiyo Satorigi

SuKe

Bell

7

M

Nobuko.M

*

Takeshi Kuma

*

Yana Toboso

❧

SpecialThanks

Yana's Mother

and You!

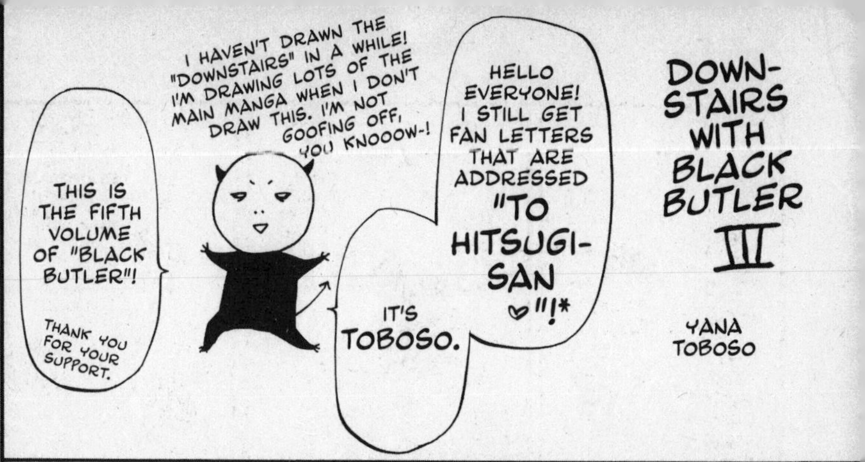
DOWN-STAIRS WITH BLACK BUTLER III
YANA TOBOSO
HELLO EVERYONE! I STILL GET FAN LETTERS THAT ARE ADDRESSED "TO HITSUGI-SAN ♥"!*
IT'S TOBOSO.
I HAVEN'T DRAWN THE "DOWNSTAIRS" IN A WHILE! I'M DRAWING LOTS OF THE MAIN MANGA WHEN I DON'T DRAW THIS. I'M NOT GOOFING OFF, YOU KNOOOW-!
THIS IS THE FIFTH VOLUME OF "BLACK BUTLER"!
THANK YOU FOR YOUR SUPPORT.

*THE KANJI FOR "TOBOSO" CAN BE EASILY CONFUSED WITH THE KANJI FOR "COFFIN."

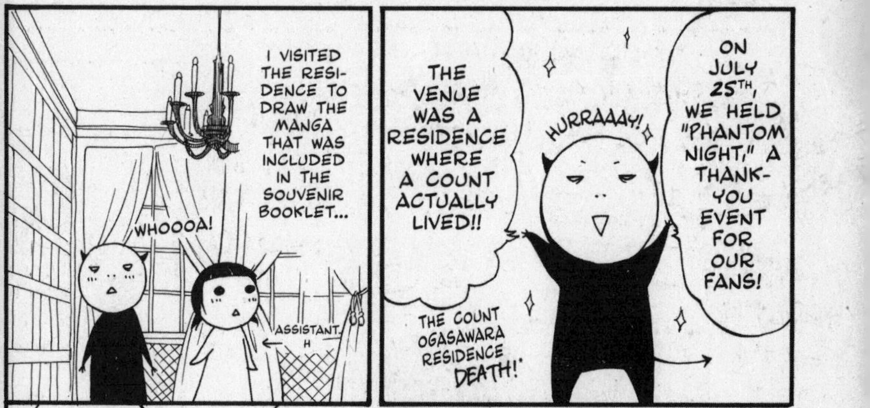
ON JULY 25TH, WE HELD "PHANTOM NIGHT," A THANK-YOU EVENT FOR OUR FANS!
HURRAAAY!
THE VENUE WAS A RESIDENCE WHERE A COUNT ACTUALLY LIVED!!
THE COUNT OGASAWARA RESIDENCE DEATH!*
I VISITED THE RESIDENCE TO DRAW THE MANGA THAT WAS INCLUDED IN THE SOUVENIR BOOKLET...
WHOOOA!
ASSISTANT H

*A PARODY OF GRELLE'S CATCHPHRASE IN JAPANESE; "DEATH" IS A HOMOPHONE OF "TO BE" (DESU)

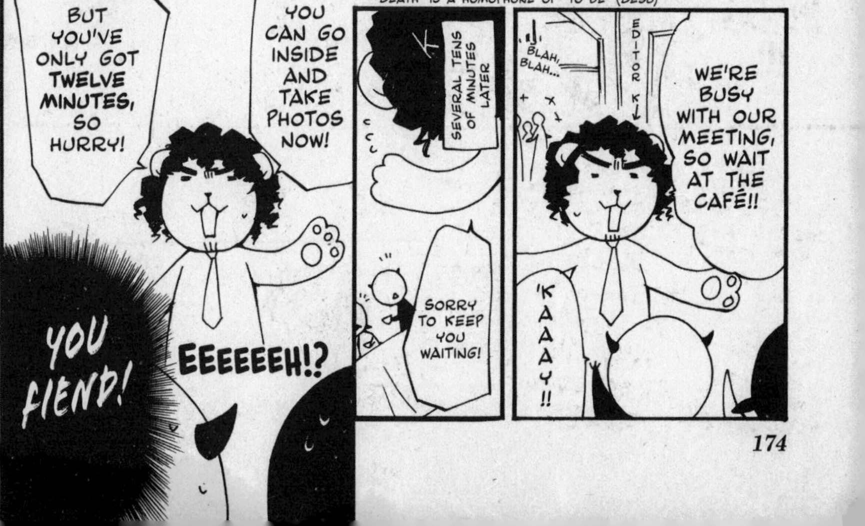
EDITOR K
BLAH, BLAH...
WE'RE BUSY WITH OUR MEETING, SO WAIT AT THE CAFÉ!!
'KAAAAY!!
SEVERAL TENS OF MINUTES LATER
SORRY TO KEEP YOU WAITING!
YOU CAN GO INSIDE AND TAKE PHOTOS NOW!
BUT YOU'VE ONLY GOT TWELVE MINUTES, SO HURRY!
EEEEEEH!?
YOU FIEND!

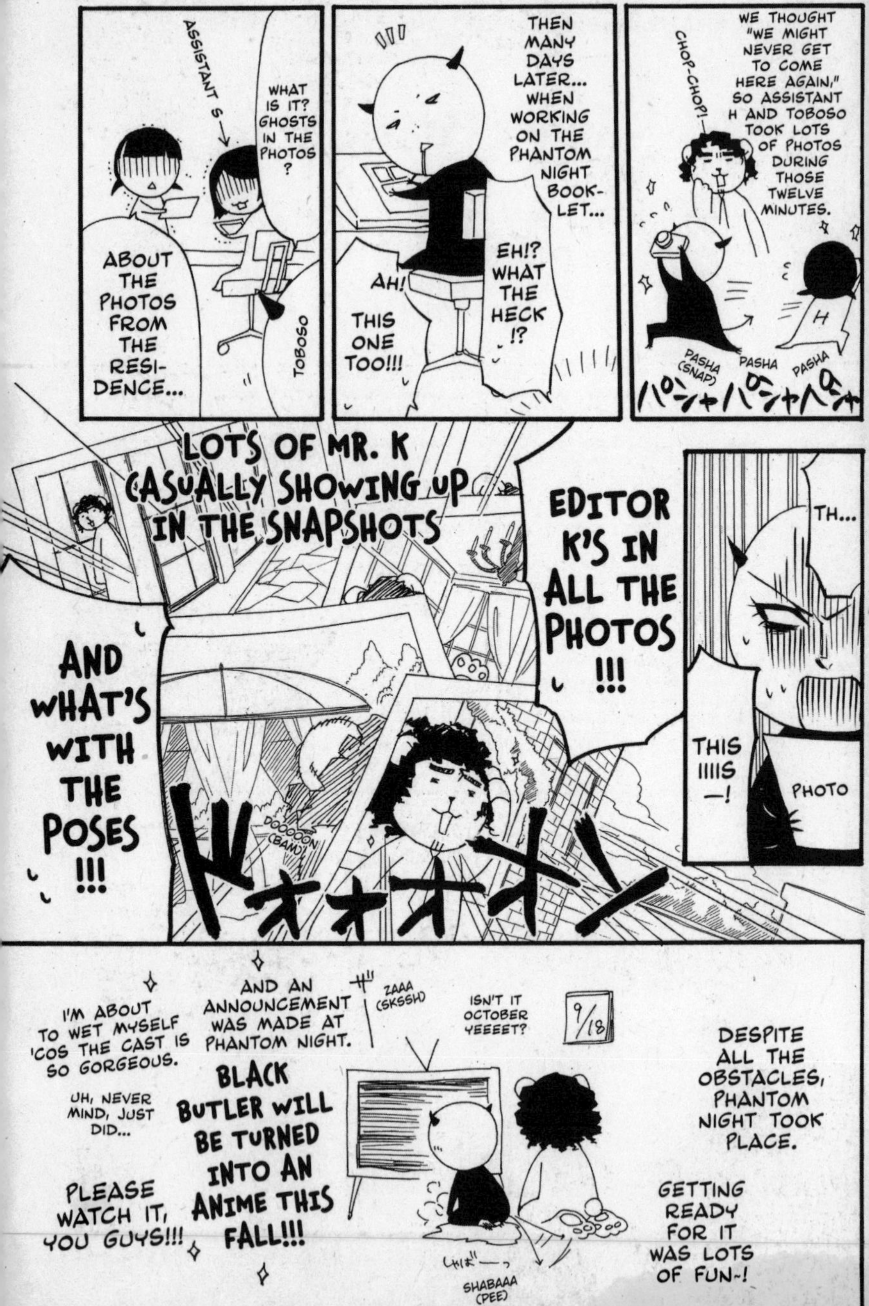
CHOP-CHOP!
WE THOUGHT "WE MIGHT NEVER GET TO COME HERE AGAIN," SO ASSISTANT H AND TOBOSO TOOK LOTS OF PHOTOS DURING THOSE TWELVE MINUTES.
PASHA (SNAP) PASHA PASHA
パシャパシャパシャ
H
THEN MANY DAYS LATER... WHEN WORKING ON THE PHANTOM NIGHT BOOKLET...
AH!
THIS ONE TOO!!!
EH!? WHAT THE HECK!?
ASSISTANT S
WHAT IS IT? GHOSTS IN THE PHOTOS?
ABOUT THE PHOTOS FROM THE RESIDENCE...
TOBOSO
TH...
THIS IIIIS—!
PHOTO
EDITOR K'S IN ALL THE PHOTOS!!!
LOTS OF MR. K CASUALLY SHOWING UP IN THE SNAPSHOTS
AND WHAT'S WITH THE POSES!!!
DOOOOON (BAM)
ドオオオン
DESPITE ALL THE OBSTACLES, PHANTOM NIGHT TOOK PLACE.
GETTING READY FOR IT WAS LOTS OF FUN~!
9/18
ISN'T IT OCTOBER YEEEET?
ザ
ZAAA (SKSSH)
しゃばー
SHABAAA (PEE)
AND AN ANNOUNCEMENT WAS MADE AT PHANTOM NIGHT.
BLACK BUTLER WILL BE TURNED INTO AN ANIME THIS FALL!!!
I'M ABOUT TO WET MYSELF 'COS THE CAST IS SO GORGEOUS.
UH, NEVER MIND, JUST DID...
PLEASE WATCH IT, YOU GUYS!!!

Translation Notes

PAGE 4
Terry Indian Cookery
Richard Terry began working at the Oriental Club in 1851 as *chef de cuisine*. Founded by officers of the East India Company who were not eligible for membership at the private clubs for military men in London, the Oriental Club was a private gentlemen's club that welcomed males who had worked abroad in the East.

PAGE 5
Edmunds' Empress Currie Powder
"The Empress" was a highly regarded blend of spices created by Joseph Edmunds, a specialist on the subject of curry by all accounts and author of *Curries and How to Prepare Them* (1903), whose manufacturing headquarters was located in Barnsbury, London. The mixture was awarded a certificate of merit in 1890 by the Royal Sanitary Institute. Also, "curry" was indeed spelled "currie" in Victorian times.

PAGE 8
Masalchi
The *-chi* suffix functions to describe occupation, like "-er" or "-ist" in English. *Masal* means "spice." Therefore, a *masalchi* is a type of kitchen servant or scullion whose sole purpose is to work with spices.

PAGE 12
Murgi'r kari
Murgi means "chicken" in Bengali. Arguably, *kari* is the Tamil word from which "curry" is derived, but in common Bengali parlance, what is popularly considered a "curry" would probably be called a *jhol* ("soup" or "gravy").

PAGE 19-20
Eating with the hands
This way of eating is a common tradition in India. Note that Soma always uses his right hand to do so; the left hand is traditionally considered unclean, as it is the hand used when cleaning oneself.

PAGE 55
Prince Albert's passing
Prince Albert died at the young age of 42 in 1861. Queen Victoria mourned his loss for the rest of her life.

PAGE 70
Le homard bleu
This royal blue crustacean is found in the wild in the waters of Brittany and the English Channel. It is highly valued as a delicacy because of its succulence and delicate flavour and is considered an aristocrat of its species by connoisseurs, hence West calling it a "noblewoman."

PAGE 81
Curry bun
More commonly known as *kare pan* ("curry bread"). A very common Japanese food that is found in convenience stores and school lunchrooms. It is typically made of Japanese-style curry inside dough, which is then breaded in bread crumbs and deep fried.

PAGE 98
Manor on the Isle of Wight
The manor to which Queen Victoria is referring is probably Osborne House, her and the Prince Consort's country home and summer retreat.

PAGE 111
The Crystal Palace
An epitome of Industrial Revolution thinking, this ill-fated but recognisable glass and iron structure was built in Hyde Park, London for the Great Exhibition of 1851. The building was moved to a different park in 1854, where it stood until 1936, when it was ruined by fire. The remaining towers of the building were demolished during World War II.

PAGE 135
Television
The television was not commercially available until the 1920s. Though development of the television was in its beginning stages at the time of the events in this volume, broadcasting of shows like *The Wild Earl* probably would not have started until the 1930s.

PAGE 155-6
Millais, Pre-Raphaelites, Waterhouse
The Pre-Raphaelite movement in the arts began in 1848 and sought to bring the arts back to a time before Raphael, whose successors were thought to be too rote and mechanical. John Everett Millais was one of the founders; his paintings were known for being extremely elaborate and nature-intensive. Today, his *Ophelia* can be found at the Tate Britain gallery in London. The painter John William Waterhouse was a later member; his famous *The Lady of Shalott* hangs in the Tate museum in London.

PAGE 162
Barnaby
Barnaby was one of the bloodhounds kept by Sir Charles Warren, who was Commissioner of the Metropolitan Police during the Jack the Ripper murders. Barnaby was being trained to track suspects in the streets of London at the time and was brought in to help with the investigation.

INSIDE BACK COVER
96422
The numbers on Baldo's hat can be read in Japanese in such a way that they sound like *Kuroshitsuji*, the original title of *Black Butler*.

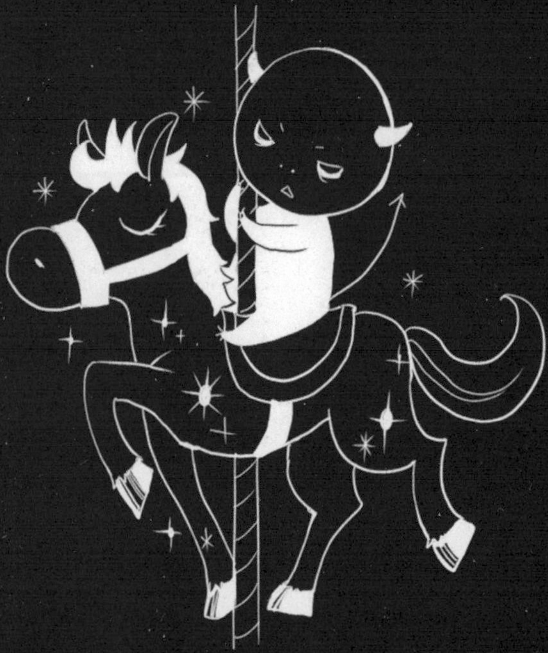

Yana Toboso

AUTHOR'S NOTE

I draw manga with the thought, "Let it be entertainment for those who read it."

Entertainments are leisure and play supporting roles in our lives. If ***Black Butler***, one such supporting player, can add colour to the leading roles that are the readers' everyday lives, even if only for a moment...... But from beginning to end, the road to perfecting a supporting role is a long and hard one, and I'm still trekking here in Volume 5.

BLACK BUTL

YANA TOBOSO

Translation: Tomo Kimura

KUROSHITSUJI Vol. 5 © 2008 Yana Toboso / SQUARE ENIX CO., LTD. All
rights reserved. First published in Japan in 2008 by SQUARE ENIX CO.,
LTD. English translation rights arranged with SQUARE ENIX CO., LTD.
and Hachette Book Group through Tuttle-Mori Agency, Inc.

Translation © 2011 by SQUARE ENIX CO., LTD.

Yen Press
Hachette Book Group
237 Park Avenue, New York, NY 10017

www.HachetteBookGroup.com
www.YenPress.com

Yen Press is an imprint of Hachette Book Group, Inc. The Yen Press name
and logo are trademarks of Hachette Book Group, Inc.

First Yen Press Edition: April 2011

ISBN: 978-0-316-08429-1

10 9 8 7

BVG

Printed in the United States of America